1. Map of China—Ch'ing (Manchu) dynasty, 1644–1911.

MANDARINS, JEWS, AND MISSIONARIES

MANDARINS, JEWS, AND MISSIONARIES

THE JEWISH EXPERIENCE IN THE CHINESE EMPIRE

MICHAEL POLLAK

PHILADELPHIA   5740 ❖ 1980

THE JEWISH PUBLICATION SOCIETY OF AMERICA

Library of Congress Cataloging in Publication Data
Pollak, Michael, 1918–
Mandarins, Jews, and missionaries.
Bibliography: p.   Includes index.
1. Jews in China—History.   2.   Missions—China.
3.   China—History.   I.   Title.
DS135.C5P6   951'.004'924   79-84732
ISBN 0-8276-0120-4

❖ To Barbara

CONTENTS

LIST OF ILLUSTRATIONS

❖ PREFACE

Now and then one reads or hears of non-Jewish families in Spain, Portugal, and elsewhere who in the privacy of their homes quietly preserve certain customs and ceremonies that stem from a distinctly Judaic heritage. Their anomalous domestic observances—lighting candles on a Friday evening, serving special foods at various seasons of the year, and the like—have lingered on for centuries, and continue even now to be handed down from generation to generation, though perhaps with diminished vigor and in increasingly diluted form. In some instances, the people who cherish these traditions are fully cognizant that there is a Jewish strain in their ancestral background; in others, they have no inkling of it at all. For neither group, of course, do these old familial usages retain any specific cultic connotations.

Although it cannot be proved, it is quite possible that a small number of Jewish folkways and religious rituals still persist in so improbable a part of the world as China, a land that is not ordinarily thought of as having fallen within the ambit of the Jewish Diaspora before the last century or two, and a land, moreover, whose indigenous credal practices, unlike those common to Caucasian countries, have no recognizable historic ties with the Hebrew Scriptures. It is even possible that the Jews of what was formerly known as the Middle Kingdom, and whose communal experience there stretches back a millennium and more, have not yet totally faded out of existence. Physiognomically, linguistically, and culturally they have all become as Chinese as their neighbors, but in the innermost recesses of their hearts and minds some few of them may still choose to regard themselves as bona fide members of the House of Israel.

This book tells the story, to the degree that it can be reconstructed, of the autochthonous Jews of China—those Jews who arrived in the country many hundreds of years ago and who, with the passage of time, blended physically and psychologically into the general population, although managing to remain until fairly recently (albeit in only one city) a distinctly identifiable Jewish entity. It does not deal with the Jews of Central Asia and the West who migrated to China in the nineteenth and twentieth centuries, except as they were involved with the very last of the several Jewish colonies that once dotted the Chinese Empire—this being the colony that was established in the Sung capital of Kaifeng, in Honan Province, between 960 and 1126 C.E. and still owned a synagogue as late as the mid-1800s. It does concern itself, however, to a considerable extent with the absurdly overblown role that the lengthy survival of a small Jewish settlement in the Middle Kingdom played in the formulation of certain political and theological hypotheses by Christians and Jews living in faraway Europe.

The study of the history of the Chinese Jews is both intriguing and frustrating: intriguing because of the sheer exoticism of the subject and the mysteries that surround it; and frustrating because the pertinent records are sparse, not easily obtainable, and all too frequently untrustworthy—difficulties, it should be added, which have not discouraged a succession of highly inventive souls from resorting to fantasy when fact was not to be had. In doing this, they have so muddied the waters that the first challenge confronting the student of Sino-Judaica is that of deciding which books and articles dealing with the subject are best ignored. The second problem, of course, is how to go about locating and retrieving those which do merit attention.

The situation being what it is, every bit of help I was able to muster in my efforts to delve into the story of the small bands of Israelites who long ago wandered into China and succeeded, as some did, in retaining their cohesiveness for centuries on end has been most welcome. I have been extremely fortunate in this regard, having enjoyed the unstinted cooperation of several distinguished scholars whose expertise in Chinese Jewish history was generously shared with me, as well as that of a number of outstanding professional librarians who, after probing the resources of their respective institutions on my behalf, not only provided me with many of the materials already cataloged in the literature of Sino-Judaica, but also discovered an array of others that had previously been overlooked.

The three scholars whose names stand out most prominently and deservedly today in the area of Sino-Judaic studies are Donald Daniel Leslie, Rudolf Loewenthal (Löwenthal), and Hyman Kublin. Each has written extensively on the subject and, as the reader will observe, the works of all three are cited time and again throughout this book. My own research, I hasten to add, could not have been carried out had it not been preceded by theirs.

Dr. Leslie's numerous contributions to the field, and especially his masterly *Survival of the Chinese Jews*, have brought together, analyzed, and summarized the bulk of the available responsible data and findings pertaining to the Jews of old China, so that no one who plans to probe at all deeply into the annals of these people can hope to succeed unless he keeps Dr. Leslie's works within easy reach. The present book, aside from attempting to offer the reader a reasonably broad overview of the Jewish experience in China, should serve as a steppingstone to the more detailed investigations undertaken by Dr. Leslie.

Dr. Loewenthal, who began his inquiries into the history of Chinese Jewry during his lengthy residence in Peking, where he was a member of the faculty of Yenching University, is the compiler and annotator of the basic bibliographies that have unlocked the door to all serious Sino-Judaic research completed since World War II; he is also the author of numerous papers dealing seminally with specific phases of study vital to the subject.

Dr. Kublin's two anthologies of carefully selected and hard-to-come-by articles and pamphlets relating to the Chinese Jews have lightened my logistical burdens immeasurably, and have done the same (and will no doubt continue to do so) for everyone else whose imagination is sufficiently touched by the bizarre saga of the extinct Jewish enclaves of China to encourage him to look deeply into it.

I have had the great pleasure of getting to know these three gentlemen personally and of corresponding with them frequently. I have benefited immensely from their guidance and owe them my sincerest gratitude. Dr. Leslie, in addition, has read the manuscript of this book and has suggested several corrections and other emendations that have since been incorporated in the text. He cannot be held responsible, of course, for any defects the reader may uncover in the finished product, but as the direct consequence of his prepublication review of the manuscript, their number and gravity are unquestionably fewer and less objectionable than they would otherwise be.

Rabbi Marvin Tokayer, formerly spiritual leader of the Jewish community of Japan and a highly knowledgeable student of Chinese Jewish lore, has been exceptionally kind and helpful in providing much of the information presented herein. He has also contributed the Appendix, outlining his interview with Lt. Col. Shih Hung-mo (ret.) of the Republic of China Air Force. To Rabbi Tokayer, my deepest thanks.

My thanks also to Marvin Stone of the Dallas Public Library and to its very helpful and efficient Interlibrary Loan Department. And to Decherd H. Turner, Jr., the director of Bridwell Library, Southern Methodist University, for his counsel and for permitting me to make Bridwell something of a second home while this book was being written; to his associate Page Thomas; and to the library's accommodating staff.

Dr. Menahem Schmelzer of the Library of the Jewish Theological Seminary of America directed me to sources I would scarcely have discovered on my own. Myron M. Weinstein, staff member of the Library of Congress, repeatedly drew my attention to others, while patiently taking on the burden of clarifying certain arcane matters lying well beyond the scope of my knowledge and, patently, well within his own.

I stand in awe of the uncanny bibliographic talents repeatedly demonstrated by Robert Singerman of the Hebrew Union College Library, as he went about unearthing a goodly portion of the materials—some already familiar to Sino-Judaic researchers and many entirely overlooked until he found them—which subsequently entered into the making of this book. Without his erudition and extraordinary professional skills to fall back on, and without his cheerful willingness to apply them in my behalf, this volume would be some dozens of pages shorter and considerably poorer. If any of his numerous contributions is to be singled out for special mention, it must be his discovery of the documentation discussed below in Chapter 9, which brought me to the abrupt realization that J. L. Liebermann's account of having visited the Jews of Kaifeng in 1867—an account upon which so much of our understanding of Chinese Judaism has hitherto been based—may be completely spurious; that Aaron Halevi Fink's very similar report of a prior visit, previously categorized by me as having been pirated from Liebermann's, was actually published a dozen years before Liebermann's; and perhaps that both accounts may be no more than outright hoaxes.

Others to whom I gladly pay my respects and proffer my thanks include my fellow Dallasites Rabbi Levi A. Olan and Rabbi Solomon Kahn Kaplan, each of whom could be counted on to clear up theological points beyond my ken; Professor Mary Kuebel of Southern Methodist University, whose mastery of matters Chinese was of invaluable assistance; Professor Luis Martín, also of Southern Methodist University, who corrected my translations from Latin and filled in the voids in my knowledge of Church history; Max Plaut, from whose extensive familiarity with both European and Jewish literature and culture I profited greatly; and my wife Barbara, Joseph L. Sanger, Homer Krueger, Cecil D. Elfenbein, and Fred Levy—all of whom served as sounding boards for some of the ideas I considered introducing into the book, and who tactfully and judiciously helped me decide which to discard and which to develop.

There are, literally, dozens of other individuals, and a lengthy array of institutions of learning as well, to whom I remain indebted and whose names I would assuredly feel obliged to catalog here, were it not for space considerations and the famous dictum enunciated by the talmudic sage Rabbi Tarphon, which asserts that "it is not incumbent upon thee to complete the task, nor art thou free to desist from it." I submit that I have made at least a beginning of listing those who had a hand in the labors that made this book possible, even if I have not completed the task by including all the names that actually belong here. However, now that I have recalled Rabbi Tarphon's time-honored admonition to their attention, the bearers of these unmentioned names will perhaps forgive me.

With exceptions here and there, the anglicizations from the Chinese occurring in this book conform to the principles of the generally accepted Wade-Giles transcriptional system or, in the case of place names, to the spellings customarily recommended by the international postal authorities.

On January 1, 1979, the government of the People's Republic of China began to transmit its English-language news releases and official notices in the Pinyin phonetic system, which its academicians have developed over the past two decades. It seems reasonable to assume that this newer method will ultimately supplant all of its several predecessors and become the standard medium for rendering Chinese ideograms into roman characters.

Rather few of the personal and place names referred to in the present work should pose serious recognition problems when encountered in their Pinyin dress. Shensi, it is true, will appear as Shaanxi, Amoy as Xiamen, and so forth. On the whole, however, the reader will have little trouble matching the Wade-Giles and "post-office" forms with their Pinyin counterparts.

Kaifeng, the city around which so much of Sino-Judaic history revolves (and which is spelled K'aifeng by Wade-Giles purists), remains Kaifeng in the Pinyin system. Honan, the province in which Kaifeng lies, undergoes a slight metamorphosis to Henan.

Michael Pollak
Dallas, Texas
April 1979

MANDARINS, JEWS, AND MISSIONARIES

A wind passes by and it is no more,
its own place no longer knows it.
Psalms 103:16

כי רוח עברה־בו ואיננו
ולא־יכירנו עוד מקומו.
תהילים ק"ג ט"ז

Prologue ❖ ENCOUNTER IN PEKING

ROM Kaifeng, the ancient capital of Honan Province, the distance to Peking is 470 miles as the crow flies, but by the less lofty mulecart and waterborne route along which the sixty-year-old mandarin Ai T'ien made his way in the spring of 1605, it was half again longer. Tedious, costly, and exhausting, the journey was not undertaken lightly; and Ai's primary reason for subjecting himself to the ordeal was to apply for a more desirable assignment in the imperial civil service than the one he already held. This was a quest in which he seems to have done well; at any rate, an old Chinese gazetteer speaks of him as entering upon a tour of duty later in the same year as superintendent of schools in Pao-ying, district of Yangchou, in Kiangsu Province.[1]

For an official of Ai's standing to travel to the imperial capital in search of promotion was a commonplace enough occurrence, but the second purpose of his trip was entirely without precedent. A district magistrate who worked in a purely provincial setting, he was in no way involved in external affairs. Not once in his life, it may be supposed, had he ever met anyone of foreign birth and, curiosity aside, would appear to have no valid reason for wanting to form a close personal association with such an individual in the remote event that he should. It could also be expected that as a government functionary and an accomplished scholar, he would be fully aware that outsiders, and above all Caucasians, were not welcome in the Middle Kingdom. A limited number of Occidentals, it was true, had been permitted to settle here and there in the country, but their presence was tolerated only because of the specialized technical skills they possessed or as part of the price that had to be paid for preserving the minimal relationships that China chose to maintain with a few backward states situated thousands of *li* beyond her most westerly borders. Yet Ai was now planning to pay a call on the small colony, which one contingent of his motherland's unwanted guests had recently established in Peking. The more xenophobic among his colleagues would have thought his conduct strange, certainly impolitic.

In effect, the extraordinary project that Ai had in mind was to seek out and get to know a tiny sect of religious enthusiasts who had come to Peking in 1601. The devotees of this cult were said to be white-skinned aliens, barbarians from the faraway continent of Europe, who had wandered about for eighteen years in various parts of China before being granted the privilege of settling in the national capital. He had read about them back home in Kaifeng, in a book called *Things J Have Heard Jell*, and he hoped that the author's report of their arrival in the imperial city was true and that they were still there.

What intrigued Ai most about these outlanders was that the faith they professed was reputed to be based on the premise that there was only one God. Reared in a culture permeated with the precepts and traditions of Confucianism, Buddhism, and Taoism, Ai could not fail to recognize that to most of his country-men the rigid monotheism of the alien sectarians whom the emperor had seen fit to admit to his domain would seem both bizarre and parochial. As far as he personally was concerned, however, there was nothing in the least unusual or constraining about the monotheistic doctrine that the Westerners preached. The fact was, he had himself been taught that very same doctrine while still a child and, unlike the vast majority of his compatriots, needed no one to remind him that there were already two religious denominations in China that demanded an unswerving commit-ment to the concept of the One God from their adherents. These faiths, each of which had been practiced in Kaifeng for hundreds of years, were Islam and Judaism. Yet, according to the book he had read, the newcomers had forcefully denied that they were Muslims. What else then could they be, Ai reasoned, knowing nothing about Christianity, but Jews—Jews, that is, like Ai himself?

He pushed the thought a step further. If, as he was now certain, the foreigners were Jews, it would not only mean that their colony in Peking was the very first Israelite settlement planted on the soil of the Middle Kingdom in many centuries but also that they were quite apt to become the medium through which the Jews of Kaifeng could logically expect to open a stirring new chapter in their own history. Not for several generations had his people welcomed even a single coreligionist from abroad or received as much as a snippet of news from a Jewish source outside their country's borders. But all this, apparently, might soon change, for if he could meet these Caucasian Jews during his pending visit to Peking, they would unquestionably be able to supply the news that he and the *kehillah* (Jewish congregation, or community) at Kaifeng were burning to hear. And if, as seemed likely, some form of continuing communication could then be instituted with the Western centers of Judaism through the good offices of the recent immigrants, Chinese Jewry would at long last be given an opportunity to reforge its severed links to the mainstreams of its faith. Such a renewal of contact, he and the leaders of the *kehillah* knew, was essential; for if it could be worked out it would boost the ebbing morale of the Jewish community of Kaifeng, help revive its dimming memories of certain aspects of its ancient heritage, and multiply its chances for survival in the long run. The implications were mind-boggling. Before leaving home, Ai must have been deluged with more advice than he cared to listen to on how to go about looking for Peking's Occidental Israelites, what to tell them, and what to ask them.

On his arrival in the imperial capital, Ai addressed himself to the business that had brought him there and, having succeeded in locating the Westerners' house of worship, proceeded to it and animatedly introduced himself to a cluster of dumbfounded bystanders as a coreligionist of theirs from Kaifeng. He had come by, he explained at some length, to pay his respects, let them know about the congregation to which he belonged, inquire about theirs, and chat about matters of mutual interest. At no point did it occur to him that the building he had entered was anything but a synagogue or that the people to whom he was talking might not be Jews. His listeners, fascinated, realized almost immediately that if the genial and loquacious gentleman standing before them attired in the robes that marked him as the holder of the coveted *chü-jen* (literary licentiate) degree turned out to be the coreligionist he said he was, he would be the first indigenous Chinese Christian they had ever seen. Impressed both by his academic and official rank and his obvious sincerity, but still a bit confused as to what to make of him, they heard him out with mounting excitement, and then ushered him into the presence of Father Matteo Ricci, the Superior of their mission.[2]

The man Ai now met, far from being the rabbi he supposed him to be, was the senior Christian cleric in China. A Jesuit priest from Italy, Matteo Ricci had by his sagacity and tact earned the trust and admiration of the Chinese with whom he had come into contact, and by virtue of his superb academic and scientific attainments was already something of a legend in Chinese intellectual circles. "Never was a man more fitted for the work he had chosen," a twentieth-century biographer was to say of him, "never did a man so labor to make himself even more fit to perform it." [3]

Ricci was profoundly moved by Ai's arrival, for here, he thought, running all the available alternatives through his mind, here at last was a Chinese who was undeniably of Christian descent. In the twenty-odd years that he had lived and labored in China, Ricci had heard occasional rumors of the presence of scattered settlements of Christians in the interior of the country. He had made several efforts to track down these elusive brethren in Christ, but without any success whatever. Now, seemingly out of nowhere, one of them had wandered into his church. It was a rare moment for the priest. He was devoutly thankful that it had come.

The situation was not without its humor. The Chinese Jew and the Italian Catholic eyed each other curiously, though with the politeness and discretion that might be expected from men of their station. While it was evident to Ai that Ricci's features were quite unlike those of his friends and kinsmen in Kaifeng, he had anticipated that this would be the case. Many of his own forebears, after all, had been Westerners, and although the Jews of China were by now a mixed strain of white and yellow there were still a fair number of them in whom the signs of Caucasian ancestry were very discernible. Ricci, for his part, was not able to rid himself of the melancholy thought that while Ai might in all honesty consider himself a good Christian, the form of Christianity he professed would never earn the commendation of the Roman Catholic church; for Ai, Ricci suspected, was almost surely a descendant of one or another of the Christian dissident sects, perhaps the Nestorian, which had found their way to China a thousand or more years earlier and had not been heard from these past several centuries. It did not cross the mind of the priest that his visitor imagined himself to be standing in a synagogue and to be carrying on a conversation with its rabbi.

The amenities having been disposed of, Ricci led his guest into the chapel. And here the comedy of errors was played out, although not quite to its denouement.

As chance would have it, Ai's visit to Ricci's church fell on the festival of Saint John the Baptist, in celebration of which a painting of the Madonna and Child had been placed on one side of the altar and a portrait of the young Saint John on the other.

Ricci approached the altar and genuflected. Ai, assuming that the individuals represented in the two paintings were Rebecca and her sons Jacob and Esau, courteously followed suit. It was not the custom of his people in Kaifeng to venerate images, he remarked to the priest, but he himself could see no harm in paying homage to one's ancestors. Then, observing the likenesses of the four evangelists that were displayed on the walls of the chapel, Ai, with Jacob foremost in his thoughts, wondered aloud whether the figures might not be those of four of the twelve sons of the infant whose portrait he had just seen near the altar. Ricci, thinking that Ai was confusing the evangelists with the apostles and was at the same time referring symbolically to the latter as the spiritual sons of Christ, tactfully refrained from offering a correction.

The two men now retired to Ricci's quarters for further talk. Both had begun to sense that something was amiss, but neither could yet understand precisely what it was that was making him feel that way. In the end, each was able to sort the matter out: Ricci, to his utter amazement, realized that his visitor was—of all things—a Chinese Jew; while Ai, not nearly as cognizant as Ricci of the significance of what was transpiring, found himself for the first time in his life face to face with a Christian. Ricci, of course, knew a great deal about Jews and Judaism. Ai, on the other hand, having not the faintest notion of what Christianity stood for, seems to have concluded that a Christian was a member of a Jewish sect—a sect, admittedly, with certain doctrines and practices that were completely strange to him, but still one which was as much a part of the House of Israel as his own congregation in Kaifeng.

The journals and letters in which Ricci chronicled his experiences in China report that he showed Ai a copy of the great eight-volume Polyglot Bible printed by Christopher Plantin three decades previously in Antwerp, and that although Ai was unable to read and comprehend the Hebrew text in the Plantin Bible, he did recognize that the characters of which it was composed were in fact Hebrew. His own schooling, Ai confided to the priest, had been devoted to acquiring a mastery of the Chinese classics, but he had two brothers in Kaifeng who, being more steeped than he in the ancestral tradition, could read Hebrew with ease.[4]

As the conversation proceeded, Ricci learned from his visitor that Jews had been living in China for many centuries and that of the various Jewish enclaves which were once dispersed throughout the country, only the settlement at Kaifeng still survived as a structured community. Even the Hangchow *kehillah*, large enough at one time to have worshipped in a synagogue of its own, had withered away. The Kaifeng colony was reduced in size, as Ricci remembered being told, to six or eight clans, presumably about 1,000 souls. They called themselves the adherents of the religion of *Yi-tz'u-lo-yeh* (a Chinese transliteration of *Yisrael*, the Hebrew term for Israel), and they had no word corresponding to the word *Jew*. Their synagogue, recently rebuilt on a grand scale, housed a number of Torah scrolls, including one said to have been written some 600 years previously. These Chinese Jews, Ricci gathered, observed most of the traditional festivals, refrained from eating pork, circumcised their infant sons and, in general, followed the law of Moses in a way that did not appear to him to be too far removed from the practices of the Jews of Europe. He surmised, nonetheless, that because of their long physical isolation from the main bodies of their people the Jews of Kaifeng would shortly be assimilated into the surrounding population.

To Ricci, the most exciting part of his talk with Ali was the impression he gained that there might be a few families in the Honan capital who were of Christian descent. This impression was reinforced when Ai came back to the church the next day with a man named Chang, a native of his own province who claimed to be of Christian lineage and who, like Ai, had traveled to Peking for the purpose of seeking a new government post. Having been told by Ai about his talk with Ricci, Chang had apparently detected certain tidbits in Ai's story that struck home and suggested to him that there could have been Christians among his own antecedents. Ricci, who did not consider this implausible, tried in the remaining six days of Chang's stay in Peking to get him to renounce his heathen ways and accept baptism, but Chang balked at the prospect. Ricci suspected that Chang's refusal to turn to Christianity stemmed from his reluctance, as a practicing polygamist, to make do with only one wife.

In December 1607 Ricci sent two Chinese converts to Kaifeng with instructions to determine whether there really were any Christians in the city and to collect whatever information they could about its Jewish community. One, adopting the name Antonio Leitam (or, Leitão), had become affiliated with the Jesuit Order as a lay brother. The other, a member of the literati class, possessed the advantage of having been born and raised in the Kaifeng region. Leitam and his companion, whose identity is not known, failed to discover any Christians in Kaifeng, but they had no trouble finding the synagogue, the Jews, and the chief rabbi. To the rabbi, whose Hebrew name is thought to have been Abishai, they delivered a letter entrusted to them by Ricci, the gist of which was that in their house of worship in Peking the Jesuits had all the books of the Hebrew Bible—and also a set of later Scriptures called the New Testament. This New Testament, the letter explained, would be of particular interest to the Jews of Kaifeng, for in it they would finally be able to read the story of the Messiah who had come sixteen centuries earlier to redeem their own people and all the other peoples of the world as well.

The reply of the rabbi left the priest bemused. He did not understand, the rabbi wrote, how a person of Ricci's vast erudition could believe that the Messiah had already arrived when it was common knowledge that he had not and, moreover, was not expected to arrive for another 10,000 years. However, the rabbi continued, the great reputation of Ricci as a man of faith, compassion, and integrity had been made known to the Jews of Kaifeng by Ai T'ien, and as he himself was now old, sick, and without a competent successor, perhaps Ricci would be interested in moving to Kaifeng and accepting the position of chief rabbi of the city's Jewish community?

The rabbi, relying on the information that had been relayed to him by Ai concerning the beliefs and practices of Ricci and his congregation, seems to have had absolutely no conception of how wide the gap between Christianity and Judaism actually was. Ricci's assurance that the Messiah had already come was apparently looked upon by the rabbi as no more than a personal idiosyncracy, much too unimportant to stand in the way of his plan to appoint the Catholic priest to be chief rabbi of Kaifeng. What did disturb the ailing rabbi and could lead to a denial of the post to Ricci was something of far greater significance, for it concerned Ricci's everyday behavior rather than any outlandish theological notions he may have picked up. He had been told by Ai, the rabbi observed somewhat testily, that Ricci had strayed from the paths of righteousness in one particular. This departure from virtue, he warned, would have to be corrected; and only if it were would the offer to Ricci of the spiritual leadership of the Jewish community of Kaifeng still hold good. He was referring, the rabbi explained, to the matter of diet. The Jesuit priest could assume the office of chief rabbi of the city of Kaifeng, the old man stipulated, on the condition that he agree to give up eating pork.

Not quite two years after this unique interchange of correspondence, three young Jews came to Peking from Kaifeng, one of them a nephew of Ai. They were graciously received by the Jesuits, who laid on a sumptuous banquet in their honor but whose efforts to convert them to Christianity did more to confuse them than to persuade them that any spiritual advantage was to be gained by acceding to the importunities of their hosts. They reported that the old rabbi had recently passed away and complained that the son who had replaced him, presumably Rabbi Jacob, was not qualified to fill his father's shoes. On the basis of his talks with the three young men Ricci, already concerned lest the Kaifeng Jews be lost to the creeds of their immediate neighbors, became convinced that the establishment of a Jesuit mission in Kaifeng would not only keep this from happening but would simultaneously reap a bountiful harvest of conversions from Judaism to Christianity. He was reluctant, nevertheless, to attempt to organize a church in Kaifeng at that particular time, having been given to understand that the mandarin who was charged with the administration of the city would be ill-disposed toward such a venture. Within the year, in any event, Ricci was dead. His position as Superior of the China Mission was assumed by his colleague, Nicolò Longobardi. Longobardi, who had met the three Kaifeng Jews during their visit to Peking in 1609, was no less anxious to bring their congregation into the fold than Ricci had been. This was a hope, however, which he would not live to see fulfilled, not so much because he lacked the appropriate facilities and manpower for dealing with the Jews, but rather because their attachment to their own heritage was to prove considerably more enduring than either he or Ricci had judged it to be.

By the opening decade of the seventeenth century the prolonged absence of any medium of communication between Chinese Jewry and the extensive Jewish settlements of Central Asia—or any other foreign Jewish settlements, for that matter—was unquestionably making substantial inroads upon the communal integrity of the Kaifeng Jews. Their congregation was by no means in peril of imminent dissolution, Ricci's fears on that score notwithstanding, but the seeds of decay were beginning to sprout. Seven or eight generations of Jews were still to live out their lives in Kaifeng before their community ceased to function as a viable religious entity, and after that a nostalgic evocation of the traditions and ethnic origins of their fathers, coupled perhaps with a sense of foreboding that they would always feel ill at ease as newcomers to an alien creed, was to induce two or three subsequent generations to profess at least a nominal allegiance to the ancient faith from which they had sprung.

As the Jews of China seem never to have exceeded a few

thousand in number or to have attained any major positions of leadership in the empire's commercial, cultural, governmental, or military affairs, it is not at all surprising that throughout the long centuries of their survival as a distinct religious community they remained virtually unnoticed by their countrymen. In fact, even those relatively few Chinese who had reason to know that certain individuals living in their midst called themselves Israelites were prone to regard them as members of an insignificant sect attached to the nation's large Islamic population. The West, of course, could scarcely be expected to fall prey to this kind of error; and no sooner did the story of Matteo Ricci's strange encounter with Ai T'ien come to its attention than a hornet's nest of curiosity was stirred up. This, in turn, engendered a long chain of speculations purporting to shed light upon the saga and way of life of that exotic offshoot of Israel that had so long ago pushed its way to distant China. These speculations, utterly unwarranted for the most part, would in the end reveal immeasurably more about the populous Jewish and Christian Occidental societies in which they arose than about the microcosmic Sino-Semitic society with which they dealt.

PART ONE

THE WORLD
AND THE
CHINESE JEWS

1 ❖ THE EUROPEAN REACTION

T HE sensational news that a handful of Christians and a small enclave of Jews had been discovered in the interior of China was brought to Rome in a letter addressed by Matteo Ricci to Claudio Aquaviva, General of the Society of Jesus, on July 26, 1605, a month or so after Ai T'ien's two recorded visits to the Peking mission.[1] Some two and a half years later, the report received by Ricci from his emissaries on their return from Kaifeng dispelled any lingering doubts he may still have entertained regarding the essential credibility of Ai's story. Although he was disappointed to learn that those few individuals in Kaifeng whom his representatives took to be of Christian descent had refused pointblank to acknowledge any connection with Christianity, he saw in this merely the natural reluctance of an uneasy minority to confide in strangers. As for the Jews of Kaifeng, he considered their community to be on the verge of extinction as a religious entity. He was of course shaping his estimate of the situation in Kaifeng on information that was skimpy and not entirely accurate. In any case, he felt justified in writing Aquaviva on March 8, 1608, that the survival in China of a sprinkling of Christians and a modest assemblage of Jews had now been confirmed.[2]

On November 23, 1610, shortly after Ricci's death, his successor, Nicolò Longobardi, wrote to Aquaviva from Shao-chun, Kwangtung Province, that the Jews of China, surpassing the Christians "in number, rank, and wealth," not only protected the Christians but even allowed them "to offer their prayers in the synagogue of Kaifeng." Having thus established a modus vivendi between Jews who unquestionably did live in Kaifeng and Christians who almost certainly did not, he then petitioned Aquaviva to assign "one or two Fathers versed in the Hebrew language" to the task of winning over the Chinese Jews to the Christian faith. "May these Fathers come," he urged, "as there are so many Jews in several provinces of China, and those of the Cross will be retrieved with them."[3]

In 1613 Giulio Aleni, a Jesuit missionary who had recently been transferred to China from the nearby Portuguese colony of Macao and would later come to be known as "the Christian Confucius," made his way to Kaifeng and introduced himself to the Jewish community.[4] His arrival aroused considerable excitement, and his reception was marked by enthusiasm and good will. Because it was the stated policy of the reigning Ming emperors to prohibit the movement of their subjects to and from other lands and, at the same time, to keep as many foreigners as possible out of China, the Jews of Kaifeng had now been completely cut off from their brethren outside the country for at least a century, perhaps for considerably longer. Several generations having thus passed since they had last met a coreligionist who was not himself a Chinese national, the sudden appearance of Aleni in their midst presented them with a golden opportunity for discovering what was happening to their fellow Jews in other parts of the globe. They seem even to have thought at first that Aleni was himself a Jew, an impression that may well have been strengthened when they learned that he could read Hebrew—and better, perhaps, than their own rabbi, whose professional competence was of necessity limited to what he had been able to pick up from his father, whose office he now held. The Jews had every reason to expect, accordingly, that Aleni would be able to clarify certain scriptural and liturgical passages that they themselves could no longer understand.

Yet when the Jesuit came to the synagogue and asked to see its sacred writings, his request was brusquely rejected. Only a few years earlier, Ricci's emissaries had experienced no difficulties at all with regard to these same texts. The Jews had gladly provided Leitam and his companion with copies of the opening and closing verses of each of the five books of their Torah, so that Ricci could have these verses compared with the corresponding passages in the Scriptures available to the West. In the case of Aleni, however, the rabbi had even refused to draw back the curtains surrounding the synagogal Torah scrolls, thus denying him as much as a glimpse of the Pentateuchs themselves.

But why? The priest had not been barred from the synagogue. What happened once he was in it?

It has been suggested that because Aleni was then unable to speak Chinese, he simply could not make himself adequately understood by his hosts. One would think, however, that at least a rudimentary form of communication might have been worked out in that language, for Aleni had begun to study it immediately upon arriving in China; or, alternatively, that even though the Kaifeng Jews had by then probably lost their ability to carry on a sustained conversation in Hebrew, Aleni should have been able to convey some basic thoughts to them by the use of a few carefully chosen common Hebrew phrases. It is not too likely, moreover, that the Jesuit priest would have been traveling across the country without a companion capable of speaking fluently one or more of the Chinese dialects and of writing and reading the language's universally accepted ideographic system as well. It is quite possible, of course, that Aleni, setting a precedent that other missionaries to Kaifeng were to follow, pressed the congregational leaders to sell or give him a portion of their biblical and liturgical manuscripts, and particularly a *sepher torah* (Torah scroll) so that he could send these on to Europe—a proposition that would scarcely have endeared him to either the rabbi or the lay authorities of the community, and might well have led to harsh words. It is also conceivable that, carried away by his zeal to convert his hosts to Christianity, he aroused their ire by blurting out in the synagogue the same kind of callous and offensive opinions regarding their theological beliefs that more than one missionary to China would later choose to express in places where the Kaifeng Jews were not apt to come across them, such as in letters destined for Rome and in books printed in Europe.[5]

Six or seven years following Aleni's rebuff at the hands of the *kehillah,* Longobardi, accompanied by Father Jean Fernandez, traversed Honan Province. Longobardi is reported by a contemporary, Antonio de Geuvea (or, de Gouvea), to have stopped over in Kaifeng and to have called on the Jews. On meeting them, according to de Geuvea:[6]

> he spoke a few words in Persian [New Persian, probably, the old lingua franca of Asiatic trade, which some of the Kaifeng Jews still knew]. Everybody was highly delighted, believing that their guest was of their own nation. And when they learned the Father was there, they wanted to invite him immediately. They fixed the day, the following Sabbath. And when the Father entered the synagogue they treated him with great honor, being certain that he was of the same stock and of the same faith as themselves.

But Longobardi's reception soon turned cold:

> So long as they thought that the Father was of their faith, they gave him a magnificent welcome and listened with great joy to the stories of the Old Testament patriarchs; but once they noticed the pictures in his Bible, abominable in their eyes, they understood he was a Christian of the Cross who worshipped Jesus, whom they called Isaï [Ersa], a name taken from the Moors, and they immediately changed about, urging the Father to leave the synagogue, which they thought had been profaned by his presence. He would have liked to discuss the Bible with them, but it was of no use. They had suddenly grown distrustful, and conversation no longer suited them.

In 1628 Father François Sambiasi established the first Jesuit mission house in Kaifeng, the administration of which was entrusted three years later to the Portuguese priest Rodriguez de Figueiredo. In 1642, the city being under attack by rebel armies, a Jesuit lay brother, François Ferreira, was sent to persuade Figueiredo to leave the beleaguered provincial capital while it was still possible to do so, but the priest refused to abandon his followers. He was never heard from again and is thought to have drowned on or about the ninth of October of the same year in the flood that was let loose when the dikes of the Yellow River were broken as part of a military maneuver designed to put an end to the stalemate, which had developed between the insurgent forces and the defenders of the city. Early in the eighteenth century the Kaifeng Jews stated that Figueiredo and also Christian Enriquez (who rehabilitated the mission in 1676, shortly after his arrival in Honan) had each been in their synagogue several times.[7] Since the synagogue, like Figueiredo's church, was destroyed by the flood of 1642, Enriquez must have visited the newer structure that the congregation dedicated on the site of the older one in 1663, or slightly before, and was to serve as its house of worship for the next two centuries. Unfortunately, nothing is known about the contacts which Figueiredo and Enriquez made with the Jews of Kaifeng other than that such contacts are reported to have occurred.

On the whole, the literate circles of Europe remained unaware that a remnant of the House of Israel had been discovered in China until the fact was brought to their attention by the publication in 1615 of Nicholas Trigault's edition of Ricci's journals. Trigault, who arrived in Peking some weeks after Ricci's death, assisted Longobardi for about three years in the administration of the Jesuit establishment in China. As part of his duties, he traveled through six of the country's principal provinces and may even have visited Kaifeng. In 1613 he was sent by Longobardi to Rome for the purpose of persuading the hierarchy of the Roman Catholic church to increase its support of the China Mission and broaden the scope of its activities. He was also to bring back a library of scientific works and a cadre of scientists, so that the Chinese upper classes could be given a taste of what Western culture had to offer. The object was to effect the Christianization of China by first converting her elite and then, with them and through them, the ordinary people of the country.

Ricci's journals, written in his native Italian, had been located among his effects not long after his death. Longobardi and Trigault quickly realized that if this literary windfall could be disseminated throughout the Christian world it would provide the reading public with an intriguing, sympathetic, and informative history of the Jesuit accomplishment in China. As such, it might be expected to contribute substantially to the success of Trigault's impending mission to Europe. The two priests therefore agreed that during the long voyage home, Trigault would edit Ricci's papers and translate them into Latin, the lingua franca of Western scholarship.

Trigault was unable to complete his work on the Ricci manuscripts before landing in Italy; but by January 1615 he had translated the last page, and the text was ready for submission to the printer. The book was published later that year at Augsburg under the title *De Christiana expeditione apud Sinas suscepta ab Societate Jesu*. It proved to be a bestseller, so much so that by 1648 five editions had appeared in Latin, three in French, and one each in German, Spanish, and Italian.[8] Ricci's journals were thus spread across the length and breadth of Europe. They included, of course, his account of his meetings with Ai, as well as a recapitulation of the experiences of the two representatives he had dispatched to Kaifeng, and a description of the visit made by the three young Kaifeng Jews to the mission house at Peking.

But Trigault was not the only intermediary through whom the presence of Jews in faraway China was made known to the West. Their survival in the Middle Kingdom and the odd bits of information that Longobardi and Fernandez had collected about them were recorded by the Jesuit Emmanuel Diaz in a work issued at Rome in 1624.[9] A few years later another Jesuit, Alvarez Semmedo, claimed to have uncovered traces of a Jewish community that had only recently existed in Nanking.[10] During his stay in that city, Semmedo declared, he was told by a Muslim of four Jewish families—the last Jews in Nanking—who, abandoning their faith because they no longer had a qualified religious leader, had embraced Islam. In 1642 Semmedo published a work that included a summary of Ricci's contacts with the Chinese Jews and chronicled Aleni's 1613 visit to Kaifeng.[11] This went through several editions in a number of languages.

There must inevitably have been some word-of-mouth transmission of the news of the Jesuit discovery of the Kaifeng community in addition to the written and printed reports. In any event, by the middle of the seventeenth century, virtually everybody in the West who was actively interested in either the far-flung missionary activities of the Church or the condition of world Jewry should have had ample opportunity to become

2. Title page of the first printing of Nicholas Trigault's edition of Matteo Ricci's journals [Augsburg 1615]. Ricci is portrayed on the right, Saint Francis Xavier, on the left.

aware that the Jewish Diaspora had spread to the interior of the Chinese Empire.

Actually, stories of Jews being found in the Flowery Kingdom were scarcely new. There is a hint, but only a hint, that the Arab traveler Suleiman encountered Jews there during a visit he allegedly made to the interior of China some time before 851.[12] Shortly after this, an unqualified assertion that Jews were trading with, and in, China was made by ibn Khurdadhbih, the so-called Postmaster of Baghdad, who in his description of the Jewish merchants known as the Radanites spoke of them as taking ship in Spain and France and proceeding all the way to China and back by any of four well-established routes.[13] This was corroborated early in the tenth century by the Arab geographer ibn al-Faqih.[14] A short time before 916 another Muslim chronicler, Abu Zaid al-Sirafi, writing about the capture of Khanfu (presumed to be Canton) in the year A.H. 264 (877/78), told of the massacre of "120,000 Muslims, Jews, Christians, and Magians who lived in this city and became merchants in it, apart from those killed among the Chinese inhabitants." Abu Zaid justified his seemingly improbable figure of 120,000 as being derived from the records of the taxes that were imposed upon the non-Chinese residents of Khanfu.[15] His report was based in large part on a visit to the then imperial capital Ch'ang-an (Sian), reputedly made by ibn Wahab in the last years of the ninth century. Ibn Wahab, incidentally, claimed that he was granted a lengthy audience by the emperor of China in which much of the conversation turned on the religious beliefs of the East and the West. The Arab was greatly impressed by the emperor's intimate knowledge of the tenets of Judaism, Christianity, and Islam.[16] If ibn Wahab's story is true— and there is no reason to suspect that it is not—it suggests that by the latter part of the ninth century the Chinese had already experienced enough contact with members of all three Western faiths to be able to distinguish between the doctrines these outlanders held in common and the doctrines over which they disagreed.

Apparently, Abu Zaid's description of the slaughter at Khanfu was considered authentic by later Muslim historians, for it was repeated, although with slight modifications, by al-Masudi ("the

Arab Herodotus") in 943, ibn al-Athir in the twelfth century, and Ab'lfida in the fourteenth.[17] In 1346 the Arab traveler ibn Battuta, visiting Hangchow, wrote: "We entered . . . through a gate called the Jews' Gate. In this city live Jews, Christians, and sun-worshipping Turks [Parsees], a large number in all."[18]

A Persian author of the tenth century, Buzurg ibn Shahriyar of Ramhurmuz, recorded the adventures of "Ishaq, son of a Jew," who left Oman with very limited funds and came back thirty years later, in 912 or 913, in a ship of his own, laden with cargo he had purchased in China.[19] Buzurg's tale is, perhaps, sheer fantasy, and, in any event, does not allude to the presence of Jewish settlements in China.

Whether the accounts provided by Buzurg and the Arabs reached the scholars of Europe before Ricci's meetings with Ai or, having reached them, commanded any significant attention is a matter for conjecture. But by the late ninth century, substantial numbers of Jews in Europe and elsewhere were definitely reading and talking about two coreligionists whom fate had brought together dramatically in that remote land known as China. One of the protagonists in this unlikely meeting had described it vividly in a small book of travels, which he said was composed some time after his safe return home. He called himself Eldad ha-Dani (Eldad, that is, of the Lost Tribe of Dan), and he told how he and a companion were captured by a band of cannibals. His comrade was eaten, but he was taken by his captors to China. There his plight was made known to an unnamed Jewish merchant "of the tribe of Issachar," by whom he was ransomed for the sum of thirty-two pieces of gold and brought out of the country.[20] Eldad's credibility rightly enough was challenged by many of his medieval readers, notably by Abraham ibn Ezra and Rabbi Meir of Rothenberg; but others, among them such luminaries as Rashi and Hasdai ibn Shaprut, took his claims more seriously.

A suggestion of Jewish trading with and in China, if not of residence there, occurs in the widely read narrative written circa 1170 by the Jewish traveler Benjamin of Tudela. Benjamin, whose reputation for reliability is much sounder than Eldad's, merely points out that Jews lived in certain areas from which, his readers are free to infer, access to China should have been relatively easy. This brings up the possibility, of course, that Jews could have taken advantage of the opportunity to travel to and from China, and probably did—perhaps even settling there.[21]

By the thirteenth century, Christians had already met Jews in China. Marco Polo speaks of them as residing in the country in or about 1286. Kublai Khan, he also says, ecumenically observed the festivals of the Muslim, Christian, and Jewish subjects of his sprawling empire.[22] John of Montecorvino, a Franciscan writing from China at the very end of the thirteenth century, comments rather casually that Jews live there.[23] In January 1326 Andrew of Perugia, Bishop of Zayton (Ch'üan-chou), complains of a lack of success in converting them to Christianity.[24] And in 1342 another cleric, John of Marignolli, talks of having participated in "glorious disputations in Khanbaliq [Marco Polo's Cambaluc, that is, Peking]" with both Jews and Muslims.[25] In 1546 and in 1552, rumors of a Jewish presence in China are relayed in letters written from the Orient by Francis Xavier, later to be canonized for his missionary work in that part of the world.[26] Similar rumors crop up again in the last years of the century in connection with his nephew Jerome Xavier and the famous Jesuit traveler Benedict Goes.[27] In a letter dated 1565 Galeotto Perera, a Portuguese who had been imprisoned in China from 1549 to 1561, remarks that in Chinese courts of law "the Moores, Gentiles, & Jews, have all theyr sundry oathes," and that all sects swear "by the thynges they do worshyppe."[28]

Matteo Ricci's letters and journals yielded more details concerning the Jews of China than all the older reports put together. They also suggested that Jews had been living in the country for so many generations that nobody could really say when they first arrived there or from where they originally came. However, in the years immediately preceding Ricci's encounters with Ai, the early references to a Jewish presence in China seem to have been discounted as outdated, the presumption apparently being that whatever forms of Judaism may once have flourished in the Chinese Empire must long ago have disappeared. But now, with Ricci's testimony to draw upon, it was concluded that the Jews had been settled in China "since time immemorial,"[29] a chronological determination sufficiently vague to encourage the promulgation of a strange two-pronged theory to the effect that the Chinese Jews were descended from the Ten Lost Tribes of Israel and had been living in utter isolation from the rest of the Jews of the world since long before the establishment of Christianity.

This was a concept eminently suited to the temper of the times, and it was not disputed. In short order, moreover, it led certain Christian theologians to speculate that the sacred texts of the Kaifeng synagogue might well be identical with those of the ancient Hebrews—perhaps as pristine, they saw fit to suggest, as the Scriptures that had circulated in Judea for some centuries antedating the birth of Christ.

The European theologians, at least half convinced that the Torah scrolls and other biblical manuscripts of the Chinese Jews would turn out to be the oldest scriptural texts in existence, or at least true and faithful copies of such texts, now began to see a compelling need for comparing the Kaifeng Bibles with their own. Ricci's emissaries had been given copies of the opening and closing portions of each of the books comprising the Pentateuchal texts used by the *kehillah,* and no differences could be found between these passages and the parallel Western verses. But such samplings were too limited to permit any meaningful evaluations. What was needed was a complete Torah scroll from the ark of the Kaifeng synagogue and, if possible, exemplars of the community's other biblical books as well.

The point was that many non-Jewish European scholars sincerely believed the Hebrew Scriptures, with which they were familiar, to be neither complete nor reliable. Christian polemicists had been insisting for well over a millennium that the contents of the Hebrew Bible were not to be fully trusted—that they had been tampered with.[30] The logic of these scholars was quite simple. To begin with, the New Testament contained several quotations which although purporting to be from the Old Testament could not be found in the Old Testament. Therefore, the Old Testament texts that were available to them were incomplete. Moreover, it was utterly inconceivable to men of their convictions that the Jewish Scriptures could have failed to foretell the coming of the Christ in very specific terms; and as the texts they owned lacked any prophecies relating to this epochal event (or, at any rate, as others saw the matter, prophecies so clearly enunciated that even the Jews would not be able to deny them), it was self-evident that all such prophecies must have been excised or re-written. The Christian theologians therefore concluded that the rabbis of the talmudic era had blasphemously expunged or altered a number of verses predicting the birth and ministry of Jesus of Nazareth.

The Jews, of course, fought back with every weapon at their command, for an accusation of this kind struck at the very foundation of their faith and provided their enemies with a marvelous excuse for harassing or even destroying them. An impressive array of Jewish scholars had methodically and indignantly refuted the calumnious indictment—but it would not die and was in fact coopted by the theologians of Islam who, beginning with Muhammad himself, grandly extended the indictment to include the New Testament. Their claim, quite simply, was that both Christians and Jews were guilty of having edited out of their respective Scriptures numerous verses foretelling the coming of the Prophet.[31]

In 1510, after the Christian version of the old canard was revived as part of an onslaught launched against the Talmud by the Dominicans of Cologne with the assistance of the Jewish apostate Johann Pfefferkorn, the faculty of the University of Mainz went on record as advising the emperor Maximilian to order the burning not only of the Talmud but of the Hebrew Bible as well. The faculties of Erfurt and Cologne, though not averse to seeing the Talmud destroyed, were willing to allow the Jews to keep their Bibles.[32] The Jews, fortunate enough to have such distinguished and influential humanists as Johann Reuchlin, Ulrich von Hutten, and Erasmus on their side, moved heaven and earth in defense of both Talmud and Torah.[33] In this instance the Jews prevailed, more or less, but prudently began to build up a system of internal prepublication censorship in the hope of forestalling even more drastic action on the part of the Church. Here they were not successful: apart from the Bible itself, nearly all Hebrew texts published in Europe were soon to be subjected to a clerical censorship more stringent by far than that imposed upon non-Jewish works, and often administered by hostile incompetents who had only the vaguest comprehension of what they were reading.

Time passed and the dispute over the textual integrity of the Hebrew Bible simmered on. Caught in the throes of the bitter conflict that raged between the forces of Protestantism and Catholicism, European Jewry suffered excruciatingly. In the fury of the counter-Reformation the venom of the more reactionary elements within both Christian camps was relentlessly directed against the helpless Jewish minorities living under their control. Old repressive measures were dusted off and applied more harshly than ever before, and new ones were introduced. Persecution became the order of the day, with censorship and book burning emerging as commonplace weapons in a continuing campaign designed to bedevil the Jews and plug the wellsprings of all nonconformist thought, both Jewish and Christian. In the struggle for the intellectual emancipation of Europe's Christians, let alone her Jews, the question of whether to destroy the literature of Judaism or permit it to survive mushroomed into an issue of sufficient importance to induce one twentieth-century historian to venture the opinion that "it was the controversy raging about the burning of Jewish books, the *cause célèbre* of sixteenth-century Europe, that divided Scholasticism from Humanism, the obscurantists from the tolerants, religious fanaticism from enlightenment—and the Middle Ages from the Modern Era." [34] The controversy spilled over into the next century and well beyond that, and while it ran its course hundreds of thousands of Hebrew volumes were consigned to the flames—not only works of a religious bent, such as prayer books and tractates of the Talmud, but in many instances anything at hand that had been written or printed in Hebrew characters, even medical and scientific treatises. When listings of condemned books were prepared by the authorities, the Hebrew Bible was generally excluded, but as they desecrated synagogues and looted private dwellings the rampaging mobs, led as often as not by crucifix-wielding members of the holy orders, burned or defaced every Hebrew text in sight. Torah scrolls were not spared.

The leadership of the Roman Catholic church was repeatedly urged to issue a formal denunciation of the "corrupt" Hebrew

Bible. During the pontificate of the ruthlessly anti-Jewish Paul IV (1555–59), for example, the hoary charge that the Torah had been falsified was once again raised, this time in the virulent pages of Franciscus Torensis's *De sola lectione legis et prophetarum Judaeis cum Mosaico ritu, et culta permittenda*. Yet, while Pope Paul embittered the lives of the Jews, ordered them locked up in ghettos, martyred them at Ancona and elsewhere, and burned tens of thousands of their books, he stopped short of decreeing the wholesale destruction of the Hebrew Scriptures. However, in 1570 and 1571 at Antwerp, the Duke of Alva, not content with the index of forbidden Hebrew books promulgated by the Council of Trent in 1564, augmented it with the sweeping Spanish restrictions "against all books written in Hebrew."[35] This ban, of course, included the Torah.

A powerful political or military leader like Alva might outlaw or destroy the Hebrew scriptural texts to suit his own fancy, but the hierarchy of the Church was forced to tread more warily. The fact was that Rome found herself impaled on the horns of a dilemma: by ruling that the Jewish Bible was textually acceptable, the Church would be rendering aid and comfort to a faith she condemned; by ruling, on the other hand, that the Jewish texts were unreliable, she would be undercutting that vital portion of scriptural writings on which her own legitimacy was predicated and which she chose to call the Old Testament—that is, the Testament that had been supplemented and in many ways even supplanted by the New Testament.

In 1578 Cardinal Guglielmo Sirleto was assigned the task of compiling an index of prohibited Hebrew works. Sirleto, well trained in Hebrew and better qualified to carry out such an assignment than perhaps any of his colleagues, designated the Italian Jewish talmudist and physician Lazarus de Viterbo to draw up a brief defending the purity of the Hebrew Bible against its detractors. Lazarus, in no position to demand that the burden of proof be thrust upon those who were proffering the charges rather than upon those who were being herded into the defendant's dock, reconstructed the more persuasive of the classic rabbinic arguments on behalf of the integrity of the received text and submitted these to Sirleto.[36] However, no clear-cut statement of policy came out of the prelate's deliberations, so that the Church was still left officially uncommitted, neither affirming nor denying the integrity of the Hebrew scriptural texts. The Church's failure to take a firm stand in the matter, whether intentional or not, encouraged those clerics who either distrusted the Hebrew Scriptures or simply loathed everything Jewish to keep on challenging the right of the synagogue to use them.

The retrieval of a pure and authentic version of the Scriptures, the Church's biblical scholars hoped, would lead to the resolution of certain apparent discrepancies in the text which, although of relatively minor interest to anyone but a specialist, were still disturbing, and could eventually raise problems extending well beyond the confines of the library or the lecture hall. More important by far, however, it would facilitate the task of converting the Jews of the world to Christianity, for once confronted with the lost or altered passages, and thereby with incontrovertible evidence that they had been betrayed by the rabbis of the Talmud, they would be left with little choice but to flock to the baptismal font. And it was such a mass conversion of the Jews, the Christian writers were convinced, that would signal and pave the way for the ardently awaited Second Coming of the Christ. Many Christian theologians were optimistic that the long-sought-for "corrections" would be found in the Chinese Torahs.

One of the more obvious defenses against the Christian charges that the sages of the Talmud had deliberately falsified the Hebrew Scriptures was based on the proposition that it would have been logistically impossible for such an action to be carried out with any appreciable degree of success. The rabbinical authorities of the Middle Ages had pointed out that in the era in which the decision to alter the Bible was purportedly made there were already enormous numbers of the various books of the entire Hebrew scriptural canon circulating in virtually all parts of the known world. By what act of necromancy then, the Jewish writers demanded, could the talmudic scholars have effected a simultaneous excision of all the christological prophecies from all the multitudinous and widely dispersed books in which they supposedly occurred?

If one were to imagine, the Jewish scholars contended, that the talmudic sages were actually guilty of having attempted to change the Word of God, then one would be forced to concede that their efforts in this connection would have provoked a storm of outrage so noisy and violent that it could not have escaped becoming prominently and indelibly etched into both the recorded history of Judaism and its legend and folklore. Why then,they asked, did the written and oral chronicles of Judaism fail to recall any of this? Moreover, it could reasonably be presumed that some Jews would not have heard of the alleged rabbinic edict to alter the text of the Holy Writ, that others flatly refused to abide by it, and that numerous biblical manuscripts—many of them owned by individuals who were not Jews—survived intact for an assortment of undetermined reasons. And what about the texts that were already in the hands of the earliest followers of Christ? How could these Christians have been persuaded to obey so repulsive a decree, especially when it emanated from a non-Christian source?

One might therefore expect, the Jews argued, that large numbers of scriptural works would in no way have been affected by the impious campaign reputedly mounted for the specific purpose of revising them, and that generations upon generations of scribes would then have used these unscathed survivors as models from which to make countless other copies. All these transcripts, it followed, would have to contain the mysterious Nazarene passages that the Christian polemicists were talking about. The Jewish writers consequently challenged their opponents to produce even one authentic example of such an "untainted" biblical manuscript. The latter had of course never been able to do so.

It now appeared to the Christian theologians that the recently developed theory concerning the Chinese Jews—that bands of Israelites had reached China before the Hebrew Scriptures were "corrupted" and, being totally cut off from their brethren in other parts of the world ever since their arrival in the country, might well have preserved their Bible in its pristine state—presented a heaven-sent opportunity for picking up the gauntlet flung at them by the Jews. Among the first to recognize this—perhaps the first —was the Jesuit missionary Alvarez Semmedo, who in 1642 brought the idea to the attention of his contemporaries. The

Kaifeng Jews, he reminded them, "have no knowledge at all of Christ, so that it seemeth they were entered into *China* before he came into the World; or at least, if they have ever heard of him the memorie of it is quite lost." It was consequently imperative, he argued, that a concerted effort be undertaken "to see their *Bible,* for perhaps they have not corrupted it, as our Jews [in Europe] have done, to obscure the glories of our *Redeemer.*"[37]

Semmedo's line of thought, wide of the mark though it was, struck a responsive chord in the hearts and minds of many of his readers. Gottfried Wilhelm von Leibniz, illustrious philosopher in the Age of Reason and independent codiscoverer with Isaac Newton of the calculus, was one of those who were seduced by Semmedo's strained conjectures. In a letter dated January 1, 1700, Leibniz informed Father Antoine Verjus that he had recently requested Father Charles le Gobien to urge the Jesuit establishment in China to arrange for a thorough examination of the "Old Testament of the Chinese Jews in order to collate its text with that of the Hebrew Scriptures employed in Europe."[38] He had read about the Chinese Jews in the writings of both Semmedo and François Bernier,[39] Leibniz explained, and he hoped that it might now "be possible to come upon certain hitherto unknown details in the Chinese texts, since it would seem that for a long time the Chinese Jews have had absolutely no contact with the Jews of Europe." Hence, he went on, "the Chinese Jews may still hold some of those books or passages which the European Jews have perhaps altered or suppressed out of hatred for Christianity." If, he suggested, it were not possible to examine the complete text of a Chinese Bible, then selected portions of the opening chapters of the Book of Genesis should be copied in order to see whether its catalog of "begats" corresponded with that of the Septuagint. The need for securing the Kaifeng texts seemed so important to him that he stressed it again in at least two subsequent letters, one written circa 1705 and the other in 1707.[40]

In 1707, in the preface to the seventh volume of the *Lettres édifiantes et curieuses,* an anthology destined to run to dozens of printed volumes of correspondence received in Europe from Jesuits stationed in remote corners of the globe, le Gobien summed up the position then being taken by many Christian theologians vis-à-vis the Chinese Jews.[41] He observed that the Jews of Europe stood accused, and for reasons that seemed quite convincing to him, of having "altered the Scriptures—perhaps by omitting or transposing entire chapters; perhaps by merely changing several verses or words; perhaps by revising those passages which did not suit them; or perhaps by altering the punctuation in various passages in order to make them support their own views." Their purpose? "To confirm the interpretations already arrived at by their sect."

The existence of the Chinese Jews, he then declared, "was until recently unknown not only to Christians but also to their fellow Jews, who are dispersed throughout the nations. Consequently, the Chinese Jews may well own texts of the Scriptures which have been preserved in a pristine state and are free of those defects which our scholars and theologians believe they have found in the texts currently available to them."

It would be of immense value to Christianity, le Gobien stressed, if the West were given an opportunity to compare the scriptural texts held by the Chinese Jews with those held by the Jews of Europe and to compile a list of the discrepancies, which he was sure would be uncovered. With such a document in its hands, he reasoned, the Church would experience little difficulty in exposing the multitude of errors propounded in the Kabbalah, that mystical body of literature that had so fired the Jewish imagination—and the imagination also, he could readily have added, of the many Christian humanists who sought to correlate certain of its teachings with Christian dogma. It would be desirable too, he felt, "to gain an insight into the practices of the Chinese Jews and be provided thereby with the appropriate weapons for combating the extravagances of the Talmud." The need to discredit the Talmud was critically important, he went on, "for it is hard to believe that the customs of the Chinese Jews can be identical with those we encounter with revulsion in that monstrous jumble of frivolous, impure, superstitious, and sometimes impious statements with which the Talmud is filled. It is of course quite likely that the Chinese Jews are just as fatuously minded as the Jews of Europe, but it is simply not possible that two sets of dreamers who have absolutely no means of communicating with one another could each come up with precisely the same hallucinations."

Moreover, a detailed study of the Chinese Jews would enable the Church to prove to the Jews of Europe that their religious beliefs were based on human teachings and were not divinely inspired. "It appears to me," he declared, "that the Chinese Jews could then be easily led to the recognition of the true Messiah and into conversion to Christianity."

Le Gobien wanted desperately to break the hold of the Talmud on Western Jewry. Wrongly assuming that the Kaifeng Jews had at no time in their history been directly or indirectly exposed to the teachings of the Talmud, he easily convinced himself that their ignorance of its contents presented Christianity with a singular opportunity for discrediting the work in its entirety. He expounded his views as to how this might be accomplished:

> One of the greatest stumbling blocks to the conversion of the Jews has been their deep-seated attachment to the chimerical writings of their rabbis, writings to which they have been exposed since childhood and which arouse in them only contempt for other areas of knowledge and for the people who cultivate them. The Talmud, according to the Jewish scholars, is the only study worth pursuing, the magnum opus of divine wisdom and the soul, so to say, of the Scriptures. It is consequently futile, they claim, to look into Holy Writ itself. They believe that if one merely has recourse to the rabbinical interpretations of the Scriptures one will gain thereby a true understanding of the Bible, an understanding which would otherwise be unattainable. If we could therefore make the Jews see that the tenets of Judaism as they comprehend them are not necessarily the same as those held by Jews living in certain other regions— regions, that is, to which the teachings of the Talmud have never penetrated—we will have convinced them to stop venerating their Talmud. We might also be able to do likewise with regard to those Jews who live in China by demonstrating to them that the faith to which they subscribe differs greatly from the faith of their brethren in the West—and this, despite the fact that each group brags that the doctrine *it* clings to comes directly from God.

While the first imperatives of the Christian theologians were to bring the Kaifeng *kehillah* into the Christian fold and to secure as many of its biblical manuscripts as possible, there were other aspects to the fascination Europe developed with regard to the Chinese Jews. People were intrigued by the challenge of unraveling the mystery posed by the survival of a community of Jews in China, by the quirk in the historical process that had enabled a band of wandering Israelites to find a haven in that remote land and then preserve its communal identity for uncounted generations. There was, as might be expected, also the factor of curiosity, the desire to know what these strange Jews looked like, how they lived, and how they resembled and differed from the Jews of Europe. In short, the *kehillah* of Kaifeng had become a veritable Chinese puzzle that the West felt obliged to resolve.

Without exception, the most telling consequences of the hold exercised by the Kaifeng Jews on the Western imagination were self-imposed by the West. The suspicion that the Kaifeng biblical texts might prove more authentic than any which Europe had inherited was merely one of the earliest of a series of illusions that the West was to entertain respecting the Chinese Jews. In essence, the European exaggeration of both the age of the Jewish settlement in China and the duration of its isolation from the rest of world Jewry magnified the historical importance of the Chinese Jews many times over, with one scholar after another seeing in them things that were not there and never had been there. Inevitably, the Chinese Jews, blissfully unaware of how the very fact of their existence was being manipulated by the West for its own purposes, were made to play a succession of very strange roles in Christian thought and in certain areas of exclusively Jewish concern as well.

Until the opening decades of the eighteenth century virtually everything Europe knew about the Jewish inhabitants of China was derived from a few letters written by Ricci, Longobardi, and Semmedo, and from several brief passages occurring in Trigault's editions of Ricci's journals and in the printed works of Diaz and Semmedo. Occasional snatches of information were also gleaned from a limited number of other sources. Lumped together, it all amounted to very little.

In 1707, a letter dated November 5, 1704, and written in

Kaifeng by the Jesuit priest Jean-Paul Gozani was published in the *Lettres édifiantes*.[42] This letter, addressed to Father Joseph Suarez and printed in the volume to which le Gobien contributed his preface summarizing the reasons for the Catholic interest in the Chinese Jews, provided fresh material regarding the Kaifeng congregation and, as far as can be determined, was the first publicized written communication dealing with the Kaifeng Jews to be received in Europe directly from a Caucasian who had sought them out on their home grounds. This does not mean that there had been no personal contacts in Kaifeng between European Christians and Chinese Jews in the ninety-one years since Aleni's visit in 1613 to that of Gozani in 1704. Longobardi, according to de Guevea, was in the synagogue, apparently about 1619, and Figueiredo and Enriquez, according to the statement made by the Jews to Gozani and recorded in his letter of November 5, 1704, were there on several occasions. It would be surprising, moreover, if of the Jesuits who at one time or another resided in Kaifeng or visited there—men such as François Sambiasi, Brother Christophe, Joseph-Antoine Provana, François Ferreira, and Pierre Canevari— none had ever tried to convert the Jews to Christianity or at least enter into some form of dialogue with them. One must conclude, therefore, that the silence of these missionaries on the subject of the Chinese Jews is more apparent than real. In any case, if they did transmit any significant information to Europe it was never made public, and consequently had no discernible effect upon the West's conceptualizations of the Jews of China. Certainly, no indication has yet been uncovered in the literature published during the seventeenth century of even one tangible addition to Europe's meager fund of knowledge respecting the Chinese Jews after 1642, the year in which Semmedo's account of Aleni's visit to Kaifeng appeared in print.

The disclosure that an ancient Jewish outpost was still holding out in the interior of China elicited more response from Christian intellectuals than from their Jewish counterparts. The latter would obviously have been curious about their coreligionists who had for so long made their home in the remotenesses of China, but strangely enough only one discussion of Chinese Jewry is known to have emanated from a Jewish source in the entire seventeenth century, and this was addressed by its author, the celebrated Manasseh ben Israel of Amsterdam, primarily to Christians rather than to Jews. Almost as surprising is the fact that neither Manasseh nor any other Jewish writer of the period saw fit to make an issue of the exaggerated importance that the Christian theologians were attributing to the acquisition of a Kaifeng Bible. Knowing as they did that verse 4:2 of Deuteronomy (repeated in 13:1), "You shall not add anything to what I command you or take anything away from it," had always been understood by Hebrew *sopherim* (scribes) as an awesome injunction from on high to safeguard the purity of the received text, and convinced that no other ancient document could have been as meticulously transmitted as the Jewish Scriptures, Manasseh and his rabbinical contemporaries had little reason for experiencing any qualms concerning the essential integrity of the biblical manuscripts that might come out of Kaifeng. Manasseh did allude to the fact that Ricci's emissaries had been provided with copies of a number of passages from the individual volumes of the Kaifeng synagogue's Pentateuchs and that these verses were then found to be identical with those known to the West, but he did not dwell on the matter.[43] Nevertheless, the Jewish scholars must have been dismayed by the repeated Christian insinuations that the texts belonging to the Kaifeng *kehillah* might be markedly different from those held in Europe. In spite of this, they issued no rebuttals, realizing perhaps that such efforts would prove futile and that the matter could be resolved only when the Kaifeng manuscripts eventually became available for direct examination.

In the Christian mind, Ricci's rediscovery of the Chinese Jews, aside from laying the groundwork for the procurement of their biblical documents, presented the Church with two outstanding opportunities that cried for exploitation. The more immediate of these was to persuade the members of the Kaifeng congregation to sever their seemingly attenuated ties to Judaism and come over en masse to Christianity. Ricci had thought that this could be done fairly easily, and in 1610 a sanguine Longobardi suggested that the task might be accomplished in short order by assigning one or two Jesuits familiar with the Hebrew language to spend some time in Kaifeng working with the Jews. Yet three centuries of sporadic missionary effort, first by Catholics and later by both Catholics and Protestants, were to bring very few Kaifeng Jews to the cross. The Jews of Kaifeng did of course drift away from their ancestral faith with the passing of centuries, but those who took formal leave of it and sought new ties elsewhere chose almost unanimously to convert to Islam or to the creeds of the great masses of their countrymen rather than to Christianity.

The second opportunity opened up by Ricci had to do with the delineation of the rules governing the conduct and religious practices of all Chinese converts to Catholicism. As certain factions of the hierarchy saw the matter, the experiences of the Kaifeng Jews, by reason of their affiliation with the oldest monotheistic faith of all and their lengthy residence in idolatrous surroundings, could be of valuable assistance to the Church in the formulation of these rules. In brief, it was assumed (and quite rightly) that the Kaifeng community had found it both necessary and expedient to modify a number of its ancient traditions and practices in order to adapt them to the soil of China. The nature and extent of these accommodations, it was therefore thought, might serve as guidelines to the Church for determining how tolerant it could afford to be with regard to those vestiges of Confucianism that the Chinese converts were carrying over with them to Christianity.[44] There was, however, no inclination on the part of the Church leadership to extend this tolerance to Buddhism and Taoism, both of which were regarded as patently idolatrous. Polygamy, accepted in China, the Church would of course not permit; on this it was adamant. Nor, above all, could the Church allow open polytheism. Still, there were other problems that did not lend themselves to such simple and positive resolution. Most important of these were: (1) should Confucianist ancestor worship be condemned as idolatry or, if regarded as an essentially innocuous means of expressing a reverential attitude toward one's forebears, should it tacitly, albeit reluctantly, be permitted a place in the Chinese Catholic Church?; (2) by what Chinese terms should the Chinese converts be instructed to refer to the Deity (the Terms Question), and would it be appropriate for them to recite the Roman liturgy, particularly the Mass, in their own language?; and (3) which aspects of Confucian tradition, culture, and philosophy might these converts legitimately retain without affront to established Catholic belief?

The specific theological, ritualistic, and metaphysical points on which the Chinese Jews had found it possible to accept a degree of sinicization—and still remain well within the boundaries of normative Judaism—were thus injected into the Church's deliberations regarding the path her China Mission was to follow. Ricci, pragmatic and tolerant, urged the institution of a liberal policy with respect to the incorporation of a selected number of Confucian-based traditions and practices within the framework of the Catholicism he was trying to introduce into China, arguing that while such a course would not do any noteworthy damage to the general structure of the Church it would encourage mass conversion. He did not ask, however, that the customs and beliefs of Buddhism and Taoism be recognized, categorizing these as completely out of the pale. Most of the Jesuits who later became involved in the evangelical work of the China Mission were inclined to go along with his lenient views vis-à-vis Confucianism,[45] but the Dominicans and Franciscans, who also entered the Chinese missionary field, were deeply disturbed by his approach, fearing that it would lead to the development of a syncretistic and perhaps schismatic sect. They therefore insisted that the Chinese converts to Catholicism be compelled to abandon all Confucianist rituals, doctrines, and customs deviating in any way from those conventionally recognized by the True Church into which they were now being received.

This fundamental and irreconcilable difference in viewpoint gave rise to the so-called Chinese Rites Controversy, a bitter dispute, which together with the Terms Question shook the foundations of the Roman Catholic church, nearly nullified her missionary program in the Far East, and was not to be definitively settled for centuries—until, in fact, the eve of the Second World War.[46] On the whole, the decision then taken liberalized the earlier guidelines regarding the Rites and the Terms, but with Mainland China destined to fall soon under Marxist hegemony it no longer mattered as much as it might once have. The Church had missed a momentous opportunity.

2 ❖ RICCI'S JEWS AND CROMWELL'S PURITANS

THE implications which the famous Amsterdam rabbi Manasseh ben Israel chose to read into the bare fact that a small colony of Jews lived within the confines of the Middle Kingdom occupy a curious niche in both Jewish and English history. By 1650 Manasseh, like so many of his contemporaries, had convinced himself that the Messianic Age could not be far off. In England, where religious enthusiasms were at a feverish pitch, chiliastically oriented cults searched avidly for omens heralding the onset of the Millennium. A diversity of sects, banded together in a shaky alliance, had only recently dethroned and beheaded Charles I; but with the victory won, theological and political differences were causing the uneasy coalition to become unstuck. In certain matters, nevertheless, the earlier commonality of interests remained more or less intact: the bickering factions, for example, continued to be fascinated by messianic prophecy, to probe for their roots in the pages of Hebrew Scripture, and to profess a sentimental and spiritual attachment to the people whose ancestors had stood at Sinai.

"Not long since," Richard Willes wrote to the Countess of Bedford on July 4, 1577, "happy was he that had any skil in the greke tongue; he was thought a great scholler that could make a greke verse. Noweadayes, who studieth not the Hebrew language?"[1] Yet the same England which in 1577 was so avidly intrigued by the language of ancient Israel had three centuries earlier callously expelled from her territories the several thousands of her inhabitants who revered it as part of their ancestral heritage. And in the middle of the seventeenth century, with Oliver Cromwell in power, the country still had no Jews living in it—except, that is, for those few families to whose presence the authorities turned a blind eye, and of whose existence the world knew almost as little as it had of the Kaifeng Jews in the years just before 1605.[2] That there were to all intents and purposes no Jews left in England did not mean, however, that the old animosities against them had been permitted to subside. The pernicious legend of "Little Saint Hugh of Lincoln," allegedly crucified by the Jews in 1255, was kept alive in various popular Scottish and English ballads, and in the poignant but outrageously unfactual lines of Chaucer's *Prioress's Tale*. For those who attended the theater, there were Marlowe's Barabbas and Shakespeare's Shylock to jeer at. In the public mind, the image of the Jew remained that of a mysterious, diabolical, and unregenerate schemer.

But for many of the sectarians striving to reduce the power of the established Church, the antipathy toward the Jews was to fade to a shadow of its former self and be replaced by sympathy, and even by affection. These dissenters would come to regard the Jews as the truly chosen of God, and deserving, therefore, of the compassion and protection of all believers in Christ. With the passage of time, some of the more daring nonconformists were to demand toleration for all faiths, whether Christian or not. They would even agitate for the readmission of the Jews to England.

The pro-Jewish sentiment that was destined to sweep England had its beginnings a generation or two before the calamitous civil war, which tore the realm asunder in the 1640s. Among its more extreme proponents there were some who practiced circumcision, others who observed the Jewish Sabbath, and also a few who, having domiciled themselves in Amsterdam, asked to be received into the synagogue. "The practical effect of this movement," as Lucien Wolf pointed out, "was not only the production of a very widespread philo-Semitism, but a strong conviction that, inasmuch as the conversion of the Jews was an indispensable preliminary to the Millennium, their admission to England, where they might meet the godliest people in the world, was urgently necessary."[3]

There was more to England's intense preoccupation with the Jews than simply an expression of the nation's burgeoning sense of spiritual kinship with them. The Second Coming of Christ, it was devoutly believed, would be heralded by an epochal drama in which the Jews would step forward as the quintessential protagonists. In short, it was generally agreed that the Messiah could be expected to arrive only after the Jews, having first been scattered "from one end of the earth to the other" (Deut. 28:64), would afterward be gathered together in one place and there accept Christ. This was the messianic order of events that the English clergy had proclaimed to their believers and that found a particularly warm reception among the adherents of the so-called Millenarian and Fifth Monarchy denominations. Its conversionary and christological aspects were of course totally unpalatable to any believing Jew. Nevertheless, it provided a setting within which Manasseh ben Israel could approach Oliver Cromwell and the English Parliament and petition them to readmit the Jews to England. In making his plea to the leadership of Britain, moreover, Manasseh would rally the unsuspecting Jews of China to the support of those of their Western coreligionists who hoped to obtain refuge in England from the furies of the Inquisition, the oppression of the secular and clerical authorities throughout nearly all of Europe, and the reverberations of the murderous Chmielnicki campaigns still being waged in Poland, Lithuania, Russia, and the Ukraine.

The son of Marrano Jews who fled Lisbon shortly after the auto-da-fé of August 3, 1603, Manasseh was taken to Amsterdam as a very young child. A precocious student, he was ordained as a rabbi at eighteen, learned to read ten languages, wrote books in five, and counted among his correspondents such world figures as Hugo Grotius, Christina of Sweden, and Oliver Cromwell. He established the first Hebrew press in Holland and, as headmaster of a Jewish school in Amsterdam, was responsible for much of the early education of Benedict Spinoza. A friend of Rembrandt, whose home was across the street from his own, he commissioned the artist to etch his portrait and later to paint him in oils. In 1655 Rembrandt provided four engravings for a book Manasseh had just written, the *Piedra Gloriosa*, but for one reason or another these were not used when the book was put on press.[4]

Manasseh's views of the history of the Chinese Jews—views

3. Manasseh ben Israel. A likeness prepared by Salom Italia and reproduced in many copies of the Latin edition (1650) of Manasseh's *Hope of Israel.*

he would later bring into play as part of his effort to convince Cromwell and the Parliament to readmit other Jews to England— were expressed in a pamphlet that he wrote in Latin entitled *Spes Israelis*. From this text he prepared a Spanish version, *Esperança de Israel*, which he printed at his own press in January 1650. The work caused a sensation. In the same year in which it was originally published it was issued in two other editions. The first of these was Manasseh's Latin text, and the second, a translation into English made by Moses Wall at the instigation, it is said, of John Milton, was circulated in Britain under the title *The Hope of Israel*. Wall's translation, "corrected and amended," was soon printed twice again in London, first in 1651 and then in 1652.[5] The Latin and English editions were graced with opening remarks which Manasseh addressed "to the Parliament, the Supream Court of England, *And to the Right Honourable, the Councell of State*." Wall's three editions created a considerable stir in England. Before the end of the century Manasseh's booklet was reissued in Spanish (Smyrna, 1659) and printed for the first time in Dutch (Amsterdam, 1666), Yiddish (Amsterdam, 1691), and Hebrew (Amsterdam, 1697). That the demand for the work was of a continuing nature is evidenced by the fact that it has been published in six or more languages and in at least twenty-six editions. It is frequently referred to by its Hebrew title, *Mikveh Yisrael*. Among other things, it did a great deal to spread the news to both Jews and Christians the world over that Jesuit missionaries had come upon a Jewish colony in the heart of China.

The feat of legerdemain by which Manasseh ben Israel tied the Jews of Kaifeng to the immigration policies of Cromwell's England was born out of a deep concern for the welfare of his fellow Jews. Holland was then to all intents and purposes the only country in Europe where Jews could live in peace and practice their faith without undue fear of molestation. Amsterdam, in which the Jewish population of Holland was concentrated, had become the continent's most sought-after city of refuge for Jews fleeing from the persecution they faced in their native lands, so much so that they began to speak appreciatively of the Dutch metropolis as the Jerusalem of the North. It was essential, however, that other havens be developed. The upheavals in England raised the prospect that the new Puritan regime could be persuaded to accept substantial numbers of Jewish refugees—for commercial and military reasons, it should be added, as well as for messianic (or even humanitarian) ones. The possibility demanded investigation. Manasseh, not the man to let such an opportunity slip by, promptly took action.

On September 19, 1644, a Portuguese Marrano had arrived in Amsterdam and introduced himself to Manasseh and other notables in the city's Jewish community by both his Christian name, Antonio de Montezinos, and his Hebrew name, Aaron Levi. Montezinos explained that he had recently come back to Europe from the New World and that he had a strange story to tell. He was received as an honored guest, and his tale was listened to with great excitement.

Montezinos's story turned out to be a wild-eyed traveler's tale of the genre that was so popular throughout the Middle Ages and well into the modern era.[6] Montezinos did not bring back claims of having seen two-headed monsters or giants twelve feet tall. Instead, he told of meeting some 300 members of the Lost Tribe of Reuben in the interior of South America.

With his audience hanging on to every word, Montezinos related how in 1639 he had traveled from the port of Honda (in modern Colombia) to the province of Quito (Ecuador) in the company of an Indian cacique called Francisco and several other natives. While passing over the Cordillera mountains, he said the little party ran into a heavy storm that caused it to lose some of its mules. The muleteers, after bemoaning their losses, began to berate themselves as sinners who richly deserved whatever calamities might befall them. The bitterest retribution that had come upon them, they mournfully agreed, was the subjugation of their tribes to the brutal overlordship of the Spaniards. This, they admitted contritely, was a trouble of their own making, for they were now being treated no more savagely than they themselves had once treated the holy people of God.

Montezinos was quite unable to grasp the significance of what the men were saying, but later, while languishing in prison at Cartagena (Colombia) following his arrest by the Inquisitors as a suspected Judaizer, it struck him that the holy people who figured in the conversation of the Indian muleteers could have been none other than certain displaced remnants of the House of Israel.[7] On his release from confinement, the perfectly valid charges against him not having been proved, he therefore sought out Francisco in Honda and, at the risk of his life, told the Indian chief what he had succeeded in withholding from the Inquisition— that he was indeed a Jew. The cacique listened sympathetically. Montezinos, greatly relieved that his gamble had turned out well and that he would not be betrayed, implored Francisco to act as his guide to the land where the Israelites lived. Francisco consented.

The two men started their journey on a Monday morning, walked for five tiring days, rested on the Sabbath, and went on. On Tuesday, at eight in the morning, they came to a broad river. Here they halted, and Francisco, waving a makeshift flag, was able to attract the attention of three men and one woman on the other side. The four, all of them white-skinned, responded by paddling across in a canoe. The woman came ashore alone, talked at some length with the cacique in a tongue Montezinos could not follow, returned to the boat, and reported to her companions. The three men and the woman now left the boat, approached Montezinos and Francisco, and greeted them warmly. One man went back to the canoe. Then, to Montezinos's amazement and delight, the two men who had stayed on shore intoned the hallowed words of the *Shema*, "Hear, O Israel, the Lord our God, the Lord is One," in a language he could understand— Hebrew. The two thereupon engaged Montezinos in discussions that went on intermittently, and apparently in Hebrew, for three days. During these three days other members of their tribe also paddled across the river to visit Montezinos, some 300 in all. It was clear to the Marrano, however, that he was not being taken completely into the confidence of the people with whom he talked. They would not permit him to cross the river, nor would they give him more than a smattering of details regarding their communal history and way of living. He was asked, nevertheless, to have twelve men, all bearded and skilled in the art of writing, sent to them, presumably to serve as teachers and scribes.

What Montezinos did learn about the people who dwelled on the far side of the river was that they were Israelites of the tribe of Reuben. He was told, and this by Francisco rather than by the Reubenites, that they had been maltreated by the Indians, who in the end decided to exterminate them. On three successive occasions the Indians deployed vast armies against them, but each time the attackers were destroyed to the last man. The Indians, atributing the three annihilatory defeats of their massive forces by a mere handful of white people to supernatural intervention, concluded that their intended victims enjoyed the protection of the Deity. Yielding to the inevitable, they abandoned their murderous designs and sued for peace. The Reubenites and the remorseful Indians now lived side by side in amity, but maintained only infrequent personal contact with one another.

Some time later, Francisco and three caciques came to see Montezinos in Honda. Although the three chieftains would at first not tell Montezinos their names, they were eventually convinced by Francisco that it was safe for them to converse freely with the Marrano. Reassured, the caciques asked Montezinos who his people were. He replied that he was a Hebrew and a member of the tribe of Levi. The caciques thereupon told him that he was to think of them as his brethren and that he would see them again but might not recognize them when he did. With this cryptic remark they departed. Francisco, who had stayed behind, then informed Montezinos that he and several other caciques were preparing to travel to the Reubenite enclave. A revolt was in the offing, he explained, in the course of which the Israelites of the Cordilleras, in league with their Indian neighbors, would overthrow the hated Spaniards. Afterwards, the victorious Americans, Indians allied with Reubenites, would with the help of God release the Jewish people of the world from the odious bondage they had so long endured.

This is a curious story, but in the ears of Manasseh and his colleagues it rang true. Theirs was an age that spawned a profusion of weird tales concerning the fate and whereabouts of the Ten Lost Tribes of Israel. Many Christian writers were wedded to the belief that with the discovery of the New World, the mystery of the Lost Tribes was at least partially resolved. What they claimed, in effect, was that the family tree of the American Indians went back to those unfortunate citizens of the Northern Israelite Kingdom, who in the eighth century B.C.E. were resettled by their Assyrian conquerors "in Halah, at the [River] Habor, at the River Gozan, and in the towns of Media" (2 Kings 17:6), and elsewhere.[8] Although a hodgepodge of arguments was advanced in support of this hypothesis, these were in the main based upon reputed similarities between the customs, beliefs, and language of the ancient Israelites and those of the Indian inhabitants of the Americas. The discrepancies in skin color between the Indians and the Israelites were, however, awkward to explain away. Some writers managed, nevertheless, to do just that by changing the theory. The Indians, they claimed, were only "apparently" Jewish. How, then, did they acquire their Jewish cultural and linguistic characteristics? The answer: at some point in their history Satan, using the tricks he knew so well, misled the Indians into adopting a way of life not too dissimilar from that of the Jews.

While Manasseh was also convinced that segments of the Ten Tribes had penetrated as far as the New World, he could not bring himself to believe either that the Indians were descended from any of them or that the Indians were the first people to come to America. He proposed instead an entirely new American-Israelite theory, this one predicated upon three separate and seemingly unrelated sources: a verse from the Book of Isaiah, the strange story told by Antonio de Montezinos, and the reports he had read in the works of both Trigault and Semmedo of the discovery of a Jewish presence in China.[9] Manasseh's theory did away with the thorny problem of how Israelites, white-skinned in antiquity, could now have red skins—the Satanic nonsense he disdained to reply to—and provided him with an argument with which he would attempt to persuade Oliver Cromwell and the leadership of the British Parliament to permit Jews to return to England. It also purported to explain how and from where the Jews originally came to China, implying that this first migration took place not very long after the Assyrian destruction of the

Kingdom of Israel. This meant, if the Amsterdam rabbi could prove his case, that in 1650 Jews had already been living in China for substantially more than 2,000 years.

Manasseh's novel contribution to the field of American-Israelite literature is presented in his *Hope of Israel*. The New World, he contends, was not settled initially by Indians, as so many Christian scholars insisted, but rather by a persecuted segment of the Ten Tribes, specifically of the tribe of Reuben, which "out of *Tartary* . . . went to *China,* by that famous wall in the confines of both," and thence "to the *West-Indies* by the strait of *Anian.*"[10] Somewhat later, he then asserts, "other people of the *East-Indies* came by that Streight [connecting, he supposes, the Atlantic and Pacific Oceans], which is between *India* and the Kingdom of *Anian,*" subdued the Israelites, and eventually drove the few survivors into the Cordillera mountains, where they lived apart from their tormentors and where Montezinos eventually found them. The red-skinned Indians would thus be descendants of Manasseh's "people of the *East-Indies,*" and certainly not of the ancient Israelites.

Matteo Ricci's discovery of a Jewish settlement in China, Manasseh holds, demonstrates that Montezinos's tale is credible, for there can now be no questioning the fact that Israelitic refugees from Tartary did pass through China and that China served as a way-stop for some of them who went on to America. As for the others, those who stayed in China, his readers are left free to infer that by reason of intermarriage with the inhabitants of the country they produced a race that was no longer white. Manasseh then states that for those Israelites who chose not to remain in the Middle Kingdom it would have been relatively simple to "saile from *China* to *New-Spaine,* through the streight between *China* and *Anian,* and *Quivira,*[11] which doe border upon *New-Spaine,* and from thence . . . to the Isles of *Panama, Peru,* and those thereabouts."[12] Manasseh also suggests, as an alternate possibility, that at one time Asia and America were contiguous, so that the journeys of both the Reubenites and the East Indians might have been made over dry land.[13]

To substantiate his claim that Jews lived in China in antiquity, Manasseh now offers in evidence a quotation from Isaiah (actually, Deutero-Isaiah). Envisioning the return of the Israelites from the farflung corners of the earth to which they had already been dispersed, Isaiah proclaims: "Look! These are coming from afar, These from the north and the west, And these from the land of Sinim" (Isa. 49:12).

But what, asks Manasseh, is the land of Sinim? He turns to Ptolemy for the answer and notes that the old Greek geographer had identified the Sinim as the Chinese. Then, admitting that the authoritative biblical commentator Abraham ibn Ezra had placed the land of Sinim on the southern border of Egypt, Manasseh merely observes that in this ibn Ezra was "mistaken."[14] As far as Manasseh is concerned, therefore, there were Jews in China during or even before the lifetime of Isaiah.

Manasseh may not have been the first exegete to identify Isaiah's Sinim as the Chinese, but his application of Isa. 49:12 to the problem of dating the arrival of Jews in China was destined to be greeted with uncritical acclaim by generations of scholars, both Christian and Jewish, and even to earn the approbation of certain modern writers.[15] It was never universally accepted, however, for long before Manasseh, such widely read and greatly respected Jewish biblical commentaries as Rashi's, David Kimchi's, and the Targum Jonathan had rendered Isaiah's land of Sinim as "the land of the South." An ordained rabbi, Manasseh should have been familiar with these works—and surely was. Yet he fails to mention their interpretations of the meaning of the word *Sinim*. He is not aware, in any case, that while the prophetic career of Deutero-Isaiah is ascribed to the latter portion of the sixth century B.C.E., nobody at that time had yet associated the term *Sin*, or anything phonetically close to it, with the cluster of principalities that then made up the portion of Asia that would later become known as China. In Hebrew, it is true, *Sin* came to be the word for China and *Sinim*, the word for Chinese, but apparently not until many centuries after the time of Deutero-Isaiah. Eldad ha-Dani, writing circa 880 C.E., is perhaps the first Hebrew author to equate *Sin* with China (he employs, actually, the variants *Azyn*, or *Zyn*).[16] Manasseh would have been greatly disturbed, moreover, if he could have foreseen the discovery of the Dead Sea Scrolls, and that among them there would be found a complete copy of the Book of Isaiah in which the crucial word in 49:12 is rendered as *Sevaniyyim* rather than as *Sinim*. This Dead Sea reading suggests that *Sinim* is a scribal error introduced after the venerable Isaiah Scroll was written—that is, after the second century C.E. The Dead Sea spelling is revealing, for the identity of the *Sevaniyyim* is no mystery: they were the Syenians, a people who inhabited that portion of Southern Egypt that later came to be called Aswan.[17] The commentator ibn Ezra, who thought of the Sinim as the people who lived in the southern part of Egypt, and the others, who placed them in the "south," were much closer to the truth than was Manasseh.

Montezinos's bizarre account of having met a contingent of Reubenites in the Cordillera mountains of South America is merely one of the innumerable fables that have been concocted with regard to the Lost Tribes. Still, the legend of the Ten Lost Tribes of Israel, like so many other myths, does have a basis in historical fact—in this case, the story of what befell the Hebrews in the several centuries after they established themselves in a country of their own. The Hebrew Scriptures provided the source from which Montezinos skimmed the raw materials with which to devise his colorful fantasy; and from these same Scriptures men like Manasseh, his Jewish colleagues in Amsterdam, and many of his Christian contemporaries were able to work out their own peculiar rationale for swallowing whole the extraordinary yarn spun by Montezinos.

The Israelites, as any reader of the Bible would know, had not been in the Promised Land very long before military, political, and economic considerations compelled some of them to leave for foreign climes. There were, of course, occasional departures from the country that turned out to be no more than temporary— Naomi forsaking the famine-stricken surroundings of Bethlehem for the fields of Moab, or David fleeing from the wrath of Saul to the domain of Achish, king of Gath—but there must also have been early migrations of a more lasting nature. In all probability, however, the first permanent dispersions of any demographic consequence did not take place until the reign of Solomon, when a mercantile development program was initiated that led to the creation of extensive overland and maritime trade routes to many parts of the known world and, concomitantly, to the implanting of supportive settlements along the way.

Might some of Solomon's subjects have reached China? There would be writers, after Manasseh, who would answer in the affirmative but without offering any acceptable proof. Other writers would go so far as to suggest that Jews had come to China before the lifetime of Solomon, and even before the Deliverance from Egypt![18]

By and large, the biblical accounts suggest, the Jews did not leave their homeland voluntarily, but, having been driven from it by a succession of conquerors, were forced to seek refuge wherever it could be had. Such a fate, to be sure, was not reserved to the Jews exclusively, for they were not the first, and would not be the last, to experience the twin humiliations of defeat and exile. What was unique about the Jews was that of all the nations in history that were deprived of their territories and scattered to foreign lands, they alone succeeded in preserving their identity for generation after generation, century after century, and even millennium after millennium. This genius for survival, in the minds of Manasseh and others of the same bent, would account for the continuing presence of totally isolated Israelite communities in those faraway regions to which the accidents of history had brought them, including the Cordillera mountains of South America and the interior of the Middle Kingdom.

Emigrations that took place from Israel prior to and during the time of Solomon were minuscule in scope compared to what was to come. After Solomon's death in 933, the centralized Jewish state that his predecessors, Saul and David, had fashioned was split into two separate kingdoms—Israel, in the north, and Judah (later called Judea), in the south. The first massive deportations of Israelites from their country followed the defeat of the Northern Israelite Kingdom in 733–32 B.C.E., when the Assyrian monarch Tiglath-Pileser III carried away large numbers of them into captivity. In 721 Sargon II completed the Assyrian subjugation of the Northern Kingdom and removed 27,200 of its inhabitants to his Asian domains. The refugees who were transported eastward in the eighth century B.C.E. are the ancestors of those forlorn peoples who have become known as the Ten Lost

Tribes of Israel; and the fate of these tribes, following their abrupt disappearance from the stage of recorded history, has inspired the development of a vast literature in which conflicting evidence is presented, often quite ferociously, to demonstrate that one favored group or another is descended from them.

A child of his age, Manasseh ben Israel elected to believe that the Ten Tribes still survived as identifiable ethnic entities, that they lived in various remote parts of the globe, and that they would eventually be found. To Manasseh, Montezinos's declaration that he had recently discovered one of the Lost Tribes, Reuben, in the Cordillera mountains of South America was an exciting confirmation of the correctness of this belief. And because he was taken in by Montezinos, he was able to delude himself into perceiving the Kaifeng Jews as descendants of a segment of the tribe of Reuben, which would have arrived in China in the interval between Tiglath-Pileser's dispersion of Israel (733–32 B.C.E.) and the period in which Deutero-Isaiah prophesied (circa 525–500 B.C.E.).

The Book of Daniel foretells that a widespread dispersion of the Jews would precede their restoration to their homeland. Theologians had connected this prediction with the Deuteronomic reference to a scattering of the Israelites from one end of the earth to the other. Manasseh accepted this and, apparently, so did most of his readers. There could be no doubt at all, Manasseh was therefore able to argue, that Montzinos's claim of having found Israelites in South America was entirely believable. But how, he then asked, could these Israelites have traveled from Western or Central Asia to that remote continent without first passing through China? Now, providentially, the Jesuits had uncovered living evidence of a very early Jewish presence on the Chinese road to the New World. What better proof, accordingly, could one expect of an Israelite passage to America? With this involuted reasoning the credibility of the Montezinos claim was established, at least to the satisfaction of Manasseh and many like him, and it was now clear that the Israelites who had come to South America by way of China must be considered as having been scattered to one of the two ends of the earth and to have fulfilled one component of the two-sided dispersion requirement prescribed in Deuteronomy.

The other end of the earth, quite obviously, would have to be England; but the sad fact, as everybody knew, was that although there were unquestionably Israelites in the end of the earth that was South America there were none, at least legally, in the end of the earth that was England. The time for the coming of the Messiah, he now declared, agreeing with the Christian Messianists, was drawing nigh. "It is said," he ruefully informed his readers, "that although the Messiah were lame, he might have come by this time."[19] But he had not come—and the blame for this, Manasseh hinted rather broadly, could well be laid at the feet of the English. If the God-fearing rulers of Britain were really serious about hastening the coming of their Messiah, it followed, they would have to invite the Jews to dwell again in that end of the earth in which they themselves lived, thus arranging the sine qua non for his appearance.[20] If someone had asked Manasseh why the Messiah did not appear in the centuries before 1290, there then being Israelites in both England and America, his answer would probably have been that at that time certain other prerequisites to this cosmic event had not yet manifested themselves.

There was considerably more, of course, to the case that Manasseh assembled for the readmission of the Jews to England, but his heaviest artillery was reserved for the messianic argument.[21] His persistent efforts on behalf of the cause he had espoused brought him to the attention of Cromwell, who invited him to come to London. The Amsterdam rabbi arrived in the English capital in September 1655 and discussed the readmission question with the Lord Protector himself and with other important figures in the British government, but those who were opposed to the movement to permit the Jews to live again in England were able to forestall any positive legal action on the matter. A lurid anti-Jewish campaign was mounted, in the course of which the rumor was spread throughout the country that the Jews intended to take over the Bodleian Library at Oxford and to turn Saint Paul's Cathedral into a synagogue. They were offering £600,000 for the two properties, Sir Edward Nicholas had declared in 1648, but, it was now being said, Cromwell and his supporters were holding out for £200,000 more.[22] As Cromwell pushed his case for the readmission of the Jews, Nicholas's charge was bruited about with increasing vigor and was believed by a large segment of the country's population. In the end, the Jews were allowed to drift back slowly and quietly to England— "through the back door," as the historian Heinrich Graetz would subsequently put it. That Manasseh ben Israel's messianistically oriented arguments exercised a profound influence upon the sequence of events that elicited this vital, although unformalized, compromise cannot be doubted. Without the Chinese Jews, however, his case would have held up less well than it did, and the readmission of the Jews to England may well have been put off to a much later time.

As for the scattered remnants of the House of Israel who lived in the heart of China, it would never have occurred to them to associate the "end of the earth" in their Torahs with either South America or the British Isles. Still, those of their coreligionists who made a safe home for themselves in England in the decades following Manasseh's mission to Cromwell owed the Jews of China a debt of gratitude. This was an obligation, incidentally, which was never generally acknowledged, as very few English Jews were even aware that a branch of their faith flourished in China, let alone that it played a striking role in opening the reluctant gates of Albion to them. And, for their part, the Jews of Kaifeng had no way of knowing that they had once been conscripted to lend a helping hand in the laborious effort to push those gates ajar.

3 ❖ TESTAMENTS IN STONE

IN Kaifeng itself, the Jews knew little more about the time and circumstances of the arrival of their people in the Middle Kingdom than did the European savants. In his journals, Ricci expresses the opinion that the first entry of Jews into China took place "at an early period."[1] He had already proposed a more specific timing for one wave of Jewish immigration to the country, having been informed by Ai T'ien, as he reported to Aquaviva on July 26, 1605, that the Kaifeng congregation "preserved the tradition that many Moors [Muslims], Christians, and Jews had come with the king Tamerlane when he conquered the whole of Persia and also China 800 years ago."[2] Here, however, Ricci's chronologic sense had gone awry. In 1605, to begin with, the legendary warrior-king had been dead only 200 years. Secondly, Tamerlane did not live long enough to fulfill the ambitious plans he had made for the conquest of China. He died, actually, in 1405, in the opening stages of the campaign in which he hoped to retake the vast Sinitic empire his Mongol forebears had seized in the thirteenth century and held for a hundred years or so before being driven out. It is therefore unclear whether the Kaifeng tradition—at least in the form in which Ricci understood it—referred to a movement of Westerners into China at the beginning of the ninth century or to one occurring 600 years later. The greater likelihood is that the Kaifeng tradition applied to Genghis Khan rather than to Tamerlane and that Ricci erred in relating it to the latter; for following his conquest of China, Genghis encouraged the immigration of Jewish, Christian, and Muslim merchants and artisans, and as early as 1219 built the first of a system of highways designed to facilitate the movement of car-

開封

4. Chinese characters representing the city of Kaifeng.

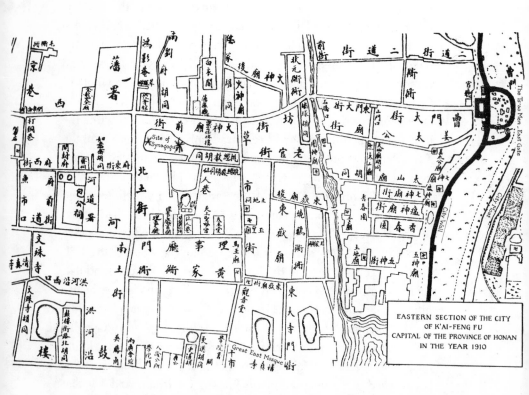

EASTERN SECTION OF THE CITY
OF K'AI-FENG FU
CAPITAL OF THE PROVINCE OF HONAN
IN THE YEAR 1910

5. Eastern section of Kaifeng, 1910. The site of the synagogue, indicated on the map, lay within walking distance of the East Gate.

6. Chang Tse-tuan. Street scene in Kaifeng. Early twelfth century.

avans to and from the West. Genghis lived, of course, 400 years before Ricci wrote his letter, not 800. Any Jews who came to the Honan metropolis during Genghis's reign would have found a thriving colony of their coreligionists already there.

Even as Ai and Ricci were carrying on their talks in Peking, the Jews of Kaifeng could stand in the courtyard of their resplendent synagogue and read two summations of their community's history and religious beliefs that preceding generations, following the custom of their compatriots, had inscribed on a stone monument erected for the edification of posterity. This stele had been set up in 1489 to commemorate the reconstruction of the synagogal compound after the devastation caused by a flooding of the Yellow River in 1461. In 1512 additional textual material was engraved on the reverse side of the same slab.[3]

In the course of time, the 1489/1512 stone, together with another that one of Kaifeng's seven Jewish clans, the Chao, erected in 1679, came into the possession of the Canadian Church of England in Honan, then headed by Bishop William Charles White. In 1912 White set up the two monuments on the grounds of Trinity Cathedral, in Kaifeng, stationing one on each side of the Cathedral's western entry. "They were dark grey limestone slabs," he later wrote, "and each stood on a large rectangular stone block. Their base blocks had both been carved in low relief with designs of lotus-flower petals, but the later one was so badly weathered as to show little of the floral design. The earlier of these stones contained two inscriptions, one dated 1489 on the front surface, and one dated 1512, on the other surface. It was five feet in height, and the stone base was twenty inches high. The two surfaces had been polished smooth, and the inscriptions, which were in Chinese script only, were lightly incised by the chisel." The five-foot-tall stele, White also noted, was thirty inches wide and five inches thick.[4] The 1679 stone was seven feet tall, and its one inscribed surface was badly disfigured, leaving much of the text indecipherable.[5]

The older stone was originally a gift to the Kaifeng congregation from two of its members, the brothers Chin Chung and Chin Yung. It was Chung who composed the lengthy text engraved on its front surface and, probably, the caption inscribed above it as well. The wording employed in the caption, "A Record of the Rebuilding of the Synagogue," is somewhat misleading, for although Chung does discuss the reconstruction of the synagogue, he devotes the bulk of his effort to explaining the precepts of Judaism. In the process, he also provides a smattering of information concerning the history of the Jewish community into which he had been born.

The Jewish religion, Chung writes, "came from T'ien-chu; in obedience to the [divine?] command it came. There were [the clans of] Li, An, Ai, Kao, Mu, Chao, Chin, Chou, Chang, Shih, Huang, Li, Nieh, Chin, Chang, Tso, and Pai, seventeen surnames (*hsing*) in all.[6] They brought Western cloth as tribute to the Sung. The emperor said: 'Come to our China, honor and preserve the customs of your ancestors, remain and hand them down in Pien-liang [Kaifeng].'[7] In the *kuei-wei* year [1163], the first year of the *Lung-hsing* period of the Sung Emperor Hsiao [Hsiao

7. Caption of the 1489 stele that stood in the courtyard of the Kaifeng synagogue. It reads: "A Record of the Rebuilding of the Synagogue."

Tsung], Lieh-wei [the] *Wu-ssu-ta* [probably Levi the Rabbi] led the religion and An-tu-la [Abdullah?; Hamdullah?] first built the temple."[8]

As the Sung dynasty maintained court in Kaifeng between 960 and 1126, it follows that the cloth which the seventeen clans brought was presented to an emperor whose reign fell within that period, and also that in 1163, when the synagogue was built, the Jews had already been living in Kaifeng for a minimum of thirty-seven years and a maximum of 203 years.[9] Where did they worship in the years before the synagogue was built? Perhaps in private homes, or perhaps in rented and less grandiose structures than those they erected in the centuries after they were authorized to build their first one.

Unfortunately, Chin Chung's text does not address itself to the questions of when the Jews originally arrived in China, what their starting points were, and where their earliest settlements in the country were located. It merely implies that the ancestors of the *kehillah* to which he belonged settled in the city of Kaifeng no earlier than 960 and no later than 1126, and it states that the Jewish religion came from T'ien-chu, a place name that has been variously translated as India (but an India encompassing an area vaster even than the modern India) and as any of several Middle Eastern countries. The text does not specify either the presence or the absence of other Jewish settlements in China when the seventeen clans began to live in the Sung capital of Kaifeng. Several Arab chroniclers—among them ibn Khurdadhbih, Abu Zaid, and al-Masudi—had of course already taken note of the existence of Jewish colonies in pre-Sung China. The contingent of Jews that paid the tribute of cloth to a Sung emperor in Kaifeng had therefore either migrated directly to the capital from a foreign country or was made up of individuals stemming from one or more of the several Jewish congregations that had for some time been domiciled in China. Yet, if the welcoming words attributed to the emperor, "Come to our China . . . ," are to be accepted at face value, they would appear to be directed to newcomers to his domain rather than to subjects who were simply moving from one part of it to another. However, if any of the surnames listed in the stele were already being used when the seventeen clans came to Kaifeng (which was probably not the case), they were presumably not recent arrivals in the country.

The 1489 inscription contains additional items of historical interest. The reader is told that the synagogue was rebuilt in 1279, during the Yüan (Mongol) dynasty, on its old site "at the southeast of the Earth-Market Character Street,"[10] and that each of the four sides of the synagogal compound measured thirty-five *chang*, or approximately 350 feet.[11] He is given the names of fourteen men who were designated by the congregation as *man-la* (spiritual leaders). He learns that in 1421 An San (a common soldier, perhaps, although he is described by the writer of the inscription as a physician) was by order of the prince Ting of Chou presented with a gift of incense; that the Jews were authorized to rebuild the synagogue; that a tablet pledging the fealty of the *kehillah* to the Ming rulers was installed in the synagogue; and that in recognition of certain valuable services he had rendered to the throne An was appointed in 1423 to an honored position in the "Embroidered Uniform Bodyguard" and was also elevated to an important office in the Regional Military Commission of Chekiang. He was, in addition, granted the right to assume the surname Chao, a very meaningful concession to be given to a person of foreign extraction since, in the first part of the Ming dynasty, foreigners were not usually permitted to adopt Chinese patronymics.[12]

The inscription reveals that in 1445 Li Jung and Li Liang provided the wherewithal for the addition of three new sections to the synagogue, and that after an inundation caused by the overflowing of the Yellow River in 1461 had leveled the synagogue to its foundations, Ai Ching and several others petitioned the government to be allowed to erect a new house of worship on the site of the old. Their request having been approved, a fund-raising compaign was initiated. This seems to have been gratifyingly successful. The four largest contributors to the building fund are listed as Li Jung (the same individual who was so generous in the 1445 expansion project), Kao Chien, Kao Jui, and Kao Hung.

Shortly after this, the text declares, "Shih Pin, Li Jung, Kao

Chien, and Chang Hsüan . . . obtained a copy of the Scriptures of the Way [a Torah scroll] . . . and Chao Ying of Ningpo respectfully brought this copy of the Scriptures to the synagogue at Pien-liang [Kaifeng]."

Reference is proudly made to the appointment of two Kaifeng Jews, Kao Nien and Ai Chün, to responsible governmental posts and to the accomplishments of the Chin clan, coreligionists living in Ningsia. A supplementary roster of donors to the building and interior refurbishing funds is then provided.

The text also supplies the names and academic ranks of the writer of the inscription, Chin Chung, and of two non-Jews: Ts'ao Tso, who prepared the characters of the text for the stone-cutters, and Fu Ju, who wrote out the seal characters for the caption.

Penultimately, it is recorded that "on a fortunate day in the second summer month of the *chi-yu* year, that is the second year of the Hung Chih period [1489], Chin Ying of Ningsia and Chin Li of Hsiang-fu [Kaifeng], descendants of the Ch'ing Chên [Purity and Truth religion—that is, Jews], have together put up this stone."

And finally: "The working masons were Wu Liang and Wu Hai," non-Jews, to judge by their names, who may have come from Wu-an Hsien in the north of Honan, an area that provided many of the masons who worked in Kaifeng.

The inscription of 1512, shorter than that of 1489, bears the title, "A Record of the Synagogue which Honors the Scriptures." It opens with the statement that it was composed by Tso T'ang and was then rewritten in vermilion (on transparent paper, to serve as a model for the engraver) by Kao Fang, and that the seal characters were the work of Hsü Ang. None of these men came from Kaifeng. Kao and Hsü were definitely not Jews; nor, almost surely, was Tso. The three, highly educated in the Chinese classics, were probably commissioned to prepare the inscription because of their superior literary and calligraphic attainments.[13]

The 1512 stele appears to have been erected at the instigation and expense of Jews living elsewhere in China than Kaifeng, presumably as a means of memorializing their devotion to Judaism in lasting form on a monument preserved in what by then may well have been the sole surviving synagogue in the country. The text more or less paraphrases the description of Judaism already inscribed on the 1489 stone, but it says rather little about the Kaifeng community itself. It does, however, allude to the building of the synagogue in 1163 and to its reconstruction in 1279.[14] Three men, identified only by their surnames (An, Li, and Kao), are credited with effecting the latest reconstruction of the edifice, and the date given for the completion of the project corresponds to August 3, 1512. Both the dating and the selection of names seem to be in error: the synagogue, to begin with, was not rebuilt in 1512, so that the dating of August 3, 1512, should in all probability have been assigned to the composition or engraving of the inscription's text, or to the dedication of the inscription; and, secondly, the surnames listed for the individuals who allegedly took the lead in erecting the *kehillah*'s newest house of worship had previously been commemorated in the 1489 lapidary text in connection with reconstruction work done during the fifteenth century.

The 1512 text also reports, no doubt with greater reliability, that Chin P'u of Wei-yang (Yangchou) contributed a Torah scroll to the Kaifeng congregation and put up the second gateway of its synagogal courtyard, and that Chin Jun of Ningsia saw to the setting up of the stele and the construction of the pavilion in which it was installed. Chin Chung, the Kaifeng Jew who composed the 1489 inscription, is believed to have been the editor of the 1512 text. The engravers are identified as Chang Luan and Chang Hsi.

In the inscription of 1512 it is plainly stated that the Jewish religion was brought to China during the Han dynasty, or between 206 B.C.E. and 221 C.E., a claim that should not be thought of as contradicting the implication in the 1489 inscription (and again in a later stele dated 1679) that the Jews came to Kaifeng between 960 and 1126, that is, while the Sung court was located there.[15] The problem is, however, that the 1512 (and 1679) reports of a Han entry into China cannot be reconciled with the equally plain statement occurring in a stele erected in the synagogal courtyard in 1663, which has the Jews arriving in China during the Chou dynasty, or circa 1122–256 B.C.E. It may be, of course, that this claim for the earlier Chou entry-time was advanced to persuade their neighbors that the Jews were not relative newcomers to the Middle Kingdom but people who had been there long enough to qualify as dyed-in-the-wool Chinese—as Chinese, so to speak, "of the Mosaic persuasion."

The noble qualities and the legitimacy of the Jewish religion are vouched for by the non-Jewish composer of the 1512 inscription in a passage which is strikingly similar in tone to the well-known opening lines of the talmudic tractate *Aboth* ("Moses received the Law from Sinai and handed it down to Joshua . . . "). "The Scriptures of the Way," he asserts, go back as far as Adam. "From creation down," he continues, imprecisely summarizing the biblical accounts of how the Scriptures were transmitted, "the Patriarch Adam (*A-tan*) handed them on to Noah (*Nü-wo*); Noah handed them on to Abraham (*A-wu-lo-han*); Abram (*Lo-han*) handed them on to Isaac (*Yi-ssu-hokê*); Isaac (*Ho-kê*) handed them on to Jacob (*Ya-ho-chüeh-wu*); Jacob (*Chüeh-wu*) handed them on to the Twelve Tribes; the Twelve Tribes handed them on to Moses (*Mieh-shê*); Moses handed them on to Aaron (*A-ho-lien*); Aaron (*Ho-lien*) handed them on to Joshua (*Yüeh-shu-wo*); Joshua (*Shu-wo*) handed them on to Ezra (*Ai-tzu-la*). From this time the religion of the Patriarchs shone with renewed brilliance."[16]

Is Judaism practiced only in Kaifeng? Not at all. "The adherents of the religion," the text explains, "are found not only at Pien [Kaifeng]; under the heavens, all who are adherents of the religion honor the Scriptures and cherish the doctrine contained in them."

Between them, the 1489 and 1512 texts reveal the names of several Jews residing in Ningpo, Ningsia, and Yangchou. It is quite possible, accordingly, that when Ai T'ien assumed his new post as superintendent of schools at Yangchou in the latter part of 1605 he found a number of Jewish families still domiciled there. As for the relatively large congregation of Hangchow to which Ai had alluded in his talks with Ricci, this was apparently in existence well before 1346, the year in which ibn Battuta wrote of having passed through "the Jews' Gate" as he entered Hangchow and of encountering Jews, Christians, and Parsees in the city, "a large number in all." By the sixteenth century, Jews could still have been living in Hangchow, even though they are not mentioned in the 1512 stone. If so, there would in all probability no longer have been enough of them there to make up an organized community.

In the first decade of the seventeenth century the Jews of Kaifeng should have been aware of a quondam Jewish presence in Hangchow, Ningsia, Ningpo, and Yangchou, and perhaps also of individual Jews living even then in one or more of these cities. They would seemingly have been aware, too, of those of their brethren whose survival in Peking was reported at second or third hand by Benedict Goes about 1595–98 and—again by hearsay only—in later Jesuit writings. These Jews in Peking, if they were really there at this time, could perhaps trace their history back to the Peking Jews of whom Marco Polo knew in 1286 and with whom John of Marignolli disputed theological doctrine in 1342.

At various periods, Jewish communities flourished in still other Chinese centers, with traces of at least one of these communities (Nanking) surviving as late as the time of Ai T'ien's journey to Peking. The Kaifeng *kehillah* would probably have known of these Jewish enclaves—Ch'üan-chou (Zayton), where Andrew of Perugia had in 1326 unsuccessfully tried to convert Jews to Christianity; Nanking, in which, if Semmedo's report is based on fact, the Jews, having been reduced in number to four families by the late sixteenth or the early seventeenth century, finally turned to Islam; and Canton, believed to be the scene of the 877/78 massacre.

Because the Jewish population of China was always so small and was frequently thought to be part of the vastly larger Muslim community, it did not figure often in the early Chinese records. Not more than six allusions to Jews and Judaism have been discovered in such documents, all of which are from the Yüan period; and of these only one relates the Jews to a specific city, this being Hangchow.[17] An entry of April 19, 1329, in the *Yüan Shih*, the official history of the Yüan dynasty, reads: "Buddhists and Taoist priests, Nestorians, Jews, and Ta-shih-man [Danishmand, or Muslim priests or mullahs] who engage in trade [are] to be taxed according to the old regulation." On November 24, 1340, the same source mentions Jews again. "Ta-shih-man, Muslims[?] and Jews," it states, "should be prohibited from marrying paternal cousins," and then goes on to prohibit for-eigners from marrying their "father's younger brother's wife." This is a prohibition that probably reflects the Mongol aversion to marriages within certain degrees of kinship rather than a means of harassing any particular ethnic groups. And in May–June 1354, this decree is noted: "The skilled archers of Ningsia and wealthy Muslims[?] and Jews from the various places were sum-moned to the capital to volunteer for military service."

The *Yüan-tien-chang*, a code of statutes prepared during the Yüan period, has a long section dated January 27, 1280, which, although directed primarily at Muslims, names the Jews too. "Henceforward," one passage declares, "Mussulmen and Jews, no matter who kills the meat, will eat it, and cease killing sheep by their own hands, and will cease the rite of *Sunnah* [circum-cision?] . . . [and] the *namāz* [prayers] of five worships a day."[18] The same code, in July–August 1320, orders "Muslims[?], Nestorians, Jews, and Ta-shih-man, except those in actual charge of temples and services, to pay taxes."

There is, finally, a reference to Jews in the *Shan-chü hsin-hua* by Yang Yü, a work whose preface is dated 1360 but which deals with the period circa 1277–94: "The officials in the Hangchow sugar board were all rich Jewish and Muslim[?] merchants." These traders, Yang reports, were punished by the authorities for having misconducted themselves in their commercial transactions, apparently by resorting to the use of false weights. The Jews whom ibn Battuta met in Hangchow before 1346, or thereabouts, were thus members of a community that had been established no later than the last quarter of the previous century, and probably well before then.

Donald Daniel Leslie suggests that there may once have been a Jewish colony in Nanchang, capital of Kiangsi.[19] He also points out that "in 1277 offices for foreign traders were established in Shanghai, Kan-pu, Ch'üan-chou, and Ningpo; and, in 1293, also in Hangchow, Wenchow, and Canton. In addition, an office for the *Wo-t'o* [*Ortaq*] Muslim merchants was set up in 1283. The importance of the Muslims in the Chinese foreign trade and probably internal finance at this time was considerable, though what part the less numerous Jews took is impossible to estimate."[20] Wherever, in any case, there were large numbers of Muslims in China, Jews may have lived near or among them.

There must surely have been enclaves of Jews elsewhere in China than in those cities for which credible indications of their presence have so far been discovered. With the passage of the centuries, Jewish families would occasionally have settled here and there in the country for a variety of reasons. Perhaps other families joined them, perhaps not. Most of the Jews who held military or civil service appointments would have been required to leave the communities in which they were born and raised, and resettle themselves in new surroundings. The 1489 inscription thus relates that Kao Nien, recipient of the licentiate degree of the *kung-sheng* grade, was appointed district magistrate in She, Ahnwei Province; and that Ai Chun, recipient of the *chü-jen* degree, was appointed subdirector of studies in Ch'ung-ming, Kiangsu Province, and also administrator in the household of Prince Te, perhaps at Shantung. Of the families transplanted in this fashion, some no doubt returned to their native hearths, but others may have stayed on, eventually becoming assimilated into the local population.

There is every reason to believe that although Ai T'ien and his kinsmen had no means of communicating with even one of the many thousands of Jewish communities situated beyond the borders of their fatherland, it was still feasible for them to keep in touch with perhaps a half-dozen scattered Jewish outposts within China itself—diminished, each of them, to no more than a few families—and with a fair number of individual Jews living in scattered sites throughout the country.

In the early part of 1642 a massive attack was launched against Kaifeng by a rebel army led by Li Tzu-ch'eng. Li had already tried twice to capture the city, but was repulsed each time. Unable to overrun his objective by direct assault, he now resorted to siege tactics, hoping thereby to starve out the million or so inhabitants of the metropolis and force them to their knees.

The suffering within the beleaguered city was intense. Because its stocks of provisions were soon depleted, the meager supplies of food that had been hoarded by local profiteers or could be smuggled through enemy lines were sold at prices high enough to make even the wealthiest buyers flinch. In desperation, many of the less affluent inhabitants are alleged to have turned to cannibalism; for not only would it later be said that in the time of the siege human flesh was openly hawked in the marketplaces of Kaifeng, but it would also be reported that some of the besieged considered it "an act of piety to deposit corpses in the streets, where they could at least be of service in sustaining those who would otherwise soon starve to death."[21]

After six horrendous months, the city fell to the insurgents. The Chinese accounts of how this happened differ widely. One story has it that the officer in charge of an imperial relief column that reached the outskirts of Kaifeng (or, in a variant rendition, the officer in charge of the forces within the city) ordered the destruction of a section of the dikes lining the Yellow River in the belief that the rebel army would be engulfed by the unrestrained waters but that Kaifeng itself would not be significantly harmed. Unfortunately, so this story goes, when the commander of the besieging army discovered what his counterpart had in mind he moved his men, animals, and equipment to higher ground and issued the command to breach the dike at a different point— an action that, as he saw it, would weaken the defenses of Kaifeng while leaving his own troops unscathed. Both sides, the tale concludes, demolished their segments of the dikes at about the same time, setting off a flood immensely more catastrophic than either had intended. Another story assigns the sole responsibility for having the dikes ruptured to the governor of Kaifeng.

Regardless of where the blame lies for the inane decision to let loose the furies of the Yellow River, the results were ghastly. The river, greatly swollen by heavy rains, broke down the Northern Gate of the massive city wall and disgorged itself into the hapless metropolis, inundating most or all of it. Estimates of the number of people killed by the onrushing waters range as high as 300,000, though even if this figure is exaggerated (and it may not be) the carnage must still have been awesome.

Damage to property was of course correspondingly high. Thousands of residential and public buildings were utterly destroyed. The synagogue, located fairly close to the river, was swept away by the raging waters. The Jesuit mission house, established by Sambiasi in 1628 and situated not far from the synagogue, was also lost, and with it Rodriguez de Figueiredo, the dedicated priest who had been in charge of it for the past dozen years. In 1645 the city was retaken from Li's forces by imperial armies under the command of General Yi, but not until 1676 did it become possible for the Jesuits to return there and open a new center from which to propagate their faith. The Jewish survivors of the flood, staying on just outside the ruined city, had by 1653 recovered sufficiently from their human and property losses to be able to come back and begin the construction of a worthy replacement for their old synagogue. In the long interval between the flood and the completion of the new synagogue, they met for worship in a rented house on the north side of the river.

In 1663 the congregation memorialized the rebuilding of the synagogue by dedicating a stone monument on which the historical data provided in the earlier steles were augmented and brought up to date. The new slab, engraved on both sides, was erected in a pavilion standing in the southern half of the synagogal compound, while the 1489/1512 stele (or perhaps a copy of it) was positioned in a similar pavilion in the northern section of the compound. The front surface (1663a) of the 1663 stone bore the same caption as the 1489 text, "A Record of the Rebuilding of the Synagogue." A briefer text was inscribed on the reverse side (1663b). This was captioned "Names Inscribed on the Reverse of the Stone."[22] It lists the names of no less than 241 members of the *kehillah*. The *chang-chiao* (chief rabbi) is Li Chên, and there are eight *man-la* (spiritual leaders), five novice *man-la*, five ritual slaughter *man-la* (apparently the *shohetim* who prepare the community's meat), and two "incense and devotion" *man-la*.

Eight of these twenty-one synagogal leaders are of the Li clan, and seven are of the Kao. Thirty-eight of the complete roster of names are those of civil and military officials.

The text of 1663a was composed by Liu Ch'ang, a non-Jewish scholar and high officeholder, and was then transcribed in vermilion ink on transparent paper as a guide to the engraver by another official, Li Kuang-tso, who was not Jewish. The seal characters were prepared by Hou Liang-han, a non-Jew. Wang Chien-yu, also not Jewish, did the actual engraving.

In 1663a, Liu first presents a brief review of Judaism as it was known and practiced in Kaifeng. Then, cavalierly disregarding the statement in the 1512 inscription that the Jewish religion was introduced to China during the Han dynasty (206 B.C.E.–221 C.E.), he ascribes this event to the more remote Chou period (circa 1122–256 B.C.E.). As for the date of the building of the first synagogue in Kaifeng, Liu assigns this to the year 1163 (as do the 1489 and 1512 texts, neither of which he alludes to in his own text).

Liu then turns his attention to more recent times. He chronicles the 1642 siege of Kaifeng and in a few sentences describes how the ordeal affected the Jewish community. "Pien [Kaifeng]," he begins, "was submerged in the waters. Pien being submerged, then the synagogue also was destroyed. The synagogue being destroyed, then the Scriptures also were swept away, floating on the waves of the flood."

The surviving Jews, now barely "more than a couple of hundred families," Liu goes on, made their way to the north bank of the Yellow River. There "they wandered about, separated the one from the other."

When it became possible to do so, he reports, certain Jews returned to the site of the synagogue and undertook a search for the sacred books that had been washed away by the flood. Their efforts did not go entirely unrewarded, the young scholar Kao Hsüan, a *kung-sheng*, being able to retrieve "several rolls of the Scriptures of the Way and twenty-six items of miscellaneous Scriptures." (1663b credits Kao with salvaging seven Torah scrolls, and adds that Li Ch'êng-chün recovered three others.)

The recovered Torahs and the other manuscripts, all severely damaged, were dried out and entrusted to Li Chên, the rabbi of the congregation, and the *man-la* Li Ch'êng-hsien. Assisted by Chao Ying-ch'eng, the two men succeeded in piecing together from the bedraggled sheets one usable Torah scroll and "several volumes of the square scriptural portions, and some tens of items of miscellaneous Scriptures."[23] These restored writings were installed in the large rented structure that served as the congregation's temporary house of worship.

Liu then states that a Jewish officer, Major Chao Ch'êng-chi of the Middle Army of the Ta-liang (Kaifeng) Route, who had commanded troops in the defense of Kaifeng and returned to the city after its recovery in 1645 by General Yi:

> repaired the roads, built bridges, and summoned the people to return to their occupations. Fearing that the members of the religion, owing to the ruin of the synagogue, might disperse and never come together again, and unable to contemplate the work his ancestors had built up and preserved through the centuries suddenly destroyed in a single day, he sent troops to patrol and protect the [ruins of the] synagogue day and night. Moreover, the younger brother of Ying-ch'eng, Chao Ying-tou, who had entered Pien to take his examinations, together with him found in the midst of the tangled ruins the actual foundations of the synagogue. The [non-Jewish] people of Pien who returned to their homes had daily increased in number, so Chao Ch'êng-chi frequently urged the members of the religion also to return home. Accordingly, Li Chên and Chao Yün-chung returned to Pien, bringing remnants of the Scriptures. This took place in the year *kuei-ssu* of the Shun Chih period [1653].

Permission was received from the authorities to rebuild the synagogue. Major Chao and numerous others contributed generously to the construction fund, and when the new edifice was finally completed, "nobody who saw it," Liu roundly declares, "failed to be aroused to a sense of solemn respect."

Twelve new Torah scrolls were written and placed in "the Ark of the Revered Scriptures" together with the scroll which had been assembled from the various salvaged Torahs.[24] Chao Ying-ch'eng, the most important Jew ever born in Kaifeng, wrote a commemorative work, *A Record of the Vicissitudes of the Holy Scriptures,* and his younger brother Chao Ying-tou prepared a book ten chapters long bearing the title *A Preface to the Illustrious Way,* presumably a description of the tenets of Judaism. Unfortunately, no copy of either of these works has yet been found.

A number of horizontal and vertical tablets, most of them displaying a brief laudatory or pietistic comment and the names of the contributors (many of these non-Jews), were composed and set up throughout the premises.

On his return home from an assignment with the West Route Army in Shensi Province, according to Liu, Major Chao was overwhelmed by the sight of the synagogue that had been completed in his absence. "The glories which have been established for some hundreds of years," Liu quotes him as saying, "have now returned, and we behold their abundance; and when later generations look back on this day, will it not be as we today look back on the men of earlier times?"

Liu now explains his own role. Major Chao, he says, "fearing that after a lapse of time this story would not be handed on, desired to have it cut on stone to be transmitted to future generations, and asked me to compose the inscription." Liu then presents his qualifications for undertaking such an assignment, pointing out that he is a native of Kaifeng, is very familiar with the religion of Israel, and has long been "on terms of intimate friendship" with the leading members of the *kehillah.* He says that he studied the old records and "added in and completed them, so that men might know the origin and history of the Way [the Law of Moses], and seeing the restoration of the Scriptures and the synagogue of today, may recognize that the merit of all the members of the religion is such as cannot be obliterated. And so this inscription is recorded."

Still another stone was set up in 1679, but not on the grounds of the synagogue. It bore the title "A Stele Record of the Story of the Past of the Ancestral Hall" and also a subtitle, "A Preface to the Establishment of the Chao Archway of the Synagogue and the History of the Origin and Development [of the Synagogue] from its Foundation Onward."

The 1679 inscription, written by Chao Ying-kun, was not known to Western visitors to Kaifeng until about 1899, when it was finally brought to their attention. The stone was embedded in the outer wall of a house belonging to a member of the Chao clan and situated on the southern boundary of the synagogal enclosure. The text engraved on the stone repeats some of the material found in the 1489 and 1663a steles and, for the rest, deals almost exclusively with the Chao and their position in the community.

By ill luck, the 1679 stone became a gathering point for the children of the neighborhood who over the successive generations used its exposed surface as a backdrop for their coin-tossing games and otherwise damaged it. As a result, the inscribed text was severely disfigured, much of it being made illegible.

Around 1904, the stone was removed from the wall of the Chao residence. Some years later, this stone, together with the 1489/ 1512 stele, was turned over to the Canadian Mission at Kaifeng and was immediately transferred to the courtyard of the city's Trinity Cathedral. At the time, Bishop White was away. He returned, as he wrote:

> to find the city in an uproar, with placards posted on public walls stating that the Anglican Bishop had obtained the stones and intended to send them out of the country. The head Jew, Chao Yün-chung, had been thrown into prison, and members of all the Jewish clans were clamoring for his release. The authorities were insistent that Chao should request the return of the stones, and finally offered him a bribe of eight hundred dollars if he would do so.[25]

Chao, according to White, refused to accept the bribe. The Jewish religion was no longer practiced in Kaifeng, the bishop has him say, and the Anglicans could be trusted to take proper care of the Jewish relics. His fellow Jews, White declares, backed him up strongly, even though they were subjected to considerable abuse for doing so and repeatedly threatened with imprisonment and physical violence. Eventually, Chao was released and a compromise worked out. Since the governor of the province was unwilling to permit the title to relics of such historical importance

LEFT: 8. Chao Yün-ching, leader of the Kaifeng Jews, 1919.

BELOW: 9. Three Kaifeng Jews, 1919, standing next to the synagogal stele of 1489. The 1512 inscription is on the other side of the stone. The man to the left is Ai Ju-lin. To the right are a father and son of the Shih clan. The photograph was taken on the premises of the Anglican Cathedral, Kaifeng.

to pass to foreigners, it was agreed that White and his successors would act as custodians of the steles, be responsible for their maintenance, and make them accessible for study by authorized scholars and officials. Under no circumstances, however, were the stones to be taken out of Kaifeng. Presumably, they are still there, but the fate of the 1663 stone, which the Canadians never saw, is unknown.[26]

The portions of the 1679 text that are decipherable deal with the precepts of Judaism and tell something of the history of the *kehillah*, paying particular attention to the Chao contributions to that history. In all, the stele adds a few minor details to the materials already presented in the earlier inscriptions, but is primarily of interest for its corroboratory restatements of certain of the specifics mentioned in the previous texts and the materials it presents regarding individual members of the Chao clan.

4 ❖ GUIDELINES FOR ROME

S PURRED on by the entreaties of the biblical scholars and the prospect of uncovering fresh evidence with which to shore up their endangered position in the Chinese Rites Controversy, the leaders of the Society of Jesus instructed the Superior of their mission at Peking to get in touch with the Kaifeng Jews, probe into their background, ask them a series of questions bearing on the Rites and Terms disputes, and try to secure samples of their scriptural and liturgical works, above all a Torah scroll. And if, *Deo volente*, the Jewish community of Kaifeng could be induced to seek salvation in the arms of the Church, so much the better.

It was the Rites affair, actually, which lay uppermost in the minds of the Jesuit authorities in 1703 as they requested Peking to enter into talks with the Kaifeng Jews, hoping thereby to elicit certain information relating to the *kehillah*'s beliefs and practices that would prove helpful to the Jesuits in their longstanding quarrel with the Dominicans and Franciscans. Such a move—to consult Jews regarding their views and customs in connection with Church matters that did not concern them at all—was unusual; but it was not without precedent. At the suggestion of his experts in canon law, to give one example, Henry VIII had sent the Cambridge humanist Richard Croke to Italy to solicit the cooperation of both Christian and Jewish scholars in the preparation of a brief that was to be submitted to Pope Clement VII, in support of Henry's petition to have his two-decade-old marriage to Catherine of Aragon annulled—and this at a time when Jews were not permitted to live in the country over which he ruled. One of the questions Croke asked the Jews was whether their interpretations of two seemingly contradictory passages in the Bible, Lev. 18:16 and Deut. 25:5, would permit a woman to marry her deceased husband's brother. Croke hoped for a negative response, the point being that such a response would mean that because Catherine was the widow of Henry's brother Arthur her marriage to Henry was unsanctioned by Holy Writ and was consequently null and void. In any event, since Jewish scholars had been called in to provide theological opinions that would presumably bolster the English cause, a group of Church officials antagonistic to Henry deemed it expedient to appeal to other Jewish authorities who, they hoped, might be induced to offer dissenting interpretations. The religious laws and traditions by which Italian Jewry lived were thus curiously injected into the crucial politico-theological struggle that eventually created the Anglican schism.[1] Another serious problem, although not quite as potentially explosive as that arising out of Henry's marital difficulties, had now come to a head in the debate over the Chinese Rites, and it was thought by the Jesuit theoreticians that if they could show that the Kaifeng Jews did not look upon the teachings and rituals of Confucianism as incompatible with Mosaic law, the Vatican might be influenced to resolve the Rites dispute along the lines advocated by their Order.

In the opening years of the eighteenth century, the Chinese Rites Controversy had developed into a festering sore on the body politic of Catholicism, a cancer menacing the overall health of the Church and threatening to terminate all her evangelical activities in the Orient. From one end of Christendom to the other, lay and clerical writers fought bitterly and relentlessly over the Rites issue, embarking with a monotonous frequency upon polemic excursions launched from premises of the most dubious validity. It was not uncommon to hear Dominicans and Franciscans speak derisively of the Chinese neophytes recruited by the Society of Jesus as "Jesuit converts," the implication being that although these people were perhaps something more than heathen they were still something less than Christian. Not surprisingly, this attitude did not sit well with the Chinese newcomers to the faith and boded ill for the Church's future in their country. To the dismay of the moderates, moreover, the clashing ideologies of the concerned parties had become so rigidly frozen in place that there no longer seemed to be much point in striving for any sort of compromise.

The Sinification Policy, as it came to be called by both its supporters and opponents, was initially proposed by Ricci and subsequently adopted by the Jesuit Order for the twin purposes of drawing the Chinese into the orbit of the Church and keeping them there. Ricci preferred to regard most Confucian rituals and customs as devoid of all theological content, asserting that they were social and civic practices and mores stemming from the secular aspects of Chinese culture. Having concluded that the ceremonies of Confucianism were inherently nonreligious in nature, it became possible for him to take a further step and argue that these Confucian ways could be benignly tolerated within the framework of the Sino-Catholic Church, which he and his colleagues had recently begun to build. Certain Confucian teachings, he willingly conceded, had with the passage of time become overlaid with accretions of Buddhist and Taoist origin, and were obviously tainted by idolatry. He urged, however, that once these objectionable encrustations were scaled off, the precepts of Confucianism could no longer be considered unacceptable, and the Chinese should not be required to give them up as a precondition for admission to the Church.

To the Dominicans and the Franciscans, Ricci's stand had nothing to commend it but expedience. They agreed that the broad concessions he was prepared to offer the Chinese would make it much more attractive for them to come over to the Church, but deplored the quality of conversions obtained under such excessively permissive terms. The compromises he advocated were also fraught with danger, they insisted, for regardless of what he and his supporters claimed, the Confucian Rites were cast in a distinctly heathen mold and, if tolerated, would enable pagan philosophies and practices to worm their way into the lifestream of the Church.[2]

At one point in the frothing turmoil over the Rites several French Jesuits, known collectively as the Figurists, contended that they had uncovered evidence suggesting a Judaic origin for China itself.[3] The so-called heathen ceremonials of the Chinese, they maintained, included no less than forty that were distinctly Hebraic. Confucius, they added, had envisioned the coming of the Messiah, and the ancient Chinese writings might properly be thought of as foreshadowing both the Old and New Testaments. They also insisted that faint glimmerings of the Christian doctrine of man's fall and redemption, and even of the immaculate conception, could be discerned in the Chinese literature of ancient times. The tenor of their arguments, understandably, left many of their colleagues in the Society of Jesus with the uneasy feeling that in their zeal to buttress the Jesuit position on the Rites, the Figurists had pushed much further than they should have. The Dominicans and Franciscans, aghast, thundered that the Figurist stand provided a grim harbinger of the kind of blasphemous attitudes that would come to the fore if the Chinese Church were ever to fall into the hands of people who could bring themselves to tolerate Confucianism.[4]

"It is true," Rowbotham has pointed out, "that the bitterness injected into the [Rites] controversy was stimulated by animosities which had grown up elsewhere between the [Jesuit] Order and the rest of the Church, but in China the struggle was protracted and opportunities for compromise were ignored, because both parties felt that the issues involved were a matter of life and death to the Faith in the empire."[5]

The basic difference in outlook apropos the Rites inspired a series of maneuvers within the Church that left the two parties locked in an agonizing and seemingly endless struggle, with the power and prestige of each Order now apt to be measured by its success or lack of success in persuading the Holy See to endorse its particular approach to the problem of converting China. The Rites Controversy was thus made to undergo a strange metamorphosis, one consequence of which was that numerous observers in and out of the Church came to think of it not so much as a theological dispute but as a weathervane indicating the direction in which the winds of ecclesiastic power were veering.

The Kaifeng congregation was not the only source from which the Jesuits hoped to extract support for their position on the Rites. The Peking mission had gone so far as to approach the emperor K'ang Hsi, in his capacity as titular head of the religious establishment in China, and petition him to supply it with a clarification of the philosophy underlying the Confucian ceremonies to which millions upon millions of his subjects were so profoundly attached. A memorial was submitted to the emperor by the Peking Jesuits that, while purposely sidestepping all mention of the vehement intra-Church battle being waged over the Rites, left the impression that the Western interest in Confucianism was purely scholarly in intent and totally unrelated to practical affairs. Viewed in this light, the Jesuit petition would appear to give the emperor no cause to suspect that his reply might be employed to influence the thrust of Europe's missionary efforts in China or to tilt the delicately poised balance of power within the Church to the advantage of his petitioners (who would, no doubt, quietly dispose of his reply, should it turn out to reinforce the position held by their opponents). In all probability, however, the sophisticated and well-informed K'ang Hsi saw through the Jesuits' stratagem. For reasons of his own, he nevertheless deigned to answer the questions posed to him by the Jesuits, and in a form that would please them.

Essentially, the Jesuit memorial urged the emperor to define the term *T'ien* (the Divinity), as it was used by the Confucian philosophers, and to explain whether the rituals and customs of Confucianism fell within the realm of the sacred or the profane. The document presented to the Son of Heaven concisely sums up the Jesuit attitude toward both the Rites affair and the Terms Question, which was inextricably associated with it; and the shrewd care with which it was drafted reflects the deep need felt by the missionaries at Peking to elicit a favorable response that was swathed in the trappings of authority and could be used to confound their Dominican and Franciscan adversaries:

> We, your faithful subjects, although natives of distant lands, respectfully beg Your Majesty to give us positive information on the following points.
>
> The scholars of Europe have learned that in China ceremonies are performed in honor of Confucius; that sacrifices are offered to Heaven, and that special rites are performed to the Ancestors. Persuaded that these ceremonies, these sacrifices and these rites are based on reason, European scholars, who

are ignorant of the true meaning of these matters, are urgently begging us to enlighten them concerning them.

We have always judged that Confucius is honored in China as a legislator; that it is to this end and solely with this in view that the ceremonies established in his honor are performed. We believe that the rites which are performed to the Ancestors are established only with a view to communicating the love in which the latter are held and to consecrate the memory of the good which they accomplished during their lifetime.

As for the sacrifices to Heaven (*T'ien*) [the term the Jesuits were urging the Pope to permit Chinese converts to use for the Divinity], we believe that they are addressed not to the visible Heavens that we see above us, but to the Supreme Ruler, Author and Preserver of Heaven and Earth, and of all that they contain.

Such is the meaning which we have always given to the Chinese ceremonies. But as foreigners cannot be expected to be capable of pronouncing upon this important matter with the certitude of the Chinese themselves, we take the liberty to beg Your Majesty not to refuse the enlightenment which we need. We await your elucidation with respect and submission.[6]

K'ang Hsi's rejoinder, brief and to the point, sustained the Jesuit view that the Confucian practices were essentially of a secular nature and that the term *T'ien*, as it was employed in Confucian rituals, had no material connotation. "What is written here," he replied, "is without fault. It conforms to our holy doctrine. To honor Heaven; to serve the prince and parents; to honor one's master and one's superiors is the universal doctrine of the empire. In all this [petition] there is not a word which needs changing. Respect this."[7]

The correspondence between the Peking Jesuits and the emperor was made public in Rome late in 1701. Although the reaction was initially favorable, the Jesuits might nevertheless have been better advised to leave the emperor out of the affair, as they soon found themselves being severely criticized for having sought out the opinion of a "heathen" in a matter being even then adjudicated by the Holy See.

Nearly a century earlier, Paul V (1605-21) had bestowed his apostolic seal of approval on most of the Rites concessions that the Jesuits had seen fit to recommend, but during the pontificate of Innocent X (1644–55), the Franciscans and Dominicans succeeded in having Paul's decree revoked. Then, during the papacy of Alexander VII (1655–67), the pendulum swung back, and the Rites were again allowed.

The reversal of policy ordained by Alexander did not end the struggle between the Orders. In 1669 a troubled Clement IX, anxious to work out a truce that both factions could be induced to honor, promulgated a decree stipulating that all papal decisions previously enunciated regarding the Rites were from then on to be adhered to "according to circumstances." This vacillating approach, naturally enough, satisfied nobody and settled nothing. It merely passed on the responsibility for resolving the problem, and the parallel Terms Question as well, to his successors. The despair and bewilderment of one of them were eloquently summed up by Robert Browning in this soliloquy concerning the Terms aspect of the affair, which he put into the mouth of Innocent XII who, having ascended the Throne of Peter in 1691, was now in the fifth year of his papacy:

Five years long, now, rounds faith into my ears,
"Help thou, or Christendom is done to death!"
Five years since, in the Province of To-Kien [*sic*],
Which is in China, as some people know,
Maigret, my Vicar Apostolic there,
Having a great qualm, issues a decree.
Alack, the converts use as God's name, not
T'ien-chu but plain *T'ien* or else mere *Shang-ti*,
As Jesuits please to fancy politic,
While, say Dominicans, it calls down fire,—
For *T'ien* means heaven, and *Shang-ti* supreme prince,
While *T'ien-chu* means the lord of heaven: all cry,
"There is no business urgent for despatch
As that thou send a legate, specially
Cardinal Tournon, straight to Pekin, there
To settle and compose the difference!"[8]

"The period from 1700 to 1702," Rowbotham writes, "is the high-water mark of the [Rites] controversy in Europe. Printing presses were kept busy with a flood of pamphlets on both sides. The Missions Étrangères and others were pressing for an immediate and unmistakable pronouncement from the Holy See."[9] And it was as part of their campaign to secure a favorable pronouncement that the Jesuit leaders decided to have the Peking mission contact the Chinese Jews apropos the Rites and the Terms. It was already too late, however, to stave off defeat, for in 1704, before a reply could be received from Peking, a verdict was rendered at Rome by the Congregation of Rites proscribing all the concessions with which the Jesuits planned to attract myriads of new converts in China and keep those Chinese who had accepted baptism from sliding away.

The Congregation of Rites condemned the Confucian rituals as both alien and antagonistic to the spirit of Christianity, and warned all members of the Church that such ceremonies were forbidden entirely. It also ruled on the Terms Question, making it crystal clear that the only acceptable Chinese term for God was to be *T'ien-chu*, or "Lord of Heaven." The use of *T'ien-chu*, the Congregation felt, would remove the ambiguity that had hitherto surrounded the Chinese designation *T'ien*, "Heaven," for it was possible to understand *T'ien* as the physical heaven, while *T'ien-chu* could mean only the Master of that heaven.

K'ang Hsi, offended by the terms of the ruling of the Congregation of Rites as they drifted back to him, retaliated in 1706 by ordering the Catholic priests in his empire either to continue abiding by the toleration policy instituted by Ricci or leave the country. The majority of the Jesuits in China chose to disregard the decision of the Congregation of Rites rather than face expulsion, an act of insubordination that eventually drew a threat of excommunication from Clement XI (1700–21). An even more telling blow to the Jesuit position was delivered on July 11, 1742, when Benedict XIV, in his papal bull *Ex quo singulari*, formally and unequivocally rescinded all earlier concessions relating to the Rites.

It took Rome nearly two centuries—until December 8, 1938, to be exact—to reverse Benedict's decision, but by then it was too late. As one historian has noted, "where Christianity had failed either to accommodate with or to eliminate Confucianism, Communism is to a great extent succeeding. Fr. Columba Cary-Elwes, O.S.D., in *China and the Cross*, writes of the controversy: 'The tragedy itself is the loss of China to the Church.' But for the Rites Controversy, who can say what China would be now?"[10]

In 1704, Rome's directive to initiate talks with the Kaifeng Jews having arrived at the Peking mission, the responsibility for carrying it out was delegated to Father Jean-Paul Gozani in a letter forwarded to him at Kaifeng by his superior, Father Joseph Suarez.

In the course of an earlier tour of duty in the Honan capital, Gozani had considered asking the Jews for permission to inspect the ancient Bible which was said to be preserved in their synagogue. However, as he subsequently explained in his report to Suarez, it had then seemed wiser to leave the matter in abeyance, because he knew no Hebrew and believed, moreover, that the congregation would never accede to such a request. Transferred back to Kaifeng, where he received Suarez's letter, he tried without too much success to brush aside his earlier forebodings and proceeded, though still painfully conscious of the linguistic difficulties lying ahead, to do the best he could to fulfill the obligation that had just been thrust upon him. He did surprisingly well, considering the circumstances, and by the fifth of November was able to send Suarez a lengthy report yielding substantially more information about the Chinese Jews than the West had managed to accumulate in the century that had now passed since Ai T'ien first knocked on Matteo Ricci's door in Peking.[11]

Gozani was gratified by the readiness with which the *kehillah* responded to his overtures. He encountered no problems in arranging for an exchange of courtesy visits, during which he entertained the chief rabbi and other prominent leaders of the congregation in his church and was himself received as an honored guest in the synagogue. He held long talks with the Jews and was given free rein to examine their Scriptures. These, of course, he could not read, but their lapidary inscriptions, composed in Chinese characters, posed no difficulties. In the synagogue itself he studied the various horizontal and vertical tablets, and transcribed a number of those which had been written in Chinese. He was even admitted to the Bethel, the sanctuary in which the congregation's thirteen Torah scrolls were kept and to which, he understood, only the rabbi was normally permitted entry.[12] There he saw the Torah scrolls, each resting on its own table and enclosed by a small curtain. It was explained to him that twelve of the Torah scrolls were dedicated to the respective Twelve Tribes of Israel and that the thirteenth and oldest, the Pentateuch collated from the sheets fished out of the floodwaters that destroyed the synagogue in 1642, was sanctified to the memory of Moses. Two of the Torah scrolls were unrolled for his inspection. One, the Scroll of Moses, had been badly damaged when the skins of which it was composed were submerged. Many of its characters, he noted, were almost bleached away by the action of the waters.

Elsewhere in the synagogue, Gozani was shown two or three old chests containing numerous small-sized volumes, some in good condition, others worn out. This collection, he was informed, was made up mainly of prayer books (*siddurim*) and booklets representing the individual weekly portions of the Pentateuch (*parashioth*). He was deeply impressed by the respect that the Jews accorded to these treasures. The congregation's books, he later wrote to Suarez, "are preserved with greater care and attention than if they were of gold and silver." He was told, just as Ricci had been told a hundred years earlier, that the Kaifeng synagogue was the only surviving Jewish house of worship in all of China.

As he was guided through the synagogue his eye was caught by a plaque honoring the emperor, an ornate pulpit, and a dais ("chair of Moses") from which public readings of the Torah were made during worship services on the Sabbath and other holy days. The congregation, he learned, faced west in prayer, toward Jerusalem. (In Europe and America, of course, the worshippers faced east, still in the direction of the Holy City.) The synagogue, like its Western counterparts, was unadorned by statues or images.

The Terms Question, quite naturally, was not overlooked by Gozani. He asked the Jews to repeat the Chinese names by which they spoke of the Divinity, and was told that they habitually employed, among others, the names *T'ien* and *Shang-ti*, both of which they had learned from their Confucian countrymen. For the Jesuits in Peking and Rome, he knew this was to be a welcome piece of news, for they would now be able to point out that the Jews, the watchword of whose faith was the cry "Hear, O Israel, the Lord our God, the Lord is One," did not look upon these traditional Confucian appellations for the Divinity as inconsistent with monotheism or conveying any hint of idolatrous leanings on the part of the people who voiced them. To the Kaifeng Jews, *T'ien* was not the material heaven but a figurative designation for the One God who dwelled in that supernal sphere, and *Shang-ti* was the Supreme Ruler. Why then, the Jesuits could now ask, should the right to continue using these same terms be denied to the Chinese followers of Confucius once they embraced Christianity?

The Dominicans and Franciscans, on the other hand, had been saying that in the Confucian system *T'ien* represented the physical heaven and that *Shang-ti*, far from having a monotheistic con-

10. Model of the Kaifeng synagogue in the Beth Hatefusoth Museum of the Jewish Diaspora, Tel Aviv, based on details derived from the early Jesuit reports, Domenge's drawing, and the journals of the Chinese delegates.

notation, referred to one of the four distinct categories of spirits meant to be worshipped by man. It followed, accordingly, that Confucianism had arrayed itself on the side of polytheism and could under no circumstances be considered the secularly oriented system Ricci had called it. Its principles were irreconcilable with the doctrine of monotheism; its ceremonies had absolutely no place in Christian worship; and it was imperative that the Deity be addressed as *T'ien-chu*, the Lord of Heaven, and certainly not as *T'ien* or *Shang-ti*. The Jesuit rebuttal to this position would of course now be that Gozani's discovery that the Kaifeng Jews had no qualms whatever about applying the customary Confucianist names *T'ien* and *Shang-ti* to the God of Israel completely demolished the Dominican and Franciscan thesis that these terms were idolatrous conceptions arising out of a movement that was inherently heathen and, as such, theologically repugnant—a movement whose teachings and practices should therefore be kept as far away from Christianity as possible.

In a separate hall outside the sanctuary, Gozani walked by rows of incense bowls, some large, some small, and consecrated, each of them, to the memory of a revered biblical figure: Abraham, Isaac, Jacob, Jacob's twelve sons, Moses, Aaron, Joshua, Ezra, "and many others, both men and women." The inference to be drawn, Gozani immediately realized, was that the Jews did not deem it inconsistent with monotheism to burn incense in honor of these august personages or, as he also learned, in honor of their more immediate ancestors—and even in honor of Confucius himself! And this, the Jesuits could therefore argue, was further evidence that the Dominicans and Franciscans were wrong in describing these particular rites as the idolatrous worship of ancestors and the apotheosization of Confucius. These rites, the Jesuits could now reiterate, and with more reason than before, were merely a ceremonial means of expressing the respect due to one's forebears and to the man who was esteemed as China's greatest sage. Why then make the road to Christianity virtually impassable for China's millions by insisting that they cease participating in those innocent rituals and traditions that held such great allure for them?

On the conclusion of his initial tour of the synagogal premises, Gozani was escorted by his hosts to the "guest room" for a discussion of comparative theology. He had brought along a Bible that contained a list, printed in Hebrew, of the Jewish scriptural canon. The rabbi who, in Gozani's words, "is deaf and speaks through his teeth," scanned the titles and admitted that although he did have most of them in the synagogue and had heard of a few others, there were several that were entirely unknown to him.

The priest and the rabbi—whom Gozani did not identify by name in his 1704 letter, but who was a member of the Kao clan and bore the Hebrew name Phineas—now sat down to the task of comparing and analyzing a series of parallel passages in their respective Bibles. Their discussion, which must have left both of them physically exhausted and emotionally depleted, probably sounded more like a disorganized shouting and hissing match than a placid and decorous meeting of scholarly minds. Gozani's European-accented Chinese, loudly delivered, fell on ears that did not hear well, while the Chinese, whistling past the clenched rabbinic teeth, might have tried the patience of a native-born listener, let alone that of a foreigner. Still, the rabbi and the priest talked, tried as best they could to understand each other, and somehow managed to work out the problems they had set for themselves.

Gozani opened his Bible to Genesis. The rabbi turned to the same text in one of the synagogal manuscripts. Between them, they then checked out "the descendants of Adam down to Noah, with the age [at death] of each," a procedure that Leibniz had recommended in his letter of January 1, 1700, to Antoine Verjus. They discovered, as Gozani reported to Suarez, that "all was in agreement." They then ran through "in a summary manner the names and main points of chronology" of each of the Five Books of Moses. There were no discrepancies.

"What surprises me most," Gozani lamented to Suarez, "are the many idle tales and stories that they or the ancient rabbis have mixed with the true facts of Holy Scripture, even in the Five Books of Moses. This made me suspicious that they have among them Talmudic Jews and have corrupted the Bible. And to have a clear picture one needs a person who knows Hebrew and the

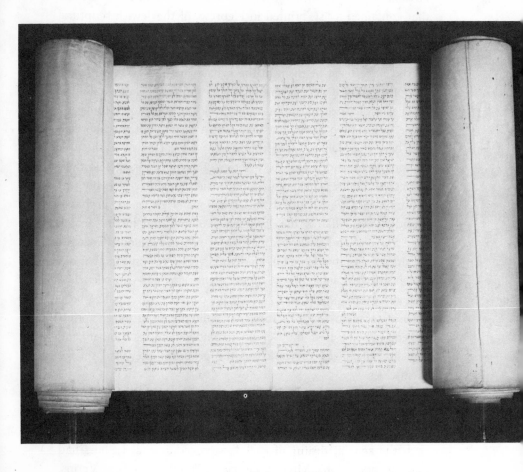

11. Mid-seventeenth century Torah scroll from the Kaifeng synagogue. The number 12, written in Hebrew as *yod-beth* on the reverse side of the last skin, indicates that the scroll was dedicated to Benjamin, the twelfth of the Twelve Tribes.

12. Details from Kaifeng Torah scroll, mid-seventeenth century.

Holy Scriptures well (which I do not). What confirms me in my suspicion [that the texts had been altered long before the Chinese Jews obtained them] is that they told me that, during the Ming dynasty, Father Rodrigo de Figueiredo and, during the present Ch'ing dynasty, Father Christiano Enriquez (both of saintly memory) went to their synagogue several times to talk with them. But (I suggest) if these two learned fathers did not bother to obtain their Bible, it shows that they found it already corrupted by the Talmudists and not pure, as it had been before the coming of the Savior." It was therefore Gozani's hesitant deduction— open to revision, as he stressed, by a competent Catholic Hebraist—that the Torahs of the Kaifeng Jews were probably no different from the Torahs known everywhere in the Christian world, and that the copies stored in the Kaifeng synagogue should be presumed, at least for the time being, to be no less corrupt than all the others.

Later in his report he again warned Suarez not to rely too greatly upon his personal evaluation of the textual integrity of the Kaifeng Torahs. "As to whether their Bible is true or corrupted, complete or partial," he wrote apologetically, "I, who am ignorant in these matters, would not be able to say: I will do and am doing my best, but I am doubtful of success."

Gozani's inability to reach a definitive conclusion regarding the purity of the Kaifeng texts did not, accordingly, satisfy the churchmen of the West. It was this, his failure to solve the vexing problem once and for all, which encouraged le Gobien to raise it again in 1707, in the preface he inserted to the seventh volume of the *Lettres édifiantes*, the work in which Gozani's report to Suarez was made known to the reading public of Europe.

While he was in the synagogue Gozani asked the Jews if they had ever heard of Jesus. They replied that they had. But it turned out, much to the priest's chagrin, that the only Jesus they recalled was Jesus ben Sira (Sirach), the author of the Book of Ecclesiasticus, also known as the Wisdom of Jesus the Son of Sira.

The fact that the Jews were familiar with the name of ben Sira may mean that they either owned or had at one time owned a Hebrew text of Ecclesiasticus, a possibility that would have enthralled both Christian and Jewish theologians, but Gozani neglected to report whether such an edition had ever been in the possession of the *kehillah*. The work was written in Jerusalem about 180 B.C.E. In 132 Jesus's grandson moved to Egypt, where he revised his grandfather's book and translated it into Greek. It was this Greek version, substantially altered by later editors and copyists, which was available to the Jews and Christians of Gozani's time, the only reliable Hebrew texts having been unaccountably lost several hundred years before his visit to the Kaifeng synagogue. Saadiah Gaon, in the tenth century, had seen a Hebrew text of Ecclesiasticus he could accept; Maimonides, in the twelfth, could no longer find one.

Although Ecclesiasticus was regarded as an extra-canonical work by Judaism and was not formally received into the Roman Catholic canon until the Council of Trent, it was always admired by the adherents of both religions for the beauty of its ethical precepts and the common sense of its utilitarian maxims. The hope that a very old Hebrew text, one likely to be far more reliable than the Greek or Greek-derived versions, might some day be discovered was therefore ever present in the thoughts of the theologians.

The scholars had another valid reason for wanting to recover an uncorrupted Hebrew edition of Ecclesiasticus. Since the date of the composition of Ecclesiasticus can be more precisely worked out than that of any other book in the canonical or apocryphal literature, a careful study of its complete text and its Hebrew style might be expected to disclose new and substantive information regarding the scriptural works to which a Jew of the early part of the second century B.C.E. could have had access; and this, of course, would be of tremendous interest to the world of biblical scholarship.

More than a century and a half after Gozani's death, that is to say in 1896, a few lines inscribed on a fragment of paper taken from the *genizah* (documentary storage room) of an old synagogue in Cairo came to the attention of the distinguished Hebraist Solomon Schechter, who promptly identified them as part of the Hebrew text of Ecclesiasticus. As soon as he could,

Schechter traveled to Cairo and installed himself in the *genizah*. Eventually, the additional Ecclesiasticus texts that he and others discovered, and the textual and linguistic analyses they undertook, enabled Schechter and his followers to argue rather convincingly that the very late chronology, which had been worked out by the nineteenth-century exponents of the "Higher Criticism" for the writing of much of the Hebrew Scriptures, was without foundation and that the time span between the composition of most of the Old Testament and the ben Sira text must be reckoned in centuries. Gozani, of course, was not looking for ben Sira manuscripts, and he may not even have been aware of the theologians' keen interest in them. Still, if the Kaifeng synagogue did contain a valid Hebrew Ecclesiasticus and if Gozani could have had its relatively short text copied, an outstanding contribution to biblical scholarship might well have been made nearly 200 years before it was.[13]

In his letter to Suarez, Gozani restricted himself almost completely to those aspects of Jewish life in Kaifeng that were in one way or another associated with religion. The Jews, he informed Suarez, practiced circumcision and observed the Sabbath, Passover, "and other festivals of the ancient Law." He reported that the Chinese called them the *T'iao-chin-chiao*, or "the sect which plucks out the sinews," because "they do not eat blood, and when they kill animals they cut the nerves and veins so that all the blood drains out." (Here Gozani was slightly in error, for although the blood must be removed from meat in order to make the meat kosher, the cutting out of the sinew is actually a custom derived from Gen. 32:25–33. This is the passage that relates the story of Jacob's struggle with the angel at Peniel, in the course of which the angel "wrenched Jacob's hip at its socket, so that the socket of his hip was strained as he wrestled with him." The last verse of the passage declares that in commemoration of this encounter "the children of Israel to this day eat not the thigh muscle that is on the socket of the hip, since Jacob's socket was wrenched at the thigh muscle.")

T'iao-chin-chiao, Gozani explained, "is the name [the Jews] are given by the Pagans, and one they accept willingly, to distinguish themselves from the other *Hui-hui* [a Chinese term including

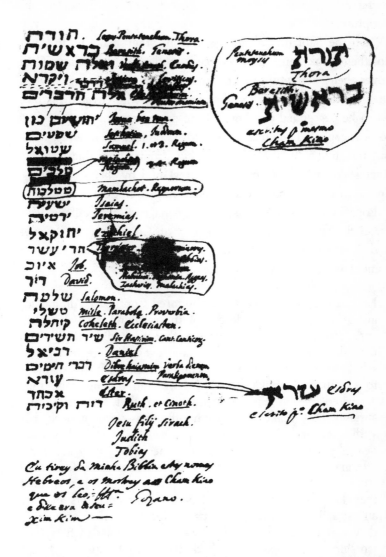

13. A list of biblical and apocryphal books known to the Jews of Kaifeng in 1704–5. Whether they still owned all of these at that time is questionable. The Hebrew is in the hand of Phineas, then chief rabbi of Kaifeng. The romanization may be Gozani's. Ecclesiasticus is included in this list.

both Jews and Muslims], who are called *tsu-mo chiao.*" In later generations, however, the congregation would be reported as preferring to be known as "the sect which adheres to the Scriptures."

"On the Sabbath," Gozani went on, "they make no fire, nor do they cook; and they prepare food on the Friday. They cover their faces with a transparent veil in the synagogue when they recite the Bible in memory of Moses, who covered his face when he descended the mountain to promulgate the Law of God to his people." They marry, he added, "among themselves, without mingling with the other *Hui-hui,* from whom they are distinguished by their *Ching* [Scriptures] and by their ceremonies, and even by their mustaches, which they do not cut."

Long before Gozani's visit to the synagogue the Kaifeng Jews were already celebrating a number of Confucian rituals over and above (or commingled with) those ceremonial rites that had come down to them as part of their own heritage:

> I asked them to tell me if they honored Confucius. All, including their *Chang-chiao* [leader of the religion, or chief rabbi], answered me without hesitation that they did indeed, and that they also, in the same manner as the greatest pagan scholars, took part in the solemn offerings which are made to Confucius. Similarly, for the worship of ancestors, they answered me in the affirmative; and that, in spring and autumn, they make the solemn offerings—without pork, but with oxen and sheep—in the ancestral hall which they have near the synagogue; and that, at other times, they make the offerings with various procelain dishes filled with food, and [that they perform the] *K'o-t'ou* [kowtow]. I asked them if they kept the customary tablets for their ancestors in their ancestral hall and in their houses. Not at all, they answered: they manage this in the same way as in the place where they worship their saints, where there are only incense bowls without tablets or images. It is only the dead, so they said, who had become mandarins, who have a tablet with their name and mandarin rank in the ancestral hall. As for burials, they preserve the custom of the Western regions and of their Law.

With regard to the history of the Jews, Gozani was informed that "the first of them arrived in China under the Han dynasty

[206 B.C.E.–221 C.E., agreeing with the timing set in the 1512 and 1679 steles]." They were once numerous, he continued, but were now "diminished to seven families [clans, actually]: Chao, Chin, Shih, Kao, Chang, Li, and Ai." Where did they come from? "They told me that their ancestors came from Hsi-yü [or Siyü, regions lying to the west of China, perhaps India or Persia—or even the Middle East] and that their own kingdom in the West is called Judah, a kingdom which, they told me, was conquered by force by Joshua after the deliverance from Egypt, and the crossing of the Red Sea and of the desert; and that the number of those who left Egypt was sixty *wan* [600,000]."

Continuing his letter to Suarez, Gozani noted that he was forwarding rubbings of "an ancient stone or *Shih-p'ei* which they possess [this was the 1489/1512 stele]," and also copies of various inscriptions he had seen in the synagogue. He alluded to the Rites dispute, although without mentioning it by name, saying that "in the [copies of the] horizontal inscriptions enclosed we have a very strong argument against our adversaries." And he ended on a cautious note: "I inform you finally that I am not sending this information to any other person outside Peking except the Vice-Provincial. Since there are many copyists in China, we must be careful so that what is written in Europe is uniform; with several pens which are not gospel it is very difficult to make the texts agree. A word to the wise is sufficient."

Whether justified or not, Gozani's fears lest his report fall into the wrong hands or reach Europe in a distorted form reflect something of the tension that the Rites Controversy had stirred up in the Catholic world. Since the Congregation of Rites announced its decision on the question of the Confucian ceremonial practices before Gozani's report arrived in Rome, his findings exerted no effect at all upon that body's deliberations. The information he furnished did, however, bring to the fore certain details not previously known to the West and aroused even more curiosity than already existed concerning the Jews of China and the manuscripts they preserved in their synagogue.

In a subsequent letter composed at Peking on August 25, 1712, but not published (and then only incompletely) until 1972,[14] Gozani reported that the Jews had recently told him that they

were descended from the tribes of Benjamin, Judah, and Levi—
the tribes that had been dispersed from the Southern Kingdom
of Judah after the Babylonian and Roman conquests of 586
B.C.E. and 70 C.E.—as well as from "others which I do not now
remember."[15] He also noted that the congregation owned a
"Decalogue written down in Hebrew in golden letters and hung
up in the synagogue," adding that:

> they do not marry except among their own men and women.
> They admit no Chinese or even Muhammadans into their
> Hebraic law which, accordingly, they do not preach to others.
> They do not print any Chinese books about their sacred mys-
> teries but they have printed only one small one in Chinese in
> which they give a brief account of their sect, for the Man-
> darins, at the onset of persecution. Their men of letters pay
> respect to Confucius, just as also all pay homage to their dead
> ancestors, whose tablets they keep in the Chinese manner.
> Within the enclosures of the synagogue, to one side, they
> have a . . . fore-court for their dead benefactors, with their
> tablets.

Gozani did not think that it would be overly difficult to secure
some of the books belonging to the synagogue. It would mean
bribing one or more of the Jews who had access to the books, he
knew, but this did not trouble him unduly. "I have no doubt," he
wrote in his 1712 report, "that with a good deal of money and
by proceeding discreetly we ought to be able to secure portions
of their Bible, particularly a Hebrew exemplar of the Pentateuch."

In 1711, four years after the publication of Gozani's 1704
letter to Suarez, Francisco Noël added a few morsels of information to Europe's meager fund of knowledge of the Chinese Jews
in his *Philosophia Sinica*.[16] No new data originating in Kaifeng
itself and dealing with the Jews who lived there were then made
available in print until 1771, at which time the Abbé Gabriel
Brotier published a synopsis of the reports that had been received
in Europe from Gozani and from Gozani's colleagues in the
Jesuit Order, Fathers Jean Domenge and Antoine Gaubil, of the
contacts they had personally made with the *kehillah* prior to
the expulsion of the Jesuits in 1724 from most of China.[17] Everything else of any value, which was printed in the West about the

Chinese Jews from the time of this expulsion until the year 1851—when the diaries of two Chinese Protestants who had recently come back from Kaifeng were published—was derived from the accounts provided by the three Jesuits who had visited the *kehillah* in the first quarter of the eighteenth century and from the Jesuit reports of the seventeenth century. The rest was either hearsay or pure fiction.

5 ❖ AN ILLUSION SHATTERED

WITH the publication of Gozani's letter to Suarez it became evident to the European theologians that the Jewish community of Kaifeng habitually celebrated a number of the Confucian rituals that the Society of Jesus was prepared to accept and tolerate in the Chinese Catholic church. Because Gozani was a Jesuit, there were those who looked askance at his testimony, suspecting that much of it had been gotten up out of the whole cloth for no other reason than to muster support for his Order's stand in the Rites affair.[1] However, while most of his readers did not question his veracity, nobody really expected the Congregation of Rites to retract its recent blanket condemnation of the ceremonial practices of Confucianism merely because a Jesuit missionary now claimed that the handful of Jews who lived in China saw nothing wrong in them.

The dissemination of Gozani's report throughout Europe whipped up even more interest in the Kaifeng Jews and their books than there already was. Gozani had himself pointed out that it would be unwise to treat his statements regarding the texts of the Kaifeng Scriptures as anything other than conjectural, his total ignorance of Hebrew having kept him from searching for the christological predictions they were thought to contain. The illusion still persisted, accordingly, that readings might some day be discovered in the Kaifeng manuscripts which, aside from revolutionizing the study of the Bible, would demonstrate to the Jews of the world that the Christian doctrine was indisputably more authentic than their own, thereby inducing them to come over to the cross—the essential preliminary, it was generally acknowledged, to the unfolding of the messianic drama. But the first step, of course, was to have a representative selection of the Kaifeng books brought to Europe for intensive examination or, if this could not be worked out, to arrange for a qualified Catholic scholar to travel to Kaifeng and study the texts there.

It so happened that at the beginning of the 1720s, there was a missionary in China, a French Jesuit named Jean Domenge, who could read Hebrew moderately well and was stationed close enough to Kaifeng to get to and from the city without undue difficulty or expense. Domenge was therefore instructed to visit the Jews, ask them a series of questions regarding their beliefs, which had been prepared for the purpose by a group of French theologians, try to procure the Scriptures belonging to their synagogue, and unravel, if he could, the tantalizing mysteries surrounding the history of Judaism in China.

Domenge's contacts with the *kehillah* began in mid-1721 and went on intermittently for a little over a year. During this period he met with the Jews on a number of occasions, attended services in their synagogue at least once, and sent back a succession of dispatches detailing his experiences and observations. He also prepared and sent on to Europe several sketches, three of which are of particular interest. The first presents a general view of the synagogal compound, the second offers an interior plan of the synagogue itself, and the third shows three Chinese Jews participating in the public reading of a Torah scroll in the course of a religious service.

The drawings made by Domenge are the only contemporary representations that have survived of either the Kaifeng synagogue or anything that took place in it. They are crudely executed, Domenge having obviously had no drafting or artistic training. A somewhat more competent draftsman, Father Joseph Brucker, subsequently reworked Domenge's two drawings of the synagogal premises. He also took it upon himself to "improve" Domenge's original sketch of the reading of the Torah by putting shoes on the bare feet of the three men who performed the ritual and by prettying up the faces and noses of two of them.[2]

Although Domenge tried time and again to persuade the leaders of the *kehillah* to sell him some of their books, they adamantly refused to let him remove even a single volume. It was the inviolable policy of the congregation, they told him, to preserve its scriptural and liturgical holdings intact. Unwilling to let them have the final word in the matter, he approached a private individual, Kao T'ing, and struck a bargain with him for a Bible that, Kao had reason to believe, he might be able to take out of the synagogue. This stratagem, to Domenge's chagrin, failed to produce any tangible results. As he explained, the synagogue's books were too closely guarded, being:

> watched over by a concierge, whom they call *T'ang-chia* in Chinese, who, however ignorant he may be, is honored with the title of *man-la*, or doctor, and would be dismissed without mercy if anything in the temple, especially the books, should get lost because of his fault. Last year [1721] I managed to speak to a Jew who is a junior official in the observatory named Kao T'ing who has not practiced his religion at all since the death of his father and who was left by his uncle (known as Kao San) a very well written Bible when he died. Unfortunately, he had deposited it several years earlier in the synagogue, as several do in order to exempt themselves with honor from going to the meetings and from other duties in the synagogue. He has made a weak effort to get it back this year, but in vain. The *T'ang-chia*, to whom he went straightforwardedly to ask for it, flatly refused to give it to him, with the reproach that he was willing to sell the Bible to a European who eats the black beast (which is what they call the pig), besides the infamy that there is in selling the Torah, . . . this being, according to them, the same thing as to sell the Lord.[3]

Undeterred by the setback he had suffered, Domenge made a second attempt to circumvent the decision of the elders of the *kehillah*, this time through the agency of a layman named Ai Wen. Ai, who had once contributed four volumes to the synagogue, agreed to reclaim the books and sell them to Domenge, but, as the priest related, "being caught in the act one festival day as he was carrying them off, he was compelled to leave them behind, and was sent away with a rebuke. He has not been permitted to see me since then and to give me hope of obtaining them sooner or later."

All in all, the leaders of the *kehillah* seem to have taken a rather dim view of Domenge's activities and to have lost their trust in him. He offered to lend them a Hebrew Bible, pointing out that from it they would be able to copy the several scriptural books they lacked; in turn, he demanded that they lend him a Torah scroll. To his surprise, his proposal was rejected outright. They would gain nothing by such an exchange, they told him, since "there was no one among them capable of copying Hebrew." This ploy, to be sure, could have been their way of averting a head-on clash with the priest, but he did not see it in that light. He concluded instead that they were incapable of transcribing any Hebrew works at all—even if it were to be done only mechanically—and in a moment of pique expressed his distaste at having to deal with "people so abysmally ignorant." In another context, however, he noted with satisfaction that it was the custom each year, shortly after the Feast of Tabernacles, for the members of the congregation to make an excellent ink with which texts were written in characters that were not only "larger and less squashed together" than those in his own printed Hebrew Bible but were also spaced so as to make "the distances between the lines . . . greater." The result, he remarked, was that the Kaifeng manuscripts were easier to read than the Hebrew Bible he usually carried with him. The statement that the Jews made to Domenge that they had nobody left who could copy Hebrew must therefore be taken with a grain of salt. The greater likelihood is that in the 1720s a few Kaifeng Jews were still capable of transcribing lengthy Hebrew texts, although not without committing numerous errors, but that they could not comprehend substantial portions of what they transcribed.

Domenge continued his quest for a Chinese Torah with dogged determination, confident that "somehow or other" he would eventually succeed in laying hands on one. He was sure, he said, that God would in time help him attain this goal, but felt that in the interim he was obligated to persist in his own efforts. He consoled himself with the thought, which he passed along to his correspondents, that "patience and perseverance can achieve anything."

But patience and perseverance did not bring Domenge the books he sought. The Jews simply would not part with any of their scriptural or liturgical works. The books, they told him, had to remain in the synagogue. He could read them there and he could copy them there, but under no circumstances would he be permitted to remove any of them from the premises. He would of course have had to devote a great deal of time to the task of transcribing a fair sampling of the texts preserved in the synagogue. In the end, he was forced to report to his colleagues in Europe that he had not been able to get away long enough from his other pressing duties to write out more than an occasional brief passage. This was a lame excuse, of course, considering the exceptional importance that was attached to the project by the people who had assigned him to it. What is more apt to be true is that when the elders of the congregation learned of the devious schemes to which he was resorting in order to obtain the synagogal books, they made it increasingly difficult for him to do much copying.

Even before he started his examination of the *kehillah*'s manuscripts, Domenge had already made up his mind that the Western transcripts of the Hebrew Scriptures were far from reliable. It was for this reason that he requested the theologians at the Missions Étrangères to send him "a list of those things for which they would like the most speedy clarification, and when it concerns controversial passages, would they please indicate at the side [in the margins of a Bible printed in Hebrew] exactly the falsifications that the European Jews have introduced." He was disappointed, accordingly, when his investigations of the Kaifeng Scriptures uncovered nothing that he could not read in his own Bible. Nor did he come across any lacunae—leaving aside, that is, the several complete biblical books which the synagogue did not possess. The discrepancies he did encounter were plainly attributable to scribal error—misspellings, for the most part—and in no instance distorted the sense of the passages involved. He also noted some minor differences in the use of vowel, accent, and other markings in the *kehillah*'s prophetic and hagiographic texts (and also in the *parashioth*), but here too the basic meanings of the contents were always left unchanged. In short, he unintentionally demonstrated that it was highly improbable that any sensational revelations would come out of the Kaifeng Bibles. His findings did not put an end to the old accusations that the sages of the talmudic era had fraudulently revised the sacred books of Judaism, but they did show that these charges could not be substantiated from any of the texts which he had personally examined in the manuscripts held in Kaifeng.

Left in disarray by Domenge's disclosures that the *kehillah's* Scriptures probably contained none of the Christ-oriented prophecies they had been led to expect, the Western scholars at first resigned themselves to the new state of affairs. Later, they tried to turn it to advantage. The position they ultimately adopted was epitomized in the closing paragraphs of the study of the Kaifeng Jews that the Abbé Brotier wrote in the 1750s.[4] "The agreement of their [the Kaifeng Jews'] Pentateuch with ours," he declared, "adds new validity to the proofs which have hitherto been adduced with so much profit from the Mosaic literature in favor of our religion." Brotier, it would appear, saw no point in reminding his readers that for the better part of a century, it had been the openly expressed goal of the theologians to discover passages in the Pentateuch of the Kaifeng Jews that were not in agreement with their own. He felt, in any event, that it would be beneficial to learn considerably more about the Kaifeng scrolls. "The missionaries," he remarked, "will put us even more deeply in their debt if they can now arrange to forward one of the Torahs from the [Kaifeng] synagogue to Europe, or at least an authentic transcript of the most ancient of these documents." His purpose was to make it possible for the theologians to catalog the relatively minor orthographic and other variants that Domenge had found in the Kaifeng manuscripts and to collate these with parallel readings originating elsewhere. What had once been hailed as a unique opportunity fraught with implications of cosmic proportions was in this way relegated to the status of a conventional academic research project. Such a venture would of course present a highly worthwhile and intriguing challenge to scholars specializing in the arcane field of comparative biblical analysis, but whatever attention it might attract from the rest of the literate world would be perfunctory at best.

Heading south to Kaifeng along the admirably constructed and tree-lined thoroughfares of Honan Province in March 1723, Father Antoine Gaubil was profoundly impressed by the villages and cities through which he passed and by the surprisingly large choice of excellent accommodations presented to the wayfarer. It was nevertheless something of a nuisance, he confided to the Abbé Etienne Souciet in a letter dated August 18, 1723, that the amenities offered by these hostels did not include bedding, making it advisable for the discriminating traveler to carry along his own.[5] Even so, he felt that in China, to which he had come some eight months earlier, travel tended to be far more comfortable than in his native France. He noticed, as the last two or three days of the trip went by, that the countryside had changed perceptibly and was less attractive and fertile than the regions that lay behind. The roads, as superb as those he had already traversed, now ran through swamplands. Traffic was increasing.

Kaifeng, which he reached on the twenty-third of March, did not live up to his expectations. He thought it "a large city, but badly built," and judged it underpopulated for the extensive area it covered. Because his stay in the provincial capital was to be limited to about two days, he did not have time enough to wander about the city in a leisurely, touristic manner. Instead, he applied himself without further ado to the business that had brought him there. Part of this business, seemingly the bulk of it, concerned the Jews who lived in the old metropolis. He was anxious to meet them as soon as possible.

After a night's sleep at the mission house Gaubil was taken to the synagogue by Gozani and introduced to the rabbi and other members of the congregation. With Gozani acting as his interpreter, his own Chinese being still of a rudimentary level, he conferred with the Jews that day and part of the next.

Gaubil, who had studied biblical Hebrew, quickly concluded that the capacity of the long-isolated *kehillah* to comprehend its own Scriptures had deteriorated shamefully. Two congregants, both of whom the rabbi described as highly knowledgeable, were summoned to the synagogue. Gaubil talked with them. It did not take him long to realize, he reported to Souciet, that "these two Jews, and their rabbi as well, were absolute ignoramuses."

The Jews proudly escorted Gaubil around the synagogue, pointing out its numerous treasures. They explained that their forebears had immigrated to the Middle Kingdom some 1,650 years earlier from "Siyü," but were unable to tell him why the move was made. Nor could they give him any clues as to the antiquity or the provenance of the biblical texts that their ancestors had originally brought with them to China; and they were at a loss to know how to respond to his suggestion that changes might subsequently have been written into these texts. They knew nothing, moreover, about the nature of the communications their remote ancestors may have carried on with Jews in foreign lands. In the end, Gaubil concluded that the initial entry of Jews into China took place "three hundred years or more before the birth of Christ," or even earlier than the *kehillah* itself had ever suggested to him.[6]

He asked to see their books, a request to which the Jews cheerfully assented. Shown a Torah scroll, the oldest one they used in their services, he observed that it exhibited signs of water damage. This Torah scroll, he was informed, was hundreds of years old and had been given to them by coreligionists residing in Siyü, following the leveling of the synagogue by fire during the Wan-li reign (1575–1620). All the other Pentateuchs now in their possession were copied from it. In the Wan-li conflagration, they said, the *kehillah* had for the second time experienced the destruction of all its books. It does not seem to have occurred to him, then or later, that the Jews had neglected to tell him how and from where their scribes obtained the models from which the community's existing prophetic, hagiographic, and liturgical texts were derived, how much of the original Torah allegedly obtained from Siyü survived the 1642 flood, or why no mention of the Wan-li fire was made in the accounts of the community's history inscribed on the 1663 and 1679 stones. (That there was actually a fire during the Wan-li reign is suggested, however, by Ai T'ien's 1605 statement to Ricci that the synagogue had recently been rebuilt on a lavish scale.)

Gaubil evidently did not think that the Siyü scroll was of non-Chinese provenance, in spite of what he was told, for he went to far greater pains to acquire it than he would have if he had thought it was written in Central Asia or the Middle East a few hundred years earlier, exemplars from this period and these locales being already available in Europe. He started by offering to buy the Siyü scroll. The Jews declined to sell it to him. He then asked them to make up a copy of the manuscript for him—a meticulous scribe takes a year, on the average, to write a complete Torah scroll—or, if they did not care to undertake so ambitious a project, to copy a large portion of it (perhaps the Book of Genesis). To this they agreed, and a fee was negotiated to cover the cost of the scribe's labors. Gozani promised his colleague that he would personally see to it that the *kehillah* carried out its part of the bargain.

Gaubil's eagerness to commission the Jews to transcribe part or all of the nearly 6,000 verses of a Torah scroll indicates that he did not really consider them the "absolute ignoramuses" he had called them.[7] Gozani, for that matter, had even noted in his letter of August 25, 1712, that the Jews "start learning how to read Hebrew from childhood, and many of them also know how to write it; I have seen them reading and writing with my own eyes." They knew enough, in any event, to ask Gaubil to resolve certain grammatical problems they were having with the conjugation of verbs and the declension of nouns.[8] In March 1723, it would therefore appear, the Jews of Kaifeng could still write Hebrew—or were at least able to transcribe it, painfully and with many errors. Not that this mattered, insofar as Gaubil's immediate goal of securing a copy of their Torah was concerned, for within the year the Jesuits, Gozani among them, were driven out of the interior of China by imperial fiat. If Gozani had managed by then to get any of the scribal work done, the finished transcripts never came to Gaubil's hands.

Continuing his letter of August 18, 1723, to Souciet, Gaubil reported that the Jewish inhabitants of Kaifeng circumcised their male progeny and habitually observed the Sabbath, Passover, Purim, and other festivals. He disapproved of the way they recited the *Shema*, describing their accent and pronunciation as strange and uncouth. "If I had not had the Hebrew text in front of my eyes," he wrote, "I would never have recognized that it was Hebrew they were reading." One gets the impression that he rather expected the Hebrew intoned by Jews living in the heart of China to have precisely the flavor of the Hebrew that had been drilled into him as a young seminarian in France.

The concept the Kaifeng Jews had of the Messiah was no more to his taste than their Hebrew diction. Their understanding of messianism, he complained, was "terribly confused." What was worse, they did not have the faintest notion of who Jesus Christ was.

The *kehillah,* he was told, consisted of seven clans, comprising a thousand or so individuals; and if there were still any other Jewish settlements in China, the Jews of Kaifeng knew nothing about them, it now being a long time since their community was last visited by a guest who was both Chinese and Jewish. They had reason to believe, they said, that a very old Hebrew Bible had once been deposited in a Buddhist temple at Peking in which foreign books were preserved, and were even able to supply the temple's name. This was exciting news but, as he soon learned, Gozani had already been given the same information and the Jesuits in Peking had not failed to look into the matter. Inquiring about the temple, they discovered that it had been demolished and its store of foreign books removed to a neighboring temple. A party of Jesuits visited this second depository, but saw only a Koran and fragments of a few other manuscripts there, all of them in bad condition. While walking by an old chest containing other manuscripts, one of the Jesuits thought that he had caught a glimpse of Hebrew, Syriac, and Chaldaic writing on the sheets. Before leaving the building he asked about these documents. The bonze charged with guiding the party about the premises insisted that the priest was mistaken, that the texts were definitely not what he imagined them to be. Since the bonze refused to take them back to inspect the chest in which the manuscripts in question were stored, the Jesuits decided that he was lying to them. There were harsh words.

The Jesuits now went over the bonze's head by petitioning the emperor to intervene and order the monk to show them everything in the temple they cared to see. The emperor acceded to their request. The Jesuits promptly returned to the temple and showed the bonze the imperial order they had obtained. Disgruntled, he conducted them through the building a second time. To their dismay, the priests could find no Hebrew, Syriac, or Chaldaic materials on the premises. They suspected that the bonze may have hidden them, but they were not completely sure that he had.

Eventually, the structure in which the contretemps between the Jesuits and the bonze had been staged was also demolished, its foreign books having first been transported to the imperial palace. The Jesuits were unable to discover what disposition was made of the books once they reached the palace.[9]

On October 20, 1723, Gaubil wrote to Souciet from Peking that he had just asked his superior, Father J. P. Hervieu, to let him go back to Kaifeng and spend fifteen days there. "I plan to bring some presents to the Jews," he remarked, "and to give them some rules written out in Chinese which they have asked for covering the conjugation and declension [of Hebrew verbs and nouns], and we will then have what we want."[10] However, his hopes of returning to Kaifeng were dashed by the travel restrictions that were imposed on all foreign missionaries—the few permitted to stay on in Peking—in January 1724. Still, he never lost interest in the Chinese Jews and often reminisced about the day and a half he had spent with them in Kaifeng. He thought at one time that he had been put on the track of an old Jewish colony in Peking and hoped that its members, who, he was told, were now Muslims, had not lost the sacred books of their ancestors, but he did not meet any of the allegedly Islamized Jews personally. Nor did he ever see the Hebrew literature they might have inherited from their forebears.[11]

It was in Peking, nevertheless, that Gaubil came closest to acquiring the texts and inscriptions belonging to the Kaifeng Jews. Several years after his visit to the *kehillah* he, Father Dominique Parrenin, and two princes of the blood were examining a collection of Russian maps of Kamchatka when the conversation was somehow diverted, perhaps on the initiative of the priests, to religious matters. This gave him the opening he needed for bringing up the story of his meetings with the leaders of the *kehillah*. It did not surprise him that the two princes had never heard of Judaism and were totally ignorant of the fact that their sprawling country harbored a tiny sect which practiced that faith.

One of the princes was sufficiently intrigued by Gaubil's description of the *kehillah's* religious views to propose a second meeting for the purpose of discussing the subject more thoroughly. In the interim, he made inquiries concerning the Kaifeng Jews through the official channels accessible to a man of his exalted rank. The responses he received piqued his curiosity even more, so that when the two priests returned, he fell in readily with their suggestion that the *kehillah* be directed to send its texts and inscriptions to Peking forthwith. He promised to transmit the necessary orders as soon as possible.

It is unclear from Gaubil's account of the second talk he and Parennin held with the prince, whether the Jews were being asked for transcripts or for originals, and whether they were to provide (or copy) their lapidary inscriptions as well as their horizontal and vertical inscriptions. In any event, the prince died before requisitioning the specific items that Gaubil had in mind, whatever they were.

Gaubil and Parennin decided that the second prince was too uninterested in the matter of the Chinese Jews to involve himself in the task of securing their writings. Bribery was considered. "Had we approached him 'in the Chinese way,' however," Gaubil wrote, "this also would have failed. But now that I think about it, perhaps we could have worked the problem out along that line."[12]

Gaubil had done everything he possibly could to secure a Bible from the Chinese Jews, but the fates seemed to be arrayed against him, and the prize persisted in slipping from his grasp. His experiences and those of the other Jesuits who had tried with just as little success to obtain the treasures of the Kaifeng synagogue were remarked upon sympathetically by Father Pierre-Martial Cibot in 1770.[13] Cibot regretted the failure of the Jesuits to gain possession of the synagogal texts and insisted that it was of the utmost importance that the West have the opportunity to examine these writings. There was nothing, however, that he or his colleagues could do. The West, it turned out, would have to wait until the middle of the next century before the *kehillah* could at last be persuaded to relinquish any of its books.

6 ❖ INTERLUDE OF SILENCE

CHRISTIANITY's fortunes in China, always shaky, were dealt a near-fatal blow in January 1724 when the recently enthroned Yung-chêng emperor put a halt to the further proselytization of his subjects and directed that all the churches in the empire aside from the four then functioning in Peking be shut down immediately. The missionaries themselves, except those few whose scientific and linguistic services were urgently required in the imperial capital, were hustled off to Canton and later deported to the nearby Portuguese colony of Macao.

The earliest of the Jesuit mission houses to operate in Kaifeng was established by Sambiasi in 1628. It stood within walking distance of the synagogue and, like it, was washed away by the flood of 1642. A new facility, built by Enriquez in 1676, served as the city's evangelical headquarters for approximately twenty years, and was then peremptorily closed by the order of a local mandarin. The next church, erected by Father Joseph-Antoine Provana between 1699 and 1701, was used by the missionaries until their expulsion in 1724, following which the building was converted, as Gaubil indignantly reported, "into a temple of idols."[1] In all, the records reveal, the Jesuits were granted somewhat more than six decades, spaced over a span of nearly a century, in which to spread their gospel in the Kaifeng area. Their presence was no secret, they went about their work openly, and they tried zealously to proselytize anyone who would listen. Given their special interest in converting the Jews, acquiring samples of the synagogal manuscripts, and learning as much as they could about the *kehillah*'s attitudes respecting the rites of Confucianism, it would be strange if in the more than sixty years of their residence in Kaifeng their personal contacts with the Jews were as few as the archives of Europe have so far indicated.

The Jews, of course, must have made repeated efforts to seek out the Jesuits for the news that only they could provide regarding the condition and the way of life of the House of Israel in other regions of the world. Having forgotten much of their Hebrew, the Jews had in 1723 asked Gaubil to write out certain rules of its grammar for them in Chinese. Might they not also have asked others among the missionaries stationed in the city to supply them with the Chinese texts corresponding to the various biblical passages that were unclear to them? And perhaps to let them examine the Chinese translations the Jesuits are believed to have made of several Old Testament books for the edification of prospective converts and those who had already come over to Catholicism? Enriquez, moreover, wrote a four-volume exposition of Christian doctrine. The language was Chinese, and he had the work printed in Kaifeng.[2] How likely is it that this book, written by a man they knew, was not brought to the attention of the Jews?

Although no Jesuit comments concerning the reactions of the Kaifeng Jews to the efforts of the city's missionaries to convert them have been found for the period before Gozani began to visit the synagogue, such efforts were surely made. They were just as surely ineffective, for had even one Chinese Jew been induced to accept the cross, the elated missionaries would have been unable to refrain from trumpeting the fact to their superiors and colleagues in Europe.

In the century and a quarter following Gozani's departure from Honan there seems to have been no direct communication between the Kaifeng *kehillah* and any individuals of Western origin. Occasional snatches of news about the Chinese Jews, hearsay in every single instance and without substance in most, filtered back to Europe and were sometimes disseminated in print, but from Kaifeng itself came absolutely nothing.[3] If the *kehillah* had been miraculously blown off the face of the earth, the event might easily have passed unnoticed in the West, and with good reason.

Throughout the greater part of this protracted interlude of

silence, reliable reports from the interior of China were almost impossible to obtain. By 1760 all foreigners doing business in the country were deliberately sequestered in a small compound adjoining Canton, travel elsewhere within the territory of the kingdom being rigidly proscribed by law. Because this restrictive policy was not administered as consistently or as assiduously as it might have been, foreign traders, and also missionaries, did succeed now and then in penetrating to regions that were supposedly out of bounds. Their trespassing, however, yielded very little intelligence from the nation's heartland, and none at all from the Jewish enclave at Kaifeng. As for the underground evangelical work that was carried on sporadically in Honan Province, neither the Chinese converts nor the European priests who participated in that perilous activity seem ever to have approached the Jews.

With the end of the Opium War and the imposition in 1842 of the Treaty of Nanking upon the defeated and humiliated Chinese, Hong Kong was ceded to the British, who also received the right, as other foreigners later did, to settle in five coastal cities, the so-called Treaty Ports. The interior continued to be sealed off until 1858, the year in which the Treaty of Tientsin was concluded, and it was only then that foreigners were permitted to go more or less where they cared to. But because the country was at the time suffering through the Taiping Rebellion (1849–64) and other military upheavals, most foreigners preferred to postpone taking advantage of their newly acquired privilege until things quieted down.

The first successful attempt to reestablish personal contact with the *kehillah* was not undertaken until 1850, when two Chinese converts to Protestantism traveled from Shanghai to Kaifeng as the representatives of Bishop George Smith of the Anglican church who, in turn, was acting on behalf of the London Society for Promoting Christianity among the Jews. The two men, usually referred to as the "Chinese delegates," were received at the synagogue, stayed in Kaifeng a few days, and then hurried back to Shanghai. In 1851 they retraced their steps and came again to the synagogue. The first Caucasian after Gaubil and Gozani to make the journey to the Honan capital and visit the *kehillah* is generally thought to have been the zealous and energetic American Protestant missionary W. A. P. Martin, whose meetings with the Jews took place in February 1866. It was then 143 years since Gozani had guided Gaubil to the synagogue and introduced him to the congregational leaders. But Martin, unlike Gaubil, never saw the synagogue, the old building having been torn down a few years before his arrival. The site on which a succession of imposing synagogues had so proudly stood for seven long centuries was now little more than a scrubby bit of wasteland. In its last years the synagogal compound had been occupied by a band of wretched squatters—a few Jewish families huddled together in abject poverty and having no other place to rest their heads than the plot of land to which some two dozen generations of their ancestors had come to pray.

With no fresh sources to tap, the Western academicians whose fancy had been caught by the Chinese Jews mulled over the old Jesuit reports, drained them of every scintilla of information they contained, and discussed their findings in learned tomes and scholarly reviews. Although what these men wrote about the *kehillah* was not always as accurate or objective as it might have been, their work was on the whole seriously and honestly done.

Still, a story as strange and intriguing as that of the Jews of China could scarcely escape being mishandled by less inhibited writers and by propagandists seeking new vehicles for the promotion of one cause or another. Quite often, even the most cautious readers of the farfetched accounts published by writers of this stamp were left with impressions of the Chinese Jews substantially at odds with the sparse facts the Jesuits had accumulated about them. On the other hand, rather few Westerners would ever have been given the opportunity to learn that a branch of Judaism could be found in the depths of the Middle Kingdom if the sensation seekers and the propagandists had not publicized the fact. Distorted or not, their portrayals of Chinese Jewry did much to spread the word that such a group existed. Their contribution, in short, was that they introduced the Chinese Jews to a much broader public than the scholars could ever hope to reach.

The literary men of eighteenth-century Europe, prolific letter writers, were not averse to airing their displeasure with what went on in Western society through the medium of chatty letters allegedly composed by erudite and urbane gentlemen traveling in, residing in, or hailing from distant and obscure lands. The more remote the country and the less known about it, the more unrestrainedly could the real authors of these letters let their imaginations roam. The countries of the Orient were especially favored as the points of origin for the bogus correspondence with which the European public was regaled.

Leafing through a sampling of such letters, or of novels or reputedly nonfiction works dealing with the same regions, the reader was apt to be informed that in certain faraway climes the culture was more advanced than at home, the economy more productive, and the laws more benign. In these blessed and enchanted domains, contentment reigned and Utopia, or something fairly close to it, had been attained. Europe, it followed, would do well to emulate the noble deportment and laudable polity cultivated by the peoples who had made all this possible. The reader did not have to believe, if it was a collection of letters he was reading, that the texts had actually been written in one of these earthly paradises—none but the most artless readers did—but the lesson was still there. And with it came such a hodgepodge of fact and fantasy as to make it well-nigh impossible for him to know what to credit as true and what to brush aside as utterly preposterous.

The veiled and mysterious empire that lay beyond the Great Wall was singled out more frequently than any other portion of the globe as the embodiment of the ideal toward which it behooved Europe to strive. Ships and travelers arriving from China brought beguilingly elegant objets d'art and superbly crafted goods, patently the fruits of a culture of the highest order. Europe's artistic, literary, and craft styles increasingly reflected the influence that the winds of change were blowing in from the land of Han. Before long, the cult of chinoiserie was sufficiently entrenched in the European consciousness to encourage certain enterprising Occidentals to establish ateliers for fabricating fanciful imitations of the rare and costly Chinese wares, the home-grown articles then being passed off, in many instances, as bona fide imports from the Middle Kingdom. Much of what was at the same time paraded about in print as authentically representative of the Chinese mind and experience had no more claim to a Chinese hallmark, actually, than the faked pieces spewing forth from the workshops of an assortment of European countries.[4]

Although the mythical letter writers who lived and traveled in China did not totally ignore either the Jews of the West or those of the East, their allusions to Judaism are with two known exceptions restricted to the plight and religion of Jews living elsewhere than China. Sometimes their remarks about Jews are reasonably accurate, sometimes they are not. In the two instances in which Asian correspondents are permitted by their creators to present information about the Chinese Jews that is supposedly authentic, no credible material is supplied that had not already appeared in the reports of the Jesuit missionaries. In the first, the then famous Jean-Baptiste de Boyer, Marquis d'Argens, has his Chinese correspondent comment briefly about the *kehillah* of Kaifeng, using data adapted without any wrenching alterations from Gozani's letter of 1704.[5] In the second, one of the foremost satirists of all time, having also studied Gozani's letter, first dismembers and then reconstructs the priest's account of his visits to the *kehillah* in order to use it for mounting a particularly scurrilous attack upon two of his favorite targets—the Jews and the Jesuits.

François Marie Arouet de Voltaire had in the course of his career become involved in two disastrous financial transactions with Jews, having entered into one of these with hands that were not entirely clean and suffered the misfortune, in the other, of holding a letter of credit against a Jewish banker who turned out to be unable to meet his obligations. Partly as a consequence of these experiences, but principally for the usual reasons that seem to make sense to the mind that has long been steeped in anti-Semitic horror tales, he developed a distaste for Jews and Judaism that colored his thinking to his dying day but was now and then permitted to lie dormant. His outbursts against the Jews, whom he delighted in depicting as rapacious and untrustworthy, were occasionally offset by less stereotyped evaluations in which, by comparison, they tended to fare not too badly. On the whole, however, he disliked the Jews, and if they happened to intrude upon his line of vision as he cast about for the next prospective victim for one of his eloquent exercises in flippancy, he simply could not resist the temptation of lashing out at them with every literary weapon at his command. One of his greatest grievances against them was that if there had been no Judaism there would be no Christianity. As for the Jesuits, he detested what they stood for, considering them the overbearingly militant arm of an all-powerful and monolithic religious establishment whose policies, goals, and methods blocked the growth of a society consonant with the moral and social principles envisioned by advanced thinkers like himself. His antipathy to the Jesuits was perhaps even more intense than his dislike of the Jews.

Interestingly, much of the ammunition for Voltaire's onslaught against the Church came directly from a Jewish source, the *Hizzuk Emunah* (The Strengthening of the Faith), a work composed in Lithuania in the late sixteenth century by the Karaite scholar Isaac ben Abraham Troki and completed on Troki's death by his pupil, Joseph ben Mordechai Malinovski. A spirited apologia for Judaism, the text did not restrict itself meekly and discreetly to defensive tactics, but daringly carried the attack to the wellsprings of Christianity by tallying up the contradictions perceived by its authors in the scriptural and patristic legacies upon which the Church justified its authority. Because of the Catholic reaction then sweeping Poland and Lithuania, the *Hizzuk Emunah* was clandestinely circulated in manuscript form (in several versions) until 1681, when Johann Christoph Wagenseil published it at Altdorf in a Latin translation. Wagenseil printed the work only so that he could refute it point by point. Voltaire, who studied Wagenseil's translation diligently, was immeasurably more impressed by Troki's logic than by Wagenseil's rebuttals. "He by himself," he wrote appreciatively of Troki, "gathered together all the textual inconsistencies which all the skeptics since his time have succeeded in amassing. In brief, even the most determined of skeptics has unearthed virtually nothing which does not already appear in Rabbi Isaac's *Strengthening of the Faith*."[6]

In the eighth of a series published in 1776 under the title *Lettres à M. Pauw,* Voltaire describes Gozani's dealings with the *kehillah* in terms that, could the Kaifeng Jews of Voltaire's time have somehow been made aware of them, would have left them wondering whether the fearsome French gadfly was not confusing their ancestors (and the missionary as well) with the denizens of another planet.

The eighth letter, allegedly written by the son of a European merchant doing business in Canton, relates that this merchant, Jean Duchemin, was asked by Gozani to join him in an expedition to Kaifeng, where the two men would then visit the Jews. Gozani is reported in the text of the letter to have been instructed in 1707 by Suarez to make the trip. This is an error on Voltaire's part, Gozani's first meetings with the *kehillah* having taken place three years before 1707. It is also the only misstatement in the entire account that can be said to be an unintentional distortion of the truth, the rest of the story being a complete and unmitigated fraud.

Gozani, who has not as much as a single *écu* in his purse, tries to persuade the elder Duchemin, twice alluded to in the text as "not a rich man," to provide the wherewithal for the two of them to go to Kaifeng and investigate the "Ten Tribes of Israel" who live there. These Israelites, he explains to the simple-minded tradesman, will some day return to the Promised Land, be joined there by the tribes of Benjamin and Judah, battle the anti-Christ, and then sit in judgment on the human race. "They will receive us with open arms," he promises, "and you will have a chance to amass a vast fortune before you are finally brought to judgment."

Duchemin is easily gulled by the crafty priest. He buys, "horses, a carriage, and sets of magnificent raiment in which to present himself decently before the princes of the tribe of Gad, Naphtali, Zebulon, Issachar, Asher, etc., . . ." He outfits the Jesuit in like manner. The two men journey to Kaifeng in grand style.

On their arrival at their destination, Duchemin and Gozani are ushered into the synagogue, where a tribunal of twelve men, sneeringly identified as a Sanhedrin, is assembled. The members of this so-called Sanhedrin are described as "a dozen beggars peddling old rags." The shabby Princes of Israel strip their defenseless guests of every coin they possess.

Gozani tries to console the chastened and suddenly impoverished Duchemin for his loss, given as 2,000 *tael* in all, by reminding him that it was only through the benevolence of the Jews—typified, apparently, by such unappealing specimens of humanity as the aristocracy of the "kingdom of Kaifeng"—that the world could ultimately be redeemed. "This doctrine," the younger Duchemin now wryly observes, "comforted my father greatly, but it did nothing to compensate him for the damages he had suffered."

Although little evidence that the Jews of Europe demonstrated more than a cursory interest in their Chinese coreligionists during the seventeenth and early eighteenth centuries has yet turned up, the endless outpourings in these dozen or so decades of Hebrew, Yiddish, and Ladino literature devoted to the Ten Lost Tribes and to curiosa of all kinds would suggest that they did. In 1650 Manasseh ben Israel had dealt rather effusively and extravagantly with the Chinese Jews in his *Hope of Israel*, a book that was not only widely read by both Jews and Christians but was also cited extensively by writers belonging to each of the two faiths almost from the time of its publication. To assume that Manasseh's discussions of the Jews of China were totally overlooked by his myriads of Jewish readers strains credibility. The greater likelihood is that what was written about the Chinese Jews during this period by European Jews, aside from Manasseh's contribution, has simply gone unnoticed by modern historians. The Jews of Europe were unquestionably just as aware of the presence of Jews in China as the Christians. From the Jewish viewpoint, however, the Chinese Jews constituted merely one more of the many exotic Israelite communities they knew of, although, admittedly, perhaps the primus inter pares of these communities and, as such, the object of somewhat more curiosity than most. The Christians were equally curious; but far more significant to them were the crucial messianic and politicoreligious problems that the news of the *kehillah*'s survival had raised, problems that Western Jews, aside, apparently, from Manasseh ben Israel and certain other kindred spirits, simply did not seriously associate with the Kaifeng community. In short, the fact that there were Jews in China had a different meaning to their brethren in the West than it did to the world's Christians.

At about the same time that Gozani was paying his first calls on the *kehillah*, Johann Schult, a young Swedish theological student who would later become court preacher to Charles XII, was present as David Nieto, the senior rabbi of the Sephardic Jewish community of London, held forth one day on the extent of the Jewish Diaspora. Schult took note of the event in his journal. Nieto, he wrote, "was discussing certain stories concerning those Israelites who were dispersed in different parts of the world. First he talked about China; and here he took his material from a Jesuit who had spoken with certain persons in China who told him that they were Israelites. He replied that he knew that their brethren in Europe were known as Jews, but they reiterated that they themselves were called Israelites, not Jews. The priest retorted that it was all the same."[7]

The distinguished Jewish literary and educational figure Naphtali Herz Wessely was born at Hamburg in 1725 and spent his early years in Copenhagen, where his father was purveyor to the court. In 1790 the younger Wessely recalled hearing about the Chinese Jews while he was still a boy. "The claims of the Gentile authors that there are Jews in the Chinese Empire," he argued in the pages of the Hebrew journal *Ha-Me'asef*, "would seem to be justified, for the king of Assyria exiled the Jews [beginning in 732 B.C.E.] to the far northwest regions [of Assyria], which lie in the direction of the aforementioned empire. [Daniel] Fenning, the [non-Jewish] geographic writer, states that in the Province of Honan . . . the Jews have a synagogue or assembly house.[8] Without doubt, they are spread throughout all the cities of the land. I remember that in my boyhood I used to hear ships' captains say, on their return to Copenhagen from the city of Canton [apparently business acquaintances of his father], a city located at the edge of China on the South Sea, that they had seen Jews there among the merchants with whom they traded, and who are called *wo-wan* [*vo-van?*] in the language of the land." He then pointed out that these Chinese Jews must stem from either the Ten Lost Tribes or from the tribes of Judah and Benjamin. If they are descendants of Judah and Benjamin, he asked whether their ancestors were among those tribesmen who were dispersed from Judea after the destruction of the First Temple (586 B.C.E.) or among those who were expelled after Titus's destruction of the Second Temple (70 C.E.). He suggested that it would be highly desirable to determine if the many biblical and talmudical texts so familiar to world Jewry were also available to the long-isolated Jewish congregations of China. It did not occur to him that his sea captains might have been mistaken, and that the merchants they dealt with were perhaps Muslims rather than Jews—or that they may have been Central Asian or even European Jews who were transients, and not old-time residents of Canton. In any case, whoever these merchants were, he was wrong in identifying them as members of the ancient Chinese Jewish communities he had read about in the accounts of Manasseh and Fenning, and to whose country, as he also reminded his readers, the redoubtable Eldad had long ago alluded.[9]

The Jews of India had known for several centuries of the presence of coreligionists in neighboring China. Ezekiel Rahabi II, lay leader of the Indian congregation at Cochin (in the modern state of Kerala) and agent there for the Dutch East India Company, shared this knowledge with Thubia (Tobias) Boaz, a Jew living in The Hague with whom he had business ties. In a letter to Rahabi, Boaz had assembled a series of questions about the Jews of Asia, one of them being whether it was true that colonies of Jews could be found in China. Rahabi's reply, composed in 1767 and printed by Wessely twenty-three years later in *Ha-Me'asef*, deals briefly and not very conclusively with Boaz's question concerning the Chinese Jews. "In connection with your eighth query, if there are Jews in the Chinese Empire," Rahabi tells Boaz, "I must inform your Lordship that we have heard from trustworthy individuals that there are Jews in Tartary. But they are Karaites, although well versed in the Holy Tongue. God alone knows how much of this is true!"[10]

One of the "trustworthy individuals" whom Rahabi had in mind may have been Leopold Emanuel Jacob van Dort, who is reported by an earnest though very unreliable nineteenth-century writer, Moses Edrehi, to have published a chronicle at Cochin in 1757, in which the claim is advanced, as Edrehi puts it, "that in several parts of Asiatic China are a great number of Jews and many synagogues, academies of science, and particularly the Talmudical and Theological, &c. They are very rich; they have nearly all the trade of that kingdom, and are masters of all the principal manufactories."[11]

"The Black Jews of India," according to Claudius Buchanan, who visited them in Cochin in 1807, "recounted the names of many . . . small [Jewish] colonies resident in northern India, Tartary, and China."[12] Buchanan also notes that the Cabul Jews who traveled from their native Afghanistan "into the interior of China say that in some Synagogues the Law is still written upon a roll of leather."[13] This statement by the Cabul Jews, assuming it to be true, probably does not refer to the Kaifeng community, but perhaps to small and hitherto unidentified pockets of Jews scattered here and there in the vastnesses of the Middle Kingdom. As late as 1807, incidentally, Buchanan could still wonder whether the old Torah scrolls belonging to whatever Jewish communities there might be in China would not demonstrate that Western Jewry had altered the texts of its Bibles "to invalidate the arguments of Christians."[14]

Rabbi David d'Beth Hillel, who visited the Cochin Jews in 1828–29, was told a story which, if it can be trusted, would indicate that toward the end of the eighteenth century or the beginning of the nineteenth, an Indian Jew traveling in China actually met some coreligionists there. D'Beth Hillel gave the details in his *Travels,* published in Madras in 1832:

A Cochin White Jew, by name Judah Ashkenazi (a German family name), told me that many years ago a Cochin Black Jew, whom he as a child had seen, went to China, and when there accompanied some of the inhabitants to a fair held without the walls of a large town. The people of this town came outside for the purpose of traffic but would not suffer any of the strangers to enter into their gates. On seeing the Jew and learning from him who he was, they professed that they also were Jews to whom the whole of the country on that side of the river belongs[!]. They would not permit him to go within the gate, but brought out food for him, and, among other things, flesh boiled in milk. Of this he refused to partake. He asked them how they, if Jews, could use food which is not customary for the Jews in India and other parts of the world to eat. They replied that Moses only forbids the seething of a kid in its mother's milk; this flesh was not boiled in the mother's milk and therefore was not unlawful to eat. He said that according to the rules of the Talmud flesh must not be eaten with milk of any kind. They replied, "Who is greater, Moses or the Talmudists?" He then ate what was set before him; and ever since afterwards used similar food, saying in reply to every remonstrance, "Who is greater, Moses or the Talmudists?"[15]

Beginning in 1760, several attempts were made by the Jews of Europe to contact the Kaifeng *kehillah* by letter. What was not always realized was that in the remote event any letters actually did get through to the Kaifeng Jews, they might refrain from replying rather than risk incurring the wrath of the authorities for becoming involved in communication with foreign barbarians. Even if the Jews did respond, there could of course be no assurance that what they wrote would ever reach the West.

The first letter sent to the *kehillah* by European Jews is believed to have been composed in 1760 by Isaac Nieto (also known as Isaac Mendes Belisario), whose father's discourse on the extent of the Diaspora had earlier proved sufficiently interesting to the young theological student Schult to merit entry in the latter's journal. Writing in the name of the Jewish community of London, Nieto asks the Kaifeng Jews in Hebrew prose so elegant as to have been far beyond their capacity to comprehend to tell him about themselves. He attaches a long list of inquiries having to do mainly with their historical background, religious practices, and beliefs. The communication also included an unsigned covering letter that, at the suggestion of the writer's friend David Salomons, was addressed to an agent of the East India Company, requesting him to do everything in his power to see to it that the letter reaches Kaifeng, and allotting him a maximum of £50 for expenses.[16]

Nieto's letter to the *kehillah* was discussed in an esoteric

14. Moses Edrehi.

work, published in London in 1863, by Moses Edrehi, a colorful, eccentric, and mystically inclined Moroccan Jew, and an indefatigable hunter for the Ten Lost Tribes. Edrehi asserts that in 1760 a letter was received by the Jews of London "from Jews who are in China, in the town of Honan [*sic*], where they are established with their synagogues, and academies, &c. An answer was sent from the Portuguese community [of London] to them. The copy of the letter signed by the late Grand Rabbin the Reverend Raphael Meldola, I have seen in the care of his son, my friend, the Reverend D. Meldola."[17] In effect, if Edrehi's text is to be taken literally, he is saying that the Nieto letter of 1760 (a copy of which was apparently made and authenticated by Raphael Meldola) was forwarded to the Jews in Honan in reply to a letter already received from them by the Jewish community of London.

Edrehi reproduces the entire text of the Nieto letter, and then relates a startling and completely unsubstantiated story. "The letter," he says, "was sent by some respectable persons, who on their return from China brought an answer in the Chinese and Hebrew languages, which was afterwards translated into the English language for the Portuguese Jewish congregation; and the original was left in the museum at the India House. I could not find the copy, and suppose it has been lost." He does not discuss the contents of the remarkable communication allegedly received from Kaifeng.[18]

Some two decades later, a far more reliable scholar than Edrehi, Marcus N. Adler, checked Edrehi's story by inquiring at India House regarding the Kaifeng letter it was once supposed to have had in its files. India House had absolutely no record of such a document.[19]

There were other letters to the *kehillah*, both from Jews and Christians, but it is almost certain that, with the possible exception of a message sent by the London Jewish community in 1815, not one of those transmitted before the middle of the nineteenth century was ever delivered. The English biblical scholar Benjamin Kennicott, engaged with his staff in a massive project calling for the collection of hundreds of Old Testament manuscripts and the subsequent preparation of a text more innocent of scribal and redactional inaccuracies than any then available, was especially eager to study the Kaifeng scriptural writings. He had written to the rabbis of numerous Western synagogues to obtain permission for himself and his representatives to examine their Torah scrolls and other biblical manuscripts. Invariably, he was granted their fullest cooperation. Around 1769 he tried to have a message relayed to the *kehillah* at Kaifeng, requesting that it either sell him a copy of its Scriptures or consent to have its Bibles compared with one of his. The request was brought to China by Sir Frederick Pigou. There, the assistance of the titular bishop of Honan Province was enlisted, in the hope that this dignitary (who had neither been permitted to visit his designated episcopacy, nor would ever be) might somehow arrange to get in touch with the *kehillah*. All of this effort, however, went unrewarded.[20]

The Danish Hebraist Olav Gerhard Tychsen also wrote to the Kaifeng Jews, first in 1777 and again in 1779, forwarding both letters to friends in Batavia who were to relay them to China. The *kehillah* presumably received neither letter; certainly nothing in the way of a reply ever came to Tychsen from Kaifeng.[21] For that matter, many a European congregation would have treated any communications from Tychsen with disdain, recalling that the scholarly Dane had once taken ungentlemanly advantage of his status as a guest in the synagogue of Altona to preach a rabid conversionist sermon to his startled and mortified hosts.

The New York *Daily Advertiser* of June 18, 1789, carried a notice by the bookseller Samuel Campbell cataloging and offering for sale a number of titles that had recently arrived from England aboard the vessel *Eagle*. Included in his newly acquired stock was an item listed as "Grosier's description of China, 2 vols." It was bought by a member of one of the seventy-two Jewish families then residing in the city. Among the topics discussed in Grosier's book was the presence of Jews in China, the pertinent data having been extracted by the author from the reports of the Jesuits who had personally visited the *kehillah* and from materials put together by later writers.

It may have come as something of a shock to the Jews of New York to read Grosier's claim in the 1790s that kinsmen of theirs had been living in the middle of China for the past thousand years or longer, but perhaps no more of a shock than the Jews of Kaifeng might have suffered if they had been told that in the not-too-distant past—in 1654, to be precise—the tents of Jacob were pitched in a remote hamlet then called Nieu Amsterdam and subsequently renamed New York.

The New Yorkers, intrigued by Grosier's account of Jewish life in China, wanted more details; and two of them, Solomon Joseph Simson and Alexander Hirsch, no doubt with the encouragement of their friends, set about composing a letter of inquiry to the *kehillah*. They asked the usual questions: How many of you are there in China? Of what tribe are you? How are you treated? What are your occupations? What books do you have? And so forth. They also advised the Kaifeng Jews that the Jews of New York had already sent a similar letter to the Jews of Malabar, and had received a reply.

The Simson-Hirsch letter, written entirely in Hebrew, was dated "New Moon, Month of Shebat, 5555" (January 21, 1795). It was addressed to the elders of the Jewish community at Kaifeng, in Honan Province, and an envelope bearing a return address was enclosed with it. The letter was sent off from New York through a Captain Howell, who was sailing for China, but was never delivered to the Chinese Jews. Instead, it was eventually returned unopened, with a notation inscribed on the envelope: "Captain Howell could not discover them."[22]

In 1815 the Jews of London tried again to communicate with the *kehillah*. A letter composed in Hebrew was forwarded to China and there entrusted to the care of the Protestant missionary Robert Morrison, who in turn gave it to an itinerant Chinese bookseller who was going to Kaifeng. The bookseller later swore that he had presented this letter to an individual in Kaifeng who was able to read its Hebrew text. The letter, he insisted, was taken away by the man to whom it was delivered, but not before the latter promised to provide a written response within a few days. When the bookseller was asked by Morrison to hand over the letter of reply he explained that he had never received it—that rumors of an impending civil war had come to his attention before his Jewish contact in Kaifeng could meet him again, forcing him to leave the city immediately.[23] Surprisingly, there may be a kernel of truth in the bookseller's story; for when the Chinese delegates visited the *kehillah* in December 1850 they were shown two letters the Jews had received from the West, one of which, presumably written in Hebrew, the delegates described as having come "from a rabbi."[24] Nevertheless, the bookseller's claim that the man to whom he gave the letter was able to read Hebrew must be discounted as untrue, there no longer being any Jews in Kaifeng at the time of the bookseller's visit there who could understand the language.

The second letter that the delegates were shown in 1850 consisted of a Hebrew original written in London in 1844 by the author and diplomat James Finn, and an accompanying translation into Chinese. Although the delegates were apparently not aware of it, the Finn texts had been transmitted to the Kaifeng *kehillah* a few months previously by Temple H. Layton, British consul at Amoy, and a reply was already in Amoy. It was this interchange of correspondence between Amoy and Kaifeng, together with the delegates' own visit to the *kehillah*, which finally put an end to the long interlude of silence separating the Jews of Kaifeng from the Jews and Christians of the rest of the world.

7 ❖ ENTER JAMES FINN

CASTING about for cheap and dependable sources from which to import the raw materials essential to their burgeoning industries and for profitable markets in which to dispose of their finished goods, the statesmen of Europe turned predatorily to the vast and crumbling Chinese Empire. The enfeebled Middle Kingdom was in turn cajoled, browbeaten, and subjected to armed incursion until, in the end, Europe's economic, political, and military demands were almost totally met. In treaty after treaty, the concessions wrung out of the hapless Chinese included stipulations guaranteeing foreigners the right to come freely to China and convert as many of the country's inhabitants as they could.

The Chinese, at ease with their own familiar religious structures, had never seen any particular advantage in exchanging them for the alien institutions being thrust upon them by people whom they tended to think of as interlopers and as agents of the presumptuous barbarian powers of the West. "I have heard of barbarians being improved by the Chinese," Mencius had said, "but I have never heard of the Chinese being improved by barbarians." It is not at all strange, then, that when the Portuguese ambassador Alexander Metello asked the Yung-chêng emperor to permit the unhampered evangelization of his subjects by the missionaries, the emperor rejected the request in no uncertain terms. Calling together Gaubil, Parrenin, and eight other priests, he explained his stand. Gaubil recorded the emperor's comments.[1] "If you had kept in better touch with Metello," the missionaries were told, "and if you had clarified my position to him, he would never have dared speak to me as he did. He demanded that I let you have your churches back and preach your law, as you were allowed to do in the time of my father K'ang Hsi. . . . Even if the pope and all the monarchs of Europe were to come here in person, I would not grant them what Metello asked for. . . . The complaints I have heard about you from my people! You yourselves I know to be honest men, but a prince less tolerant than I would have expelled you long ago. . . . Tell me, if I ever decided to send my bonzes to proselytize the people in your European provinces, would your rulers even let them in?"

A few missionaries were tolerated as necessary evils, in exchange, essentially, for the services they could render in such fields as astronomy, cartography, mechanics, and linguistics; but as the European powers increasingly brought the might of their superior military and naval forces to bear against her, China was left with no alternative but to yield to their demands and allow free entry to any and all missionaries, merchants, and travelers who chose to cross her borders. China had permitted some barbarians of this stamp to station themselves in the foreign "factory" compound that had been set up for them just outside Canton. When China lost the Opium War of 1839–42, however, it became clear that before long there would have to be an end to China's restrictive entry and travel policies.

In Europe, of course, the prospect of having the Chinese ban against Christian proselytization lifted stirred one missionary group after another into action. These included, not so surprisingly, the London Society for Promoting Christianity among the Jews, the promptings of one of its members, James Finn, having directed its attention to the Jews in Honan Province. If Jews the world over were the legitimate targets of its conversionary campaigns, the London Society reasoned, why not also the Jews who lived in China?

Born in 1806, James Finn devoted his career to diplomacy, scholarship, and the challenge of converting the errant Jews of the world to Christianity. Attracted at an early age to the work of the London Society, he became the son-in-law of one of its leaders, the Reverend ("Rabbi") Alexander McCaul, a brilliant student of Hebrew who had abandoned a promising academic career at Trinity College, Dublin, to become the moving spirit in the first of the Society's drives to bring the gospel to the Jews of

Poland. McCaul's daughter Elizabeth Anne, who was born in Warsaw during his tour of duty there, became fluent in both Yiddish and Hebrew while yet a child. Her goal in life, like her father's and her future husband's, was to hasten the Second Advent by persuading world Jewry to accept the Anglican Protestant form of Christianity advocated by the London Society.

Before his marriage to Elizabeth Anne, Finn made himself proficient in Hebrew, studied the theology and traditions of Judaism in considerable depth, and wrote a history of the Jews of Spain and Portugal. His researches brought him frequently to the British Museum, where he encountered the *Lettres édifiantes*, which the Society of Jesus had started compiling a century before his birth. Reading the *Lettres*, he came upon the reports of the Jesuit meetings with the Chinese Jews, and was so taken with the bittersweet story of Israelites stranded in the heart of the Middle Kingdom that he promptly directed his finely honed academic talents to the task of clarifying the muddled accounts that the Jesuits' experiences with the *kehillah* had inspired. The first tangible result of this effort was his eminently readable *Jews in China*, published in London in 1843 and reprinted in large part two years later at Canton in the English-language periodical *Chinese Repository*.[2] With this book, patently a labor of love, he reawakened Europe's dormant interest in the Chinese Jews and serendipitously brought the London Society a legacy of £500, which enabled it to underwrite the 1850 and 1851 visits of the two Chinese delegates to the last known Jewish outpost in their country.

"Anyone who ploughs through the literature on the Jews in the Chinese Empire before the mid-nineteenth century," the historian Hyman Kublin has written, "can only be impressed by Finn's *The Jews in China*. It is not simply that the Englishman combed patiently and methodically through all the available literature on the subject. He also possessed what many earlier writers had not enjoyed, namely, a fine grasp of Jewish history and Judaism. Careful in his evaluation of his sources, he was circumspect in the formulation of his conclusions. It is therefore not surprising that for many years, even in our own time, students of the history of the Chinese Jews have leaned heavily upon Finn's book."[3]

The tribute is entirely justified. Finn made mistakes, as has every writer in the field before and after him, but his account was clearer, more factual, and more comprehensive than any that had been previously attempted. Nearly three decades later, his second book on the subject, *The Orphan Colony of the Jews in China*,[4] corrected many of his earlier errors and summarized the several vitally important events involving the Kaifeng Jews, which had been sparked by both his pen and his persistent efforts to enter into communication with them. Unfortunately, even more nonsense has been thrown together about the Jews of China since the publication of Finn's initial study than he himself was compelled to deal with as he started his investigations in the quiet reading rooms of the British Museum. On the other hand, a gratifyingly large amount of sound information never available to Finn has also been amassed.

Finn approaches the history of the Chinese Jews with a sense of compassion born out of the conviction that Judaism is part of God's plan for the redemption of mankind and finds its ultimate expression in Christianity. Appalled by the persecutions that Jews have suffered almost everywhere they have lived, he compliments the Chinese for treating their Jewish compatriots with a humanity all too often unmet with in Europe. Even his antipathy to the Church of Rome stems to a degree from its long record of mistreatment of the Children of Israel, and he deplores the contemptuous attitudes that her missionaries displayed toward the Jews of Kaifeng. He notes twice that Semmedo, reporting Aleni's admiring comment about how neatly the Kaifeng synagogue was maintained, could not keep himself from indulging in the jibe, "if any synagogue can be free from uncleanliness."[5] He also recalls with intense displeasure Gozani's sweeping characterization of certain Jewish beliefs voiced by the elders of the *kehillah* as foolish and superstitious.[6] Equally abhorrent to him is Trigault's remark that Ricci's discovery of Jews in China indicated that "Jewish filth" was found even there.[7]

Why did the Jesuits never succeed in converting the Kaifeng congregation? Finn ascribes their lack of success to indifference, to their failure to appreciate the centrality of the Scriptures to the faith of Israel, to their preoccupation with other duties, and to "political disputes . . . with their rivals in the monkish orders."[8]

Polemics and all, in 1843 Finn's book was still the best history of the Jews of China yet written. Its author's intent, however, was not alone to compose a historical treatise but also to convince the English reading public that the time was at last ripe for attempting the Protestantization of all China. It is his thesis that although the Israelites living "amid the alien corn" of the Middle Kingdom have not themselves been brought to Christianity, they may ultimately see the light, accept baptism, and become God's chosen instruments for guiding their pagan countrymen to the cross. "The Church of God," he piously conjectures, "may even yet have the pleasure to behold them [the Chinese Jews] disseminating a saving knowledge among the heathen."[9] To Finn, of course, "the Church of God" is Protestantism, and especially the form of Protestantism practiced by the Church of England.

Finn's vision of a Protestantized China and the role of the Kaifeng Jews in bringing it about are touched upon in the preface to his 1843 book:

> We are indebted for our present knowledge of the Chinese Jews to the Jesuit missionaries in that country. Let us hope to receive new information concerning them from future missionaries, who shall be free from the least taint of idolatry; men animated with zeal for the salvation of mankind, and at the same time rendering obedience to ecclesiastical discipline. The new position of England, arising from the Treaty of Nanking, 29th August, 1842, ought to encourage many such men to proclaim Christianity in that Empire. Facilities of various kinds for such a work are now before us. The Jews there will be unimpeachable witnesses to the truth of the Old Testament . . . and we may rest assured that the Divine blessing will not be wanting to sanction every effort made in promoting the spiritual good of China.[10]

In February 1844 Finn took his first practical step toward reestablishing contact with the Jews of Kaifeng. Hearing that Temple H. Layton was about to sail for China to assume his duties as Her Britannic Majesty's Vice-Consul at Ningpo, Finn induced him to take along several copies of *The Jews in China* for distribution to missionaries and laymen whose relationships with the Chinese might afford them some opportunity for relaying a written message to Kaifeng, this to be prepared by Finn. Both men realized, of course, that the prospects for success were quite limited and that any letters addressed to Kaifeng would have to be taken there by Chinese subjects, the restrictions against travel into the interior by foreigners being still in effect.

But Finn would not let the matter rest there. Nor would it let him rest. He sought out the assistance of the French Oriental scholar Garein de Tassy in enlisting the collaboration of the Société Asiatique, but nothing came of this. He also discussed appropriate ways and means of forwarding a letter to the *kehillah* with friends in England, among them Joseph Wolff, a missionary of Jewish birth just back from Bokhara, where he was told by the local Jews of their tradition that long ago, when some of their people were expelled by Jagatai, successor to Genghis Khan, they migrated to China.[11] Another friend whom Finn consulted was the peripatetic Bible agent and novelist George Borrow. Nobody he knew, however, could really help. He realized that he would have to depend completely on Layton and hope that the consul would somehow manage to get a message through to the *kehillah*.

By November, Finn's letter to the Jews was ready, its text having been composed in "as simple and distinct a style of Hebrew as possible."[12] Three copies were made and sent on to Ningpo early in 1845, together with an English translation for Layton's benefit. The letters were addressed in Chinese characters to the Jewish community of Kaifeng.

Like those prepared by earlier would-be correspondents, Finn's letter extends the author's greetings to the Jews, wishes them well, and asks for replies to a series of queries concerning their history, their religious beliefs and practices, and their present condition.

Within three weeks after posting his packet of letters to Layton, Finn was designated consul for Jerusalem and Palestine. The appointment in his pocket, he promptly married Elizabeth Anne McCaul, and in February 1846 sailed with his bride for the Middle East, having first taken the precaution of writing

Layton that all correspondence should thenceforth be routed to him at Jerusalem via London.

Nearly five years after he consented to join hands with Finn in the Kaifeng venture, there was at last something concrete for Layton to report. He had in the interim been transferred to Amoy, and from there, on January 15, 1849, he sent Finn a synopsis of what he had recently discovered.

Layton's report is a breakthrough, the first to be achieved in the 125 years since Gozani's expulsion from Kaifeng. He has not yet been able to get Finn's letter delivered to the *kehillah*, he explains apologetically, but it now appears that success cannot be far off, perhaps no more than a year away. He has arranged with a skin and fur merchant, a Chinese who does business in a Shensi city near the Honan border, to forward one of Finn's Hebrew letters to the *kehillah*, together with a Chinese translation, by way of another merchant who goes once a year to the Honan capital. If, however, Finn wants to expedite matters, he might try sending "a learned Jew, disguised as a Chinese," to Kaifeng, or simply keep writing to the *kehillah* "time and again." There is still another alternative: it is now possible to dispatch a courier directly from Amoy to Kaifeng; but this, he hints discreetly, will take money. "I will be obliged to you to tell me to what expenses I may go," he writes, "if you wish me to send any special messenger to Kaifeng."[13]

The really significant news in Layton's letter is that he has met a native of Kaifeng, a Muslim sergeant in the Chinese Imperial Army whose name is T'ieh Ting-an and who, while growing up, lived within a half-mile of the synagogue. T'ieh, whom Layton considers a "very decent, gentlemanly mannered man" and in whose reliability he places great faith, claims to have been "well acquainted with the Jews." It is now five years since his last visit home. The information he gives to Layton in January 1849 is therefore at least half a decade old, perhaps much more.

T'ieh recalls that there were eight Jewish clans in Kaifeng, and estimates the city's Jewish population at about a thousand.[14] Of the eight clans, two, the Kao and Shih, have remained "perfect," but six have intermarried with their neighbors. Two of the six "give their daughters to the Muhammadans; the Muhammadans

15. James Finn.

do not give their daughters to the Jews." He maintains that the clans "do not know whence they came, or the period of their coming into China." The Jews, he adds, "are quite Chinese in appearance. The women exactly resemble the Kaifeng women. They have all straight features like the people in the center of China. In the Ming dynasty [1368–1644] the Jews were rich, and their customs were as of old. One of the family of Kao keeps a large spice and perfumery warehouse; and Shih (Stone) has a large silk shop. His name is Brown Jade Stone. Stone is the family name." A member of the Chin clan, he declares, holds high military rank.

T'ieh remembers that the synagogue has eight corners and that "strangers and carriers of pork cannot pass near the synagogue." One enters the building through either of two side doors. "The large door is only opened on the last day of the old Chinese year; it is then thrown open from New Year's Eve until the evening of (Chinese) New Year's Day. There is one large room in the synagogue no one dares to enter. There is a high table with the names of all the priests, a tablet put up two hundred and fifty years since, with the names of all the priests, and the name of the reigning emperor."

"I have not seen any of their ceremonies," T'ieh says. "There are no priests; there is not any form of worship. One rich man only takes charge of the synagogue. No one Jew can read or write [Hebrew] at Kaifeng. The Jews would never allow a book to be taken away." Still, "if new books and writings were given to the Jews, they would be most gladly received." He recognizes a Hebrew inscription shown to him by Layton as akin to the writing he had seen in the synagogal compound. He is confused about the Jewish Sabbath. Some Jews, he tells Layton, consider the sixth day of the week to be the Sabbath, while others celebrate the eighth day as the day of rest.[15]

Layton sends a second letter on January 20, 1849, five days after composing the one dealing with T'ieh. He tells Finn that he has distributed copies of Finn's book to several leading missionaries, but that "not one has ever seen a Jew or a man who has seen one. Consul Thom, Gutzlaff, Medhurst &c., &c., and myself all doubted their existence." However, now that T'ieh, who is away at Fuchow for a week or two, has confirmed that there really are Jews in Kaifeng, further investigation is definitely called for. But, Layton suggests, money alone "will obtain information, and perhaps Sir Moses Montefiore or some wealthy Hebrew will pay it."

For more than a year after this, nothing of consequence comes from Layton. Then, on March 24, 1850, he writes that he still has hope that things will turn out well. He has had no further news about the letter he tried to send to the *kehillah*, except that the fur dealers assure him that they have relayed it to Kaifeng, together with another letter which Sergeant T'ieh gave them for transmission to some old friends there. They believe that Finn's letter should already have been received by the *kehillah*. Fortunately, one of the merchants, an elder brother of the man who had been entrusted with the earlier letter, is now going directly to the Honan capital and will be happy to take a second copy of the letter with him and deliver it personally to the Jews. He should be back in Amoy, hopefully with a reply, "about the same moon next year."

Layton, who has searched diligently, and always without success, for a courier whom he can send "express" to Kaifeng, is delighted, and he gives the merchant the second copy. He tries to make Finn understand how totally cut off a Westerner is from Kaifeng or from any other city in the interior of China. "The great difference of local dialects throughout the various provinces of the Empire, the jealous and eager watchfulness of the mandarins over all travelers in the interior, the frequent questionings and searchings which a traveler is liable to, and the danger which he might incur should the real object of his journey be discovered, all combine to make me believe that it would be many years before such a person could be found among the Chinese natives of Amoy who would successfully undertake the task of a special visit to Kaifeng. I assure you that I do not magnify the difficulty; and were you resident in China, and a consul, you would find your every movement watched most narrowly."

T'ieh's military duties have kept him in Fuchow much longer than either he or Layton had originally anticipated, but he is now back in Amoy. He has written friends in Kaifeng for information three times in all, but has received no reply. "He has asked his friends to send a drawing of the temple, etc.," Layton writes, "such an one as may be found in the shops of Kaifeng; but I did not dare to give such a commission to the fur dealers, for I might excite suspicion of my having some design upon the city."

However, T'ieh has run into a townsman while in Fuchow, a man "ten or fourteen years older than himself, who said that he could well remember in his young days that the Jews had a priest—he had seen him on one occasion. . . . He was almost sure they had more priests than one."

Layton warns Finn that the Jews, in the opinion of a Chinese clerk who works at the Consulate in Amoy and whom he respects highly, will almost certainly be afraid to receive a letter known to have been written by foreigners, since this will leave them open to all kinds of suspicion on the part of their neighbors and the authorities.

In Jerusalem, there is now nothing Finn can do but wait for Layton's next letter and hope that it will contain the welcome tidings that a message has finally come through from the *kehillah*. He waits more than a year, and then, to his surprise, receives a letter from Mrs. Layton. It is dated June 12, 1851, and bears a London postmark. It brings the unexpected news that Layton has died in Amoy and that she has recently returned to England. As for the Jews of Kaifeng:

> You have waited long and patiently for news of real import from Honan, and I have now the pleasure to tell you that, at last, an answer has arrived at Amoy, brought by the fur merchant to whom the last of your letters was entrusted; and I will await your instructions respecting its transmission to you by post, for it seems something so precious to me that I shall hardly like to risk it when once safe in my hand. . . . The letter has been opened, and a copy taken, for the purpose of being sent to the Bishop of Victoria [Finn, however, claims that the bishop never received such a copy]. . . . The expected Chinese letter, I hear, is directed to Mr. Layton, and does not say very much more than we have already been told, viz., that the community of Jews have arrived at nearly the last stage of

decay, though less than forty years ago they must have been able to keep up the forms and ceremonies of their religion, perhaps but imperfectly, but they did keep them up someway.— Believe me, &c.

S. D. Layton[16]

Mrs. Layton now waits for the *kehillah*'s letter to be forwarded from Amoy to her residence in London, and Finn waits for Mrs. Layton to send it on to him. He continues to wait, until 1863 in Jerusalem and later in England, and gets it at long last in London—in April 1870. "The chain of occurrences which produced this delay surprises one to look back upon it," he writes, "the principal circumstances being, besides much uncertainty as to my own movements and long succeeding illness, the utter inability after a certain period to discover the existence or whereabouts of my amiable correspondent, Mrs. Layton. I have it now before me, a writing on most delicate paper, with the address upon a slip of bright red, gummed over the exterior. The translation was made by Mr. M. C. Morrison . . . who was engaged in Her Majesty's Consular Service in China until 1867. At the time of the receipt of this letter, he was employed under Mr. Layton at Amoy."

The letter on Finn's desk bears a date corresponding to August 20, 1850. Written entirely in Chinese, it is signed by the Kaifeng Jew Chao Nien-tsu. The inscription on the envelope reads: "The enclosed letter is to be delivered to His Worship Mr. Layton, H. B. M. Consul at Amoy, in the Province of Fukien, for transmission to the chief teacher of the Jewish religion. Year *Keng-hsu,* seventh month, thirteenth day. Sent from the street *Hsiao-chieh.*" Chao, then, was under the impression that the letter he was answering came from a Jew. And so, for that matter, were the other members of the *kehillah,* for four months after Chao's reply was written the two Chinese delegates who came to Kaifeng observed that during their visits to the synagogue the Jews alluded to Finn's letter as having been sent to them by "a teacher of our religion."[17] The *kehillah* had good reason to believe this, not only because of the nature of the contents of the letter and the fact that it was accompanied by an original composed in Hebrew characters, but also because the directions on the face of the envelope in which it came had read: "From the Head of the

Honourable Israelitish [Pluck-sinew religion] synagogue with instructions to inquire in Pluck-sinew lane in the Great Street within the Prefectural city of Kaifeng and give it to the Teachers of the religion in the Temple of Purity and Truth [the Kaifeng synagogue], to be by them opened."[18]

Yet although the inscription placed by Chao on the envelope containing his reply specifically states that his letter is to be delivered to a Jewish leader, all the individuals through whose hands it passed—Layton's staff, Mrs. Layton, and Finn himself—deliberately disregarded the writer's instructions. Finn, basically a decent and honorable man, is plainly ill at ease for having profited from an ungentlemanly interception of correspondence addressed to another person, and tries lamely to explain why Chao's letter was not forwarded to a responsible Jewish individual or organization. He acknowledges that "it was very natural for the Chinese writer to imagine that his answer, in passing though Amoy, was to reach 'the chief teacher of the Jewish religion,' wherever he might be." But, Finn asks, where would one find this "chief teacher of the Jewish religion?" He then responds to his own question with the strained excuse that he has no way of knowing "who, in a literal sense, would be that 'chief teacher.' Neither the principal Rabbi in Jerusalem, albeit he rejoices in the title of 'First in Zion,' nor the head Rabbi in London, could have any claim upon the epistle, which was a reply to one received in China: it belonged evidently to the person understood by the writer himself, namely the correspondent to whom he was replying."[19] Chao, however, had no way of knowing the precise identity of this "correspondent," since, as Finn himself acknowledges, the letter transmitted to the *kehillah* by Layton "bore no signature."[20] Finn, moreover, completely ignores the fact that, given the choice, Chao would certainly have directed that his reply be delivered to any "teacher of the Jewish religion," no matter who he was or where he lived, rather than to an individual who was affiliated with an alien creed.

Chao's letter, in any case, answers several of the questions posed by Finn, including those concerning the festivals celebrated by the Kaifeng Jews.[21] It also reports that the *kehillah* has fallen on evil times and is in dire danger of disintegration unless help is immediately forthcoming. The synagogue must be rebuilt, Chao says, and it is essential that teachers be sent to work with the Jews and bring them back to the faith of their fathers. "During the past forty or fifty years," he laments, "our religion has been but imperfectly transmitted, and although its canonical writings are still extant, there are none who understand so much as one word of them. It happens only that there yet survives an aged female of more than seventy years, who retains in her recollection the principal tenets of the faith."

"Morning and night," he continues, "with tears in our eyes and with offerings of incense, do we implore that our religion may again flourish. We have everywhere sought about, but could find none who understood the letters of the Great Country, and this has occasioned us deep sorrow." The unexpected arrival of a communication from Layton has given him fresh hope, for it suggests to him that the Judaism that survives in England could now become the vehicle by which Judaism might be brought back to Kaifeng. He obviously thinks that the man whose queries he is answering represents the Jewish community of England and would be astonished to discover how far off the mark he actually is.

"Our temple in this place has long been without ministers," Chao comments sadly. The synagogue itself is virtually in ruins. Poverty has kept the Jews from rebuilding it. "Daily, with tears, have we called on the Holy Name. If we could again procure ministers, and could put in order our temple, our religion would have a firm support for the future, and its sacred documents would have a secure repository. This it needs no divination to be assured of."

The preservation of the synagogue and the books is a matter of the utmost concern to Chao. "It is to be desired that some person be early deputed hither," he pleads, "for if much longer delay occur, not only will the synagogue have fallen into ruins, but we fear that the holy books may likewise be injured by decay."

To add to the *kehillah*'s numerous troubles, its membership is far from united. "It is well," Chao writes, "that your letter reached the hands of the present writer: had it been carried to others it might have remained unnoticed." Three of the Jews are trying to "mortgage or sell the temple buildings and materials." Two others have already "mortgaged portions of the building," and another three have dismantled various parts of the property and sold them. Chao gives the names of the eight offenders. He concludes by asking again that a person of authority be sent to Kaifeng forthwith. He prays that this individual will take strong measures "to put a stop to the scandalous proceedings" of the eight disreputable characters whose greed, if not checked by outside authority, may well lead to the total destruction of the synagogue and the irretrievable loss of its books.

It had taken Finn a long time to get a reply to his letter of inquiry—twenty-five years, to be exact. In the interim, much had happened, and the Jewish congregation of Kaifeng was now in even worse shape than when he started working on the problem of getting in touch with it. Chao Nien-tsu was not exaggerating when he wrote in 1850 that the *kehillah* was nearing its end. But in 1870, as Finn read the old letter, the congregation's isolation had already been broken by the visits of the two Chinese delegates and also of an American Protestant missionary and, apparently, a European Jew. It is not likely, in any case, that anything tangible could have been done for the Jewish community of Kaifeng even if Chao's message had reached Finn within a few months after it was written. And Chao, of course, had no way of knowing that his anonymous correspondent's interest in the *kehillah* was not to rebuild its ties to Jewishness but to get it to pass safely to Protestantism without falling prey to either the blandishments of the indigenous creeds of China or the lure of Rome.

8 ❖ THE CHINESE DELEGATES

FOUNDED in 1809 in the flush of the neo-Puritan evangelical fervor then sweeping the upper and middle strata of English society, and numbering among its patrons some of the most influential figures in British governmental and clerical circles, the London Society for the Promotion of Christianity among the Jews soon came to be regarded by the objects of its attention with emotions ranging the entire gamut from tolerant amusement to apoplectic rage. In short order it attracted, in addition to the earnest Christians who provided the funds and theological direction that sustained it, a motley assortment of Jewish opportunists whose motivations were more worldly than pietistic. Particularly damaging to its reputation were the scandalous activities of Joseph Samuel Christian Frederick Frey, a convert who came to England in 1801 from the Bavarian Missionary Seminary of Berlin. Installed as the first president of the London Society, Frey took advantage of his position to attempt the seduction of the wife of a recent proselyte, only to have this and other peccadilloes of a similar nature unmasked as the consequence of a police investigation of certain criminal charges being proffered against the lady's husband. It became advisable for the London Society to ship Frey off to America. There he subsequently organized the American Society for Meliorating the Condition of the Jews, a conversionary institution that included among its sponsors such luminaries as the presidents of Yale and Princeton, the first director of the Mint, and Secretary of State John Quincy Adams, soon to become president of the United States.[1]

The London Society's missionaries channeled their energies to the proselytization of Jews of all classes, but concentrated initially on the poverty stricken inhabitants of the London area. They fed and clothed those penniless Jews who would listen to their preachments, and also furnished training and employment to some of them in a textile mill and a printing plant established for that purpose. For the most part, as many Englishmen, both Christian and Jewish, were quick to point out, the very few converts enticed by the "soul-snatchers" came from the ignorant, the indigent, and the ignoble, a taunt not unlike the "rice Christian" jibe to which later missionaries working in other parts of the world were to become accustomed.

This is not to say that the London Society never attracted converts of whose sincerity there could be no question. Nor should it be inferred that the men and women who financed and administered it were in the main anything other than devout and well-intentioned souls. Unfortunately, so thoroughly caught up did they become in their zeal to do good—as they saw it—that they were utterly incapable of understanding how anyone could construe their efforts as busybody intrusions upon the personal rights of the very people they were trying to save.

The Christian critics of the London Society—and they were not few—argued that the time, money, and energy being expanded to convert a Jew here and a Jew there might more profitably be devoted to bringing some of Protestantism's own lost sheep back to the fold. Many of these critics regarded membership in the London Society as prima facie evidence of eccentricity, or even worse. Thus, in a sanity hearing presided over in 1863 by Anthony Ashley Cooper, seventh Earl of Shaftesbury, the question was posed: "Are you aware, my Lord, that she [the woman whose sanity was being questioned] subscribes to the Society for the Conversion of the Jews?" It was a question that would have been better left unasked. "Indeed," snapped back Lord Shaftesbury, "are you aware that I am president of that Society?"[2]

On the whole, the members of the London Society tended to regard all believing Jews as backward, misguided, and willful beings—as problem children, almost—who, if treated firmly but humanely, might in God's good time come to realize that it was to their advantage to give up their obstreperously sinful ways and attain salvation through Anglican Christianity. The more compassionate of the London Society's agents, when stationed in Central and Eastern Europe and in the Muslim strongholds of North Africa and the Levant, did what they could to minimize the physical abuse to which the Jews of these regions were chronically subjected. At home in England, however, the leaders of the London Society stood stoutly opposed to the extension of civil and political equality to those of their countrymen who did not happen to be Christian.

Totally convinced of the righteousness of their cause, the London Society's missionaries looked upon the anguish they occasionally inflicted upon the Jews as regrettable but unavoidable. An authorized history of the London Society, published in 1866, to give one example, records that in 1810 the London mission picked up a hungry fifteen-year-old boy, provided him with food and clothing, and persuaded him to defect from Judaism and accept baptism in the Anglican faith. When his father and mother discovered where he was and pleaded to be allowed to see him, the directors of the mission refused their request pointblank, fearing that the adolescent might be induced to recant and revert to Judaism. The Jewish community appealed to the King's Bench for the return of the youngster to his parents. The court, the London Society's historian reported with obvious satisfaction, rejected the Jewish petition after hearing the defense contend that since Judaism itself regards thirteen, the bar-mitzvah age, as the end of boyhood and the beginning of manhood, the parents could no longer be considered their son's legal guardian.[3] In this instance, and in innumerable others, the London Society proceeded from the premise that because its objectives were undeniably noble, and patently in the best interests of the Jews, its agents had the right to assume that when it came to converting the Jews the ends automatically justified the means. This logic would color the London Society's approach to the Chinese Jews.[4]

Among the more ardent supporters of the work of the London Society was Miss Jane Cook, a wealthy resident of Colchester whose contribution of more than £60,000 had made possible the construction of an Anglican church in Jerusalem shortly after James Finn's arrival there. It was this Miss Cook who provided the funds that enabled the London Society to draw back the curtain of total silence that for a century and a quarter had separated the Jews of Kaifeng from the Jews and Christians of the West. Her interest in the Chinese Jews, aroused by Finn's *Jews in China*, brought the London Society a legacy of £500, with the stipulation that the money was to be used to search out the Jews of the Middle Kingdom and effect their conversion to Protestantism. The size of her bequest, while substantial, was far less than the expense ordinarily incurred by the London Society to convert a single Jew, a figure that varied (in the second half of the century, according to the society's records) from a low of £600 to a high of £3000—an equivalent, in this period, to between ten and fifty times the yearly earning of an English textile worker or coal miner.[5] The funds advanced by Miss Cook were in any case placed at the disposal of the Reverend George Smith, an Anglican minister who had just been named bishop of Victoria and was leaving for Hong Kong, the seat of his episcopacy.

Once in China, Smith started almost immediately to investigate the feasibility of dispatching an emissary to Honan. A European who ventured into the interior, he knew, might not come back alive. The journey would present hazards even to a native of the country, but not forbidding ones. The problem, therefore, was to find a reasonably qualified Chinese who would be willing to undertake a mission to the Jews in Kaifeng.

In 1850, while visiting Shanghai, Smith discussed the matter with Dr. W. H. Medhurst, a missionary associated with the London Society. Medhurst suggested that two Chinese converts whom he knew well and who were then living in Shanghai might be persuaded to accept the assignment. As was to be expected, he told Smith, the men had no knowledge of Hebrew, but they were trustworthy and resourceful. One of them, Ch'iu T'ien-sheng, a printer by trade, had been educated in Medhurst's mission school at Batavia. The other, Chiang Jung-chi, a literary graduate of the fourth degree, was employed as a teacher of Chinese and had even taught the language to several missionaries who were newcomers to the Orient.

Ch'iu and Chiang—the Chinese delegates, as they came to be

called—agreed to make the trip to Kaifeng. They were instructed to try to purchase some of the synagogal books and to bring back as much information as they could about the *kehillah*. They were also given a Hebrew letter composed by Isaac Faraj ben Reuben Jacob in which the writer tells the Jews of Kaifeng that he is a coreligionist of theirs and a native of Baghdad, and that he had come to Shanghai some five years previously for the purpose of engaging in mercantile activities. He hopes that they are getting along well, and he asks them to reply to certain questions: Do they have a Torah scroll? Do they have all the twenty-four books of the Hebrew scrpitural canon? The Mishnah and the Zohar? What books do they use for the training of their children? From which of the tribes of Israel are they descended? He also asks if they know of any other Jewish settlements in China; and he promises to send them any scriptural and pietistic texts they lack, if they will only let him know what they are. He would like to visit them personally, but this is not possible.[6]

The delegates left Shanghai at 7:30 A.M. on Friday, November 15, 1850. They had been requested to keep detailed personal diaries during the course of the trip, and they did—Ch'iu's being written in English and Chiang's in Chinese. Early in 1851, Chiang's journal was translated into English by the Reverend Joseph Edkins. Later in the same year the two journals were printed in booklet form at Shanghai, together with an introduction prepared by Bishop Smith, and given the imposing and leisurely title of *The Jews at K'aie-fung-foo: Being a Narrative of a Mission of Inquiry to the Jewish Synagogue at K'ae-fung-foo, on Behalf of the London Society for Promoting Christianity among the Jews.*

As they proceeded northwest to Kaifeng, first by boat and then by mulecart, the delegates filled their diaries with notes on the topographical features and economic characteristics of the areas along their route and with comments on the living conditions and religious inclinations of the inhabitants. They distributed missionary tracts in one town after another, expressing the hope in several of their journal entries that the tracts would be read and do some good. There was considerable room for improvement, they felt, not only in the religious attitudes of the people through whose regions they traveled, but also in the grooming of many of the women they saw. The hair of these women, Ch'iu observed with disapproval, "was always un-combed, and instead of dressing it they covered their heads with a piece of black napkin, while some of the dishevelled hairs were just pushed in, in order to conceal their slovenliness." They were as immodest as they were untidy. "Their dress," Ch'iu primly noted, "was not very long, coming down only to about four inches below the knees, without a petticoat, such as is worn by women of other parts."

On Monday, December 9, at about 4:30 in the afternoon, the delegates passed through the East Gate of Kaifeng and quickly found lodgings at an inn. Their initial impressions of the city were more favorable than Gaubil's had been in 1723. "We could see at once," Chiang wrote, "that it was a place where merchants and men of education were numerous, and that it was not unworthy to be the capital city of the Sung dynasty. The streets, however, are unpaved, and persons belonging to wealthy families always use mule carriages; the city walls are about forty-five *li* round."

Taking their evening meal in a shop not far from the inn at which they were staying, the delegates learned from the Muslim proprietor that the Jewish community still existed, consisted of seven clans, and no longer had a "teacher." Some Jews, they were told, were very poor, but others, "having a little money," had "opened shops to support their families." They were also given directions for getting to the synagogue, which was fortui-tously nearby. Finishing their dinner, they walked the short dis-tance and soon arrived at the old structure. They found it standing, but in very bad condition. "Within the precincts of the temple," Ch'iu remarked, "were a number of . . . people, who had spread out a great quantity of cabbages in the open air, just by the side of the temple; the residents there were mostly women, some of whom were widows."[7] In all, four or five destitute families made their home in the compound. The dis-astrous flood which struck Kaifeng in 1849, the delegates later learned, had aggravated the already desperate conditions of the squatters.[8] To obtain food, they were forced to sell some of the synagogal bricks and tiles.

"Are there any of you who can read the Hebrew character?" the delegates asked. "Formerly," the answer came, "there were some who could, but now all have been scattered abroad, and there is not one who can read it."[9] Two letters had been received "some time ago" from "a teacher of our religion," they added. This would suggest that the two duplicates of Finn's letter entrusted by Layton to the skin and fur merchants had gotten through to their destination, or perhaps that one of the two letters was Finn's, the other being the 1815 communication relayed by Morrison through his Chinese bookseller from the Jews of London to the Jews of Kaifeng. Whatever the case, the squatters had no reason to believe that either of the two letters in their possession might have been written by non-Jews.

The first meeting of the delegates and the Jews was necessarily of short duration, the hour being late, but the delegates were back at the synagogue by eight o'clock the next morning.

The delegates delivered Isaac Faraj's letter to the Jews—a forlorn gesture, of course, since none of them could read its contents—and were in turn shown the two letters of which the Jews had spoken the previous evening. The delegates were informed that they were not the first strangers to seek admission to the synagogue, others having done the same in the past. Not one of these earlier and unidentified visitors had been permitted to enter the edifice, the Jews having sensed that they were "merely pretended professors of their religion." But, wrote Ch'iu, "finding that we had been sent by some of their own people and had a letter in their own character, they allowed us to see the place."[10]

The Jews guided the delegates through the shabby remains of the synagogue, and Ch'iu was given carte blanche to try his hand at copying the inscriptions. He began laboriously to write down the Hebrew characters, one after the other, but before he could get very far an old man named Ch'iao strode into the synagogue, saw what was going on, burst into a tirade, and demanded that Ch'iu and Chiang leave the premises at once. They protested vigorously, but it did them no good, and they were unceremoniously ejected from the synagogal compound.

Later in the day a Jew named Chao Chin-ch'eng called on the delegates at their inn and apologized profusely for the discourtesies they had suffered at the hands of his coreligionists. After their regrettable expulsion from the synagogue, he told them, Ch'iao had made a point of warning the Jews that their visitors from Shanghai were not to be trusted.[11] They were not Israelites at all, he shouted at the bystanders, but agents sent "by the English missionaries to examine our establishment." Be careful in your dealings with these men, he warned them, and do not let them come into the synagogue again.

Who this Ch'iao was is not clear. In Ch'iu's journal he is described merely as "a man of the name of Ch'iao who had attained a literary degree."[12] Chiang refers to him as "a literary graduate named Ch'iao who belonged to the Jewish sect."[13] The names of the seven Jewish clans noted in Ch'iu's journal correspond exactly with those provided by the Jesuits and by Westerners who were to visit the Jews after the delegates, but the patronymic Ch'iao does not figure in any listings, neither in Ch'iu's nor in the others. Ch'iao, then, was not a Jew. He may have been a local official of some kind, or perhaps simply a friend of the Jews who did not want to see them get into trouble with the authorities for trafficking with strangers. Whoever he was, it is evident that he was not a man to be trifled with, and the Jews thought it wise to accede to his wishes and expel the delegates from the synagogue.

With access to the premises barred to them, the delegates asked Chao Chin-ch'eng if arrangements could be made to have the synagogal inscriptions copied and, more important, if he could sell them any of the congregational books. "I cannot get you the [Torah] scrolls," Chao replied, "but I can give you some of the small books." In fact, he had one small volume with him, having apparently smuggled it out of the synagogue. He handed this over to the delegates.

The delegates were able to get a fair number of the small inscriptions transcribed without undue difficulty, although the 1489/1512 stele posed a special problem, the entrances to the pavilion in which it was located being blocked by large accumulations of rubbish. The problem was worked out by Chiang who, as reported in the *Narrative*, "succeeded in inducing one of the professors [of the Jewish religion], named Chao, to effect an entrance through holes in the walls, and by means of candles, he obtained sufficient light to enable him to copy the whole, which was the work of several days."[14]

Even though they were personae non gratae in the synagogue, the delegates still managed to stay in touch with the Jews. It got them into trouble. "Yesternight," wrote Ch'iu on December 13, "we had great fear, on account of the Jews who came to our inn to visit us," this coming and going of people having aroused the suspicions of three would-be police informers who were staying at the same hostelry. "As soon as the Jews had gone," Chi'iu continued, "we went to bed, and about 11 at night we heard them [the informers] talking loudly about our business; there were in one room three people, one of whom said, 'I will accuse them to the district magistrate, saying that these two men are come from Shanghai and are friends of the foreigners; that they talked last night with the Jewish people . . . and came hither as spies and breakers of the law. We will certainly bring them to the magistrate and get them beaten and put in jail; by doing which they will be obliged to give out some money.' "

Frightened, the delegates spent a miserable and sleepless night. Rising very early in the morning, while the conspirators were still abed, they prudently slipped out of the inn and found safer lodgings elsewhere.

A few hours later, the delegates "took tea and luncheon" with Chao Chin-ch'eng and his younger brother Chao Wen-k'uei at a cost, Chiang dutifully noted, of "500 cash." Chao Wen-k'uei then turned over "the key of the guest chapel of the Pure and True Synagogue" to Chao Chin-ch'eng, who took the delegates to the synagogue, surreptitiously unlocked the door to the chapel, selected eight of the synagogal books, and sold them to the delegates for an unspecified sum.

The delegates hurried back to their new lodgings, carrying the filched books with them. Having run short of money, they then sought out a friend of Chiang's father and borrowed "8,000 cash" from him. Using these funds, they immediately booked passage on a Yellow River coal boat scheduled to depart the next day. They left Kaifeng on this vessel, their stay in the city having lasted six days. Their return trip to Shanghai was marked by two unsettling adventures, one with sneak thieves and the other with river pirates, but they came out of both encounters unscathed. They arrived in Shanghai on January 8, 1851. In all, they had been gone fifty-four days.

Safely back at their starting point, the delegates turned over their precious haul to the missionaries who had originally sent them to Kaifeng: eight synagogal books, copies of several Chinese-language inscriptions, and the few lines in Hebrew characters that Ch'iu had succeeded in transcribing before he was stopped by Ch'iao. In his journal, Ch'iu spoke of obtaining nine books from Chao Chin-ch'eng, one at the first hostel in which the delegates had stayed and eight more at the synagogue. However, in the introduction he prepared for the *Narrative* in which the delegates' journals were printed, Bishop Smith acknowledged receiving only eight books. "They brought back," he wrote, "eight MSS of apparently considerable antiquity, containing portions of the Old Testament Scriptures, of which fascimiles are subjoined. These eight MSS are written on thick paper, bound in silk, and bear internal marks of foreign, probably Persian, origin. The writing appears to have been executed by means of a stylus, and to be in an antique Hebrew form, with vowel points." Six of the eight were *parashioth* (*sidroth*, or section books, of the Pentateuch): Exod. 1–6:1, Exod. 38:21–40, Lev. 19–20, Num. 13–15, Deut. 11:26–16:17, and Deut. 32. The remaining two were *siddurim* (prayer books) whose texts included, as is customary, selections from the various books of the Hebrew Scriptures.

Smith and his colleagues eagerly inspected the individual *parashioth* and the scriptural passages contained in the *siddurim*. "The cursory examination which we have been already enabled to bestow on them," he then noted, "leads to the belief that they will be found by Western biblical scholars to be remarkable for their generally exact agreement with the received text of the

Hebrew Old Testament." Any last ditch expectations that the Kaifeng Scriptures might reveal novel readings were thus dealt still another blow. Smith hoped, however, that he would soon have the privilege of announcing the acquisition of the synagogue's Torah scrolls. "Measures are already in progress," he told his readers, "for procuring these." He did not elaborate, but what he had in mind was that the delegates were being sent back to Kaifeng with enough money to tempt the starving Jews to sell their Torah scrolls, the most readily marketable assets they had.

The first reports that two Chinese Christians had penetrated to the heart of their country, met the exotic colony of Jews who were known to live there, and acquired substantial portions of their ancient Scriptures attracted worldwide attention. Journalists in Europe and America, stirred by the news, sought out the old Jesuit accounts, scanned them for background materials on the *kehillah,* and then superimposed the sensational story of how a tiny Israelite island lost in a vast sea of Oriental heathenism had just been resighted. What they wrote usually made for interesting reading, even if their facts were not always as accurate as they might have been.[15]

Half a world away from Kaifeng, Charles Dickens published an article called "The Jews in China" in *Household Words,* the popular weekly magazine he had recently begun to edit as a sideline to his novel writing. The article, which appeared without a byline and may or may not have been written by Dickens himself, was well enough received to justify being reprinted several times in the next few years.[16]

Since the writer of the *Household Words* report, whether he was Dickens or not, probably did not have the full text of the delegates' journals at hand, these then being on press in Shanghai, he was forced to base most of the piece on information extracted from letters of the Jesuits. The bulk of his presentation, actually, is derived from Gozani's 1704 report to Suarez. He was able, however, to touch on some of the high points of the delegates' trip, material which had found its way to England in newspaper accounts published in Hong Kong or Shanghai and in letters received from missionaries stationed in China.

Similar articles, most of them as sparing of details concerning the very recent developments vis-à-vis the *kehillah* as the *Household Words* piece, appeared at about the same time in numerous periodicals and in a number of languages. They added nothing of any substance to the details Dickens already presented in the magazine article.

As for Ch'iu and Chiang, they had accomplished considerably more than they probably realized. Not only did their primary mission turn out well for them, but they were among the first to bring back other information that the West, starved for first-hand intelligence about what was going on inside China, was impatiently waiting to hear. Some of the observations made by the delegates regarding the regions they traversed on their way to Kaifeng and back were available to the author of the *Household Words* essay. "Population near the Yellow River," he told his readers, "they found rare and unhealthy. Localities that figure in the geographical charts of the Empire as principal places, or as towns of the second class, are but huge piles of rubbish, surrounded by crumbling walls. Here and there a gate, with its inscription half effaced, informs the traveler that he is entering a mighty town." The delegates' report made it clear that the interior of China, or at least the parts of it through which they passed on their journey, had changed markedly, and apparently for the worse, since the embargo on travel by foreigners was imposed in 1724.

On July 20, 1851, thirteen days before Dickens's magazine published its description of their first trip to Kaifeng, Ch'iu and Chiang rode triumphantly into Shanghai with six of the *kehillah*'s Torah scrolls and fifty-odd of its smaller manuscripts— and also with two Kaifeng Jews who chose to accompany them, the brothers Chao Chin-ch'eng and Wen-k'uei. The delegates had been gone exactly two months. Two weeks of this time were taken up in negotiations with the *kehillah* for the documents, the rest in travel. The delegates had every reason to be pleased with what they had achieved in their short stay in the Honan capital. The missionaries, of course, were elated.

Presswork for the *Narrative*, the booklet containing diaries composed by the delegates in the course of their first journey to Kaifeng, was done, or nearly done, by the time they came back from their second expedition. It was decided, as a last-minute measure, to augment the text with a brief memorandum relating what had been accomplished in the aftermath of the first expedition. As soon as this was prepared (by an unidentified writer), it was printed on a small slip of paper and tipped into the book between the end of Bishop Smith's introduction and the first page of Ch'iu's diary. It announced in two paragraphs that the long quest for the Scriptures of the Kaifeng synagogue had finally been crowned with success:

> Since the preceding pages were written, the two Chinese travelers have been despatched a second time to Kaifeng. They returned to Shanghai in July, having met with complete success in their mission. Six of the twelve [thirteen, more likely] rolls

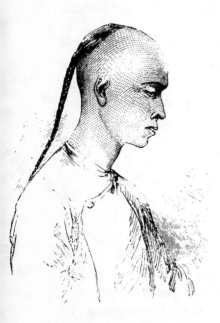

16. Two Chinese Jews. The brothers Chao Wen-k'uei (left) and Chao Chin-Ch'eng, as they appeared in 1851, shortly after accompanying the Chinese delegates from Kaifeng to Shanghai.

of the Law, which they saw during their previous visit, each containing a complete copy of the whole Pentateuch, were purchased for 400 *taels* of silver [about £140] from the Jews duly assembled to the number of 300 persons; and the Mss. were conveyed in open day from the synagogue to the lodgings of our travelers. They are each written in a fine legible hand on thick sheepskins sewn together, and are without points, or any of the modern divisions into sections or even books. They are in excellent preservation, except one which was injured by a flood during the Ming dynasty but is considered critically of the greatest value. During the first visit our travelers, by mistaking family names for individuals, greatly underrated the number of the Jewish community. Circumcision also appears to be practiced, though the tradition respecting its origin and object appears to be lost among them. Forty other smaller Hebrew Mss. were also brought away, which, on further examination, may possibly throw light on their early history and migration. [In reality, about forty *parashioth* were acquired, plus a dozen or so prayer books, two Passover Haggadahs, and a Memorial Book from which considerable information was later extracted regarding the history of the *kehillah* from about the beginning of the fifteenth century to the latter part of the seventeenth.]

Two Chinese Jews also accompanied our travelers on their return, and are residing under the roof of Dr. Medhurst at Shanghai, in order to study Hebrew, the knowledge of which has been entirely lost among them. They appear to have a great desire to reestablish the Hebrew services in their synagogue. They have expressed also a willingness to send down their children for instruction; and the Bishop of Victoria indulges the hope that he may possibly obtain hereafter two Jewish students for the Missionary College of St. Paul's at Hong Kong, now nearly completed, and instituted for the object of training native missionaries for China. A portion of the Mss. are sent to the London Society for Promoting Christianity among the Jews, Chatham Place, Blackfriars, by the present monthly steamer.

There are grounds for suspecting that the writer of the addendum tipped into the *Narrative* was apprehensive lest charges of impropriety be leveled against the London Society for the unconventional tactics by means of which the first installment of the Kaifeng texts was acquired, for the aura of respectability with which he surrounded the more recent negotiations between the delegates and the *kehillah* seems a bit overdone. The six Torah scrolls and the smaller books, he was careful to point out, "were purchased for 400 *taels* of silver (about £140) from the Jews duly assembled to the number of 300 persons, and the Mss. were conveyed in open day from the synagogue to the lodgings of our travelers." He himself was no doubt sincere, but all of his information concerning the delegates' second trip came from the men themselves and also, perhaps, from the brothers Chao—the same Jews who had taken it upon themselves to sell the delegates the eight books already in the possession of the London Society, and who were now in Shanghai. Ordinarily, of course, a protestation that merchandise has been honestly bought and paid for in the presence of a very large number of witnesses and then taken away by the purchasers in broad daylight is uncalled for. The fact, to be sure, that such a declaration was written into the tipped-in addendum to the *Narrative* should not of itself be construed as an attempt to head off accusations of wrongdoing on the part of the delegates during their second expedition to Kaifeng; but in light of their earlier dealings with the Jews the suspicion arises that it may have been the intention of the writer to do just that.

The composer of the insert to the *Narrative* stresses that 300 Jews were on hand when the Torah scrolls were sold. He is claiming, in short, that the books were disposed of with the knowledge of the entire *kehillah*. But is it possible that he was misinformed, and that the sale of the books was arranged by a small clique within the congregation rather than by the majority of its membership? Is it possible that there was collusion between the two Chaos and the delegates, and that the 400 *taels* of silver ended up in the pockets of the brothers or was split with the delegates?

As a matter of fact, specific charges that the delegates had cheated the *kehillah* of its manuscripts would later be made by the Kaifeng Jews themselves and repeated in a letter (of dubious authenticity, however) addressed by a Jewish resident of China to his cousin, the chief rabbi of Alsace, as well as in a report sent by a London resident, whose religious affiliations are not known, to a Jewish newspaper in New York.[17]

In 1867, when as he would later claim the Silesian Jew J. L. Liebermann was in Kaifeng, he discussed the transfer of the synagogal documents with several members of the *kehillah* who told him, as he put it, that they "used to have several [Torah] scrolls, but foreigners who came here, and of whom we did not know whether they were Israelites or not, took them from us. But when they once had possession of them, they kept them."[18] Liebermann, however, was not inclined to believe this story. "It seemed to me," he wrote, having been told by a local Muslim leader that money had changed hands when the books left the synagogue, "that these [Torah] scrolls were purchased for a very high price from the poor of that town." Liebermann was apparently left with the impression that the Jews with whom he talked were reluctant to admit to a fellow Jew that they had traded away their sacred texts for money, and that they were trying to cover up the sale by attributing the loss of the books to a fraudulent act perpetrated by the delegates. Yet, while he challenged the veracity of the charge that the strangers had absconded with the Torah scrolls and the other manuscripts, Liebermann did not take issue with the claim of the Jews that they were not sure whether these same strangers "were Israelites or not."

The decision of the Chao brothers to leave Kaifeng and accompany the delegates to Shanghai sheds no light on the questions posed here. They may have left under suspicion, or in the expectation that they soon would find themselves suspect. Chao Chin-ch'eng, the older and less educated of the two, remained in Shanghai for a relatively brief period and then subsequently returned home. Chao Wen-k'uei, a teacher, stayed on in Shanghai permanently. On his death, he was buried in the communal cemetery which the nineteenth-century Jewish emigrants from Central Asia and Europe had established in Shanghai.[19]

Although the Jews of Kaifeng may not have understood precisely what a Christian was, those of them who were present when Ch'iao expelled the delegates from the synagogue had heard him castigate the men as agents of an English missionary group and should have known that the delegates were not Jews. Any proposal to sell the six Torah scrolls and the smaller manuscripts should, moreover, have engendered considerable opposition within the *kehillah*, no matter who the prospective buyers were. Chao Nien-tsu, the author of the poignant letter to "the chief teacher of the Jewish religion," as well as those others who felt as he did, would certainly have raised their voices against it, and their opposition would in the end have had to be decisively overridden by the rest of the community. This may have happened, but it may also be that no more than a few Jews participated in the sale and profited from it—perhaps the poorest ones, who were wondering where their next meal was coming from, or perhaps only the brothers Chao. With the evidence currently available, in any case, it cannot be demonstrated that the transfer of the second group of Kaifeng synagogal books was carried out by means as shady as the first—or, for that matter, that it was not.

As for the Torah scrolls themselves, one was deposited in the library of the Missionary College at Hong Kong. It has since disappeared. The others, together with the smaller books, were sent to the London Society's headquarters. The London Society retained the small books and two of the Torah scrolls, and donated one each to the British Museum, the Bodleian Library at Oxford, and the University Library at Cambridge. Of the two Torah scrolls retained by the London Society, one is now at Bridwell Library, Southern Methodist University, Dallas, and the other is lost. The surviving small books are, with two known exceptions, in the possession of the Hebrew Union College, Cincinnati.[20]

Once the Torah scrolls were in Western hands they were minutely examined. They were found to contain numerous misspellings and to exhibit occasional scribal stylisms not normally occurring in scrolls written for synagogues in other parts of the world. The texts themselves, however, were in no way exceptional. The Chinese Jews, it became clear, had done their best to obey the old Deuteronomic injunction, "You shall not add anything to what I command you or take anything away from it, . . ."; and, leaving aside copyist errors, which grew more numerous as their knowledge of Hebrew waned, the texts they passed on from generation to generation were whole and unchanged. Had Domenge, Gozani, or Gaubil been able to acquire one of the Kaifeng Pentateuchs and to forward it to Europe, the theologians who studied it would quickly have discovered that nothing had been added to its text, nothing had been changed in it and, more to the point, nothing had been removed from it.

9 ❖ THE ORPHAN COLONY

B
Y the middle of the 1860s it was again possible for foreigners to venture into certain regions of China that had been
almost totally sealed off to them since 1724, first as a matter
of national policy and more recently because of the unsettled
condition of the countryside. The stretch of land lying between
Peking and Kaifeng was among the areas that could now be
traversed with a modicum of safety, and the American Protestant
missionary W. A. P. Martin became one of the first Caucasians
since the time of Gozani and Gaubil—if not the first—to cross
it. His most immediate concern, as he started on the long and
demanding journey from the imperial to the provincial capital,
and beyond, was to visit the Jews.[1]

Martin left Peking late in January 1866 or early in February.
The highways to Kaifeng, he soon realized, were far more
crowded than he had foreseen. He took tallies of the oncoming
traffic and estimated "the number of vehicles passing in the
course of a day at two hundred, employing four to five hundred
mules," all this in addition to the numerous "caravans of pilgrims
mounted on camels" which were making their way to the shrines
of Shansi. But how much better it would be, he mused, if he and
all his companions on the road could enjoy the amenities of
travel by rail rather than relying on camels or being condemned,
as he was, to alternate the whole day long between sitting in a
jolting mulecart and plodding along on foot. And why was there
no railroad? He placed the blame for this squarely on the
shoulders of the politicians and bureaucrats who controlled the
country. It was solely because of their senseless and pigheaded
stand against technological innovations, he told himself, that

there were as yet no modern transportation facilities paralleling the route he was taking.

The hostelries that a century and a half earlier had impressed Gaubil as superior to those of France held no attractions for Martin. "To arrive at a miserable inn with sore feet and aching head after driving from five in the morning till nine at night to make out a distance of forty miles," he complained, was bad enough. But, then, to have "to throw yourself down in an apartment . . . without windows, without a fire, . . . and without a softer spot than a pavement of brick on which to rest your weary limbs"—this was absolutely unbearable. He had not heeded, it would seem, or perhaps was not aware of Gaubil's sage counsel that one should carry along one's own bedding when traveling through the interior of China.

Martin tossed about fitfully night after night on the floors of inn after inn and dreamed wistfully of watching the miles roll by from the hedonistic splendors that a Peking-to-Kaifeng rail service would presumably lavish upon its passengers—only to have his reveries rudely interrupted each morning "when the crowing cock" awakened him "to another day of toil and pain," and it was again time to rise and set out dauntlessly in the direction of Kaifeng. He arrived there on the seventeenth of February, thoroughly exhausted but impatient to catch his first glimpse of the synagogue.[2] He found lodgings in the city and immediately inquired of the innkeeper how one went about getting in touch with the Jews. When the landlord could not give him a satisfactory answer, he had his bearers take him to one of the city's six mosques, where he put the same question to the mufti. The mufti, it turned out, knew about the Jews but had nothing good to say about them; to him the Jews were unbelievers. As for their synagogue, he announced with relish and to Martin's dismay that it was no longer in existence. The mufti said it had been totally razed and that the people who once worshipped there were now impoverished and dispersed. He told Martin how to get to the site it had formerly occupied.

Leaving the mosque and instructing his bearers to conduct him to the old synagogal compound, Martin was carried "through streets crowded with curious spectators" to an open square, in the center of which there stood a solitary stone. The mufti had not misled him: the synagogue was no more, having been torn down in the interval between the delegates' 1851 visit to the *kehillah* and his own. The stone was the 1489/1512 stele. He examined the inscriptions on both surfaces. Then, resting one hand on the monument, he turned to the large group of onlookers who had clustered about him and told them why he had come to Kaifeng. He recorded what ensued:

"Are there among you any of the House of Israel?" I inquired. "I am one," responded a young man whose face corroborated his assertion; and then another and another stepped forth, until I saw before me representatives of six out of the seven families into which the colony is divided. There, on that melancholy spot where the very foundations of the synagogue had been torn from the ground and there no longer remained one stone upon another, they confessed with shame and grief that their holy and beautiful house had been demolished with their own hands. It had, they said, for a long time been in a ruinous condition. They had no money to make repairs; they had lost all knowledge of the sacred tongue; the traditions of the fathers were no longer handed down, and their ritual worship had ceased to be observed. In this state of things, they had yielded to the pressure of necessity and disposed of the timbers and stones of that venerable edifice to obtain relief for their bodily wants.

That evening several Jews came to see him at his inn. He had rashly told them earlier in the day that he knew Hebrew. Having no reason to doubt his word, they had brought along a Torah scroll, from which they now asked him to read aloud. He could not, and was forced to sputter out whatever lame excuses came to mind. A few years later, as he explained in a footnote to the account he wrote of his meetings with the Jews, he had the opportunity of examining the texts of two Kaifeng Torah scrolls. "After a little practice," he commented, he was able "to read them with sufficient ease; the chief difficulty being the want of vowel-points." An extraordinary accomplishment this—unless, of course, he had made a point of learning basic Hebrew after his linguistic misadventure in Kaifeng.

17. The Rev. W. A. P. Martin, as he arrived in New York in October 1900 in the "siege costume" he had worn during the Boxer attack on Peking earlier in the year.

On the next day two Jews came again to visit Martin. This time they gave him no Hebrew texts to read or translate. He summarized what he learned from them:

> Two of them appeared in official costume, one wearing a gilt and the other a crystal button; but, far from sustaining the character of this people for thrift and worldly prosperity, they number among them none that are rich and but few who are honorable. Some, indeed, true to their hereditary instincts, are employed in a small way in banking establishments (the first man I met was a money changer); others keep fruit stores and cake shops, drive a business in old clothes, or pursue various handicrafts, while a few find employment in military service. The prevalence of rebellion in the central provinces for the last thirteen years has told sadly on the prosperity of Kaifeng, and the Jews have, not unlikely owing to the nature of their occupations, been the greatest sufferers.
>
> Their number, they estimated, though not very exactly, at from three to four hundred. They were unable to trace their tribal pedigree, keep no register, and never on any occasion assemble together as one congregation. Until recently they had a common center in their synagogue, though their liturgical service had long been discontinued. But the congregation seems to be following the fate of its building. No bond of union remains, and they are in danger of being speedily absorbed by Mohammedanism or heathenism. One of them has recently become a priest of Buddha, taking for his title *pen tau*, which signifies "one who is rooted in the knowledge of the Truth!" The large tablet that once adorned the entrance of the synagogue, bearing in gilded characters the name Israel, has been appropriated by one of the Mohammedan mosques; and some efforts have been made to draw over the people, who differ from the Moslems so little that their heathen neighbors have never been able to distinguish them by any circumstances than that of their picking the sinews out of the flesh they eat—a custom commemorative of Jacob's conflict with the angel.

Martin identified one of his visitors as "a son [grandson?] of the last of their rabbis, who some thirty or forty years ago [actually, about sixty years] died in the province of Kansu." Because the *kehillah*'s knowledge of Hebrew died with its last rabbi, the Jews had recently considered "exposing their parchments in the marketplace in hopes they might attract the attention of some wandering Jew who would be able to restore to them the language of their fathers." Whether they really did display any of the Torah scrolls in this manner is not known, but it would obviously have accomplished nothing. Circumcision was no longer practiced by any of the Jews, and intermarriage was common. Not all the old holidays and religious rites had been forgotten but none were still formally celebrated.

"Near the margin of the Poyang lake [Kiangsi Province]," Martin observed:

> there stands a lofty rock, so peculiar and solitary that it is known by the name of the "little orphan." The adjacent shore is low and level, and its kindred rocks are all on the opposite side of the lake, whence it seems to have been torn away by some violent convulsion and planted immovably in the bosom of the waters. Such to me appeared that fragment of the Israelitish nation. A rock rent from the sides of Zion by some great national catastrophe and projected into the central plain of China, it has stood there, while the centuries rolled by, sublime in its antiquity and solitude. It is now on the verge of being swallowed up by the flood of paganism, and the spectacle is a mournful one. The Jews themselves are deeply conscious of their sad situation, and the shadow of an inevitable destiny seems to be resting upon them.

Martin's sentimentally felicitous likening of the plight of the *kehillah* to that of a parentless waif caught the fancy of his readers and led Finn to call his 1872 book on the Kaifeng congregation *The Orphan Colony of the Jews in China.* The term *orphan colony* was subsequently adopted by other writers as an apt designation for the foundling *kehillah* of Kaifeng and is still used for that purpose.

Questioned by the Jews "about the destruction of their holy city and the dispersion of their tribes," as well as other vital historical matters which were fading from their collective memory, Martin "endeavored to comfort them" with the explanation that Judaism's mission on earth had not been in vain, their ancestral faith having already fulfilled much of its purpose by providing "the root" from which "Christian civilization, with all its grand results, had sprung." He did not comment on the Jews' reaction, but evidently came away from Kaifeng feeling that they could not be considered likely prospects for immediate conversion to Christianity. He concluded that a very serious and sustained effort would have to be mounted if they were ever to be brought to the cross. He preferred, in any case, to see them restored as a first step to Judaism than be lost irrevocably to Islam or any of the Chinese "heathen" creeds, and in a letter sent two years later to a Jewish newspaper in New York urged its subscribers to come at once to the aid of their lapsed coreligionists in Kaifeng. "Nothing can save them from a speedy extinction," he declared, "except the rebuilding of their synagogue, which is indispensable to give them a visible existence or rallying point and a bond of union. For the honor of Israel and of Israel's God, this ought to be done."[3] It was therefore Western Jewry's duty, he argued, to proceed without delay to finance the reconstruction of the Kaifeng synagogue.

Martin's was scarcely the voice that the readers of a Jewish periodical could be expected to heed, whether on the subject of the Chinese Jews or anything else. He was, after all, a missionary, and the people to whom he was addressing his plea would have had to be exceptionally naive to believe that he honestly wanted the members of the Kaifeng *kehillah* to become sincere and pious Jews again. The truth was, of course, that he wanted nothing of the sort. He had, in fact, already candidly defined his true objective—the Christianization of the *kehillah*—in a letter which he had sent to a colleague in Shanghai named Kaufmann and which was soon afterward reproduced in print.[4] It would be highly desirable to dispatch a missionary to the Kaifeng Jews, he told Kaufmann, and, luckily, it should not be overly difficult to find a qualified man for the job, for the dialect commonly spoken in Kaifeng was virtually the same as the one used in Peking. But, he also warned Kaufmann, it was futile to hope that any conversionary successes could be scored until there was a synagogue in Kaifeng to draw the Jews together. Once this synagogue, which need not be "so large or splendid as its predecessor," was in place, a missionary ought to be able to bring its congregants to Christ. Then, quoting from the prophet Haggai (2:9), "the glory of this latter House [the Second Temple] shall be greater than that of the former one [the First Temple]," he assured Kaufmann that Haggai's words could be made to come true in a Chinese Jewish setting if a missionary were on hand to see to it that Christ also "would be there."

The extraordinary stories brought back by the delegates and by Martin did not escape the notice of the Jews of the West, but neither did the spate of wild tales that sprouted like weeds around the ancient offshoot of the House of Israel that had so incredibly been transplanted to the alien soil of China. The most widely circulated and persistent of these fables surfaced early in the 1860s and reemerged intermittently until 1911, and perhaps beyond that. It alleged that during the Opium War of 1839–42 a British naval commander piloted his vessel deep into China and there discovered a previously unknown city of a million inhabitants, every last one of them a Jew. Understandably, the names of the officer, his ship, the waterway along which he sailed, and the city he found were never revealed. In some tellings, the story was made even more colorful by having the commander of the English war vessel portrayed as being himself a Jew.[5]

Another absurd tale of this genre was advanced by I. J. Benjamin in a book of travels that was published initially in French, in 1856, and then translated into German, English, and Hebrew.[6] Benjamin, who wandered indefatigably over much of the world seeking out exotic Jewish settlements, wrote of his experiences under the nom de plume Benjamin II, a harmless conceit conveying the implication that he was treading in the footsteps of the famous twelfth-century traveler Rabbi Benjamin of Tudela.

Benjamin II says that while he was in Canton he was told by some Jewish (Caucasian) traders that "on the other side of the Yellow River" there lived a people who every two or three years sent caravans to Canton to deal in spices, dyes, tea, and other commodities. These people, Benjamin states, are thought to be Jewish, but since it is not possible for him to visit them his readers will have to be satisfied with a few pertinent comments provided by someone other than himself. He has a copy of a letter, he explains, which Rabbi Arnaud Aron of Strasbourg received from his cousin Aaron, a resident of one of the coastal cities of China, presumably Shanghai. The copy in Benjamin's possession was made for him in Strasbourg by Rabbi Aron on November 13, 1855. It concludes with a declaration by the rabbi that he had personally transcribed the text "character by character from the letter written by my esteemed cousin Aaron, who sent it to me from the land of the Chinese." Benjamin prints the rabbi's transcript in its entirety.

Aaron tells his rabbinical cousin that he has had several meetings in the past year "with brethren of ours of the House of Israel, Honan Province," whom he entertained in his home, with whom he conversed in Hebrew, and who presented him with some of their Hebrew books. He offers several tidbits of information concerning the Kaifeng *kehillah*—including the fact that its members have forgotten their Hebrew—which he has obviously derived, although not always without error, from the diaries of the delegates. He does not explain, however, where his house guests acquired their ability to speak the language of their forefathers. Presumably, the Jews who visited him—if any did—were the brothers Chao; and if they carried on any discussions with him in Hebrew, they would have had to pick up their ability to speak the language from missionaries to whom it was probably no more a conversational medium than Ugaritic.

According to Aaron, there are Jews in many parts of the Chinese Empire. In "Kang-chiou" there are 10,000 of them; in "Chang-chou," 1,000–2,000; and in "Arnoy," for which no specific figure is given, their numbers are merely represented as being very large. As for the delegates who have sought out the Jews, they are "stealers of Jewish souls" and are guilty of having robbed the *kehillah* of an ancient Torah scroll that has since been forwarded to England. The delegates, Aaron asserts, first asked the *kehillah* for the loan of the Torah scroll in order to copy it, but once they had it in their hands, they demanded that the congregation set a price for it. This was simply a swindler's ruse, he claims, since the delegates had already decided to embezzle the funds that had been entrusted to them for the express purpose of buying the congregation's books and had no intention of paying the Jews for them. Prudently, they decamped from Kaifeng with both the Torah scroll and the money their principals had allocated to them. This very year, Aaron goes on, several Jews have come here from Kaifeng to reclaim their Torah. As the missionaries refuse to arrange for its return, the Jews plan to come back in three months to present their case before the British consul in the hope of obtaining redress for the shameful injustice being inflicted upon them by the missionaries.

Why, one wonders, did Benjamin print such a letter? If it was completely a figment of his imagination—and there is absolutely no basis for believing this—he was painting himself into a corner by attributing the preparation of its transcript to Rabbi Aron, who besides being well known in Jewish circles by virtue of his position as chief rabbi of Alsace was perhaps even better known as the compiler of the very popular *Prières d'un coeur Israélite*. The rabbi would surely have become vociferously and publicly indignant if a letter falsely linked to him showed up in print, and it is of course unlikely in the extreme that a man of his stature would concoct such a letter and forward it to Benjamin. The probability is that a cousin of the rabbi did actually write him from China and claim to have spoken in Hebrew with Jews from Kaifeng, and that both the rabbi and Benjamin believed his story. This cousin may merely have been embellishing a wild tale he had heard by asserting that he himself had been involved in dealings with the Chinese Jews. Or he may have been an out-and-out hoaxer. His hoax, if it was no more than that, was successful enough to create quite a stir in the ranks of European and American Jewry and to be accepted as totally factual by nearly everybody who read Rabbi Aron's transcription of his letter or heard of it.

Another letter, this one originating in London and printed in a New York journal in 1859, told a story somewhat akin to that related to Rabbi Aron by his cousin.[7] The author, identified merely as J. C., did not claim to have met any Kaifeng Jews himself but, having picked up some information about them from an unnamed acquaintance who said that he had personally met several, explained that he wanted to pass it along to readers in America:

They [the two Jews who accompanied the delegates to Shanghai] arrived there in July 1851, and soon afterwards my informant became acquainted with them. On visiting them he found them in possession of six fine Scrolls of the Law, one of them of very considerable dimensions, and several other manuscripts. With four of these they had subsequently to part. The two Jews, one of whom was a merchant and the other the schoolmaster of the colony, paid frequent visits to my informant, and even stayed for some length of time in his house. He described them as well-informed men, of great command of language, and most gentlemanly in their bearing, especially the schoolmaster, in whose conduct there was an extraordinary propriety. They strictly observed the Sabbath, and seemed scrupulously to adhere to the dietary laws, as they never would take their meals with their host, and always superintended the preparation of their food. They were, however, unacquainted with Hebrew, the last rabbi who understood it having died about fifty years ago; nor did they practice circumcision, as no man knew how to perform the operation. The colony had dwindled to two hundred, who intermarried among themselves. They carried on all kinds of trade, but were exceedingly poor. Their standard of education was nevertheless very high, much higher than among the rest of the population, their small colony numbering eleven graduates. . . .

Their second visit, in 1852 (the teacher did not come, but instead of him a brother of the merchant, who was blind in one eye), turned out most unsatisfactory to them. Differences arose between them and Dr. Medhurst, the former maintaining that they had never intended to sell the precious relics of their ancestral literature, which they prized above everything, but only to allow the doctor to examine or copy them; and the latter asserting that they had been purchased for him by his emissaries. It is most probable that the Jews were defrauded, and the doctor deceived by his Chinese messengers. This is the belief of my informant himself, who has a very poor opinion of Chinese morality in monetary matters. Nothing is more likely than that the two Chinese, who acted as brokers in the matter, pocketed the purchase money handed to them by the doctor, and made him believe that the manuscripts entrusted to him for examination were his property. The disappointment and grief of the Jews may be imagined when they discovered that their Scrolls had been shipped to Europe. Disagreeable scenes took place between them and the doctor, and they would have had to return to their native city penniless, had my informant not humanely assisted them with fifty dollars.

J. C. was evidently not aware that the two Jews who came to Shanghai in 1851 with the delegates were the brothers Chao. The teacher, Chao Wen-k'uei, is known to have remained in Shanghai until his death. The merchant would have been Chao Chin-ch'eng, but who the man with the bad eye was—the one identified by J. C. as "a brother of the merchant"—is unclear. As J. C. explained it, in any event, the merchant and his brother, "before they left in October 1852 . . . agreed with my informant to send six youths to Shanghai, four of them to be sent to America, and two to be educated there by the missionaries of that denomination. A strict observance of all Jewish rites in the education of these youths was stipulated by them. Nothing, however, my informant told me, has since been heard of them. This, he said, was probably owing to the outbreak of the Chinese rebellion, which soon afterwards took place, the insurgents being in possession of several important places on the road between Kaifeng and Shanghai, and thus intercepting all communication between these towns."

The Jews presented his informant, J. C. added, "with two of their Hebrew manuscripts, which are now here in London." One, he discovered, contained a portion of Deuteronomy, the other a prayer for the New Year, according to the Sephardic rite. J. C. who, like so many others, exaggerated the age of the Jewish settlements in China and the length of their isolation there, did not know what to make of the prayer. "The historical problem to be solved," he wrote, "is how did a form of prayer of comparatively so modern a date reach a colony which has professedly been isolated for at least eighteen centuries, as may be inferred from the circumstances that it had never heard of Christianity until the missionaries, in comparatively modern times, spoke of it?"

As early as 1842 Occidental Jewry was already discussing the feasibility of stationing a representative in Kaifeng, Henri Hirsch announcing that year in Paris that he was prepared to travel to China and serve as teacher to the *kehillah*. The Opium War had just come to an end, leading Hirsch to conclude—much too prematurely, as it turned out—that the Chinese would now permit foreigners to wander about freely in all parts of the empire. He was compelled to abandon his project, in any case, because of ill health.[8]

When the accounts of the delegates' two trips to Kaifeng reached London, Dr. Nathan Marcus Adler, chief rabbi of the British Empire, wrote to the directors of the Shanghai branch of the Sassoon banking house requesting whatever information they could provide concerning the *kehillah*, and also asking their opinion of a plan then fermenting in his mind for assigning one or more rabbis to the task of establishing a Jewish school in Kaifeng. The Sassoons' response was far from encouraging. "We beg to state," they replied on July 21, 1853, apropos Adler's first request, "that we are hardly qualified to satisfy Your Reverence on that point, regarding which ourselves, if not all our neighbors, are quite in the dark." Nor could they see much hope for getting one or more rabbis to Kaifeng. "As to our opinion on the probable result of able ministers being sent out for the purpose of recalling and receiving into the bosom of Judaism all such scattered brethren," they informed Adler, "we beg to state that little or nothing could be done unless such ministers are masters of the Chinese language, and have means to get into the interior of the country, where they may, by constant and habitual intercourse with the natives, meet with some of them, but this, we think also impracticable at the present time."[9]

The desire to resurrect the Kaifeng *kehillah* was not restricted to Adler alone, numerous other Jewish leaders in Europe and America having become equally interested in the problem.[10] In the United States, Rabbi Isaac Leeser, then editor of the Jewish periodical *Occident*, deeply moved by the plight of the Chinese Jews, appealed to American Jewry for funds with which to rescue them from oblivion. "The Jewish mind in America," he told his readers, "will not be so entirely selfish as to close itself against the appeals of religion and humanity." He also sounded the alarm. Time was short, he warned, and if the Jews of America did not bestir themselves on behalf of the *kehillah*, there were others who would, and in ways that American Jewry would find shameful. "The agents in China of the Mission Society of the Seventh-Day Baptist sect," he reported sadly, were preparing "to *benefit* the poor Hebrews" of Kaifeng. How? By bringing them over to Christianity. To prove his point he reprinted a letter fowarded by a representative of that denomination, Solomon Carpenter, to its journal, the *Sabbath Recorder*, urging that a Seventh-Day Baptist missionary be dispatched to the *kehillah*. Carpenter had met the Chao brothers in Shanghai and gotten to know them well. "They seemed to feel much at home with us," he wrote, "on account of the identity of our Sabbath day and theirs. They manifested a desire for instruction, both for themselves, their children, and their people. As often as circumstances would allow, while in Shanghai, they attended our little meeting on the Sabbath. My teacher Tong, who was deeply interested in them, as we all were, using their dialect, took great pains to instruct them."[11]

In London, Adler, just as fearful as Rabbi Leeser of losing the *kehillah* to the missionaries, sent off a letter to a Jewish merchant who lived in Hong Kong and had business connections in Shanghai, asking more or less the same questions he had put to the Sassoons. The merchant's reply was as pessimistic as the Sassoons' had been, but he suggested that the practical course, at least temporarily, might be to help the *kehillah* by providing funds for its sustenance, an act which would not only keep it from falling apart physically but might also encourage it to hold on until Western Jewry could eventually come to its spiritual rescue. Disappointed, but bowing to the inevitable, Adler transmitted the merchant's words of counsel to Leeser, who promptly issued a plea to the American Jewish community to provide the necessary funds. "We appeal again," he wrote, "to our leading men and our ministers, and indeed to all who may see these few lines, to endeavor to do something to wipe away the disgrace which would forever attach to our name should we, one and all, leave our castoff brothers to the cruel mercy of those who endeavor to ensnare them. For once, we beg our leading men, lay aside your jealousies, your want of confidence in each other, and act for the

Lord's sake, since strangers to our faith strive to deprive many of God's law."[12]

Deeply disturbed though he was by the efforts of the missionaries to convert the *kehillah*, Leeser nevertheless found a measure of consolation in the texts they had recently published of the synagogal prayers secured by the delegates. His readings of these ancient prayers—far older, he deduced, than any yet discovered—bolstered his argument, it seemed to him, that the objections being raised by the leaders of the Reform movement regarding the legitimacy of the prevailing liturgy of the Orthodox synagogue were utterly without foundation. In a confrontation between the advocates of Reform and the upholders of Orthodoxy, he therefore informed his readers, "the adherents of the ancient system of worship would come off conquerors in the argument, if the form of prayer of the Chinese Jews is to be appealed to as the umpire."[13]

Leeser's continuing publicization of the abject condition of the Chinese Jews brought him some surprising if belated intelligence about them from a most unexpected quarter, the gold country of California. The news was provided by Samuel Hyman Cohen who, having served as founding secretary of Congregation Shearith Israel in San Francisco, still retained membership in the synagogue although he had since moved to the small mining settlement of Auburn, Placer County, more than a hundred miles away.

Cohen had spent six years in China, four of them in Shanghai. In June 1849 he sailed for San Francisco, drawn there, apparently, by the exciting reports that gold had just been discovered in California.

During his stay in Shanghai, Cohen wrote Leeser on August 25, 1853, he became acquainted with a native of Kaifeng who identified himself as a Jew and who, as a much too trusting Leeser put it, "finding that Mr. C. did not understand *shehitah* [the ritual method of slaughtering meat] refused at first to have any conversation with him, because he pronounced him unclean, and wondered how a Jew could travel away from his native land without knowing this. But when Mr. C. had satisfied him that he was a Jew by exhibiting his prayer books, *mezuzoth, arba kanfoth,* and *tefillin,* he gave him an invitation to come and see him at Kaifeng. . . . As far as Mr. Cohen recollects, he was told by the Jew that the city in which he lived is situated about 900 or 1,000 miles inland from Shanghai on the Yellow River, and that about 2,000 Jews resided in his district, and again as many 100 miles farther. The man whom Mr. Cohen conversed with understood Hebrew."[14]

Anxious to visit the Jews, Cohen applied to the British Consul at Shanghai for a passport, only to have his request turned down on the grounds that the treaty then existing between China and England contained a clause prohibiting foreigners from traveling inland. Undeterred, Cohen appealed to three leading Protestant missionaries to intercede in his behalf: Dr. W. H. Medhurst, Rev. Samuel S. Schuck of the Seventh-Day Baptist Mission, and Bishop William J. Boone of the American Episcopal Church. They could not, or would not, help him; but although he was forced to give up his plans to go inland, he remained convinced that individuals with more influence than he personally possessed could secure the necessary permission "by giving a sufficient fee to the Governor and paying the expense of the men to be sent as a protection, which would not be much."

Cohen thought that the journey could be accomplished with considerably less danger than had been suggested. He himself had ventured seventy miles out of Shanghai without encountering any difficulties, and he saw no reason why others could not do the same, and even get as far as Kaifeng. He warned, however, that a Westerner should not try to travel deeply into the interior without a suitable disguise. Chinese dress would have to be worn, and the traveler would be wise "to have the hair shaved to the crown and wear what is left in a long tail, as the Chinamen do when they come here, and to remove part of the eyebrows also, and to wear no hair on the face." The safest part of the year for attempting an expedition to Kaifeng, he advised, was the winter season, since a Westerner could then mask portions of his face, as the Chinese were accustomed to do. "In the cold weather," he told Leeser, "the Chinese wear a cover over their heads, which partly conceals their face."

Cohen's letter persuaded Leeser that sending a teacher or rabbi to Kaifeng was not to be ruled out as either overly perilous or necessarily doomed to failure. He was especially interested in Cohen's evaluation of the effectiveness of the missionaries he had met during his four years in Shanghai. "Mr. Cohen," he observed, "does not speak in very flattering terms of the labors of the Protestant missionaries who, he says, live at their ease in fine houses, with good salaries, and seldom venture more than eight or ten miles from town, and convert the [local] Chinese, whom they send out in their stead." When it came to the Jesuit missionaries, however, it was an entirely different matter. Five Italian members of the Society of Jesus had arrived in Shanghai in 1845, five more in 1846, and still another five in 1847. These men went personally into the countryside. By May 1849, Cohen estimated, the fifteen Jesuits had converted "upwards of 40,000 Chinese to their faith." A Father Buffo had even told him that the figure was actually "upwards of 60,000." What would happen to the *kehillah* if these awesomely effective Jesuits should decide to extend their sphere of action to Honan Province?

Horrendously exaggerated though they were, Cohen's statistics alarmed Leeser. A Jewish expedition to Kaifeng, he thundered, must be launched immediately, before the Christian missionaries— Catholic or Protestant, it made no difference to him—could subvert the *kehillah* once and for all. American Jewry, Leeser stressed, would "present a sorry figure before the world" if it sat on its hands and let the missionaries destroy China's Jews. "We owe it to ourselves," he concluded, "not to be asleep on our post when our aid is so much needed."

On November 11, 1853, Robert Lyon, editor of the Jewish periodical *Asmonean,* reprinted the story Leeser had written about Cohen. Although less enthusiastic than Leeser regarding the feasibility of getting one or more Jewish emissaries to Kaifeng, he was swayed by Cohen's insistence that it could be done, and now added his voice to the growing clamor for sending an expedition to the *kehillah.* But within days after the Cohen account appeared in the *Asmonean,* Lyon received a copy of the letter the Sassoons had written to Rabbi Adler on July 21, 1853, the letter that stated pointblank that travel into the interior of China was still far too hazardous to be risked. Lyon reproduced the Sassoon letter on the twenty-fifth of November.

The Sassoon letter made it clear to the more practical-minded Jewish leaders in both Britain and the United States that other means for providing help to the Kaifeng Jews would have to be found than that of dispatching teachers or rabbis to them. Nevertheless, some outstanding Jews refused to accept the Sassoons' opinion as the final word on the matter and kept demanding that a program be immediately instituted to bring the *kehillah* back into the mainstream of Judaism. Leeser, among those who refused to stand still, continued to prod the Jews of America to take on the responsibility for rescuing the remnants of Chinese Jewry.

The Jews of New Orleans were the first to respond to Leeser's plea for help. Under the leadership of Rabbi James K. Gutheim, and with the financial backing of the ever-generous Judah Touro, they chartered an organization known as the Hebrew Foreign Mission of New Orleans, whose express purpose was "the amelioration of the spiritual, social, and political conditions of the Jews in foreign lands." As an integral part of its program the newly founded society proposed to sponsor missions to remote Jewish communities and to establish and maintain schools "to rekindle the expiring lamps of religion in such settlements." Since the *kehillah* at Kaifeng was to be the starting point for its ambitious plans, the society obligated itself to contribute £100 to Rabbi Adler, "to be expended by him in educating the Chinese Jewish young men."[15] How Adler was to get this done was not spelled out, but the society may have felt that he would be able at the very least to have the *kehillah* send some of its young people to Shanghai or to the West for the schooling they so sadly lacked.

The American response was not limited to New Orleans, whose efforts on behalf of Kaifeng Jewry were in any case interrupted by the devastating yellow fever epidemic that swept Southern Louisiana shortly after the formation of the Hebrew Foreign Mission. Funds were collected from Jewish congregations in various parts of the United States. Philadelphia, Atlanta, and

Richmond made their contributions. The city of Mobile promised fifty dollars. New York wondered whether to organize a missionary society similar to the one in New Orleans and to include the Chinese Jews in its program, but decided for one reason or another to put the matter off. In San Francisco, the most fervid supporter of the campaign to rehabilitate the *kehillah* of Kaifeng turned out to be Rabbi Julius Eckman. In 1852, either unaware of the dangers involved or willing to risk them, he had written Adler from Mobile (from which, two years later, he moved to California) that he was personally prepared to travel to Kaifeng and, once there, devote several years of his life to the task of teaching the tenets of Judaism to the *kehillah*. He did not know a word of Chinese, Eckman confessed, but he was sure that this minor handicap could be fairly easily overcome. He intended to take along an Anglo-Chinese dictionary, he explained to Adler, from which his prospective students would in short order undoubtedly succeed in teaching themselves enough English to follow the course of instruction he proposed to offer in that language.[16] Adler, understandably, did not consider Eckman's plan either practical or prudent. Disappointed that he could not gain the support of the chief rabbi, Eckman now raised his voice on behalf of any and all efforts designed to help the Jews of China. Nearly a decade later, however, he might have been able to search out eight Kaifeng Jews who had come to California and try to persuade them to become his pupils—if the notices of their arrival there that appeared in the *Jewish Chronicle* (London) are to be credited. "We reported about a year ago," the *Chronicle* declared on August 30, 1861, "that there was a Chinaman at Sacramento who did not work on the Sabbath day." Now, however, the *Chronicle* announced, the latest vessel to dock at San Francisco following a voyage from China had carried "two Hebrew merchants . . . who stated that there were seven Jewish Chinamen brought to California in the ship as coolies." How did the *Chronicle* learn about the seven very recent Chinese Jewish arrivals in California? Through "Mr. Benjamin, the traveler, from whom we have the report. As there is no doubt of its truth, inquiries will consequently be made."[17]

The American movement to rescue the Kaifeng Jews was

brought to an abrupt halt by the outbreak of the Civil War. After Appomattox, with peace restored, the matter came to life again when the *Occident* printed an article reviewing the steps previously taken in the United States, with respect to the Chinese Jews, and reminding its readers of Judah Touro's bequest of $5,000 to the New Orleans society for use in its missionary program.[18] The *Occident* expressed the hope that the Touro legacy had been invested soundly and had "escaped the wreck" experienced by so many Jewish organizational investments in the course of the war. If the money was not lost, the article went on, it would now be appropriate to dip into it on behalf of the Chinese Jews. But the New Orleans Hebrew Foreign Mission chose to react unfavorably. Beset by urgent problems much closer to home than the Orient, and no longer in any position to carry out the terms of its charter, it decided instead to disburse the Touro legacy in Louisiana to Jewish families that had been impoverished by the fighting. In the aftermath of the war, numerous other Jewish communities, North and South, were similarly compelled to restrict their philanthropic endeavors to the rehabilitation of their own people, and the enthusiasm for rushing to the aid of Chinese Jewry subsided.[19] Nevertheless, their interest in the *kehillah* did not flicker out entirely, and in 1869 the Board of Delegates of American Israelites contributed $200.00 to a fund then being raised to send the French rabbi Joseph Halévy to Kaifeng. In this venture the Board of Delegates was working jointly with the Alliance Israélite Universelle and Rabbi Adler's group, but the project was abandoned when the several other Jewish organizations that were invited to participate declined to do so.[20]

As the American Civil War raged on, European Jewry realized that whatever assistance could be provided for the *kehillah* in the foreseeable future would have to come from Europe rather than America. In 1864 Benjamin II, then in London, let it be known that he would gladly undertake the risky trip to Kaifeng if funds could be found to cover the out-of-pocket expenses which would be incurred. This was not the first time he had volunteered to return to the Orient and seek out the various exotic Jewish communities said to be there, especially the one in Kaifeng. Four years earlier, while in New Orleans, he was sure that he had finally gotten the financial backing he needed for such an enterprise. On April 19, 1860, Rabbi Gutheim, acting in his capacity as secretary of the city's Hebrew Foreign Mission, had even written him of the board of directors' decision, arrived at on the tenth of the month, "that the sum of $300.00 be paid annually to Mr. Israel Joseph Benjamin from Falticeni in Moldavia from the treasury of this society, for three successive years, to defray the expenses of this seasoned traveler in his contemplated voyage to Arabia, Malabar, and China for the purpose of discovering the condition of our fellow Jews in those lands and to report upon it."[21] And on the twenty-ninth of April, appropriate announcements having been published two days previously in the local newspapers, the Jews of New Orleans met and voted to form the Benjamin Society, whose sole raison d'être would be to help subsidize the traveler's trip to the Middle East and the Orient. "Thirty-five members," Benjamin subsequently reported, "were accepted immediately and paid their dues at once [$5.00 annually, per member]."

So far, so good—and for the moment it looked as if Benjamin's financial problems were solved. But, he then went on, the money was turned over "to a member of the Executive Board and, for all I know, he may still have it. Not only was the money not received by me, but I have the loss of about $18.00 to complain of in this affair. I was billed for the announcements and for the hall in which the meeting was held. I paid these bills believing that I

18. I. J. Benjamin (Benjamin II).

would surely be reimbursed out of the money that had been collected; but, when I asked the member of the Board for what I had spent, he refused to pay me. I believe I know the probable reason: it lies in what took place later."

What took place later was that once the discussion regarding the financing of Benjamin's trip was concluded, S. Friedlander, president of Shaarei Chesed Congregation, asked the audience to remain a bit longer for the purpose of considering a proposal, which had recently been submitted to him, for having the New Orleans Jewish community commission a bronze bust of its deceased benefactor Judah Touro. Benjamin, outraged, leaped to his feet and in no uncertain terms denounced the proposal as an impious violation of the old Jewish ban against graven images. His outburst broke up the meeting.

A day later, Benjamin buttonholed Rabbi Gutheim and demanded that he come out publicly against the plan for the erection of the bust—and was scandalized when Gutheim not only refused to do so but even declared himself in favor of the project. As far as he was concerned, the rabbi explained, the prohibition against graven images was outdated, and he could see nothing sinful in setting up a likeness in bronze or stone of the most philanthropic Jew in the history of New Orleans.

Before long, Benjamin succeeded in making the Touro memorial project a cause célèbre in Jewish circles on both sides of the Atlantic. He started by firing off an indignant letter to the editor of New Orleans's Jewish newspaper the *Cornerstone*, in which he forcefully demanded that Touro's memory be perpetuated by giving his name to a new hospital or orphan asylum, arguing again that under no circumstances could it be either appropriate or permissible to set up a bust to honor a Jew.[22] A contrary opinion appeared a few days later in the local daily the *Picayune*, this one written by Benjamin da Silva, sexton of Gutheim's synagogue. Benjamin II retaliated with a slashing attack on da Silva in the next issue of the *Cornerstone*, with the result (as he charged) that da Silva's son threatened to murder him. Undaunted by the younger da Silva's threat, the prospective victim went openly about the city for the next few days, daring his would-be assailant to make the attempt. Nothing happened.

Within a matter of weeks, Benjamin's persistence brought the problem of the Touro memorial to the pages of the *Occident,* the *Jewish Messenger,* and other widely distributed Jewish periodicals. This, in turn, made it advisable to have the matter adjudicated by a group of impartial rabbinical authorities—Adler (London), Samson Raphael Hirsch (Frankfurt-am-Main), S. L. Rapoport (Prague), and Zacharias Frankel (Breslau).[23] In the interim, the Benjamin Society was quietly disbanded by the mortified and irate Jews of New Orleans, leaving their brethren in faraway Kaifeng to live out their days without having the pleasure of meeting the irascible Mr. Benjamin or any other emissary from the Crescent City.

With the hubbub over the Touro memorial receding from memory, Rabbi Adler, S. D. Sassoon, and a coterie of other leading English Jews, agreeing that Benjamin was still the most qualified man they had to send on a mission to the Jews of Kaifeng, organized a society to sponsor such a venture and inserted an appeal for contributions supplementing their own in the *Jewish Chronicle* of April 29, 1864,—precisely four days before Benjamin died unexpectedly of an ailment he had contracted some weeks previously. Adler thereupon wrote again to David Sassoon & Company, this time to suggest that a few of the *kehillah*'s youngsters be fetched to Shanghai for preliminary indoctrination and then be transferred to Europe or the United States for more advanced schooling. The goal he had in mind was to provide the *kehillah* with qualified teachers of its own. All that came out of his efforts, however, was that two Kaifeng boys were brought to Shanghai as guests of the city's Caucasian Jewish community, where, to the dismay of all concerned, they soon became so homesick that it was decided to send them back home.

Toward the end of March 1867, three young Kaifeng Jews arrived unexpectedly in Peking, bringing with them three of their people's remaining Torah scrolls. These they deposited in the custody of the Reverend Joseph Edkins, both for safekeeping and for display to potential purchasers. Whether they were acting on behalf of the *kehillah* or had simply expropriated the Torahs for their own gain is not known. W. A. P. Martin bought two of the Torah scrolls, retaining one for himself and letting his friend S. Wells Williams have the other. The third was acquired in 1870 by the Austrian diplomat Karl von Scherzer.[24]

In Peking, the young visitors met the Reverend (later Bishop) Samuel Isaac Joseph Schereschewsky. Schereschewsky, by birth a Jew and thoroughly schooled in the academic disciplines of Judaism before he went over to Protestantism, was now working as a missionary in China. He did not have a high opinion of the three youths. They had expressed an interest in being taught the principles of Judaism and Christianity. This pleased him. "But," he observed caustically, "they are perfectly unconscious of the difference between Judaism and Christianity. . . . They take it for granted that the religion preached by the missionaries here is identical with their own forgotten belief."[25] It was not their ignorance alone which distressed him, however, but their general attitudes as well. Even worse, two of them turned out to be opium addicts.

The sudden appearance in Peking of the three young Jews, coming as it did on the heels of Martin's visit to the *kehillah*, suggested to the missionaries that an investigation should be conducted in Kaifeng itself to determine if the time was ripe for the establishment of a permanent mission there. Since the dangers associated with travel to the interior seemed for the moment less appreciable than they had been in the past, Schereschewsky was urged to go to Honan and look into the matter. He agreed to make the trip and, as his biographer relates, "shaved the front of his head in the Chinese manner, donned Chinese costume, and went."[26]

Schereschewsky's formal report of his visit to Kaifeng is no longer extant, but a summation of his experiences there, composed by his friend Blodget on July 23, 1867, has been preserved:

> Mr. Schereschewsky has returned from his visit to the Jews in Kaifeng. He was fifteen days on the road in reaching the place and spent about twenty-five days there. He reports that there are in the colony 200 or 300 families of Jewish descent and that a fair proportion of them are in good circumstances. . . . They have entirely lost their religion and are scarcely distinguishable in any way from the heathen. They have idols in

their houses, and ancestral tablets. One has become a Buddhist priest. They intermarry with the natives and have ceased to practice the rite of circumcision. In features, dress, habits, religion, they are essentially Chinese. . . . They cannot read the Law, although the manuscripts are still in their possession. . . . It is not known that they have ever had any religious works in the Chinese language.

Mr. Schereschewsky was well received by literary men from regions distant from the city, and they visited him in great numbers to obtain books and converse. The natives of the place, however, felt differently. The literary men were jealous of him as the propagator of a foreign religion. One pasted a vile placard abusing him and foreigners generally. At last they raised a mob, . . . frantic with rage, threatening violence, beating an old priest, his host, and vociferating, "We are the disciples of Confucius and Mencius." He [Schereschewsky] was compelled to leave.[27]

Schereschewsky seems to have made no great effort to meet any representatives of the *kehillah* during his unnerving stay in Kaifeng, even though this was one of the principal objectives of his trip. His allusions to the city's Jews, as recorded by Blodget, are consequently based on what he learned about them at second hand in conversations with non-Jews.

On an unspecified day in July 1867, either shortly after Schereschewsky's departure from the Honan capital or perhaps while he was still there, the Jewish merchant J. L. Liebermann came to Kaifeng and made himself known to the *kehillah*. He is generally thought to be the first non-Chinese Jew to have visited the congregation in centuries. He was perhaps also the first Westerner in modern times, Jewish or Christian, who traveled to Kaifeng to see the Jews on his own initiative rather than on behalf of a religious organization.

Still, as is all too often the case with stories dealing with the Kaifeng Jews, there is some question as to whether the claim later made by Liebermann of having traveled to the Honan capital and met its Jews is to be taken seriously or brushed aside as totally untrue. Historians have been prone to accept his notes describing his expedition to Kaifeng as an authentic account of a trip that was actually made, with the result that Liebermann's report has become one of the most trusted primary sources in the entire field of Sino-Judaic studies. As far as is known, its first appearance in print occurs in the 1878–79 annual report of the Anglo-Jewish Association, where it is captioned "Notes on the Jews of China (translated from a portion of a Hebrew letter [from a series of ten letters, actually] addressed by Mr. J. L. Liebermann to his father in Bielitz, Austrian Silesia)."[28] A footnote explains that "Mr. J. L. Liebermann, a merchant in Vienna, traveled in 1867 in China, where he was engaged in the pursuits of commerce, and at the wish of his father he prepared there the present notes of his travels. He was the first European Jew who had communications with the remnants of the Jews in China. . . . In 1877 he called on the Rev. A. Löwy, who requested him to send him these notes of travel, which, it was thought, might be translated for insertion in the Annual Report. Mr. Liebermann having complied most obligingly, Mr. Löwy is desired by the President and the Council to tender Mr. Liebermann their cordial thanks for this valuable and important contribution to a knowledge of the condition of the Jews in China."[29]

Yet the *Jewish Chronicle,* which reprinted the Löwy version of the Liebermann report in its issue of July 11, 1879, had nearly twelve years earlier published a three-part English rendition of a somewhat emotional Hebrew letter dated 2 Heshvan 5628 (October 31, 1867), Shantung Province, and signed by an early professional photographer, one Aaron Halevi Fink, telling of a visit he purportedly made to the Kaifeng Jews for an eleven-day period beginning 2 Tammuz 5624 (July 6, 1864).[30] The original Hebrew text of Fink's letter appeared at about the same time as the *Jewish Chronicle*'s English version in the Hebrew journal *Ha-Maggid,* and was later reprinted in a book called *Metziat Aseret ha-Shebatim* [Discovery of the Ten Tribes] (Warsaw, 1900) and again in a second edition of the same book, this time entitled *Sefer ha-Brit ha-Hadash* [Book of the New Covenant] (Petrikov, 1911). Fink's story differs in no more than a few minor respects from Liebermann's; and not only are the revelations in the two accounts uncannily similar in the details they offer, but the order and manner in which they are presented (and some of the phraseology as well) are also very much alike. It is obvious to even the most casual reader that the tale told in one of the two letters was either plagiarized from the other or that both stories were pirated from an unknown third source. A week after they had completed the printing of the Fink account, incidentally, the editors of the *Jewish Chronicle*, totally unaware at this time of the existence of Liebermann, stated that they considered Fink's report entirely factual.[31] When they published the Liebermann material in 1879, however, they seem to have forgotten completely about Fink.

Which, if either, of the two tales should be believed? Fink's has the advantage of priority, since it was printed more than a decade before Liebermann's. Yet Liebermann may really have been in Kaifeng in July 1867 and may have had his account published immediately afterward in an as-yet unnoticed place, and Fink may have found the inspiration for his story in that source; or perhaps he was shown the letters Liebermann had written to his father before they were posted to Bielitz, and took his materials from them. On the whole, Liebermann's report appears to be the more plausible, though perhaps because it does not include (at least in the Löwy rendition) the plea for financial assistance that Fink's does—a plea, it should be recorded, which is expressed in embarrassingly fervid prose. To this should be added the consideration that after meeting Liebermann and presumably questioning him at some length about his experiences in Kaifeng, Rabbi Löwy was willing to devote a good deal of his time and effort to editing and translating Liebermann's account and then risk his own professional reputation by submitting it for publication to such an esteemed organization as the Anglo-Jewish Association.

Historians have somehow overlooked Fink's claim to have been in Kaifeng in 1864, but have made a great deal of Liebermann's tale of having been there in 1867. The recent reemergence of Fink's account therefore raises the question of which of the two men (if either) was the first Jew to meet the *kehillah* in modern times, and requires thorough investigation.[32] In the interim, Liebermann's remains the less objectionable version and is presented here as if it were essentially true, though with the caveat that it may not be, or that it describes a visit to Kaifeng made by someone other than Liebermann.

Liebermann, in any case, like so many other Central European Jewish laymen of his generation, had been given very extensive training in Judaic law and lore as a youth. Traveling in China, he tried hard to acquire the dialects of the localities in which he found himself and was apparently capable of carrying on conversations with the Kaifeng Jews, although with some difficulty. His account of his contacts with the *kehillah*, it should be added, has all the earmarks of authenticity when he refers to things he claims to have witnessed personally, but for those matters in which he was dependent on others for his information, his reliability (as he himself acknowledges) suffers considerably.

Liebermann had come to China for business reasons, and it was business—and perhaps the prospect of meeting the Jews—that brought him to Kaifeng. While traveling to the city, he had found it wise to maintain a low profile. "I assumed the garb of the natives," he informed his doubtlessly bemused father, "and plaited my hair in the Chinese fashion. I . . . had placed myself under British protection, and was therefore supplied with a permit to visit the interior of the country. Although I had been furnished with such a document my safety was often endangered owing to the existence of feuds in different districts. Sometimes I was regarded as a spy, and had many miraculous escapes. I was on some occasions fortunate enough to receive letters of protection from the leaders of the hostile parties."

On his arrival at the gates of Kaifeng, Liebermann's papers were minutely scrutinized. When they finally passed muster, he was placed under armed guard and escorted directly to "the foreigners' inn." In a way, he was relieved to be taken there in protective custody, distasteful though this was, since, as he noted ruefully, "the inhabitants of this place behave fiercely and cruelly towards Europeans." In all, he spent eleven days in the city, fearing constantly for his life. He could not leave the inn, he informed his father, "without being surrounded by a countless mob of men, women and children" by whom he was hooted at as "the ghost of a stranger"—as an Occidental, that is. Implored by his terrified landlord to give up his lodgings and depart forthwith, he refused but from then on never ventured outside the walls of the inn without a weapon at his side. On the eleventh day of his residence at the inn, the building was surrounded and he was expelled from the city. He had been there longer than he had anticipated. "Ordinarily," he explained to his father, "a stranger is not permitted to remain longer than three days."

Steeling himself to disregard the perils that beset him day and night, Liebermann went about the city as best he could. Given the circumstances, it would speak well of the man's courage and determination if he was actually able to accomplish all he said he did—holding several meetings with the Jews, inspecting the site of the synagogue, paying a visit to a mosque, and engaging in bouts of trading with the local merchants.

Where there had once been a synagogue, Liebermann found nothing but mounds of rubble and traces of an entrance court. In the rubble he came upon a stone lintel on which there had been inscribed in Chinese the words "the House of God and the religion of those who extract the sinew from the flesh." He also saw a stone inscription, again in Chinese, cautioning persons "not of the Israelitish religion" to refrain from trespassing on the premises. The site of the synagogue, he observed with dismay, was almost totally "covered with mire and pools of water."[33]

In Kaifeng, he was told by the Jews, their number ran to about 400 families, in Peking there were 200 more, "and in Hansho [apparently Hangchow] and near Ningpo, as also in other places, many were likewise scattered." Not all the Jews who left Kaifeng had done so voluntarily. "The ravages of war," he noted, "had carried off many Jews. Some of them had held high military posts and Government offices. Through following a military career and through being scattered, the majority of the Jews had become so entirely ignorant of their religion that they abandoned its tenets. Yet their descendants still abstained from eating swine-flesh and any meat killed by a stranger. They abstained from the use of blood, and the eating of anything impure of beasts, birds and fishes. They also refrained from intermarrying with persons of other creeds. They still have a burial ground of their own."

Liebermann offered to buy whatever manuscripts or other relics the Jews still retained, but they insisted that they had nothing left other than a stone tablet that had formerly been attached to one of the walls of the synagogue. This tablet, they said, "was inscribed with characters which none of them could read." He urged them to let him see it. They were perfectly willing to show it to him, but would not let him accompany them to its hiding place for fear that their neighbors might learn where it was kept and then steal it. Instead, they brought it to his inn. It was black, thirty-two inches long, sixteen inches wide, and eight inches thick, and on it was a Hebrew inscription placed vertically in two lines. One line he readily identified as part of Deut. 8:3, "but that man may live on anything that the Lord decrees." The other line, which he could not make out completely, he translated as, "written on the fourth of Sabbath by me, Soonan[?], on the day of . . . one thousand nine hundred."

"In the synagogue," he wrote to his father, "according to the tradition of their ancestors, there was a golden bell, on which was inscribed in Hebrew characters the time when the synagogue was built, the place where they came from, why they had come hither, and some other matters unknown to them." They could not show it to him, they explained, because "the Muhammadans of the place had stolen the bell, and also the books, which were originally in the synagogue."

Hoping to see the bell and the books, Liebermann went to the mosque in which, the Jews maintained, the purloined relics were kept. He talked at length with the mullahs. They would not admit to having the bell, but he was finally shown a single manuscript, a Hebrew section book of *Va-era* (Exod. 6:3–9:35). At the end of this manuscript there was a colophon of two lines, also in Hebrew: "Done according to a vow of Rabbi Phineas, the teacher, the son of Israel, the son of Joshua, the son of Benjamin. For thy salvation I have waited, O Lord." This Phineas, although Liebermann would probably not have known it, was the hard-of-hearing and teeth-clenching rabbi with whom Gozani had sat down in the synagogue in 1704 to compare biblical texts.[34]

The Jews complained to Liebermann that they had been swindled out of several of their Torah scrolls by strangers, presumably the two delegates. Informed by the mullahs that this was untrue, he concluded that the Jews were distorting the facts and that the Torah scrolls were purchased from them legitimately. He surmised, moreover, that their denial that they still owned any biblical documents or synagogal artifacts was not entirely sincere, and that if by any chance they did have some in their possession—as, indeed, they did—they were not prepared to take him into their confidence about it. They attributed the loss of some of their manuscripts to the fact that "two hundred of their families had removed to Peking and had taken with them three Scrolls."

Although they no longer conducted any formal worship services, the Jews still considered themselves adherents of "the religion of Moses." As for the God they recognized, they called Him "Ye-cho a-cha" (Jehovah). Their synagogue, which they wrongly described as having been built "on the model of the Temple in Jerusalem," was of course no longer in existence, but notwithstanding the fact that in 1851 the delegates had reported the edifice to be reasonably intact, the date of its demolition was represented to Liebermann as falling within the period 1840–50. Why had they not rebuilt the synagogue? Because, the Jews said, most of them were poverty stricken and, in addition, they had forgotten so much of their liturgy that it seemed pointless to erect a sanctuary in which they would not even know how to go about presenting their prayers. The authorities had directed them to display a Torah scroll in the marketplace with a poster "offering a reward and a leading position to anyone who would be able to explain the wording of the Scroll," and they had later made "similar offers in other places, but to no avail."[35] Frustrated, they gave up all hope of rebuilding the synagogue. They claimed, also, to have been ordered "not to adopt another religion before the arrival of persons who could read the Law, and who might reintroduce amongst them the knowledge now fallen into oblivion."

The Jews assured Liebermann that they would be overjoyed if facilities for studying Judaism could be made available to them. He suggested as a beginning that they petition the authorities for permission to receive a foreign teacher "who should bring them back to their ancient religion," but an old man immediately raised the objection that it would be virtually impossible to persuade the government to allow a European to be stationed in Kaifeng. "Nearly all of us," he pointed out, "are poor and engaged in menial labor. It would, therefore, not be practicable to afford all the instruction that is needful. Besides this, . . . the presence of Europeans would have no other effect than that of exciting suspicion." Other Jews, agreeing that the prospects of securing permission for a foreigner to live in their community were rather dim, proposed that they or their children be taken to Europe for the training they could not be given at home. One man, however, took Liebermann aside and warned him not to expect too much from this suggestion. It had been blurted out on impulse, he said, and would soon be regretted, for the Jews had no desire to leave their native land. It might be more realistic, someone else volunteered, if they simply gave Liebermann a letter of introduction to their kinsmen who had in recent years moved to Peking, where, he explained, they enjoyed far greater freedom than the Kaifeng Jews did. There was not time enough, in any case, for such a letter to be drafted, since Liebermann was ejected from the city the very next day. Circumstances, moreover, did not permit him to visit Peking. If they had, he might have found a few Chinese Jews there, but certainly not the 200 families he was told about in Kaifeng. He might also have found the three Torah scrolls that, the Jews claimed, had been taken to the imperial capital—but he would have discovered that they had very recently been brought there by three young men and not, as the Jews insisted, by 200 families.[36]

10 ❖ TOO LITTLE, AND MUCH TOO LATE

WITHIN the short span of seventeen months, three Westerners had journeyed to Kaifeng with the expectation of visiting the *kehillah*. Of the three, only Martin came back believing that it was not too late to keep the old community from fading away into the creeds of its neighbors. He warned, however, that whatever efforts were mounted to achieve this objective must be neither too little in scope nor too late in coming; otherwise, the *kehillah* would disappear completely. Schereschewsky and Liebermann, on the other hand, were far less sanguine about the prospects for restoring the communal integrity of the *kehillah*, though perhaps because the abuses and perils to which they were subjected during their stays in Kaifeng made them realize that in the foreseeable future no foreigner—whether priest, minister, rabbi, or layman—could be expected to carry out a mission to the city's Jews without incurring considerable risk to his own person and endangering the Jews as well.[1]

Martin had been lucky, not only while traveling to and from Kaifeng but also while he was there. The discomforts of the road, to be sure, wore him down physically, and the report that came to his attention of a recent robbery in one of the regions through which he was passing caused him some twinges of alarm. The slight uneasiness he felt might have been allayed by the many police stations and signal towers he saw along the way—one every mile or two—had he not noticed that these were too sparsely manned to hold the local desperadoes totally in check. The days, however, went by quietly, and whatever minor fears he did develop along the route were quickly dissipated. No one seems to have tried to molest him or to interfere with his movements. In

Kaifeng, too, he appears to have exhibited no special concern for his safety or to have had any limitations placed upon his activities. He had no reason, in short, to conclude that others would be prevented from meeting the Jews and working with them. All that was needed, he decided, was the will to make the necessary effort.

Yet only a little more than a year later the climate had deteriorated sufficiently to induce both Schereschewsky and Liebermann to attempt to pass themselves off as natives as they proceeded to Kaifeng, hoping by this stratagem to be left in peace, if not by all potentially hostile Chinese then at least by those who did not peer at them too intently. Their disguises, so easily penetrated, did them little good once they arrived at their destination; and because the aversion of the citizenry of Kaifeng for the white barbarians was now expressed so openly, Schereschewsky was unable to meet the Jews at all and Liebermann was compelled to restrict his excursions from the foreigners' inn to a minimum and carry a weapon at his side when he did chance one. Each man, moreover, was hustled out of the city under circumstances that were as frightening as they were humiliating.[2]

The antiforeign agitation worsened, with the missionaries serving as the particular targets of those sectarians who saw all outlanders as obnoxious intruders into areas of Chinese life where they did not belong. Stories were circulated charging the missionaries with a panoply of crimes, the most lurid of these being that they habitually kidnapped Chinese children and cut out their hearts and eyes for use in perverted cultic services and for the concoction of certain mysterious magical potions—accusations strongly resembling the ritual murder denunciations, which for centuries had been hurled against the Jews of the Occident, and against which they were even then being called upon with tragic frequency to defend themselves. The situation was so bad that the Caucasian who wandered into the interior of China never knew when he might be set upon by howling mobs bent on his destruction. Understandably, only the most daring or the most reckless Europeans were prepared to court disaster by venturing outside the coastal cities in which their own governments could afford them some reasonable measure of protection.

Because travel conditions had become so dangerous, twenty-one years went by from the time of Liebermann's involuntary departure from Kaifeng before another Westerner came to the city and tried to meet its Jews. The traveler was an unidentified Christian who on arriving at Kaifeng in May 1888 was not even permitted to pass through its gates and promptly vented his displeasure with the local authorities by dashing off a letter from outside its forbidding walls to inform the editors of the *Jewish Chronicle* of what had just befallen him.[3]

For eighteen years, this anonymous traveler explained, he had been eagerly awaiting an opportunity to go to the Honan capital and meet the Jews who lived there. It had taken him and a Chinese companion, whom he described merely as his "Manchu fellow traveler," five long weeks of travel by shanks' mare to get from Peking to Kaifeng, counting several stopovers enroute. "The people with whom we conversed on the road and who had visited Kaifeng," he wrote in the opening lines of his letter, "were well acquainted with a street bearing the name of *T'iao-chin-chiao*, i.e., the street of the sect who pluck out the sinew. None, however, knew any followers of a religion bearing such a name. My intense interest in the subject had to wait for its personal gratification."

But the *Chronicle*'s correspondent was to be denied the "personal gratification" he longed for, and for a reason he had never anticipated. The second paragraph of his letter explained why: "The foregoing lines were written outside the city's walls before daybreak. Shortly afterwards, when the gates were opened, I sought to enter, but was repulsed at the very outset. Under no conditions, except by special instructions from the emperor, could a foreigner be admitted. I tried another of the five gates of this great and wealthy city, but it was of no use. My name was shown to me as having been transmitted to the guards of the city gates on its four sides, and they were prepared for me."

The exclusion edict, fortunately, did not apply to his "Manchu fellow traveler," who, the writer reported, was allowed to enter the city. There he found "in a dustheap the site of the synagogue, which once faced the street known as *T'iao-chin-chiao Hu-T'ung*. The land does not seem to have been alienated, but has become a public urinal. A small slab in the center [the 1489/

1512 stele] tells the tale of the ruined synagogue. My deputy was able to read the inscription on rubbing off the dust and dirt, and was greatly strengthened in his belief as to the truth of the scripture records. He saw two families of the sect, who had become secularized, and he was also informed of the existence of two other families. Living as they did at a distance, he did not come across them."

The Jews to whom the "Manchu" spoke also told him that "the students of Hebrew" were dead and that two Jews had moved to Shanghai (the Chao brothers?). "But of the ten who were taken as students to Peking twenty years ago [?]," the writer to the *Chronicle* added, the "Manchu" learned nothing.

The letter closed with the cheering statement that because a telegraph line had recently been extended to Kaifeng, "it cannot be long before foreigners will gain access" to the city and learn more about its Jewish inhabitants.

The writer's disappointment at having come so close to meeting the *kehillah* and then failing to do so shows through very plainly in his letter, but the high note of optimism on which he closed—the prediction that other foreigners would soon be able to succeed where he had not—was fully justified. His disconcerting experiences at the gates of Kaifeng, in any case, marked the end of the *kehillah*'s isolation from the West—leaving aside occasional intervals of civil unrest—until the seizure of the city by Communist forces shortly after World War II.[4]

The Reverend Dennis Mills, who arrived at the gates of Kaifeng only a year after the *Chronicle*'s anonymous correspondent, was allowed free entry into the city. He remained there only two days, perhaps the maximum period allotted to him by the authorities, encountering friendliness on the part of some of its residents and unfriendliness on the part of others. Inquiring about the Jews, he was told that the seven clans enumerated by earlier visitors still lived there, making up about 200 families among them, and that they were being rapidly assimilated into the general population. "Many of them," he lamented, "now intermarry with the heathen, and are given to idolatry." He met a Jew by the name of Kao who volunteered the information that he and his family had lived in the Protestant Gospel Hall at Peking for two years. Mills offered Kao copies of the Old and New Testaments, which Kao politely refused to accept. "We tried to interest him in the promise made to Israel, and the offer of salvation in Christ," Mills complained, "but to all this he seemed perfectly indifferent! 'I know all about it,' he said." The *kehillah*, the missionary added, was torn by dissension, and one Jew was in prison awaiting trial for the murder of a coreligionist.[5]

In 1893, during a short stay in Kaifeng, a representative of the National Bible Society of Scotland, A. S. Annaud, came to see the plot of ground on which the synagogue had stood and noted that Jews still lived in its vicinity. He spoke to a man called Kao Hui-k'uei, perhaps the same Kao with whom Mills had talked, "who had some Jewish features." He was told by Kao that the *kehillah* could now count only six clans, the Chang having apparently moved away or become completely assimilated. In all, the Jewish population was said to consist of 500 individuals. However, some Muslims with whom Annaud also spoke put the figure at under 250.[6]

Other Westerners who in the next decade visited the *kehillah*, or what was left of it, described it as well on the way to extinction. In 1899, one of them, Monsignor Volonteri, then Apostolic Vicar of the Honan Vicarate, was able to buy a Torah scroll and several smaller documents from an elderly Jewish widow. This scroll was the last of the ten which are specifically known to have passed into foreign hands. Volonteri sent his purchases to the Siccawei Mission, a Catholic institution near Shanghai, from which the scroll was shortly forwarded to France for detailed study. It has since disappeared without trace.[7]

On June 10, 1900, Hermann Marcus, chief rabbi of Britain, received a letter from S. J. Solomon, a Jewish merchant living in Shanghai, relaying certain information he had just obtained about the *kehillah* from the Reverend Robert Powell. Powell, who was stationed intermittently in Kaifeng over a period of several years, estimated the number of Jews still residing there at 140, a figure that seems excessively low, unless it represents only adult males, or perhaps even adults of both sexes. "Their condition, socially," he wrote to Solomon, "is not very high. Once they were the richest and most influential people in the place, but through internal dissension they have dwindled down until now they are very poor, and, I am sorry to add, have not a very good reputation. One of them is a Buddhist priest, and is in the position of a small mandarin—that is, he manages the affairs of all the other priests."

The members of the *kehillah,* according to Powell, knew virtually nothing about the faith of their ancestors. "They do not observe any of the ordinances of their religion," he reported to Solomon, "neither do they, with the exception of the Buddhist priest, observe the idolatrous practices of the heathen; they do, however, intermarry with them."[8]

That the Kaifeng Jews were in so sad a state of disarray was the unpleasant news, Solomon informed Adler, but he had some unexpected good tidings to soften the blow—a colony of 500 Jews had just been discovered in Tang-chwang, a city located about 100 miles southwest of Kaifeng. The honor of finding this settlement belonged to a Colonel Lehmann (first name not given) of the German army.

But Solomon's good news was not a scoop, the secretary of the Shanghai chapter of the Royal Asiatic Society having reported, in a letter dated November 18, 1899, that:

> the Jewish colony has spread to other towns. Their occupation as silk weavers took some of them to a distance. Some families were well-to-do through connection with this trade. One of the moderately large towns near Kaifeng, where there is a colony of Jews, is called Tang-chwang. It is a mile and a half long, and is about 100 miles southwest of Kaifeng. The Jews are all people well-to-do. They weave the silk fabric called ling, and take it or send it to Peking.[9]

Neither Solomon nor the Shanghai official of the Royal Asiatic Society volunteered any significant details regarding Colonel Lehmann, but from the confused accounts that appeared in print it was evident that he was a Jew. The story allegedly presented by Lehmann was either totally or partially a hoax, and although it was believed on the whole by many of the people who read it, there were others who scoffed at it, a few going so far as to suggest that Colonel Lehmann was himself the product of someone's overworked imagination. Who, they asked, had ever heard of a Jew being permitted to hold the rank of colonel in the Kaiser's regular army? And if a Jewish settlement did really exist in Tang-chwang, how was it that nobody after this Lehmann was ever able to rediscover it?

The second objection of the scoffers was valid; the first was not. There was a Jewish officer by the name of Lehmann, a reservist assigned to the German forces in China, but he was, at least in 1899, a captain, not a colonel. He was in fact Jonas (also known as Jon) Lehmann, son of the prominent rabbi and literary man Marcus Lehmann and elder brother of Rabbi Oskar Lehmann.[10] Jonas, born in Mainz in 1865 and thirty-four years old when his visits to Kaifeng and Tang-chwang are supposed to have taken place, gained a modicum of renown as a publisher, playwright, and poet after his five-year-term of military service, and died at Breslau in 1913.[11]

Not only is the story attributed to Lehmann shot through with implausibilities, but there is not even any agreement of what, precisely, that story originally consisted. In a lecture on the subject of the Chinese Jews delivered in London on June 17, 1900, Marcus Nathan Adler, son of one of England's chief rabbis and brother of another, merely paraphrased Solomon's statements regarding Lehmann, telling his audience that "a certain Colonel Lehmann, who was in Kiatschou, had been a few months ago in a place about 100 miles southwest of Kaifeng, where there were about 500 native Jews, most of whom were engaged in the silk piece goods trade."[12] Adler then read to his hearers the excerpt dealing with the Chinese Jews from the report prepared by the secretary of the Shanghai section of the Royal Asiatic Society. If Lehmann was ever in Kaifeng, Adler either knew nothing about it or, improbably, did not think it important enough to merit inclusion in his talk.

Yet the *Chicago Inter-Ocean* had seen fit, some months before Adler's lecture was delivered, to print a first-person account by one "J. J. Liebermann" describing a visit this Liebermann had recently made to Kaifeng and containing no hint whatever of a stopover in Tang-chwang.[13] The *Inter-Ocean's* article was re-

19. Col. Jonas Lehmann, of the German army of occupation in China.

printed two weeks later by the *American Hebrew* which, in its introductory remarks to the story, identified the author as "Herr J. J. Liebermann, an officer of the German army of occupation in Kiatschou, China," and in an accompanying editorial observed that "Col. Liebermann, the German officer who recently visited this remnant of Israel, is a layman of limited knowledge, as he confesses, but he has paved and pointed the way for the Jews of the world to take up the subject, and we hope that in the interest of Judaism it will be done under the auspices of a Jewish organization."[14]

If the man who figures in the two newspaper reports was mistakenly meant to be J. L. Liebermann, the account he supposedly presents clashes sharply in many details with those offered in Albert Löwy's 1878/79 translation and condensation of the Hebrew letters that the Austrian merchant of that name is reputed to have written to his father in 1867—thirty-two years before a German Jewish officer is alleged to have visited Kaifeng. The officer to whom both the *Inter-Ocean* and the *American Hebrew* referred was undoubtedly Lehmann, but whether he ever was in Kaifeng and met any Jews there is highly questionable. Whether he personally wrote the article attributed to him is equally questionable.

Lehmann, if it is assumed that he did write the article, explains that during a visit to Kaifeng he gained the impression that some of its inhabitants were "of pronounced Semitic type." Curious, he asked his guide who these people could be, and was told that they were the *T'iao-chin-chiao.* "Are many of these strangers living in town?" he then asked. "They are not strangers," the guide replied. "They have always been with us. There may be 500 left. We will reach their quarter shortly."

Before long, Lehmann and his guide came to a moneychanger's shop, in front of which was displayed a sign bearing several Chinese characters and a lone Hebrew word. Lehmann construed the Hebrew word as "the place where God assembles his people"—a bizarre and inappropriate term, one would think, to apply to a commercial establishment and, incidentally, not expressible in a single Hebrew word.

The moneychanger, "a patriarchal man with a big hook nose,"

was introduced to Lehmann as "the high priest" of the Jews. His people had come to China, this "high priest" told the officer, in the very last part of the Han era (58–75 C.E.), about three years after the destruction in 70 C.E. of the Second Temple. The refugees, he then declared, had "traveled to China via Persia, through Khorasan and Samarkand." They were kindly received by the Chinese.

The "high priest" now conducted his visitor to the site of the demolished synagogue and showed him all that remained of it—mere rubble. Even though he was the nominal rabbi, or high priest, of the Jewish community, the old man confessed to Lehmann as they poked about the rubble, he had no knowledge of Hebrew. Why? Because the rabbi before him "was also innocent of the historic tongue for the reason that his father died at an early age, and when the child's, his hereditary successor's, education had scarce begun."

The next stop was at the "priest's" house, where Lehmann was shown three old chests. "There," he reported, "encased in pieces of thick, soft silk, I saw numerous papyrus and parchment rolls, the oldest probably written twenty-two or twenty-three centuries ago[!]. I recognized a copy of the Pentateuch on very large parchment. The titles of the others I could not decipher, but the Patriarch told me that among the Scriptures were many dealing with the last years of Jewish independence and the beginning of the Roman occupation of Palestine."

In the Jewish quarter Lehmann met "makers, tailors, dealers in fruit, and petty storekeepers." They wore the local costume, including the pigtail. They had begun to marry Chinese women, he was told, only about fifty years previously. The Sabbath was still kept, however, and weekly prayer meetings were held in the "rabbi's" house, in a room set aside for that purpose. They practiced circumcision and celebrated several of the old festivals.

Although Lehmann claimed that he could translate the one Hebrew word he saw on the moneychanger's sign and, by virtue of what he called his "half-forgotten schoolday lessons," was also able to transcribe a few hundred Hebrew letters from an inscription he was shown, he could not, he explained apologetically, read enough Hebrew to identify any of the venerable manuscripts in the "priest's" house, except in the case of a Pentateuch, or to make sense out of almost everything else that was paraded before him in that language. A perplexing admission, this, coming as it reputedly did from a man who was the son of a famous rabbi and who, at his father's funeral a few years earlier, had delivered a eulogy adorned by a number of appropriate Hebraicisms—and was a few days later described in the columns of Germany's leading Orthodox Jewish periodical as "a colleague on our journal (*ein Mitarbeiter unseres Blattes*)."[15]

Several Westerners who were in Kaifeng around the turn of the century reported that because the title deeds to the site of the synagogue were lost during the Taiping Rebellion, the Kaifeng Jews received replacement documents for them in the mid-1890s, although only after engaging in lengthy wrangling with the authorities.[16] The Jews, apparently, still looked upon themselves as a distinct community, or at least as a segment of the population entitled to be counted as a communal entity for legal and financial purposes, and the authorities were still willing to recognize the right of the Jews to identify themselves as such.

The French diplomat Phillippe Berthelot, who met the leaders of six of the clans in 1905, listed the occupations of four of the men as that of tea merchant (Chao), shoe seller (Ai), bricklayer (Kao), and soldier (Li). The Ai clan, who were not doing well, and the Shih, concerning whose status Berthelot offered no comment, were the most numerous. The Chang he did not see, for, as previous visitors had noted, in the past two or three decades they had either left the city or become totally assimilated. The six remaining clans, Berthelot observed, regarded themselves as Jewish, although they no longer came together as a group and remembered none of their Hebrew. He was told that the 1679 stele (later to be transferred to the care of Bishop White) had been taken out of the wall of a Chao home the year before by Edward Jenks, a visiting American engineer.[17]

Abbott Lloyd, an American who lived in Kaifeng from 1902

to 1914, described the Jews as indistinguishable in dress and deportment from their Muslim neighbors. He counted twelve to fifteen stalls or shops belonging to them, in which they sold hot water and a few sweetmeants. The stock-in-trade of a typical shop of this kind, he pointed out, might not be worth more than an American dollar or two.[18]

The English writer Oliver Bainbridge was cordially received by the Jews in 1906. He learned that they had sold one Torah scroll to a missionary (presumably Volonteri). Another Torah, the Jews complained to him, was borrowed from them by a mullah who, instead of returning it, insisted that it was swept away by a gust of wind and wafted to the heavens. Bainbridge took a series of photographs of the Jews, and also succeeded in obtaining a cylindrical Torah scroll case from a mosque, which had somehow gotten possession of it.[19] The case, which he brought to London, was for a time owned by the book dealer J. Jacob, and is probably the same case that is currently in the Los Angeles branch of the Hebrew Union College. (A second case, bought later by Bishop White, is owned by the Royal Ontario Museum, Toronto.) Before he left Kaifeng, according to a newspaper report that appeared after Bainbridge's return to London, he was entrusted by the Jews with "a petition to their brethren across the seas, praying for assistance to rebuild their synagogue and to raise them from the decadence and poverty into which they have sunk." The petition and the case, the report continues, "may be seen at Mr. Jacob's bookshop."[20]

Early in 1900, a letter from Dr. Timothy Richard was delivered to S. J. Solomon in Shanghai, bringing the news that Monsignor Volonteri had recently purchased a Torah scroll and several other manuscripts from the Kaifeng Jews and sent them to the Siccawei Mission. A committee of Shanghai Jews promptly visited the mission and inspected Volonteri's acquisitions. The sight of these irreplaceable Hebrew treasures in a non-Jewish setting, a shattering blow to the conscience and pride of the Shanghai deputation, awakened it to the realization that prompt and drastic action would have to be taken—if it was not already

20. Torah scroll case from the Kaifeng synagogue.

21. A Kaifeng Jew, early twentieth century.

too late—to reverse the tide of decay engulfing the Kaifeng *kehillah*, and that it was Shanghai Jewry's responsibility to get to work on the problem at once.

On March 13, 1900, Solomon, David Ezekiel Abraham, and forty-four other Shanghai Jews signed their names to a letter drafted in Hebrew and provided with a Chinese translation, both of which they sent to Kaifeng. The letter chided the *kehillah* for having strayed so far from the old Jewish ways and offered the assistance of Shanghai's Jewish community in bringing it back to its ancestral faith:

> You have forgotten everything, and have gone so far as, three or four months ago, to have sold a Scroll of the Law, which our own eyes have seen in the hands of those who are not of the seed of Israel. And we are further told that you are about to dispose of three or four more Scrolls [an error— there were probably no more Torah scrolls in Kaifeng] because you are in dire distress, and urge as your excuse that you and your children cannot read.
>
> Now, verily, sorrow and anxiety filled our hearts when we heard these evil tidings, that affliction and want have brought you to this pass, so that Sabbath and festivals are forgotten, and that you are becoming mixed up with the heathen around you, and that you forsake the covenant, and the way your forefathers have walked for two thousand years in this land of your settlement. Tidings such as these caused the ears of every one of us that heard [them] to tingle, and we have roused ourselves to come to your help.
>
> Some of us were willing to come to you to find out wherefore all this evil has befallen you, and to see what we could do to heal the breach. But we are told that there would be danger to us on the way [because of the Boxer Rebellion], and that if we did come in your midst, our presence would arouse anger and excite the Gentiles among whom you dwell; therefore we decided to write you this epistle, and to ask you to send us an answer, either by letter or by word of mouth, through a member of your community.
>
> Now, we assure you that we are eager to help you according to our ability, so that you may walk again in the footsteps of your forefathers. If you desire to rebuild the House of God, which is now become a waste place, we will collect money

and send it to you; if you want a teacher to instruct you, we will send you one; if it should please you to come hither and settle here in the city of Shanghai, we will help you to do so, and put you in the way to earn a livelihood by starting you in trade, and all that you may require we will endeavor to supply you with, for there are in this city men of our faith— great and wealthy men of affairs and business—who can help you to maintain yourselves and your sons and daughters.

Therefore we beg you not to part with the Scrolls still left to you. On this letter reaching you, send two or three men to us whom we may question, and from whom we can find out what we can do for you. We will give them their sustenance, and pay them their expenses until they reach again your city.[21]

On the fourteenth of May, thirty-one Shanghai Jews met in the home of E. M. Ezra and formed an organization to which they gave the name the Society for the Rescue of the Chinese Jews. The objectives of the new organization, as spelled out in its by-laws, were "to study the origin, development, and history of the Jewish Colonies in China; to preserve such sites and monuments [as still exist]; [to] erect monuments where advantageous; and to bring back to Judaism all Chinese Jews lineally descended from Jewish families."[22]

The letter of March 13 was intercepted by the Boxers, but a duplicate sent some months later was received by the *kehillah*. To the delight of the Shanghai Jews, it yielded a reply, this from the flour merchant Li Ching-sheng, who indicated that he and others among the Jews of Kaifeng were interested in hearing more about the Shanghai offer of aid.[23]

On April 6, 1901, after some further exchange of correspondence, Li arrived in Shanghai with his son Tsung-mai, a cheerful boy of twelve who seems to have captivated the hearts of all who met him. Father and son remained in Shanghai for about three weeks before returning home.

The elder Li, about fifty-two years old when he came to Shanghai, had little to tell his hosts about the *kehillah* that they did not already know. He estimated the number of adult Jews in Kaifeng at 140. (Powell had recently given the same figure, but he may have gotten it from Li.) Li also told the Shanghai

Jews that his Jewish townsmen no longer extracted the sinews from the meat they ate, had given up observing the Sabbath and the festivals, and did not circumcise their infant sons. In spite of all this, he stressed, they were not idol worshippers, and they still refrained from eating pork.

The Society for the Rescue of the Chinese Jews renewed its efforts, and by March 10, 1902, Li and his son were back in Shanghai, this time with six other Kaifeng Jews who ranged in age from sixteen to sixty-one.[24]

Now, to its intense embarrassment, the society discovered that it had been excessively optimistic regarding its ability to raise the funds that rebuilding the synagogue would take. The initial cost, it turned out, ran to about £5,000, and much more would be required later on. The society appealed to the Jewish community of Britain for help, but was not able to collect the money needed to make its brave promises of assistance to the *kehillah* come true. "We here in London," the chief rabbi of England was compelled to write in response to the society's request for financial assistance, "can do but little to aid your pious undertaking. We are absolutely overwhelmed by the Russian Jewish immigration which is continuing, and to which now has been added the influx of our brethren from Rumania."[25] The situation was no better elsewhere, Western Jewry being preoccupied at this time with the more immediate problems of succoring the Jews of czarist Russia, supporting the great masses of poverty stricken immigrants flooding into the ghettos of New York, London, and numerous other European and American cities, and providing aid to the hard-pressed Sephardic Jews of North Africa and the Middle East. There simply was not enough money to meet these overpowering demands, and certainly none to spare for so quixotic an enterprise as the rehabilitation of a cluster of self-styled Israelites lost somewhere in the depths of China. One irate Shanghai Jew, N. E. B. Ezra, later laid the blame for the failure of the rescue society to save the *kehillah* squarely at the feet of his own community. The Shanghai Jews, he charged in 1906, were so exceedingly remiss in the discharge of their responsibilities to the Kaifeng *kehillah* that they had failed to reimburse the secretary of the rescue society for the thirty dollars he had been obliged to lay out of his own pocket each month to support the Kaifeng Jews who had come to Shanghai as guests of the city's Jewish community.[26] Nevertheless, Ezra refused to absolve the rest of the world's Jews from bearing a goodly portion of the guilt. As for the rescue society, he would write in 1913:

> [it had] long ceased to exist, owing to the disorganized state of the Shanghai Jewish community and the want of unity prevailing among them, due to want of a capable lay or spiritual leader. There was every reason to hope of some help being extended to the poor and helpless Jews of Kaifeng by their affluent coreligionists in Shanghai, but, alas, the want of foresight and a little consideration on their part has played an important part in killing every chance of success in this direction. Paraphrasing a Biblical injunction, Jewry throughout the world in general, and the Shanghai Jewish community in particular, cannot say with a clear and calm conscience: "Our hands did not destroy this community, nor have our eyes seen who did it."[27]

Disappointed by the news that the rescue society would not be able to rebuild their synagogue, the six Jews who in 1902 had accompanied the elder and younger Li to Shanghai started back home, having spent about three months in the port city. One of the six underwent the rite of circumcision while in Shanghai and was given the name Israel. The elder Li, who died there in 1903, was buried in its Jewish cemetery. Li Tsung-mai remained in Shanghai. After his father's death, he was raised by one of the city's Jewish families. On the occasion of his circumcision, he was assigned the Hebrew name Shmuel. Later, he was enrolled as a student at the Shanghai Jewish School. As an adult, he demonstrated little or no interest in Judaism. Employed in a minor clerical capacity in the offices of a Jewish firm, he continued to live in Shanghai until the end of the Second World War. He then returned to Kaifeng, where he died in 1948.

With the passage of the years, other Kaifeng Jews came to Shanghai. A cousin of Shmuel, known as Jacob, was given employment by E. D. Sassoon & Co. Still another cousin worked as a watchman in the home of a wealthy Jewish family. The three cousins and their numerous progeny, Mrs. R. D. Abraham recalled in 1962, participated in merely one Jewish custom—and passively at that. "Their only recognition of Judaism," she observed ruefully, "was that they received gifts on Purim [from their employers, apparently] instead of on the Chinese New Year!"[28]

While all eight of the visitors from Kaifeng were still in Shanghai, they were sought out and interrogated by various members of the local Jewish community. Edward Isaac Ezra, who would shortly write a lengthy article about the visiting Jews and their ancient *kehillah*, had them at his home on the evening of March 26, 1902 and subjected them to two hours of intensive questioning.[29] He learned very little that was not already generally known. Shortly after this, the scholarly merchant S. M. Perlmann met several of the Kaifeng delegation in either Ezra's house or that of another Shanghai Jew. A group of Caucasian Jews was also present; and the guests from Kaifeng, Perlmann was amused to note, "were proud" that they and the rest of the company were all "members of one tribe ('brethren,' as the Chinese usually call members of the same tribe), that we were all of the Jewish nation and creed, and all descendants of Abraham."[30]

Perlmann was appalled by the backwardness and ignorance of the men from Kaifeng. "It was very apparent," he regretfully reported, "that the visitors were of low intellect and lacked education. It was too much to expect these people to understand how deep an interest is taken in the Chinese Jews by their coreligionists, as well as by sociologists in the West." As to their way of life? "They proceeded to tell me that they abstain from pork, extract the sinew from the slaughtered cattle [contradicting Li's statement of the previous year], and mostly marry among their own tribe, but that all other Jewish rites have come into oblivion; even circumcision of their newborn sons is not exercised any more. They bury their deceased in coffins, but of a different shape than those of the Chinese are made, and do not attire the dead in secular clothes as the Chinese do, but in linen."[31]

The leaders of the Shanghai rescue society, depressed though they were by their inability to raise enough money to rebuild the Kaifeng synagogue, called new meetings, hoping against hope that a practical solution to the problem of reviving the moribund

22. A family of Kaifeng Jews, early twentieth century.

kehillah might somehow be worked out. In 1903, one of the society's members, S. I. Shekury, offered to go to Kaifeng. At about the same time, Nahum Silas, a Hebrew scholar then in Hong Kong, A. May, a Jewish resident of Tientsin, and General William Mesney, editor of the *Chinese Miscellany*, volunteered to establish a Jewish mission in Kaifeng.[32] In the end, however, nothing was done, perhaps because it was realized that only by erecting a new synagogue and providing it with a full-time Chinese-speaking resident rabbi, one who would be compassionate enough to appreciate the difficulties besetting his unique congregation yet strong enough to overcome them, could any success be anticipated. And since the rescue society, for all its good intentions, had neither the wherewithal for constructing the needed synagogue nor the proper rabbi to head it, it was left with no alternative but to suspend its operations, a course of action—or, rather, inaction—which was reluctantly decided upon during its last meeting, held during March 1904. Two decades later, however, a fresh and optimistic generation of Shanghai Jews would reconstitute the society—though, despite its great hopes, it too would accomplish nothing. The ancient *kehillah* of Kaifeng, in its unchecked descent into oblivion, had by then slid well beyond the point of no return.

11 ❖ BEYOND THE POINT
OF NO RETURN

O
F all the Westerners who were destined to meet the Kaifeng Jews, the one who came to know them best was Bishop William Charles White of the Canadian Church of England. Born in Britain in 1873 and raised in Canada, White took orders in 1896 and made his initial visit to the city of Kaifeng and its Jews in the following year. Consecrated the first Anglican bishop of Honan Province in 1909, he administered his church's mission in Kaifeng from its establishment in 1910 until his retirement in 1933. Returning to Canada, he embarked upon a second career at the Royal Ontario Museum, Toronto, serving first as assistant professor of Chinese archaeology and keeper of the museum's East Asiatic collection, and subsequently as assistant director of the museum and director of its school of Chinese studies. A manuscript and several synagogal artifacts that he had acquired from the Kaifeng Jews were given a home in the museum. In 1942, after years of preparatory and research effort, he published his *Chinese Jews,* a three-volume collection of excerpts from numerous works dealing with the Jewish experience in the Middle Kingdom, augmented by comments of his own on the subject and samplings of the fresh data that he was personally able to amass in the course of his talks with the Jews.

During the quarter of a century of his residence in Kaifeng, White's relationship with the Jews was warm enough to permit him to visit them frequently in their homes and to receive them just as often in his own. Their forefathers may have thought that Christianity and Judaism were more or less the same, but they themselves had met too many representatives of both faiths in Kaifeng and elsewhere to make the same mistake. White's ultimate purpose in seeking them out, they recognized, was to convert them to the Christian faith, but although the Judaism of their ancestors was now little more to them than a hazy folk memory, they had no intention of severing their tenuous connection with it in favor of Christianity. As for White, he liked them and had every reason to believe that they also liked him. Encouraged by their manifestations of friendliness, he urged them time and again to reconstitute their old *kehillah*, hoping that their next step might take them en bloc into Protestantism. In any event, he would have preferred to see them reunited as a community of professing Jews than be left to drift individually into the creeds of the people among whom they lived. The Kaifeng Jews, however, remained stolidly indifferent to his proddings, perhaps because at heart they were not really interested in becoming actively Jewish, perhaps because they remained skeptical that a non-

23. Bishop and Mrs. William Charles White, standing beside a sedan chair, in Fukien Province in the late 1890s.

Jewish Moses could or would lead them to a second Sinai. Whatever their reasoning, their ostensible lack of concern for reclaiming
their birthright disturbed White. "No spark of interest in their
history and in the divine heritage of Israel could be aroused in
them," he later complained. "They were Jews no longer, either in
a religious sense, or even as a community."[1]

In 1910, when White was looking about for a site on which
to build his mission house, the Jewish clans of Kaifeng, frag-
mented though they were, still held legal title to the tract of land
from which their synagogue had been removed long before most
of their members were born. Convinced that there could be no
place in all of Honan more symbolically appropriate for the
erection of a Christian evangelical center than the little corner of
consecrated soil on which Judaism had held sway for so many
hundreds of years, White tried to buy the property from the Jews.
To his regret, he was unable to work out a mutually satisfactory
arrangement with them and was compelled to set up his mission
elsewhere in the city. In December 1912 the 1489/1512 and 1679
steles were entrusted to his care with the understanding that they
would be maintained properly and kept from harm. The transfer of the stones to the Canadians raised a hullabaloo throughout the city and led to the imprisonment of Chao Yün-chung, the
leader of the remnants of the old *kehillah*. A compromise was
finally worked out whereby the Anglicans agreed that they would
never remove the stones from the province. Chao was released,
and the steles were turned over to the Canadians.[2] Shortly afterward, the Jews offered to sell the synagogal site, with the result
that in 1914 the Canadians took title to the plot of land that had
then been the property of the Jewish colony of Kaifeng for three-
quarters of a millennium, and perhaps even longer.

Once the ownership of the site was transferred to the Canadian
mission, the land was drained of the stagnant pool that disfigured
it, leveled, and cleaned. Part of it was then converted to use as a
children's playground under the auspices of the city's Young
Men's Christian Association. White had tried, though unsuccessfully, to persuade the Jewish community of Shanghai to provide
funds for the construction of a hospital on the synagogal site.
The institution would be jointly owned, he had proposed, by the

ABOVE: 24. The site in Kaifeng on which a series of synagogues stood for 700 years, beginning in 1163. Photo taken in the early 1900s, shortly before Bishop White acquired the property and the two surviving synagogal steles for his mission. The 1489/1512 stele is in the middle foreground.

RIGHT: 25. Jewish women, Kaifeng, 1919. All, including the child, have bound feet.

Canadian mission and the Occidental Jewish inhabitants of China, but its administration would be left to the missionaries. He could not understand why the Shanghai Jews would not go along with the plan.[3]

In 1919 White issued a call to the Jews of Kaifeng to convene as the guests of the mission for the purposes, as later spelled out in a Chinese missionary periodical:

1. of making them mutually acquainted and organizing them;
2. of making them acquainted with their own history;
3. of making them acquainted with the religion of their fore-fathers and the Scriptures;
4. of making them realize their connections with their core-ligionists throughout the world; and
5. of teaching them that Jesus Christ was a Jew, and that he came to save the world.[4]

Whether the Jews were told about the fifth purpose behind the invitation is dubious, but they must have sensed it. Their response, in any case, did not meet White's expectations. A relatively small contingent showed up at the meeting—some "scores of men and women of Jewish descent," in his words, out of an estimated population of several times that number. All seven clans were represented, including the Chang, the same Chang who had previously been reported as having either left the city or become assimilated into other faiths. The ties between the clans were now so attentuated that it became necessary to introduce a number of people to one another and even to distribute identifying name cards to pin to their clothes.

The conference took place in May 1919 and went on for three days "of discussion and social friendship," but, as White ruefully admitted, "it failed to achieve its purpose, and not a spark of interest in the glorious past and the prophetic future of Israel could be evoked. Chinese Israelitism had definitely come to an end." His attempts to turn the situation around were unsuccessful. "A hall and club rooms were prepared for their use," he wrote, "and an informed Chinese teacher, who was interested in

26. Women and children of the Jewish community of Kaifeng, about 1912.

the Israelites, was engaged to shepherd this remnant of Israel, but all to no avail, and in a year or so these special activities were ended, and only individual contacts were maintained, which have continued more or less to the present."[5]

Several of the Jews who attended the conference brought along their "three-generation" tablets, these being the listings of parents, grandparents, and great-grandparents, which individuals were required to present as a precondition to obtaining government employment. The head of the Shih clan, whose son was a student at the mission school, showed White a family register going back more than two centuries and containing several hundred names. So large a genealogical chart would suggest the existence of a fair-sized body of Shih descendants in Kaifeng, but of these only ten took the trouble to come to the meetings. As for those Shih who stayed away, White doubted (though perhaps with too little justification) that any of them were even aware of the Jewish element in their background.

Among the Occidentals who came to Kaifeng in the decade or so following the First World War and left published accounts of their contacts with the Jews were the American diplomat Charles D. Tenney (1918), the American traveler Harry A. Franck (1923), E. M. Berthel (1924), the Shanghai editor Arthur Sopher

(1924), the Shanghai Jew A. Horne (1924), and the Soviet military officer A. Klimoff (between 1925 and 1927). Their reports revealed little of value.

Tenney, who was disappointed in finding so few Jews remaining in Kaifeng, noted that those he saw were impoverished.[6] Franck doubted that as many as a hundred were left, though the man he called "the present head of the clan" had suggested to him that the number might go as high as 200. Franck observed that their assimilation was by now almost complete and that they knew virtually nothing about the traditions of their fathers. "Several portions of Hebrew Scriptures," he wrote, "have been found on the streets for sale, evidently as mere curios."[7]

Berthel's visit to the Jews, in January 1924, was his second, the first having taken place in 1903. The story he told of his more recent experience with them was preposterous. Invited to "an old Sabbath-eve dinner" at the home of a Jew who worked as an accountant for a large oil firm, he tactfully reminded his would-be host that he was not Jewish. The accountant politely waved the objection aside. "At the subsequent dinner in a well-furnished private house," Berthel recalled, "I met a very patriarchal-looking host and a score of persons of both sexes, garbed in Chinese dress and apparently belonging to the better class." Some of the guests, he decided, looked Jewish. The dinner did not include pork. Then: "After dinner my venerable host permitted me to inspect a large chest filled with ancient scrolls and books in Hebrew characters. My query whether these documents were for sale met with a refusal and a hasty closing of the chest."

There had been another Jewish colony in Hangchow, Berthel declared, whose synagogue was destroyed during the Taiping Rebellion and never rebuilt. He did not explain where he picked up this false bit of information, and may actually have believed it to be factual. As far as he knew, there were no longer any Jews left in Hangchow.[8]

Sopher, introduced as a fellow Jew to a Mr. Chao (perhaps Chao Tzu-fang), owner of a tea shop near the site of the old synagogue, was greeted with the remark, "Hah! A member of the same tribe?" He took photographs of various individuals and groups which were later printed in his booklet on the Chinese

Jews, but inserted nothing about his own visit to Kaifeng aside
from the one sentence describing his encounter with Chao.[9]

Horne, like Sopher a member of the Shanghai Jewish community, found the Jews of Kaifeng "a terrible disappointment," and
Jewish "in name only." He estimated their number at 150 and
observed that they now lived "in different quarters of the town,
never meeting together for religious or communal purposes."
They followed no Jewish customs at all, he lamented, nor had
"the faintest conception of what it means to be a Jew."[10]

Klimoff, who was in Kaifeng with a team of Russian military
advisers, remarked that the Jews he and his companions met
looked typically Chinese and remembered nothing of their heritage except the injunction against eating pork. He believed,
nonetheless, that certain religious rites were still practiced,
though presumably without any appreciable understanding of
their meaning.[11]

In Shanghai, meanwhile, after two decades of somnolence, the
Society for the Rescue of the Chinese Jews had finally bestirred
itself and come to life again. Meetings were held in July, August,
and October of 1924, and in January and June of 1925. Enthusiasm ran high among the participants, but because the communal ties of the Kaifeng Jews had by now totally disappeared
and the reconstituted rescue society's financial resources were no
more adequate than the original organization's, nothing of enduring value was accomplished.

Shortly after his return from Kaifeng, Sopher delivered an illustrated lecture before a group of interested Shanghai Jews in
which he reviewed the colorful history of the Chinese Jews and
told of his personal contacts with them. Sharing the podium
with him was George A. Sokolsky, later to become one of
America's most widely read political columnists, who presented
an analysis of how the ancestors of the people Sopher had just
met made their way to the old Sung capital.

Galvanized into action by the eloquence of the speakers, the
newly reorganized Shanghai rescue society resolved to send a
representative to Kaifeng without further delay, have him get in

touch with as many of its Jews as possible, let them know that there were coreligionists in Shanghai who were eager to help them, and try to find out how this could best be done. The man selected to undertake the mission was David Levy, formerly assistant sexton of Shanghai's Ohel Rachel Synagogue. He was the most extraordinary emissary any Caucasian body had ever dispatched to the Jews of Kaifeng.

Like the delegates who were sent to the Honan capital by Smith and Medhurst three-quarters of a century earlier, David Levy was Chinese; but, unlike them, he was, or pretended to be, a member of the House of Israel. To non-Jews he was better known by the surname Wong, and he claimed to be a native not of Kaifeng but of Khotan, the famed oasis and supply center, which sat astride the ancient silk trading route linking the countries of Central Asia, Europe, and the Levant to China. Khotan, approximately 2,000 miles to the west of Kaifeng, was in Sinkiang Province; and in both Sinkiang and its neighboring Kansu, Levy asserted, thriving colonies of Jews could still be found.

Neither Sopher nor Sokolsky saw any reason for disputing Levy's testimony. Not long after Levy left Shanghai to carry out the assignment allotted to him by the rescue society, Sokolsky wrote as follows about him and the people to whom he allegedly belonged:

In Kansu and Sinkiang—that is, in that vast area which is roughly called Chinese Turkestan—the Jews still remain a flourishing element. Before the war [World War I] these Turkestan Jews carried on commerce, principally in Russian Turkestan and thence to Siberia. The war forced some of them to face eastwards to the interior of China. They then followed the old trade routes known to their ancestors, from Turkestan to Sianfu, from Sianfu to Kaifeng, from Kaifeng to Shanghai.

These Jews of northwest China are in every respect like other Chinese of the region; even their beards are of that peculiar copper hue common among the Moslems of Kansu. One of these Turkestan Jewish traders, a native of Khotan, I knew quite well. His Chinese name was Wong (Prince), and this, he said, was the family name taken by the Levites when they settled in China. In Hebrew, his name was David Levy. He could speak Mandarin, Turki and some Russian. He could read Hebrew. He was seventy years old, but looked like a man of forty. He said that in his part of the world men lived long, principally off goat's milk. In Shanghai he performed the incredible task of learning to speak better than "pidgin" English in three months. For a time he acted as assistant *shammash* to the Ohel Rachel Synagogue. Then he traded in wool and was finally sent into the interior of China by the Society for the Rescue of the Chinese Jews, with which he corresponded until he disappeared. Unless he died or was killed by soldiers (he was always in war territory), he is undoubtedly somewhere in Honan, Shensi or Kansu with Marshal Feng Yu-hsiang's Northwestern army. For David Levy was an amazingly versatile gentleman, who could be all things to all men and make money as he went along. He told us that he had raised $10,000 in Chinese currency for the establishment of a synagogue and Hebrew school in Kashgar [nearly 300 miles to the northwest of Khotan] and that his principal donor was the Tuchun of Charhar, General Ma Fu-hsiang, a military man of considerable importance, whose father is said to have been a Jew, but whose mother was a Moslem.[12]

Sokolsky feared for Levy's safety, but as Sopher was able to report, the indomitable agent whom the rescue society had chosen to make the journey to Kaifeng arrived at his destination unharmed. Once there, moreover, he sought out the Jews and, gaining their confidence, was soon able to write the society that:

> on the 13th of August [1924] we took a picture in the garden of the American Church Mission [Trinity Cathedral, apparently] at which more than ten people were present, all of them heads of families. The next morning at ten I gave a talk at the Mission attended by about a thousand people, Jews and Christians. After the meeting I asked two Jews, Mr. Chao and Mr. Shih Chung-yung, to make a plan of the synagogue and to write the enclosed report.[13]

The report accompanying Levy's letter recognized only ninety-nine persons in Kaifeng as Jews, most of them very poor. Their names, ages, and occupations were listed. The enclosed sketch of the plot of land that had once encompassed the synagogue showed that several private dwellings and other buildings still stood on it, the playground having been allocated the remainder of the space.

On his return to Shanghai, Levy was able to tell the society that the Jews to whom he had spoken would welcome whatever assistance might be offered to them. They had suggested, he said, that a start be made by setting up a school in which their children could be taught the essentials of Judaism. Levy volunteered to move himself and his family to Kaifeng as soon as the necessary funds for the organization of such a school could be raised and spend his remaining years working with his coreligionists. For one reason or another—perhaps because they had begun to suspect that Levy was an impostor—the Jews of Shanghai decided to defer further action on the matter.

Can Levy's claim for the existence of Jewish enclaves in Sinkiang and Kansu be believed? Noach Mishkowsky, who met Levy some years before the reconstitution of the rescue society, never doubted the man's Jewishness but failed to interrogate him about the Sinkiang and Kansu settlements of which he had time and again told the Shanghai Jews. "In Shanghai," Mishkowsky wrote, "I met the *shammash* of the synagogue in the French Concession. Also a Jew, one of 'the old ones.' He, for a change, knew a little about Judaism, could even read a bit of Hebrew, and had some appreciation of Jewish law and tradition; but he picked up his Jewish 'expertise' not from his own brethren, the Chinese Jews, but from 'our' Jews—from the Sephardic Jews, that is. It was they who enlightened him and made him cognizant of Jewish ways."[14] Sokolsky's "amazingly versatile gentleman, who could be all things to all men and make money as he went along," had, it would seem, taken in not only Sokolsky but also a fair number of others in the rescue society.

Before meeting Levy, Mishkowsky had already run into two Chinese outside of Shanghai who called themselves Jews. The first he chanced upon in a Manchurian town served by the Chinese Eastern Railroad.[15] The man was a grocer, he told Mishkowsky. His forefathers had believed in the One God. They had extracted the sinews from the meat they slaughtered and had salted it.[16] He himself, however, was totally ignorant of the teachings of Judaism, Mishkowsky realized. He knew that there was a language called Hebrew but did not remember ever seeing the characters in which it was written. His wife was a Buddhist. As for his two children, he regarded them as Jewish.

But what, Mishkowsky demanded, did their Jewishness consist of? The man did not know, but as far as he was concerned he and they were of Jewish descent, and that made the three of them Jewish. Where had his forebears lived? Mishkowsky either failed to ask the question or neglected to record the reply.

On another occasion, in Chalantun (also in Manchuria), Mishkowsky was in the process of buying a basin of some kind. He asked its price. The vendor, turning the utensil over, glanced at two characters traced on its bottom and gave Mishkowsky the figure. Curious, Mishkowsky looked at the markings—and immediately recognized the two letters as the Hebrew *kaph* and *heh,* the numerical equivalent, in the sequence in which they were written, of twenty-five. Astounded, he asked the tradesman to tell him how the characters had come to be inscribed on the basin. The merchant explained that he had always used characters of this kind for his price coding, and so had his father and grandfather before him. Quizzing him about the individual letters of the Hebrew alphabet, Mishkowsky discovered that while the man was thoroughly familiar with their numeric values he had absolutely no conception of their names or the phonemes they represented.

Mishkowsky's merchant, like the grocer, spoke of ancestors whose faith had been monotheistic. He also knew that these ancestors rested one day a week and shied away from polygamy.

Did he think of himself as Jewish? Yes! Were there any other Jews in the area? Perhaps, but he had never met any. He understood, however, that far away, in the (unnamed) region from which his grandparents came, there were many Jews.[17]

The question of whether there were still a few Jewish communities elsewhere in China than Kaifeng when David Levy was a young man or, even later, when Mishkowsky was wandering about the country, remains unanswered. Donald Daniel Leslie, referring to stories emanating from India and Afghanistan in the early 1800s, which hint at the presence of occasional clusters of Jews in unidentified regions of China, theorizes that in recent centuries "a renewed migration (Drang noch Osten) through Central Asia into Kansu and other areas might have occurred." He suggests that because "one comes across odd references to Chinese Jews not from Kaifeng," it is possible to infer that "perhaps among the large Muslim population of China small pockets of Jews still exist."[18]

On a November afternoon in 1932, after a seven-hour flight originating in Lanchow, capital of Kansu Province, David A. Brown, the publisher of an American Jewish periodical, disembarked at Kaifeng from a Junkers transport placed at his disposal by T. V. Soong, minister of finance in the national government headed by his brother-in-law Chiang Kai-shek. Brown, whose sole reason for stopping off in the Honan metropolis was to investigate the status of its Jews, was greeted at the landing strip by a large delegation of local officials, lured or directed there, no doubt, in deference to his standing with Soong. Also on hand to welcome him was Bishop White, in whose mission house he stayed for the duration of his visit and who summoned the Jews to assemble at the mission and hear what their American coreligionist had to say. This convocation, although neither man realized it at the time, was to be the last formal communal gathering in the long history of the autochthonous Jews of China.

Brown, who was especially anxious to inspect the old synagogal site, was given an opportunity to do so while the final arrangements for bringing the Jews together were being worked out. With White at his side, he watched "the little Chinese children of the neighborhood play games and make mud-pies, as do children the world over," but his thoughts were far removed from the childish scamperings going on about him. The experience was unnerving, he later confessed, arousing emotions bordering on the atavistic. In his mind's eye, he saw the area covered not by a playground but by "buildings much in the form of the Temple in Jerusalem, yet with a touch of Chinese architecture." Allowing his imagination to roam free, he conjured up a vivid scenario of "Chinese Jews conducting their services daily, on the Sabbath and on the holy days, worshipping the One God, the God of

Israel, [and] offering their prayers facing west, towards Jerusalem, just as millions of other Jews have done these many centuries."[19]

From the synagogal site the Canadian churchman and his American guest walked to the nearby teashop of Chao Tzu-fang, at seventy-five the oldest Jew in Kaifeng, and quickly discovered that he was only sketchily acquainted with the story of his people. As his home was close to his place of business, they were able to visit it and meet his family. His son, well educated, proved to have a better grasp of the history of the Kaifeng Jews than the old man, though not enough to provide White and Brown with any details they considered worth recording. The younger Chao complained that their last Jewish visitor had more than eight years previously promised them assistance that never materialized.[20]

Five clans were represented at the 1932 meeting: the Chao, Ai, Li, Shih, and, as at the 1919 conference, also the Chang. All the Jews looked characteristically Chinese to Brown, aside from those of the Chao clan and one elderly lady, the Widow Shih. With her oval face and wide eyes, Brown felt, she "could pass without trouble for a Baghdad or Indian Jewess, except for her bound feet."

Brown talked to the Jews through his own interpreter, G. Findlay Andrews, who, born in China, spoke several of the country's dialects fluently. Through Andrews, he told the Jews that the Hebrew Union College of Cincinnati, with which he was associated, had acquired many of the manuscripts formerly owned by their forefathers and that he himself was in Kaifeng because he was intensely interested in learning as much about his Chinese coreligionists as he could. At this point he was interrupted by a Mr. Ai, who explained that the Jews already knew why he was there. Many of the people present, it turned out, had read about Brown's reason for coming to Kaifeng in the Chinese press.

Brown asked the Jews what their most pressing need was. "A school for our children," Ai replied, "so that they may learn who they are and in what respects they are different from the other Chinese. We know we are Jews, and that our people came here many centuries ago, [and] that we once had a synagogue and a rabbi. But we have lost all knowledge of this, and we are anxious that our children shall walk in the footsteps of those ancient people from whom we have sprung."

Was this mere talk, Brown demanded, or were they serious? Could he count on their becoming practicing Jews again if the synagogue were rebuilt and a school established for their children?

The questions unleashed a Babel of excited voices. "They all responded in the affirmative at once," Brown recalled, "and Mr. Ai was quite emphatic in stating that a congregation of over 200 souls could be brought together in time." Hearing this, White must have been thunderstruck. Thirteen years earlier, at his own meetings with the Jews, he had been forced to conclude that "no spark of interest" in matters Judaic could ever be aroused in them. Now, suddenly, they were acting in a way he had never foreseen.

Why did the Jews express no interest at all in reorganizing their *kehillah* during their talks with White and do precisely the opposite when they were face to face with Brown? Was it, in the one instance, that they preferred to conceal their true feelings from a man whose obvious goal was to get them to stop being Jews, even in name alone, and start being Christians? Or, in the other, did they simply think it politic to tell American Jewry's representative (and, also, apparently a friend of the powerful T. V. Soong) what he seemed to want to hear? Or, when all is said and done, did they merely hope that the Americans might be induced to help them out financially? The questions remain unanswered.

Asked by Brown to define the religious status of the Kaifeng Jews, Ai replied that "as a body they had no religion; but, when asked of what faith they are, they claim to be Jews." They had no leader, "but in the event that a school and synagogue were projected, they would get together and elect a chief man with full power to represent them." They called themselves the religion that plucked out the sinew, Ai also told Brown, but others called them the people who followed the Scriptures.

The Widow Shih was a find. Even White had never heard of the lady. Brown was quite taken with her. She wanted to know if he had ever been in the Holy Land. Yes, he said, he had been there twice. She was greatly pleased. Could he read the Bible in Hebrew? He had to confess that he could not, but assured her that it was available in English, in Chinese, and in many other languages. She knew this, she sighed, but what a pity it was that the Chinese Jews had lost their own scriptural manuscripts. Her late father-in-law, born around 1810, had on numerous occasions repeated to her what had been passed on to him in his youth about the synagogue and the worship services that were held there in times gone by. She could remember him saying that there were no galleries in the sanctuary, but that the sexes were separated during worship services. Both men and women were dressed in long white gowns while at prayer, the men also wearing a turban of sorts. A deceased Jew was wrapped in a plain cloth, placed in a coffin, and interred. On the anniversary of the death of an ancestor, incense was burned and special offerings were made before a tablet set up in the family home. The person who was to conduct the memorial service was first required to purify himself ritually by immersing himself in a large wooden tub.

As to the occupations of the people at the meeting, Ai said that he was a painter; Li described himself as a postal clerk; Chao, as Brown already knew, owned a small tea and candy shop; and the Widow Shih declared that her husband had been a teacher. The Shih penchant for scholarship, she wanted Brown to know, was more than 200 years old, and her son was carrying on the family tradition—he too had become a teacher. Another widow, also a Shih, admitted that her husband had been a mere businessman, not a scholar. However, she quickly added, her daughter, as yet unmarried, was in the teaching profession.

A Mr. Chang told Brown that he worked as a carpenter. He was born, he said, in Tung-ming, ninety miles northeast of Kaifeng, in Hopei Province, and was brought to Kaifeng while still a youngster. It was only when his father began to make inquiries about the Jews, he explained, that he himself discovered that his family was of Jewish extraction. His story suggests that the reports provided by several visitors to Kaifeng of an exodus of the Chang from the city may have had a degree of substance to them, and also that the memory of their Jewish ancestry had faded completely from the minds of at least some of the displaced Chang.

The meeting was terminated before sunset so that Brown could take photographs of the participants. Ai apologized to him for the limited amount of information the Jews had been able to supply, and pleaded for the help that would enable the community to find its way back to the House of Israel. There were large numbers of Jews scattered throughout the length and breadth of China, he pointed out, and if Judaism were ever revived in Kaifeng many of them could be expected to return to their ancestral faith. In response, Brown made it clear that it was by no means in his power to set up a school or replace the synagogue, but promised to publicize the plight of the Kaifeng Jews and urge the outside world to send them the assistance they so desperately needed.

A little later, as White, Andrew, and Brown were passing through the mission grounds, they stopped for a moment at the two historical monuments that had originally belonged to the defunct *kehillah* and were now the property of the Anglicans. The bishop turned to Brown. "Are you Jews really interested in saving these people?" he demanded. Brown could not give him a direct answer. "This is a question I am going to ask my people in the United States upon returning there," he told White. "I will let you know."

12 ❖ OUTRIGHT LIES, TALL TALES, AND A FEW TRUTHS

L ONG before Brown undertook to publicize its plight, the Jewish community of Kaifeng was already a community in name alone, and Jewish only in the sense that it thought of itself as such and was made up, however loosely, of people who had never seen fit to disassociate themselves willfully from their ancestral faith by becoming formally affiliated with some other religious entity. Jewish religious law, the *halakhah*, defines a Jew as a person who was either born of a Jewish mother or has in good faith passed through the prescribed rites of conversion, which include, when the proselyte is a male, the rite of circumcision. The practice of halakhically converting non-Jewish women who married into the *kehillah* would not have been carried on beyond the period 1800–10, when the last of its rabbis died, and may well have come to an end even before then. Leaving aside the occasional individual who underwent the rite of conversion in Shanghai or elsewhere, few if any of those Chinese who in recent generations persisted in identifying themselves as Jews could successfully have withstood a strict halakhic investigation of their right to do so.[1]

From the point of view of the West, none of this mattered much. The missionaries who came to Kaifeng imbued with the desire to proselytize its inhabitants could scarcely be expected to concern themselves with the halakhic status of the tiny remnant of Israel they found there. As for those Jews in the Caucasian world who were appalled by the justifiably pessimistic reports filtering through to them concerning the status of the ancient *kehillah*, what they wanted first of all was to fan the sparks of Judaism still flickering in the hearts of their lapsed coreligion-

ists until the strong flame that once burned there could be re-
kindled. This done, halakhic problems might readily be resolved
and the strayed brethren welcomed back to the fold as coequal
sharers in the heritage of Israel.

There were others, of course, whose interest in the Jewish
community of Kaifeng was not restricted to proselytization or
did not include it at all. The Jesuits, on the Christian side, and
Manasseh ben Israel, on the Jewish, had tried to inject the
Kaifeng *kehillah* into theological and political arenas of whose
existence it had never even heard. Serious scholars, of whom
there were not a few, looked forward to examining its scriptural
manuscripts and studying its history. Voltaire saw nothing rep-
rehensible about denigrating the Kaifeng Jews and using them
Samson-like as a convenient weapon with which to smite his foes.
He was not the only writer who deliberately misrepresented the
story of the Chinese Jews to suit his own ends, but most of those
who did so tended to concoct relatively harmless fantasies about
them, often for no other reason than to provide entertainment to
the casual reader. At times, however, the motives of the Occidentals who addressed themselves to the question of what to say
or do about the Jews of Kaifeng were unclear, or even dubious,
as in the case of Aaron Halevi Fink, whose impassioned plea for
funds with which to rescue them may or may not have been
entirely selfless. At other times, the motives turned out to be
absurd, as when the Japanese, who held Kaifeng during World
War II, dispatched two separate intelligence missions there to
determine if its few dozen faintly Jewish adult residents, presumably no admirers of Japan's *Herrenvolk* ally, posed a threat to
the security of the forces who occupied the city. And, unfortunately, the motives occasionally became totally obscene, as
when the Nazis, already wallowing in the blood of masses of
Jews nearer home, coolly offered a venally adulterated version
of the long history of the small *kehillah* of Kaifeng as evidence
that the world would be a more congenial place to live in if only
it were *Judenrein*. It need scarcely be said that they were not
the only anti-Semites to misuse the Chinese Jews in this fashion.

The most disturbing fact about the stories that grew up around the Chinese Jews—even in those years during which access to their midst was not denied to Westerners—is that so few can be trusted, completely and without question. The report attributed to Lehmann and believed by Marcus N. Adler and others may of course be rejected as an out-and-out hoax, but even Liebermann's account, so long taken as totally reliable, must now, it seems, be subjected to reexamination. Yet, the essentially identical stories told by him and by Fink fall at least within the realm of the possible, and their uncannily similar descriptions of the Jews they each say they visited in Kaifeng do not appear to have been plucked wholly out of thin air. A European Jew did perhaps go to Kaifeng in the mid-1860s and did spend some time with the *kehillah*, but who he was—Fink, Liebermann, or a third party—and the year in which his trip took place are still to be determined.

Quite different from the Fink-Liebermann story, and without a shred of truth to it, is the tale of Adolph Stemp (f) el's visit, also in the 1860s, to a Chinese city inhabited by a remnant of the Ten Lost Tribes. Pure fiction from beginning to end, Stempel's narrative—or, more accurately, the first-person account ascribed to him—is presented as straightforward reportage, though it was drawn up, in reality, to promote the view that the rightful place of the Jew is in agriculture, not in the petty trades or commerce of any sort. Its starting point is the ancient Jewish legend that tells of a wondrous river called the Sambatyon and the Ten Lost Tribes who inhabit the regions lying beyond it.[2]

It was to the far side of the Sambatyon, so the legend goes, that the Ten Tribes were ultimately dispersed. That the Sambatyon's whereabouts are shrouded in mystery is of no particular practical significance, for even if the river were found, not a single observer of the Law of Moses, whether of Judean or Israelite extraction, would be able to cross it. For the Sambatyon is a temperamental and forbidding stream, the like of which is not to be met with anywhere else in the world. Six days a week, enormous stones spew forth menacingly from its surface. On the seventh day, the Sabbath, the turbulence subsides and the waters grow placid, but the traveler, bound by Jewish law, must on that day break his journey and take his rest. The river is thus rendered impassable at all times and in either direction, leaving the Ten Tribes who are stranded on its more remote bank effectively sealed off from all contact with the Two Tribes on the closer bank. As to how the Ten Tribes accomplished their original crossing to the trans-Sambatyonic lands they now occupy without violating the Sabbath, on this the legend remains frustratingly silent.[3]

Stempel, however, has the answers to the perplexing problems posed by the Sambatyon. He claims to have discovered where the storied river is, and also how the Ten Tribes managed to cross it—on a weekday, of course—and he passes on the good news in a series of letters addressed to the Jewish banker in Calcutta who for the past several years had been sponsoring Stempel's search for Israelite settlements in the Middle Kingdom. The fabled stream, Stempel announces, is almost surely the Irawadi River, which, as everyone knows, may be crossed safely on any day of the week—though, he now explains, not necessarily at all points. The boatman who had just ferried him across the Irawadi has informed him that for a small distance above and below the place of their crossing the Irawadi always flows quietly for intervals of two weeks, following which, for two or three days, great rumblings disturb its tranquillity. The uproar caused by the disturbance is earshattering, loud enough to be heard a parasang away. Stempel theorizes that subterranean volcanic eruptions might be responsible for the unconventional behavior of the stream and that the compilers of the Sambatyon folktale may have misconstrued the nature and periodicity of the commotions that shook the body of water separating them from the Lost Tribes. He had not realized before crossing the Irawadi that it was in ancient times known as the Sambatyon, but the boatman's story had made it abundantly clear to him that such was the case, and also presaged what happened almost immediately afterward when, beyond the river and on the other side of the Chinese border, he discovered a city full of Jews. He is now in that city, he writes his sponsor, and he has no reason for doubting that the people who live in it are of the stock of Israel. Why? Not only because the legend declares that one can expect the population of the trans-Sambatyonite regions to include large numbers of Israelites, but also because the local rabbi, obviously an honorable man, has assured him that his congregants are directly descended from the tribes driven out of the Northern Kingdom of Israel in the eighth century B.C.E. The rabbi, moreover, has a massive collection of ancient communal documents with which to back up his claim.[4]

Stempel was living in Calcutta when his banker friend, excited by the report that a British naval commander had recently chanced upon a Jewish metropolis on the soil of China, commissioned him to go find it. Neither man foresaw how long the search would take; but now, after several years of unprofitable wandering about the country, Stempel's luck has at last changed. He is elated at having found his first Sino-Israelite settlement, the more so since he has also learned that there are many others like it not very far away.

The precious communal manuscripts entrusted to the care of Stempel's Chinese rabbi are prominently displayed in the rabbi's house. There they are pointed out to Stempel, large numbers of them standing side by side in their neat sky-blue binders. A half-decade of Chinese Jewish history is recorded in each binder. Speaking fluent Hebrew, the rabbi describes the procedure by which the contents are assembled. At five-year intervals, every rabbi in China is required by ancient custom to transmit to the chief rabbi a summary of all the significant events that have transpired in his particular community since the submission of his last report. The materials thus collected are then compiled into one volume, a copy of which is deposited with each *kehillah* in the empire. The count of quinquennial chronicles amassed by the Jewish communities of China now runs to about 450; and the texts of the earliest volumes, Stempel asserts, prove beyond a shadow of a doubt that the Ten Tribes have been settled in the Middle Kingdom for well over two millennia!

That the Chinese rabbinate accepts the responsibility for preparing and preserving the historical records of the people it serves surprises Stempel greatly. "If only our European rabbis would do the same!" he exclaims wistfully to his host—who, dismayed by the revelation of his Occidental colleagues' remissness in so vital a matter, expresses the hope that the salutary example set by the rabbis of the Middle Kingdom will encourage the rabbis of the West to turn over a new leaf and begin at once to chronicle the experiences of their people.

Stempel's conversation with his Chinese rabbi is for the most part devoted to comparing notes on how Jews earn their daily bread in Europe and in China. The rabbi is stunned by Stempel's disclosure that European Jewry is almost totally divorced from the land, and is engaged instead in petty trade and the handicrafts. In China, he tells Stempel, no self-respecting Jew would ever dream of becoming a merchant. Of necessity, some Jews work as skilled craftsmen, but the overwhelming majority devote their efforts to tilling the soil. Agriculture, he reminds Stempel, was the principal vocation of ancient Israel and has always been the loftiest economic pursuit to which man can aspire. It is common knowledge, he points out, that the merchant's goal is to accumulate wealth, a shabby ambition that dulls a person's sense of morality and often incites him to despoil his fellow man. The farmer, on the other hand, is not exposed to temptations that might lead him to do harm to his neighbor, for the improvement of his own lot is not conditioned upon the taking away of a jot or tittle of what belongs to someone else. The farmer's is thus a nobler life than the merchant's. Since dignity and virtue are what all Jews should strive for, and since these are more apt to be attained if one's thoughts and energies during the working day are dedicated to agriculture, Jews have no business being elsewhere than on the land.

To this, Stempel agrees wholeheartedly; but when the rabbi asks why, now that many European Jews are at last being permitted to buy land, they do not organize agricultural schools for the training of their youth, Stempel is left shamefacedly silent.

Stempel is of course putting into the rabbi's mouth the two-sided message that he, a self-appointed spokesman for the Haskalah (Enlightenment) movement, wants to drive home to European Jewry—that it must return to the land, and that the first prerequisite for doing so is to establish vocational centers in which to prepare its young people for the agricultural careers he hopes they will pursue.[5]

The series of letters allegedly written by Stempel traveled back across the Sambatyon-Irawadi and in due course came safely to the desk of his patron in Calcutta. The banker read them with rapt attention and decided that the startling revelations they contained must not be withheld from the Jewish press of Europe. With this in mind, he posted the letters to the Paris representative of his bank, one Jacob Elsa(e)sser, with the request that Elsasser see to their publication.

By one of those remarkable coincidences that defy the imagination, it turned out that Adolph Stempel, on the banks of the Sambatyon, and Jacob Elsasser, on the banks of the Seine, had known each other in their youth. At any rate, that is what Elsasser told the editors of *Archives Israélites,* to whom he forwarded the letters and who published them without challenging their credibility from November 1867 through January 1868. An English translation of the French text that had appeared in *Archives* was printed a few weeks later in the *Jewish Chronicle,* whose editor, to his credit, suggested that the authenticity of the material was still to be demonstrated. At about the same time, *Der Israelit,* in Mainz, published a German version. A Hebrew version also appeared in *Ha-Maggid,* declaring the letters to be completely factual. The *Ha-Maggid* text was reprinted in the aforementioned collection dealing with life in China, *Metziat Aseret ha-Shebatim* (1900), also known as *Sefer Brit ha-Hadash* (1911).[6] No doubt the same letters were also printed elsewhere and in still other languages, and no doubt they were taken literally by more people than one would expect.

The innocuous hoax dreamed up by Adolf Stempel—or Jacob Elsasser, or someone else—was followed by numerous others of the same genre. Sometimes these seem to be goodnatured attempts on the part of individual Chinese to have a bit of fun at the expense of a foreigner; sometimes they are harmless tall tales told by Westerners and by Chinese. There is, for example, the case of the Chinese florist in Shanghai who urges an English Jewish lady late one afternoon in 1940 to make her purchases quickly so that he can close shop and prepare for the Yom Kippur fast, which begins that evening. She takes his little joke much more seriously, apparently, than he had anticipated. And there is also the story that crops up time and again, though in an assortment of versions, about the Caucasian Jew who enters a synagogue in a Chinese city, finds a seat, looks about him, and realizes that all the other worshippers in the sanctuary are Orientals. At the conclusion of the service, the rabbi approaches him and invites him to come again, adding that non-Jewish visitors are always welcome. The Occidental indignantly retorts that he is as much a Jew as the rabbi. Whereupon the rabbi adjusts his spectacles, peers intently at the stranger's face, and then exclaims—"Really? But you don't look Jewish!"[7]

The Japanese army that marched into Kaifeng in 1938 remained there until 1945. During the seven years in which it held the city it kept a vigilant and baleful eye on the civilians who had come under its control and did the usual things that an occupying force does to ferret out all potential challenges to its authority. In the course of its administration of the old provincial capital, it ran into the Jews and did not quite know what to make of them. Were they as few, as weak, and as disorganized as they appeared to be? Or were they, as Japan's German ally insisted all Jews were, part of a powerful, evil, and hydra-headed international conspiracy that had to be destroyed at all costs?

Whatever the case, the traces of Judaism still existing in Kaifeng seem to have drawn far more attention from the Japanese military than the circumstances warranted. As a consequence, at least two investigations were launched—both, apparently, on behalf of Japanese intelligence agencies—for the purpose of determining just how dangerous the city's Jews might be. Portions of the information uncovered by the Japanese inquiries were published in Tokyo in 1941 in two separate articles, one prepared by Shizuo Sogabe and the other by Teichō Mikami. Both men had been in Kaifeng during the autumn of 1940.[8]

The articles themselves yield little that is new about the Kaifeng Jews. Mikami concludes that they number only about a hundred persons (out of an estimated citywide population of some 300,000), and reports that those he met told him that they were Buddhists, Taoists, or Confucianists.[9] Sogabe counts 180 autochthonous Jews in the city, but speaks of eighty more in Shanghai, also under Japanese domination at this time. Both writers use the term *ch'i-hsin pa-chia* ("the seven names or eight clans") in connection with the Kaifeng community, and each states that there are two clans named Li and that the whereabouts of the Chang cannot be ascertained.

What is most striking about the Sogabe and Mikami investigations is, of course, the mere fact that they took place—that the Japanese authorities, already holding power over several tens of thousands of Caucasian Jews living in other occupied Chinese cities, should have gone to the trouble and expense of checking out so obviously feeble and disorganized a collection of Jews as the one in Kaifeng. The most plausible explanation that can be offered for the inflated concern displayed by Japanese officialdom in connection with the remnants of the ancient *kehillah* of Kaifeng is that some of the more gullible members of the Japanese bureaucracy had been taken in by the poisonous anti-Semitic campaign that the Nazis were then carrying on in Japan itself, and were acting as if the Nazi fantasies about the satanic powers of the Jews had some substance to them. On the whole, the Japanese treatment of the Western Jews who came under their control during World War II was of course infinitely more humane than that accorded to Jews in German-held lands.[10]

Some months after the visits of Sogabe and Mikami to Kaifeng, the Nazis would also have something to say about the descendants of the Jews who came to the city so many centuries earlier, but their way of saying it would not be at all as dispassionate or fair-minded as Sogabe's and Mikami's. For in the case of at least one of the academicians within the Hitlerite camp, no less averse than his colleagues to distorting historic and scientific fact in order to justify the racial policies of the Führer, the propagandistic potentialities inherent in the story of the old *kehillah* were much too tempting to ignore. That he was himself of Mediterranean rather than Nordic ancestry did not restrain him from endorsing the Aryan superman mythos of which his German counterparts had become so fanatically enamored. He was Troilo Salvotti, a member of the Italian nobility, and in setting his own standards of racial "purity," he went even further than the infamous Nuremberg Decrees of 1935, which did not overly concern themselves with blood lines going back more than two generations. It was Salvotti's contention, in short, that once

Jewish genes were introduced into a non-Jewish biological strain, the damage resulting from such an act of miscegenation could never be undone, regardless of how many generations might go by. It followed, therefore, that if even a few Jews were permitted to mix their blood with that of their neighbors, the impact on the biological and moral health of the totality of the community would be catastrophic.

Salvotti's outstanding contribution to the war effort of the Axis powers was a scurrilous diatribe to which the Nazis enthusiastically lent their imprimatur. Translated into German and heralded as a serious scholarly study, it was printed in Berlin in 1941 under the title *Juden in Ostasien* (Jews in East Asia). It consists, actually, of a long tirade directed against the great Jewish banking house of Sassoon. According to its author, the Sassoons, pro-Communist to the core, are conniving with international Jewry, the British, and the Chinese to bring down all that is worthwhile in the civilized world.[11]

Salvotti opens his book with a survey of Chinese Jewish history. His familiarity with the subject leaves much to be desired. He believes, or pretends to believe, that the Jews were already established in the Middle Kingdom well over 1,500 years before the 1605 meeting of Ai T'ien and Matteo Ricci. The first Jewish immigrants to China, Salvotti holds, intermarried with the native Chinese shortly after being permitted to settle in the country. A large number of generations has therefore passed since the process of assimilation was initiated, he says, but in spite of this the physically and socially obnoxious biological traits of the Jew are still very evident in those Chinese unfortunate enough to be descended from the early Jewish arrivals in China.

Ricci, Salvotti points out, observed that even though his visitor from Kaifeng looked Chinese he nevertheless exhibited certain physiogonomical characteristics that were distinctly Jewish. The Europeans who subsequently met Ai's kinsmen, Salvotti notes, made similar observations. "In spite of their marked Chinese-Mongolian appearances and yellow skin," Salvotti laments, the Chinese Jews "nevertheless display clearly recognizable Jewish racial characteristics. These facts merit our special interest, for they prove that Jewish racial traits can never be assimilated. The other racial 'substance' associated with the Jews is in fact so insidious that 2,000 years of living together with the Chinese and intermarrying with them have created a blood mixture in which the Jewish elements have triumphed, so that today the Jewish bloodlines tend to be the dominant ones."[12]

The alarm sounded by Salvotti had of course been heard often enough in the Nazi world, though not quite in the form presented by him, and with genocidal effect. Salvotti, it is true, does not specifically urge a program of slaughter on his readers to keep the Jews from infecting the bloodstreams of the planet's superior races, but the implications emerging from his discussion of the impact of the Jews on their Chinese hosts are terrifyingly clear —total isolation or, if a more foolproof course is preferred, Final Solution.

Revolting though Salvotti's bigoted attitude and his misuse of the Chinese Jews as a medium for spreading anti-Semitism are, later efforts to follow in his footsteps make the Italian Fascist's seem tame by comparison. Two illustrations will suffice.

The first is taken from a disjointed rabble-rousing "sermon" delivered by one Wesley A. Swift in a California church in the early 1970s and afterward issued as a booklet by a publisher based in Georgia; the second is provided in a pamphlet distributed by a Louisiana anti-Semitic organization which attributes its authorship to a Hungarian "researcher" named Itsvan (Istvan?) Bakony and represents it as a translation made in 1969 from the Hungarian and subsequently "brought up to date by the author."

In his California talk, Swift charges the thirteenth-century Jewish community of Venice with sending Chepe Noyon, whom he identifies as a Chinese Jew, on a mission to Genghis Khan. (Actually, one of Genghis's foremost military commanders was a Mongol named Chépé.) Through their Chinese coreligionist, the Jews of Venice offer Genghis all the financial and military backing world Jewry can muster, if he and his Mongols will first overrun China and, once that great nation is incorporated into his own, proceed to invade Europe and put an end to Christianity. To this proposition Genghis agrees. Before long, his forces advance eastward, their task made easy by the Jewish residents of a succession of Asian population centers, who swing open the city gates to them. On one night of infamy, the Jews of China open the gates of the Great Wall, an act of treachery, in the words of the concoctor of this sleazy tale, which takes place "while the Chinese people are asleep." When the sun rises and the unsuspecting Chinese creep out of their beds and rub the sleep from their eyes, he goes on, it is too late for them to offer any resistance, the Mongols having by then penetrated no less than eighty miles into China.

As soon as the country is firmly in Mongol hands, the story continues, Jews from other lands arrive "with their goods and merchandise and open up their stalls beside the great gates inside the Chinese Wall." Later, the Mongols fulfill their end of their bargain with Venetian Jewry by sweeping into Europe. Their Jewish confederates, naturally, now open the gates of the Christian cities in which they live. Multitudes of innocent Christians, caught unaware, are slaughtered by the barbarian hordes. In the massacres, the Jews are never touched, since the yellow armbands they wear identify them to the Mongol butchers as friends and collaborators.

Bakony's charges against the Chinese Jews are even more paranoid in nature than Swift's. Bakony's method is to take statements out of context and use the resulting distortions to prove to his readers that Judaism's ultimate goal is the subjugation of the entire human race. Among the authors whom he victimizes in this fashion are S. M. Perlmann, Benjamin II, Alexander Wylie, the distinguished Orientalist Édouard Chavannes, several contributors to two Jewish encyclopedias—and, while he is at it, the composer of the Book of Esther. Madame Sun Yat-sen and her sister Madame Chiang Kai-shek, he calls Jewish. The former he accuses of conspiring to have a Chinese Jew, "or at least a Gentile Chinese easily manageable by the Jews . . . succeed Mao Tsetung when he dies." She and her Chinese coreligionists, whose numbers he estimates as "2 million people at most," are determined, he declares, to bring the masses and resources of China under the yoke of "the Jewish socialist imperialists of Moscow," thus endowing the Kremlin with the additional strength it needs to conquer the world for Judaism.[13]

Brown's 1932 encounter with the Kaifeng Jews was by no means their last direct contact with a Westerner.[14] They were in frequent touch with Bishop White until his departure from their city in 1933, and occasionally talked with other Caucasians passing through or living in Honan. The journalist and photographer Harrison Forman, who reached Kaifeng in 1938, shortly after its occupation by the Japanese, spoke with several Jews and observed that they knew little or nothing of their heritage except that it was "different" from that of their neighbors.[15] The French diplomat Pierre Gilbert, also in the city at this time, later told President Yitzhak Ben-Zvi of Israel of meeting a few Jews who were engaged in camel transport and agriculture. They preferred to speak of themselves, Gilbert remembered, not as Jews who happened to be Chinese, but as Chinese who happened to be Jews.[16]

In 1943, Father Antonio Cattaneo, rector of the Regional seminary of the Catholic Mission at Kaifeng, wrote to Dr. Rudolf Loewenthal, then teaching at Peking's Yenching University, that a small number of Jewish families were still left in and about the old provincial capital, and that the Shih clan had gone over to Catholicism in 1924. In 1941, Loewenthal learned from another source, one of the Shih had enrolled in Cattaneo's seminary with the intention of becoming a priest, only to change his mind and withdraw from the school.[17] In any case, how many of the Shih accepted baptism in 1924 remains a mystery, for eight years later several members of the clan were still sufficiently interested in Judaism to meet with David Brown and discuss the prospects for establishing a Jewish school in their city.

Relatively little of any credibility has been heard about the condition of Kaifeng's Jews since the end of World War II. A friend of Ben-Zvi, Joseph Buchholder(?), told the president of meeting a Jewish guide in Kaifeng in 1948, and also a Jew who held the post of deputy to the city's chief administrative official.[18] Two American reporters, Jimmy Burke and Archibald Steele, visiting Honan in 1948, took photographs of a number of Jews but had little of note to say about them.[19]

From Shanghai, the physician Dr. Joseph Preuss, corresponding in 1948–49 with two colleagues practicing in Honan Province, asked them about the status of the area's old Jewish community. Dr. Ernest Lippa replied that five families (clans?) still considered themselves Jewish. Dr. Rudolf Hoferrichter noted that all the Jews he had ever met looked entirely Chinese, except one old lady of the Chao clan. He had once called on her, he wrote Preuss, but "at home, unfortunately, were only mother Chao and several daughters, who were all purely Chinese looking. The only sign out of the ordinary was the slightly curly hair of the old T'ai-t'ai, which one doesn't see very often among the Chinese."[20] Timoteus Pokora, a Czech sinologist who was in Kaifeng for a few days during February 1957, counted about 100 families with 200 dependents (presumably children) who classified themselves as Jews. They earned their livelihood, for the most part, as petty entrepreneurs—not yet absorbed, apparently, in the new order— and they no longer sequestered themselves in one quarter. They viewed their Jewishness as a nationality rather than as a religion. A number of them attended Muslim or Buddhist services.[21]

Also visiting Kaifeng at the same time as Pokora was a contingent of foreign students who were then enrolled at the University of Peking. René Goldman, later to become a member of the faculty of the University of British Columbia, was among them. "In the course of this visit," he recalled, after the passage of twenty-one years, "two of us had to be quite persistent in our entreaties with the city Cadres before they acknowledged that indeed the Kaifeng Jews existed. They informed us that there were some 2,000 persons in Kaifeng of Jewish ancestry, of whom only 700 acknowledged this ancestry. How they came to that figure is a mystery, considering the history of the Kaifeng Jewish community."

In the end, however, the Chinese softened their position and offered to introduce the students to a Jewish couple. "One afternoon," Goldman was therefore able to write, "they drove several of us who were interested in the question to visit one such family which still lived in the ancient lane of the Chinese Jews, *T'iao-chin-Chiao Hu-T'ung*. We were received by an elderly gentleman surnamed Lee [Li] and his wife: unfortunately, because of the presence of the Cadre, the discussion was formal and reserved. Nevertheless, when upon leaving the house I discreetly whispered

27. A Jewish couple of the Li clan, 1957.

to the old gentleman that two of us were Jewish he beamed effusively and shook our hands. Later in the day I saw the two old Jewish steles still standing in front of the former Canadian Anglican church."[22]

Occasional snatches of information about the Kaifeng Jews have been conveyed to other visitors to Asia in the years that have elapsed since Goldman's visit to the old Sung capital, but these tend to have little significance or are utterly unfounded. In 1968, for example, Dr. Lev Rubashov wrote of having been told by a Chinese Jew in Hong Kong that some Kaifeng Jews had fanned out from their native city to other parts of the country, where "they mingled with the general Chinese population." Rubashov's informant added that although these Chinese Jews differed little from the people among whom they lived, they continued "to keep to their traditional faith."[23] Whoever this informant was, his testimony regarding the enduring piety of the Chinese Jews is as little to be relied upon as that of the Italian missionary who in the late 1940s declared that the Kaifeng Jews had been holding services in their own synagogue as recently as a decade earlier.[24]

Still, no specific day, year, or decade can be singled out as the one in which the *kehillah* of Kaifeng breathed its last. It died slowly, and of an assortment of ailments, the most lethal of which was its lengthy isolation from the rest of the Jewish world. Its memory lingers on, however faintly, challenging those who care to do so to extract whatever lessons they can from its long and bittersweet history. Reminders of its demise are brought up now and then, usually by foreigners who happen to be visiting China, but sometimes by Chinese who happen to be in countries far from home. In 1974 or 1975, to give one illustration of the former, the German writer Walter Spiegel, sitting at lunch in Peking with several highly knowledgable Chinese, interjected the old Jewish colonies of China into the conversation, only to find out that his table companions had never heard of them. "Jews?" they asked. "In China? What Jews? We know about Jews like Ben-Gurion and Golda Meir, and there are a few million of them in the Soviet Union, which mistreats them and won't allow them to emigrate."[25]

On the same order is the poignant note sounded by Rabbi Bernard S. Raskas of Saint Paul, Minnesota, who, toward the end of 1976, making inquiries in Shanghai about the status of China's Jews, was told that two Jewish women, presumably of Kaifeng origin or descent, had just died in one of the city's homes for the aged. There was still a single elderly Jew in the same institution, and arrangements were made for Rabbi Raskas to meet him. However, as the rabbi put it, "something came up," with the result that the meeting never took place. When this man dies, Rabbi Raskas concluded, Chinese Judaism will die with him.[26]

But autochthonous Chinese Judaism was of course already dead long before Rabbi Raskas's institutionalized elderly Jew was even born. What lives on of Judaism in today's China is merely the faintest of memories of a Judaism that once was. Nevertheless, not all human traces of the people who practiced the religion seem to have disappeared as yet, nor have all the customs associated with it. A case in point may perhaps be made from the odd story of the sailor on a vessel that some years after World War II was part of the fleet belonging to the Lury family, Jews from Siberia who had established themselves in Japan. Caught gambling in the ship's boiler room (a prohibited pastime), the man was found to be wearing a *tallith katan* (a small undergarment worn by the pious Jew to which *zizith*, or ritual fringes, are attached). Asked to explain how he had come by it, he replied that it was traditional in his family to wear such an undergarment. He had no notion of the significance of the *tallith katan* and, for that matter, had never even heard of a people called the Jews.[27] That he and the men of his family wore such a garment does not of course prove that they were of Jewish descent.

Of a somewhat different order, and also from the postwar years, is the story told by Rabbi L. I. Rabinowitz of meeting a Chinese (Taiwanese) consul in Johannesburg who mentioned the fact that he owned a copy of Bishop White's *Chinese Jews* and offered to lend it to the rabbi. Asked why the subject of Chinese Jewry should interest him, he explained that he himself was of Kaifeng Jewish extraction, of the Li clan. His interest, however, was essentially perfunctory, and his Jewish heritage meant nothing to him.[28]

If, by any chance, there are any people left in China who seriously think of themselves as Jews, as there may well be, they are few and far between. Hundreds, or even thousands, of individuals in the country must no doubt have a vague appreciation of the fact that some of their antecedents belonged to a religious sect known as Judaism. Here and there, a Jewish custom may even now be practiced, though by families who, if they stop to wonder about it, probably have no inkling that there are any religious connotations to what they are doing. Chinese Judaism, in short, is no more, but occasional vestiges of it probably do linger on, even if they are not usually recognized for what they are.[29]

PART TWO

THE WORLD OF THE CHINESE JEWS

13 ❖ THE BEGINNINGS OF
JUDAISM IN CHINA

So very little is known about the early history of Judaism in China that invention and conjecture have all too often been called upon to fill in the blank spaces. When did the influx of Jews to China begin? In how many waves did they arrive? Why did they come? From where? By what routes? In which cities did they settle? To these questions there has been no lack of responses, some worth taking seriously, some not.

That Jews did occasionally reach China before the Babylonian Captivity (586 B.C.E.)—perhaps by way of what later came to be spoken of as the Silk Route, perhaps by sea—is highly improbable, but not entirely impossible. A nineteenth-century Russian churchman, Hieromonach Alexei Vinogradoff, surmised that occasional enterprising Hebrews may have been making the passage to the Middle Kingdom even before the birth of Moses, and was sure that it was being done with some frequency during the reigns of the first kings of Israel.[1] His bizarre suggestion of pre-Mosaic Hebrew visits to China seems, however, to stem from a misreading of the 1489 stele of the Kaifeng synagogue. His theory that Jews traveled to China in the early Hebrew monarchical period is derived from two sources: a biblical verse recounting an episode that took place 3,000 years ago, and a poem that, so he says, was part of the folklore of the Chinese Jews. "King Hiram of Tyre," the scriptural passage reads, "sent envoys to David with cedar logs, carpenters, and stonemasons; and they built a palace for David" (2 Sam. 5:11). The poem, according to Vinogradoff, enlarges upon the meager details provided in Samuel by relating that among the gifts received by David from his Phoenician ally were some that had originally been sent to Hiram by no less a personage than the emperor of China. Such royal gifts would seemingly have included silk, that most favored of all Chinese commodities.

Vinogradoff is convinced that commercial ties existed between the Middle East and the Orient in the reigns of David and Solomon. Once this thesis is allowed, it becomes reasonable to assume that the Phoenicians, then the outstanding maritime people of the Mediterranean littoral, took an energetic hand in the transport of cargo to and from China, and that their Hebrew friends and neighbors, who in the time of Solomon already possessed a substantial navy and merchant marine, did not remain aloof from the same activity. Moreover, even if the merchandise was carried overland between the Levant and the Far East, by caravan rather than by sea, the trading nations of the Mediterranean, the Jews among them, would scarcely have failed to carve out a niche for themselves in the presumptively lucrative enterprise. There is no indication, incidentally, that the Chinese customarily ventured any great distance beyond their borders in pursuit of trade. All the evidence points to goods being hauled to and from China by merchants based in Central Asia and elsewhere.[2]

The fragile projections presented by Vinogradoff do not by any means justify his contention that Jews penetrated as far east as China three millennia ago, and would certainly not support a claim for Jewish settlements in the country as early as that. Still, farfetched and strained as his hypotheses may be, they are no more fanciful than those of a succession of other writers who have maintained that there was substantial Jewish travel to China (and, by extension, perhaps even one or more communities there) during the Solomonic or immediate post-Solomonic era—that is, as remotely as the tenth to the eighth centuries B.C.E.[3] Insisting that silk was then known in Israel and Judea, these enthusiasts reach out to three scriptural verses allegedly referring to the costly fabric and to several old Jewish legends also having to do with the product to bolster their cause—failing to note, in the process, that the precise meanings of the two biblical terms that are conventionally translated as silk are still to be resolved and that the legends are of a much more recent manufacture than the periods with which they deal.[4] This silk, these writers then say, could have come only from China. Therefore, there were links between the Middle East and the Far East some 2,800 to 3,000 years ago, and Jews were undoubtedly involved in the comings and goings between the two regions.

These arguments are, in any case, scarcely convincing, for if any silk actually reached the Near East so far back in history, it need not have been transported there directly from its place of origin. It may have been relayed across Asia through a chain of middlemen scattered throughout the vast expanse of land separating the Middle Kingdom from the Levant.

It has never been demonstrated, for that matter, that Solomon or his immediate successors ever enjoyed the use of silk. This does not necessarily mean that they were totally unfamiliar with it, but it is highly unlikely that what little there may have been of the material in Israel and Judea would have been shipped there as part of a trade pattern rewarding enough to encourage the movement of Middle Eastern merchants all the way to China and back. In fact, a full thousand years after the death of Solomon the number of Caucasians who had been to the Middle Kingdom was still so small that the West had not even then succeeded in unraveling the jealously guarded Chinese secret of what silk was and how it was produced. Had there been any travel of consequence between the areas, the great Roman geographer Pliny, who lived in the first century c.e., might have been spared the indignity of being posthumously twitted for writing that the luxurious commodity from the Orient was a form of plant fiber, rather similar to cotton. Nor is it likely that he would have placed himself on record as saying that to obtain silk the Chinese "remove the down from leaves, with the help of water, and then the women have the double task of unraveling and weaving. It is thanks to these complicated operations in far-off lands that the Roman matron is able to appear in transparent garments.[5]

The misidentification by writers like Manasseh ben Israel of Deutero-Isaiah's "land of Sinim" as the Chinese Empire convinced generations of readers that Jewish colonies were flourishing in the country before the end of the sixth century b.c.e., and continues even now to gain converts.[6] Another misconception, although not met with as frequently as the Sinim error, makes use of the custom of the levirate marriage to "prove" that Jews were definitely in the Middle Kingdom in the pre-talmudic period and, therefore, most likely during the lifetime of Deutero-Isaiah as well.

Levirate marriage, still practiced today, was common to many ancient polygamous cultures, though not always in precisely the same form. In some instances its purpose was essentially economic, while in others, as in the case of the Israelites, it was employed primarily as a means of perpetuating the name of the male who died without issue. In its biblical format, the practice requires a man to marry his brother's widow in the event that she reaches that state childless. The first-born son of this second union is then considered to be the offspring of the deceased brother. The contention that levirate marriage was introduced to China by Jews, where it was subsequently adopted by various indigenous peoples, has no credible evidence to support it. Nevertheless, the contention has not only been made, but it has also been asserted that levirate marriage was necessarily brought to China before the era in which the Talmud was developed, the point being that had the Jews introduced the practice to China at a later date their descendants would have been aware of the rulings contained in the tractate Yebamot, which reinterpreted and liberalized certain of the more rigid aspects of the code. There are, however, three fallacies here: first of all, there is absolutely no evidence that it was the Jews who brought the custom to China; secondly, no one has ever shown that the *kehillah* guided itself by precisely the same levirate rules as those that held sway in Israel before the centuries-long discussions that culminated in the formulation of the Talmud; and, finally, the entire thesis that the practice of levirate marriage was taken to China prior to the talmudic period is tied by its advocates to the equally erroneous notion that the Chinese Jews were from the start left in total and unbroken ignorance of what was going on in the rest of the Jewish world.[7]

The 1663a lapidary inscription attributes the first entry of Jews to China to the Chou dynasty (circa 1100 B.C.E.–221 B.C.E.), while the 1512 and 1679 stones have them coming there, though not yet to Kaifeng, during the Han dynasty (206 B.C.E.–221 C.E.).

The claim for an arrival during the Chou dynasty may be discounted as either an error or a protective maneuver designed to bestow a more ancient Chinese pedigree upon the Jews of the Middle Kingdom than they were actually entitled to claim.[8] The efforts of various Western scholars to draw sociological, linguistic, and cultural similarities between the Chinese and the Jews is no more convincing than is the information on the 1663a inscription.[9] Nor are other writers on firmer ground when they point to figurines crafted by Chinese artists of the T'ang dynasty (618–907), which depict foreign merchants with Semitic and Persian facial features and then offer these as evidence that Jews traveled to the Middle Kingdom during the T'ang dynasty; for the models after whom these artifacts were fashioned may just as readily have represented any of a number of non-Jewish peoples who were active in the commerce then being carried on between Central Asia, the Middle East and the Chinese Empire.[10]

Every search through T'ang or pre-T'ang Chinese sources for allusions to Jews has so far yielded nothing, notwithstanding the readiness of certain writers to attest that they have found some. One such writer was the Shanghai merchant S. M. Perlmann. The first known reference to Jews, he declared, comes from a historian living during the Sung period (420–79) who mentioned "a house at Kaifeng set apart for prayers to the heavenly spirit." A second Chinese literary man, Perlmann added, later wrote of "a foreign Temple of Heaven at Ch'ang-an [Sian] in Shensi Province, which, it is said, was erected in 621 C.E."[11] In the end, however, Perlmann was unable to offer any plausible reasons for identifying these old houses of worship as synagogues or the people who frequented them as Jews.

The only safe statement that can be made regarding Jewish travel to China in biblical times or in the several hundreds of years following the canonization of the Hebrew Scriptures is that there are at present no valid grounds for accepting or rejecting that occasional subjects of the kingdoms of Israel or Judea ventured into the country, either on their own or in the company of non-Jews. The prospects that such visits did take place increase as the centuries go by and large numbers of Israelites and Judeans are dispersed to the east. As for the dating of the earliest Jewish settlements in China, neither the affirmations of their establishment during the Han period inscribed on the 1512 and 1679 steles nor the statements made to Western visitors by the Kaifeng Jews that a contingent of Judeans made a home for itself in China during the reign of the Han emperor Ming Ti (58–75 C.E.) should nevertheless be brushed aside as mere legend so long as convincing proof to the contrary is not forthcoming. It is conceivable, and entirely feasible, that Jewish settlers could have wandered into China during the Han period—and even more so that they may have arrived in its latter years, perhaps not too long after the 70 C.E. capture of Jerusalem by the Romans.[12]

While the oral tradition of the Kaifeng Jews cannot be admitted as definitive evidence for the founding of a Jewish colony in China during the Han dynasty, their folk recollections are at least as persuasive as any of the widely ranging chronological estimates that have been derived from comparisons of the languages, religious practices, beliefs, and ways of life of the ancient Jews and the ancient Chinese, or from either the Sinitic interpretation of Isa. 49:12 or the supposed references to Jews taken from the old Chinese writings. However, the earliest authentic contemporary record of any kind that specifically indicates the presence of Jews in China is from the eighth century C.E. The next such record is from either the same or the following century. Both are of Jewish provenance. The first was discovered in 1901 by the Hungarian-born British Jewish Orientalist and archaeologist Sir Marc Aurel Stein at Dandan-Uiliq, near Khotan, in Chinese Turkestan. The other was extracted by Paul Pelliot in 1908 from a massive trove of documents, also discovered by Stein, in the Caves of the Thousand Buddhas, not far from the desert oasis of Tun-huang, in western Kansu Province.

The Dandan-Uiliq find has been ascribed to the year 718 or thereabouts. It consists of thirty-seven lines of Judeo-Persian text (Persian in Hebrew characters) written on paper, a product that in 718 was made only in China. The sheet on which the lines appear is ragged and torn, about sixteen inches high, and varies in width from four to eight inches. Portions of the wording are missing, but the surviving text makes it clear that the author was a Persian-speaking Jew. He was evidently addressing himself to a fellow Jew associated in some manner with the court of the Ispahud, or ruler, of Tabaristan, far to the west in Persia, in the hope that this man would help him dispose of some sheep of inferior stock that he had the misfortune to own.[13] The cache of ancient manuscripts discovered by Stein at Tun-huang was, as he later described it, "a solid mass of manuscript bundles rising to a height of nearly ten feet, and filling, as subsequent measurement showed, close on to 500 cubic feet."[14] It was one of the greatest bibliographical finds ever made, so great that Stein and the Orientalists who followed him were able to cart away more than 25,000 separate items, all dating to the period 406–995 C.E. One of these items, as Pelliott discovered, was a single leaf of paper bearing a *selihah* (Hebrew penitential prayer) composed of passages from the Psalms and the Prophets. It was written in the eighth, or perhaps the ninth, century.[15]

By the ninth century, the trade carried on between the West and China was handled mainly by Muslim entrepreneurs, many of whom sailed from Persian Gulf ports, skirted India, Sumatra, and Tongking (Vietnam), and then landed their goods at Canton, Ch'üan-chou, Hangchow, and other Chinese coastal cities. There they founded colonies, a number of which ultimately grew to considerable size. Sharing in this trade, though on a lesser scale, were Jewish merchants, some coming by sea alone, while others, as is made clear in the descriptions given by ibn-Khurdadhbih of the routes favored by the Jewish Radanite traders, traveled "from west to east, from east to west, partly on land, partly by sea."[16] These Radanites had the option of breaking their journey in one Asiatic city after another, there to replenish their supplies and enjoy the hospitality extended by the local Jewish communities. Arriving in China, they, like the Muslims, may well have been greeted by coreligionists already established in the country.

The presence of fair-sized Jewish colonies in China from the ninth century on is further suggested by the evidence provided in the melancholy account, originally written by Abu Zaid and accepted as factual by later Arab historians, of the 877/78 massacre of the foreign residents of Khanfu, Jews among them. Eldad ha-Dani's story of being ransomed from captivity in China by a Jew of the tribe of Issachar in the ninth century may be

28. Letter written in Judeo-Persian, circa 718, by a Jewish merchant and discovered in 1901 at Dandan-Uiliq, near Khotan, in Chinese Turkestan, by Sir Marc Aurel Stein.

29. *Selihah* (penitential prayer) leaf, in Hebrew, eighth or ninth century. Discovered in 1908 at Tun-huang, Kansu Province, China.

dismissed as pure fantasy, and so perhaps may Buzurg's tale of the Chinese voyage of "Ishaq, son of a Jew." Pelliot, however, sums up the matter of a Jewish presence in China in this period very aptly when he concludes, after analyzing the Chinese trade carried on by Muslims, Christians, and others in the T'ang era and pointing out that these foreigners could invariably expect to meet coreligionists on their arrival in the Middle Kingdom, that this would also have applied to the Jews. "It would be strange," he observes, "if the Jews were the only ones left out of this flowing traffic."[17]

Although the twelfth-century travel account of Rabbi Benjamin of Tudela does not of itself prove that Jews were then sailing to and from China, it gives reason to believe that they were and that other Jews could at the same time have been living in the country on a permanent basis. For this relatively late date, of course, Benjamin's unwitting contribution to Sino-Judaic lore has interest only in that it suggests that he may have known of Jewish ties to several of the port cities of China—cities, that is, other than Kaifeng, where, as Benjamin was writing his book, there was already an established *kehillah* and a synagogue as well. In the next century, according to the traditions that the Jews of Bokhara and Samarkand related to foreign visitors, unspecified numbers of Jewish natives of the two regions escaped persecution by fleeing to the Middle Kingdom.[18] But if these traditions tell of events that truly took place, as they may, what happened next? Did the refugees found new communities of their own once they arrived in China? Were they perhaps absorbed into existing Jewish communities? Or did they soon become assimilated into the popular creeds of the country? The Bokharan and Samarkandian folk-tales, unfortunately, do not appear to have included the answers to these questions.

The Chinese records which refer to Jews living in the empire circa 1277–94, and in 1280, 1320, 1329, 1340, and 1354, have them spread about in "various places,"[19] with one specifically identified as Hangchow. Christian and Arab sources confirm a modest dispersion of Jews within the great land mass of the kingdom: Peking (Marco Polo, 1286, and Jean de Marignolli,

1342), Ch'üan-chou (Andrew of Perugia, 1326), Hangchow (ibn Battuta, 1346), and one or more unspecified metropolitan centers (John of Monte Corvino, circa 1300, who could, however, have been referring to Peking, Ch'üan-chou, or Hangchow). A fair rule of thumb may be that wherever there were fairly large concentrations of Muslims—Kaifeng, Hangchow, Peking, Canton, Ch'üan-chou, Nanchang, Ningpo, Yangchou, Nanking, Ningsia, Shanghai, Kan-p'u, Wenchow, and so forth—Jews were also apt to be found.[20]

There are no known references indicating the presence of Jews in China for the two centuries following the promulgation of the 1354 imperial edict conscripting them into the military service, except of course for those provided for this period by the Kaifeng community through its steles and oral tradition. The few allusions to the Chinese Jews that are encountered in the second half of the sixteenth century attest merely to the survival of some of them, but reveal nothing else of value. It is only with the coming together of Ai T'ien and Matteo Ricci in 1605 that further information emerges, though everything else that relates to Sino-Judaic communities in cities other than Kaifeng is from then on expressed in the past tense. Even more frustrating, from the point of view of the historian, are the obstacles raised by the endless misrepresentations of fact, which have been commingled with the story of the Jews of China and which confuse the entire matter by making it extremely difficult to sort out the true from the false. Given this situation, it does not seem likely that a definitive chronology of the rise and fall of Chinese Jewry will ever be reconstructed.

The Kaifeng traditions of a first entry of Jews into China during either the Chou or the Han dynasties give no inkling of where they settled or how many generations passed before they disappeared as a distinct religious and ethnic entity. Could they have been the organizers of the Khanfu congregation, fated to be decimated or perhaps entirely wiped out in 877/78 by the forces of the rebel Huang Ch'ao? Or of the Jewish communities that were established at Peking, Ch'üan-chou, Hangchow, and elsewhere? Were their numbers sporadically reinforced by the arrival of coreligionists from outside China? If so, to what extent? The questions cannot be answered.

A not unreasonable scenario would have Jews dribbling into the Middle Kingdom both individually and in groups over a time-span that is measurable in centuries. They come from a variety of places, and by whatever routes seem most expedient. They travel to China by land and by sea, as do vastly larger numbers of Arabs and Persians, in the T'ang, the Five Dynasty period that followed it, and the Sung. Some are merchants, like those of the Jews arriving in Kaifeng during the Sung dynasty, who deal essentially in cotton or, like the Radanites, who handle a diversity of goods. Others, if the Bokharan and Samarkandian allegations of a flight of many of their ancestors from the persecutions insti-gated by Genghis Khan's second son Jagatai are true, are refugees. A few may be religious functionaries, teachers, and communal envoys (*shelihim*) from non-Chinese Jewish centers who stay on. Others may even be loose-footed adventurers.

The Jewish merchant's letter discovered by Stein in Dandan-Uiliq, the *selihah* leaf retrieved by Pelliot from Stein's find at Tun-huang, and also the tombstones and other artifacts excavated after World War II in Afghanistan, which bear witness to the presence there of Persian-speaking Jews circa 1150–1300, all argue for the use of any of several overland routes for passages to the Middle Kingdom.[21] The establishment of Jewish commun-ities in a number of China's port cities suggests arrivals by sea. In sum, Jews kept trickling into China over a period of hundreds of years, some coming by ship, some by overland caravan, and some by a combination of both.

It is generally agreed that those Jews who settled in Kaifeng reached the city, as their descendants claimed, during the Sung dynasty, that is to say, no earlier than 960 and at least thirty-seven years before 1163, the year in which they were permitted to build the first of their synagogues. Most scholars believe that they came from Persia or perhaps Bokhara. Nevertheless, the logistics are such that it was possible for them to have made the journey either by sea or by land. Christian historians, on the whole, bear-ing in mind the Jewish communities that grew up in the coastal cities of China, favor the sea route, followed by an overland march from the point of entry to Honan. Jewish writers, on the other hand, more keenly conscious of the large number and wide diffusion of Jewish communities throughout Central Asia, tend to hold that the route taken by the Jews to Kaifeng was overland, and perhaps by way of Afghanistan.

Although most writers, from the Jesuits on, have leaned to a Persian origin for the Kaifeng Jews, the synagogal inscriptions hint at an Indian homeland, while the synagogal liturgical texts point to a Yemenite background. The reasons advanced for a Persian beginning are mainly linguistic, the Kaifeng Jews having repeatedly used Judeo-Persian rubrics in their synagogal manuscripts, retained some knowledge of Persian throughout all the years in which they were in contact with the Jesuits, and pronounced their Hebrew in a manner betraying a Persian influence. The matter is, however, not yet definitively resolved.[22]

Shih Hung-mo (k), also known as Samuel Stupa Shih, earned four academic degrees, rose to the rank of lieutenant-colonel in the air force of the Republic of China, and taught classical Chinese literature at a Taiwanese university. Although ill health made it necessary for him to retire from active military service in 1973 or 1974, he subsequently found the strength to begin studying Chinese medicine. A roster of the languages of which he at one time or another claimed to have a working knowledge would include Chinese, Japanese, English, Portuguese, Sanskrit, Mongolian, Tibetan, Turkish, Danish, Icelandic, Malayan, Urdu, Hindi, German, and Hebrew. The great interest of his life has been Judaism, and it has pleased him to be known as "the only Chinese Jew in Formosa," a phrase he has applied to himself in print and in correspondence on a number of occasions. He has, moreover, propounded certain theories that, if they can be proved, will make it necessary to revise radically the hitherto known history of the Jews of the Middle Kingdom.

Shih's first public announcement of his Jewish background was in the form of a letter to the editor of the *Jerusalem Post,* in 1952.[23] "I am the only Hebrew of Chinese nationality in Formosa Island," Shih declares. He has traveled, he says, to seven

30. Lt. Col. (ret.) Shih Hung-mo. Photograph taken in Taiwan in 1974.

foreign countries and has visited fourteen of the provinces of China. He confesses, to his sorrow, that even though he is now a mature man he is "still living in [an] unmarried state." The establishment in 1948 of the State of Israel, he continues, was a source of boundless joy to him and he is anxious to find friends in the Holy Land with whom to correspond. He hopes they will send him "stamps, postcards, photographs of historical and religious sites of Tel Aviv, Jerusalem, etc., obsolete banknotes and lottery tickets, tram and bus tickets, theatre tickets, photos of Israelitic friends themselves, etc."

Several months later, a similar letter appeared in the United States, in the monthly publication of the B'nai B'rith, together with the author's photograph in uniform.[24] "I am enclosing my picture," he informs the editor, "so that you may see what a real

Chinese Jew looks like, but I should add that not all Chinese Jews look like me."

On this abrupt note the letter ends, but in an article outlining his novel version of the history of Chinese Judaism, which Shih contributed in mid-1953 to an Indian journal, he repeats the statement, adding, "I am considered the second best-looking fellow in my military unit of 117!"[25]

Shih returned to the subject of his Judaism in 1954, this time with a piece in a Hong Kong magazine, where he complains that it is hard to be a Jew in Formosa. "I have no kosher food to eat," he laments, "no Talmud, Zohar, Halakha, Midrash, etc. to read and no synagogue to go to. I am also still unmarried because it is impossible to find a Jewish girl in Formosa."[26]

The story of Shih's personal career—as it emerges from his letters to the two editors, the Indian and Hong Kong articles, interviews granted in 1974 in Taipei to Rabbi Marvin Tokayer,* and occasional other sources—is not entirely consistent, but the discrepancies are of no great consequence and may be easily explained away as minor lapses in memory. What is far more disturbing is that everything he alleges about his genealogy and the wanderings of his ancestors must be judged entirely on his own unsupported testimony. Here are the autobiographical notes that he provides in his 1954 article:

> My full name in Chinese is Shih Hung-mok. *Shih* is my family name, *Hung-mok* is my personal name, and preceded by *Shih* means "carry out the great plan."[27] Whilst living in foreign countries I called myself Samuel Stupa Shih. *Samuel* is the English version of the Hebrew name which means "Heard of God"; *Stupa*, my middle name, is the well-known Sanskrit word [*Mound*]; and *Shih*, of course, is again my family name, only this time, Western fashion, at the end.
>
> I was born in 1924 at Kunming City, Yunnan Province (Southwest China), into the leading family among the Jewish communities in Yunnan Province who belong to the first batch [of Jews] that came to China in A.D. 620. When still a very small child I was circumcised at the order of our Patriarch.
>
> At the age of eleven by Chinese reckoning (nine years ac-

*See below, p. 347, "Appendix: Interviews with Shih Hung-mo," for a summary of Rabbi Tokayer's talks with Shih.

cording to Western calculation) I left Kunming, and China itself, and traveled abroad with my maternal uncles.

We first visited Siam, where we saw many Buddhist temples, and a few Christian churches and Muslim mosques; but my uncles forbade me to enter any of these places. When I asked them for the reason, they explained to me that I was a Chinese of Hebrew blood and origin and therefore should avoid the gentiles' places of worship. They also taught me all they knew about Judaism.

A year later we moved westwards through Burma to India. A few months later we left India for Angola (Southwest Africa), whence, after six months, we traveled to Portugal, which we left two years later for Iceland. After yet another two years we returned to Asia, namely, to Hokkaido, Japan, where I studied at the University and became by far the most highly educated among my family.

Owing to my long stay in foreign countries I can read and write, apart from Chinese, also Japanese, Sanskrit, Mongolian, Tibetan, Malay, English, Portuguese, Danish, and a little German.[28]

After World War II, I returned to China and served in the Army. In 1949 I was evacuated from Shanghai to Formosa, where I am now an Assistant Professor teaching Chinese Classics, and also 1st Lieutenant in the Chinese Air Force. I am a Nationalist and an extremely patriotic supporter of the Republic of Free China.

Shih divides the waves of Jewish immigration to China into three, the most recent consisting of refugees from Hitlerism. The descendants of the first two waves of immigrants intermarry over the centuries with the Chinese and become the "autochthonous" Jews of China. He summarizes the history of the earlier two "batches" (as he calls them) as follows:

In the year 1056 B.C. [!] 114 people (the first batch) left Israel and traveled to Babylonia, where they remained settled for a long time.[29] In A.D. 139, a couple of generations after Judea's defeat by the Romans and the destruction of the Second Temple, this batch, now numbering 160, continued eastwards. After some time they reached India. Some centuries later they left the Ganges Valley and traveled slowly eastwards again to arrive in 620 A.D. at Chang-an City [Sian] in China proper. About 200 years later they moved eastwards again to Shangchiu City and lived there for about 500 years, until, at the beginning of the Ming Dynasty, they moved to Yunnan Province and settled there at Kunming City and Tali-fu.

The Jews in Yunnan Province, 85 souls in all, were sub-divided into four clans—their surnames were Shih, Li, Ai, and Ha.

According to tradition, the second batch came to China from India in the 8th century A.D. Chinese history books, however, say that they arrived from Eastern Turkestan some time in the 12th century as bearers of tribute to the Emperor of China and settled in the then capital city, Kaifeng-fu.

The present-day descendants of the second batch number about 200. Most of them are dwelling in *Chiao-ching Hu-T'ung* (Lane of Scripture-Teaching). They have their Rabbi, their Talmud in the Chinese language[!].

They also had a synagogue, which, however, they had to sell a few decades ago to the Christians as a Church for the Episcopal Mission, in order to keep off starvation, at the brink of which they stood all the time, being very poor.

The second batch of Jews of Kaifeng-fu were divided into eight families belonging to seven clans with six different surnames: Chao, Chin, Chang, Ai, Kao, and Li . . . . [30]

The Jews of the first and second batches were closely related in many respects. Both are called "Blue Mussulman" by the Chinese (in China, all Semites, and West Asians in general, are called *Mussulmans*, whether Muslims or not). Both batches spoke Mandarin (the standard language of China). Both referred to their synagogues as "Mosques" (like Muslims), and the Judaic religion of both batches was called the "muscle-cutting religion" by the surrounding population because they picked out the tendons and ligaments from the meat.

In his 1974 talks with Rabbi Tokayer and in a series of letters to the rabbi and the author, Shih adds more details. He tells Tokayer that he once owned a family genealogical chart traced out on a wooden tablet and apparently embellished with either a reproduction of a menorah or a collage of Hebrew lettering. This tablet, and all his family documents as well, fell overboard with much of his other baggage during the hasty loading of the ship in which he escaped from Mainland China to Taiwan. His engagement to a Taiwanese girl was brought to an abrupt end, he confides to Tokayer, when the lady's parents were confronted with the startling and bewildering news that their prospective son-in-law was a Jew.[31]

Rabbi Tokayer believes that Shih's assertions are made in good faith, that there is a ring of truth to them, and that it would be advisable to suspend judgment as to the validity of Shih's claims to a Jewish background until further details become available. When it was suggested to Shih that he might be of distant Kaifeng extraction, he insisted that this was not so—that his people had lived in Kunming for centuries and were not related to any Jews in Kaifeng.[32] Asked if he himself had ever been in Kaifeng, his reply was: "In the year of 1947, I have visited the city of Kaifeng and stayed there for a week and talked with some of the local Jews who survived the long discrimination and absorption."[33] Asked why no outsider seems to have ever run into traces of the Jewish community he places in Kunming, he answered:

> As for the matter that why there is not any record about a long-established Jewish colony in Kunming or in any other cities besides Kaifeng, I can tell you a truth here—a true Chinese autochthonic always hides his Jewishness unless he has made certain that the visitor or the inquirer is also a Jew. [Here Shih explained the reason for the Jews' caution—the contempt with which the Chinese Jews were often treated by some of their neighbors.] From this fact, it is easy to understand that there must be some other communities of Chinese Jews in other big cities which remain undiscovered; and the reasons why I can find some Chinese Jews in Kaifeng while others could not. The Kaifeng Jews began to be known to the world only by Mr. Ai T'ien, who thought that he had the same religion with the Jesuit priest Matteo Ricci and visited the priest and talked fully with him.[34]

Shih seems to have made a considerable effort to find allusions to Jews in Chinese sources. He claims to have discovered several. "I have tried to find some historical references on the first batch of Jews," he writes in his 1954 article. "There is some mention here and there regarding the second batch and, of course, there are complete records regarding the third batch. There is no record about the immigration of the first batch into China in any of the formal Chinese historical works, apparently because their number was very small. Nor did they attract the notice of historians later as (except for some time during the Yüan Dynasty) no thing ever existed in China as racial discrimination, and therefore no particular attention was paid to the minorities. However, some information about the first batch of Jews can be found in the historical records of the Mongols and in the folktales of Eastern Turkestan."

The Mongol records to which Shih refers are dismissed by Donald Leslie as dealing with Muslim *wo-t'o (ortaq)* commercial associations rather than with Jews.[35] As to the "folktales of Eastern Turkestan," Shih fails to explain what they are.

The fact remains that neither Shih's claim to descent from Jewish immigrants to China nor his reconstruction of the history of Chinese Jewry is backed up by corroboratory evidence. His allegations are intriguing, his expertise impressive, his sincerity unquestionable, but he offers no tangible proof to support either the statements he makes concerning the community into which he was born or the experiences in centuries gone by of what he calls the "first batch"—the Jews he takes to be his own ancestors. Shih's version of the history of Chinese Judaism, as Rabbi Tokayer suggests, may have some basis in fact, but the most suitable judgment that can be applied to it, at least for the present, would be the old Scottish verdict—"not proven."[36]

14 ❖ THE SYNAGOGUE ON THE
EARTH-MARKET CHARACTER STREET

For almost 700 years, the several synagogues that stood southeast of the intersection of Kaifeng's Earth-Market Character Street and the Fire God Shrine Street served as the focal points of the spiritual and communal life of the city's Jewish colony.[1] The site was always the same, though not the structure. When a synagogue was destroyed by fire or flood—a catastrophe that struck on at least three occasions—it was rebuilt from the ground up. On other occasions, existing structures were refurbished, renovated, or enlarged. If the Jewish community of the old capital city owned a synagogue before 1163, nothing is known about it. From their arrival in Kaifeng until that year, when they were authorized to erect a house of worship at the Earth-Market location, the Jews presumably assembled for prayer in either a private dwelling or in rented facilities.

The steles commissioned by successive generations of Kaifeng Jews tell of a number of synagogal remodelings and rebuildings. The 1163 structure underwent repair in 1279. It was again repaired in 1421, this time with the assistance of Su, Prince of Chou (also known as Chou Ting-wang), who, while his support of the project was in all probability anything but enthusiastic, was apparently left with little choice but to put as good a face on the whole affair as he could. His involvement seems to have arisen out of an incident that nearly cost him his life. Serendipitously, the same incident was destined to do a great deal toward removing the civil disabilities still clinging to the Jews by reason of their foreign descent and enable them to play a disproportionate role —though, considering how few they were, not a very significant one—in the country's administrative, military, and educational systems. This improvement in status would have marked effects on the community's life in ensuing centuries.

In 1420, Su, a nephew of the reigning emperor Ch'eng Tsu, was accused of engaging in treasonous activities, his complicity having been exposed by a small group of subordinates, among them the Jewish soldier An San (An the Third, a name connoting low birth and alien origin). Recalled in disgrace to the imperial capital, Su confessed his guilt, expressed remorse for what he had done, and freely admitted that the offense merited the death sentence. His recantation was accepted, more or less, and he was pardoned, perhaps because of his family connection with the emperor. He was also reinstated to his old post of power in Kaifeng, although his handling of the office was no doubt thenceforth scrutinized much more closely than in the past. An San, in the meantime, was rewarded for demonstrating a greater sense of fealty to his emperor than to his more immediate master by being assigned the dignified name of Chao Ch'eng (Chao the Honest) and by being elevated to officer rank. Dr. Irene Eber has suggested, and quite reasonably, that it was "perhaps through coercion, or in order to neutralize An San as a still potentially dangerous foe, [that] the prince was subsequently instrumental (it is not clear how) in having the synagogue restored in 1421."[2]

Three sections of the Front Hall were rebuilt in 1445 with funds provided by the Jews Li Jung and Li Liang. In 1461, when the Yellow River overflowed its banks, the synagogue was among the many structures within the city that fell victim to the raging waters. Ai Chin and several other members of the *kehillah* petitioned the authorities to issue a statement confirming the right of the Jews to erect a new house of worship on the ruins of the old, pointing out that the legal basis for allowing them to replace a demolished synagogue had been set for all time in 1279, when they were given official sanction to make the synagogal repairs then needed. The authorities admitted the justice of the Jews' argument. The reconstruction that was subsequently carried out was financed in great part by the same Li Jung who had opened his purse so generously in 1445.

Three sections were added to the rear hall in 1465–68, the funds having been made available for the purpose by Kao Chien,

Kao Jui, and Kao Hung. There seems also to have been some alteration work done on the building in 1489, when Chin Ying underwrote the purchase of a piece of land adjacent to the synagogue, this being needed, apparently, for excavations having to do with the foundations of the building.

As construction and repairs proceeded, in the years following the 1461 flood, money was raised by public subscription to provide repositories for the Torah scrolls, a tripartite arch that was to stand on a table in front of the Torahs, and an array of utensils appropriate to synagogal use. The 1489 stele was erected in commemoration of the completion of the work necessitated by the flood.

Neither the 1663 nor the 1679 stone records any untoward event in the life of the *kehillah* during the Wan-li reign (1573–1620). Yet in 1605 Ai T'ien remarked to Ricci that the *kehillah*'s house of worship had not long before been rebuilt at great cost, and in 1723 Gaubil was told by the Jews that the synagogue was gutted by fire during the Wan-li period. The inference to be drawn is that even though the writers of the 1663 and 1679 inscriptions are strangely silent regarding the matter, the synagogue was burned down and rebuilt sometime between 1573 and 1605.

When the Chinese delegates came to Kaifeng in 1850 and again in 1851, they found the synagogue that had been built in the two decades following the 1642 flood still standing, though in deplorable condition, with several desperately impoverished Jewish families living on the grounds. When Martin arrived there in 1866, the building was gone. In 1910, the Chinese historian Chang Hsiang-wen, visiting the home of an old Jew belonging to the Chao clan, was told that "seventy years ago [*sic*], a military student by the name of Kao, who was more vicious than a tiger, so recklessly trampled upon his coreligionists that he destroyed the synagogue and sold the materials. We could do nothing to prevent him. Several workmen, who were tearing down the synagogue, fell, and were killed. That was due to the God of our religion, who cast His anger on to them."[3] How much credence should be placed in this explanation of why the synagogue was demolished is questionable, but it is known that tiles and other materials from the decrepit edifice were sold to other religious groups in Kaifeng and that a number of the synagogal books and accoutrements were somehow acquired by various mosques and temples in the city.

The tragic effects of the 1642 flood on the *kehillah* and the demolition of its synagogue are recorded in the 1663 and 1679 steles. The largest individual contributions to the rebuilding of the synagogue were apparently made by Major Chao Ch'êng-chi, Kao Teng-k'uei, and Chao Ying-ch'eng. All seven clans subscribed to the fundraising program, and the building was completed no later than 1663, the year in which a commemorative stele was placed in its courtyard.

In 1678, an archway was erected in front of the main gateway to the synagogue by members of the Chao clan in honor of their kinsman Chao Kuang-yü and his two sons, Ying-ch'eng and Ying-tou. The Chinese scholar Ch'en Yüan asserts that there was further construction or remodeling in 1688, but does not say where he obtained this information.[4]

Practically nothing is known about the synagogal building that was lost in the 1642 flood. It was of recent construction, Ai T'ien told Ricci in 1605, and it was costly and imposing. Semmedo's account of Aleni's set-to with the elders of the congregation in 1613 has the communal Torah scrolls stored in a special sanctuary reserved for periodic devotions performed by the chief rabbi alone—though this would perhaps imply that only he could take the Torah scrolls out of the Ark for the Sabbath and other public readings and then replace them. The premises of the synagogue, Semmedo grudgingly acknowledged, were kept spotlessly clean. The responsibility for maintaining them, and also for safeguarding their contents, was in the hands of a *shammash* (sexton).

A fair number of the manuscript sheets belonging to this synagogue have survived, and conceivably several of its artifacts too. Some of the Torah scroll skins, scriptural sections, and prayer books washed away in the 1642 inundation were retrieved, restored, and put to use in the synagogue that was erected on the ruins of the older edifice. The Torah scroll preserved in the American Bible Society, New York, includes numerous skins that are disfigured by the severe waterstains acquired during the flood. Many of the parchments of this Torah, and perhaps certain of the extant sectional and liturgical works, may even have been rescued from the flames that gutted the synagogue preceding the one to which Ai T'ien belonged at the time he met Ricci. It would follow, if this is the case, that a portion of these manuscripts first saw service in the synagogue erected in 1461, were later salvaged and installed in the Wan-li edifice that replaced it, and were still later retrieved from the 1642 flood and placed in the structure that was put up after that disaster.

The 1489/1512 and 1679 steles, which Bishop White obtained from the Jews in 1912, may still be standing in Kaifeng, or elsewhere in China. It is equally possible that the 1489/1512 monument and certain other surviving artifacts, such as the stone lavers that White presented to the Royal Ontario Museum, Toronto, and the Episcopalian cathedral, in Washington, D.C., were originally made for an earlier synagogal structure than the one erected after the 1642 catastrophe.

Considerably more information has been handed down about the last of Kaifeng's synagogues than about any of its predecessors, and more of its manuscripts and accoutrements have survived. The 1663 and 1679 steles chronicle many of the steps taken by the *kehillah* to construct and furnish it. From the descriptions of the synagogue provided by the Jesuit visitors to Kaifeng and the Chinese delegates, the verbal statements made in later years by various Jews, and the data presented in the steles themselves, a reasonably clear and reliable image of the *kehillah*'s last synagogue can be pieced together.

The occasional allegations by the Jews that their synagogue was patterned after the Second Temple were no doubt made in good faith, but there was no substance to them. Generally speaking, synagogues tend to take on the architectural and ornamental characteristics indigenous to the areas they are intended to serve. The structure erected by the Kaifeng *kehillah* in the aftermath of the 1642 flood was no exception: its outward form and most of its furnishings were thoroughly Chinese in both concept and construction, but its spirit was unquestionably Jewish—though with strikingly Confucian overtones. The architect, in any case, knew enough about the traditions associated with the construction of a synagogue to orient the building properly. Instead of having it face south, as Chinese temples ordinarily do, he planned it in such a manner that its most sacred section, the Ark of the Revered Scriptures, would be close to its western wall, thus requiring the worshipper to face west, in the direction of Jerusalem.

The synagogue erected after the 1642 flood was situated on a plot measuring some 400 by 150 feet. It was, according to the 1663a inscription, "more complete" than the one it replaced. In Domenge's plan of the compound in which it stood, the viewer is presumed to be facing west from the street later known as the T'iao-chin Chiao Hu-T'ung (Lane of the Sinew-Extracting Religion) and preparing to enter the east gate (1, in Domenge's sketch of the exterior of the synagogue, illustration 32, p. 282) of the compound.[5] Over this gate were inscribed the Chinese characters *Ch'ing-chen-ssu* (The Temple of Purity and Truth.) Domenge did not sketch or indicate the two large stone lions that stood guard at the entry, one on each side. In the mid-1800s, when the

31. The synagogue of Kaifeng, as drawn by an anonymous and highly imaginative Italian artist in 1827, for an Italian edition of the *Lettres édifiantes*.

synagogue was demolished, they would find a new home in a Buddhist temple.[6]

Once through the east gate, the visitor to the synagogue passed under the memorial archway (2) erected by the Chao clan in 1678. Next, he walked through the Great Gateway (3), which was flanked by two fanning ornamental walls and two smaller doors. This took him to the first courtyard.

The visitor now had three choices. He could continue straight ahead through the second gateway (4), pass under the memorial archway of the Ai clan (6) into the third courtyard, and go between the 1489/1512 stele (7), to his right, and the 1663 stele (7), to his left. He would then walk past two marble lions astride their pedestals (13), a large incense tripod of iron (14), two carved stone bowls (15),[7] and a well (19).[8] Next, was an open terrace lined by marble balustrades (10), in which the communal *sukkah* was set up at the Feast of Tabernacles.[9] Stepping up to a verandah (11), the visitor could now proceed through a lattice arrangement (9) into the front hall (8) of the synagogue proper. Or, before leaving the first courtyard, he could take his pick of two side doors (5), the left leading to the entry to the second courtyard (5, also toward the west end of the compound) and the other to the entry to the fourth courtyard (5, again, toward the west end of the compound).

Spaced along the north and south sides of the area were several buildings of varying size. On each side, as the visitor made his way beyond the Chao archway and headed for the synagogue, were small residences occupied by members of the *kehillah* (24). Beyond these, on the north side, were the Li(?) clan's ancestral hall (23), the north lecture hall (16), and the kitchen (18). Ranged along the south side were the ancestral hall of the Chao clan (22) and the south lecture hall (17). The synagogue itself was located close to the western extremity of the compound. It was separated from the property line by the rear hall (12), which formed an integral part of the synagogue and was the area in which the Torah scrolls and other scriptural works were kept. To the north of the synagogue, and connected to it, was a chamber dedicated to the memory of Abraham and known as the "hall of the founder of the religion" (20). Positioned to the south, and also connected to the synagogue, stood the "hall of the holy patriarchs" (21), in which incense bowls were maintained as tributes to the ancient leaders of Israel, to some of the ancestors of the *kehillah*, and to Confucius. In all, as Domenge's drawing indicates, the compound was impressively and tastefully arranged.[10]

The central synagogal structure was about forty feet wide and some sixty feet deep. Running through the center of the building for nearly its full depth was a nave which was separated from either side of the hall by a pair of balustrades (3, in Domenge's sketch of the synagogal interior, illustration 33, p. 283), both of them broken at intervals by wooden pillars rising up from the floor and extending to the roof. As one entered from the east, the first object encountered was the main ceremonial table (1), on top of which stood a censer (A), two flower vases (B), two candlesticks (C), and two oil bowls (D), each mounted on its own stand—the very same arrangement that could be seen in most Chinese temples. On the floor, to the right of the table, was a stone drain (13), over which the hands were laved in preparation for the performance of certain rituals. Like the front wall of the chamber, the walls paralleling the nave were made up to a great degree of latticed partitions (12).

Slightly beyond the main ceremonial table stood the "chair of Moses" (2), the lectern on which the Torah was positioned upright and read to the congregation during worship services. The ceiling above the chair contained a small latticed dome (16). Behind the "chair of Moses," a canopy designated as the "dragon's pavilion" (6) enclosed a table on which the Ch'ing (Manchu) Emperor's tablet (4) was displayed.[11] Another table, placed just in front of this table, bore a censer and a pair of candlesticks. Behind the Ch'ing tablet was the Ming Emperor's tablet (5, not seen in Domenge's drawing). It too stood on a table, and was faced by another on which there was a censer, but no candlesticks. White saw one of the imperial tablets in 1912 in Kaifeng's Tung Ta Mosque, the Muslims having bought it from the Jews when the synagogue was torn down.[12] Such tablets were installed in all sanctioned houses of worship throughout China. Above the Ch'ing tablet (15), emblazoned in letters of gold, were the hallowed words of the *Shema* ("Hear, O Israel, the Lord our God, the Lord is One"). The placement of the *Shema* above the im-

32. Exterior view of the Kaifeng synagogue. Revised by Joseph Brucker, S.J., from a drawing prepared on the site in 1722 by Jean Domenge, S.J.

33. Interior view of the Kaifeng synagogue. Revised by Joseph Brucker, S.J., from a drawing prepared on the site in 1722 by Jean Domenge, S.J.

perial tablet was not casually decided upon. Obeisance to a tablet honoring the emperor was required by law, but to the Jews (and also to the Muslims) this smacked of paganism, of the apotheosization of a human being. As they paid homage to the *Shema*, which is of course Judaism's eternal affirmation of the unity and uniqueness of the Divinity, the Jews could thus give the appearance of acknowledging the loftier-than-human status of the emperor even as they inwardly restated their unequivocal dedication to the concept of monotheism.

Still in the nave, and slightly deeper into the sanctuary than the Ming tablet, was a table bearing the tripartite arch (7). Immediately beyond this was the Bethel (8), or Ark of the Revered Scriptures. In it were stored the thirteen Torah scrolls used in the synagogal services, each enclosed in a Torah case.[13] A rack (9) in a recess to the right of the Ark held the individual portions (*parashioth*) of the Scriptures read on the Sabbath, Mondays, and Thursdays, and on festival days. Another rack (10), to the left of the Ark, held the Miscellaneous Writings (*San-ching*), the collective term employed for the various non-pentateuchal works owned by the *kehillah*, and its prayer books. Above the front of each of the two recesses was a Hebrew inscription (14). The texts of both inscriptions were the same: the *Shema*, followed by the verse with which it is traditionally associated, "Blessed be the glorious name of His kingship for ever and ever." Two gilt circles were inscribed over each rendition of the *Shema*, one on the right and one on the left. The left bore the word *kamon*, the right the word *shemesh*.[14] Other inscriptions, some on horizontal plaques (*pien*), others on vertical (*lien*, or *tui-lien*), were placed at appropriate positions within the synagogue and also elsewhere in the compound.[15]

The two halls that comprised part of the synagogue, the one consecrated to Abraham and the other to the outstanding heroes and heroines of the biblical period, housed a large array of incense bowls. These had been set up, Father Gozani was told, to honor Judaism's "great men or great men of the Law." Nearby the *kehillah* had also stationed other bowls memorializing a select group of its more recent ancestors, and had even added one as a tribute to Confucius. The reason given to Gozani for the singling

34. Stone bowl from the synagogue of Kaifeng. Acquired by Bishop White during his residence in the city.

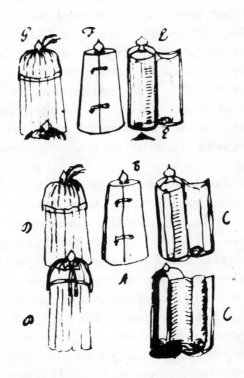

35. Torah scroll and case, Kaifeng synagogue, circa 1722. Drawing by Jean Domenge, S.J.

out of a non-Jew to be so honored was that the congregation revered him as a universal sage and as one of history's foremost legislators.[16]

Buildings can of course be rebuilt and what has once been written down can be written again, so that after both the synagogue and a substantial portion of its literary treasures were destroyed in the disaster of 1642, the leaders of Kaifeng Jewry proceeded energetically and painstakingly to restore the damaged. Not only did they rebuild the synagogue from the ground up, but they simultaneously saw to it that additional copies were made of much of the literature that had been retrieved from the flood-waters. As for those works that were entirely lost, since the *kehil-lah* could no longer turn to external sources for replacement texts it was from that point onward forced to get along as best it could without them. The disappearance of these texts dealt the community a catastrophic blow from which it never recovered, for among them were a goodly number of Judaism's seminal works, including, one would surmise, most or all of those tractates of the Talmud that may perhaps have been amassed in centuries gone by. If, indeed, the *kehillah* had possessed any significant portions of the Talmud and had lost them, the blow would have made it all the more difficult for its membership to retain its old familiarity with Judaic doctrine and could also have been respon-sible in some degree for the eventual collapse of Judaism in Kaifeng.

The effort launched to preserve and transcribe the salvaged texts was far more ambitious than might ordinarily be expected, considering the small size of the community and the severe maul-ing to which it had just been subjected. By the time the new syn-agogue was dedicated, twelve Torah scrolls had been rewritten—in itself a remarkable accomplishment—and numerous other works of lesser extent as well. Nor did the congregation's scribal endeavors come to a complete halt once its more urgent textual replacement needs were met, for a half-century later additional copying projects, albeit on a comparatively modest scale, were still being attempted, notably by Rabbi Phineas. But by then, of course, rather few of the worshippers who came to the synagogue could read the books they found there, and most of those who could were incapable of doing more than sound out the words without understanding what they meant. As far as is known, the congregation had never prepared a Chinese translation of its scriptural or liturgical holdings either before or after its penultimate synagogue was destroyed. Perhaps it was constrained from doing so because of a mistaken belief that to render the Sacred Writings into an alien script would be the height of impiety; or perhaps the translations were actually made and the vernacular texts later lost.[17] Whatever the case, the community might have lasted even longer than it did if the survivors of the 1642 flood had seen fit to provide themselves and their heirs with a set of translations of those of their synagogal manuscripts that came out of the tragic event unscathed or, better still, if they (and their descendants) had faced up more resolutely to the challenge of keeping their Hebrew from slipping away.

As for the many inscriptions that were set up throughout the rebuilt synagogue and its grounds, rubbings and other reproductions of all of the five known lapidary texts are extant. However, of the far more numerous horizontal and vertical tablets (the *pien* and the *lien*, respectively) the texts of no more than twenty-four of the former and seventeen of the latter have been preserved. Some of these were transcribed at the beginning of the eighteenth century, almost certainly under the direction of Father Gozani, and then sent on to Rome from Peking by the Jesuit Philippe Grimaldi. Others were copied in 1850 and 1851 by, and on behalf of, the delegates. A few additional texts were acquired by Volonteri in 1899. All or nearly all of the tablets were originally presented to the synagogue either as tributes to locally prominent individuals or to pay homage to the institution of religion and to the ethical way of life that religion advocates.[18]

The *pien*, generally from three to five feet wide and two or more feet high, were of wood. They were painted or lacquered, the inscriptions being chiseled into the wood and usually filled in with gilt. Typically, a *pien* held three or four Chinese characters, to which were appended the name and official title of its donor or composer and, more often than not, the year in which it was written or presented to the *kehillah*. Of those inscriptions that were attributed to specific donors (leaving aside the *pien* mounted on the archways erected by the clans), eleven bore the names of officials who were not Jewish and one the name of an official who was—Chao Ying-tou.

Several of the sentiments expressed in the *pien* were taken directly from Confucian sources—for example, "He Daily Regards this Place," or, "With Enlightenment Serve the Supreme Ruler." Others were not Confucian—"Religion is Derived from Heaven," or, "The Supreme Doctrine [Judaism] Comes from the West." Still others merely identified the areas in which they were hung—"Hall of Perfect Instruction" (apparently a reference to the alcove in which the Miscellaneous Writings were stored), or, "Temple of Perfect Purity" (the rear hall).

The significance of the *pien* lies less in their religious content than in the names, titles, and dates they provide to the scholar interested in reconstructing the history of seventeenth-century Kaifeng. Wang Yüan-tu is thus listed in 1656 as assistant defense commandant of the Ta-liang (Kaifeng) circuit of Honan and senior counselor; Hsi Shih is identified as prefect of Kaifeng in the same year; and Shên Hsü is district magistrate of Kaifeng in 1676. The tablet prepared by Chao Ying-tou, dated 1670, and reading "Honor and Fear August Heaven," lists the title he then held as district magistrate of I-liang in Yunnan Fu.

The *lien* were also of wood. Some were flat, while those mounted on pillars were shaped to fit the rounded contours of the uprights to which they were attached. These *lien*, like the *pien*, were presentation pieces, and each bore a couplet in Chinese characters. All seventeen surviving *lien* texts display the donors' names, with six of them also noting the year in which they were contributed to the synagogue: one in 1663, one in 1676, and four in 1688.

On the whole, the sentiments expressed in the *lien* are more Judaic in inspiration than those of the *pien*. Three of the seventeen were written by Shên Ch'üan, whose name betrays a non-Jewish origin but whose efforts are essentially Jewish in attitude, though one ecumenically includes an encomium to Confucianism, Buddhism, and Taoism; the other fourteen were written by individuals who were unquestionably Jews. Of these fourteen, Ai

Fu-shêng wrote eight; Chao Ying-tou composed two; and Chao Tso-mei, Ai Shih-tê, Ai Ying-k'uei, and Ai T'ien one apiece. Later, Ai T'ien's *lien* (which must have been composed long before the 1642 flood and then rescued from it) was restored by his grandson, the physician Ai Hsien-shêng, who appended an appropriate statement of his own to complement his grandfather's text.

Although most of the recorded *lien* couplets are thoroughly Jewish in outlook, a sampling runs the entire gamut from pure Confucianism to unadulterated Judaism:

Acknowledging Heaven, Earth, Prince, Parent and Teacher, you are not far from the correct road of Reason and Virtue. Cultivating the virtues of Benevolence, Righteousness, Propriety, Wisdom, and Faith, you reach the first principle of Sages and Philosophers.

—Chao Ying-tou

From the time of Noah, when beauteous creation arose, until now, talented men of Western India[?] have sought the principle that produced Heaven, Earth, and Man. From the time of Abram, when our Religion was established, and subsequently, men of China have diffused instruction, and obtained complete knowledge of Confucianism, of Buddhism, and of Taoism.

—Shên Ch'üan

The Heavenly Writings are fifty-three in number; with our mouth we recite them, and in our hearts we hold them fast, praying that the Imperial Domain may be firmly established. The Sacred Script has twenty-seven letters: these we teach in our families and display on our doors; desiring that the Commonwealth may continually prosper.[19]

—First sentence by Ai T'ien; second added by Ai Hsien-shêng

The Way [Torah] has its source in Heaven, and the fifty-three sections record the facts concerning the creation of Heaven, Earth, and Man. The Religion is based on holiness, and the Twenty-seven Letters are used to transmit the mysteries of the Mind, the Way, and Learning.

—Ai Fu-shêng

靈
陽
玉
磬

36. Black jade chime used to call the Jews of Kaifeng for worship.

37. Reading the Torah at the synagogue of Kaifeng. The original drawing (top) was made by Jean Domenge, S.J., who visited the synagogue in 1722. The revision (bottom) by Joseph Brucker, S.J., inaccurately puts shoes on the feet of the participants and "improves" the original by straightening their noses.

The worshipper is summoned to prayer by the beating of a resonant jade chime shaped very much like the body of a violin.[20] Before entering the synagogue he bathes himself ritually in the adjoining *mikveh,* or ablutions building, and changes his garments.[21] This helps him "dull the ardor of sensual desire and quieten his spirit."[22] He then"adjusts his robes and his headdress, and adopts a dignified deportment."[23] Once in the synagogue, he prays side by side with other men only, the sexes being separated for the duration of the service.

"To the present," says the 1489 lapidary inscription, "the robes and headdress, the rites and music, all conform to fixed regulations for each season." Whether the "robes" are prayer shawls is moot,[24] but the music, following the tradition, is vocal only, never instrumental. By Domenge's time, if what he says is correct, sacramental clothing is no longer worn during services, except on Simhath Torah, when the rabbi drapes a red silken sash across his chest, from above his right shoulder to below his left arm. Also, the person reading the Torah at the "chair of Moses" keeps a cotton veil over his face, the reason presumably being that Moses covered his face with a veil when he came down from Mount Sinai and presented the Law to the Children of Israel (Exod. 34: 31–35).[25]

According to Domenge, the men wear blue caps at prayer, but no shoes.[26] His original sketch of the reading of the Bible at a synagogal service in 1722 has the three participants standing at the "chair of Moses" shoeless. Father Brucker's revision of Domenge's drawing puts shoes on the men.

The 1663a inscription tells of chanted prayers and silent prayers. Ritual swaying seems to be indicated in the same inscription, and in both the 1489 and 1663a texts the worshipper is made to step forward and backward as he intones certain unspecified portions of the liturgy. He also bows and kneels.[27]

The Kaifeng congregation's calendar of worship services, at least in the centuries before its members begin step by step to neglect their old rituals, is basically the same as that of any other Jewish community. Morning, afternoon, and evening services are held in the synagogue daily. Since the surviving prayer books include the liturgies for the Sabbath, New Year, Yom Kippur, Passover, Shevuoth, Sukkoth, Hanukkah, Purim, Tishah b'Av, and the New Moon, it would appear that the traditional services associated with these festivals are read in the synagogue, so long, at least, as the *kehillah* remains active. As the old ties slacken, the synagogue counts fewer regular worshippers and the hallowed rites so meticulously observed within its precincts by earlier generations fall into disuse. The process is, of course, gradual: first one holy day disappears—and with it its liturgy and custom—and then another and still another, until all are gone. The names of festivals, and also a little of the lore surrounding them, linger on nostalgically in the folk memory for some decades or even centuries, but with nothing tangible to peg them to they are in the end completely forgotten.

While the community flourishes, however, the holy days are very strictly observed. Yom Kippur, understandably, is regarded as the most sacred of all. The writer of the text of the 1663a stele tells how the Jews of Kaifeng observed the sacred day:

> At the end of autumn [the Jews] close their doors for a whole day, and give themselves up to the cultivation of purity, and cut themselves off entirely from food and drink, in order to nourish the higher nature. On that day the scholar interrupts his reading and study; the farmer suspends his work of ploughing or reaping; the tradesman ceases to do business in the market; and the traveler stops on his way. Desires are forgotten, attainments are put aside, and all apply themselves to preserving the heart and nourishment of the mind, so that through direction there may be a restoration of goodness. In this wise it is hoped that while man remains at rest his heavenly nature will reach perfection, and his desire abating, his reasoning faculty will develop.

A custom practiced in the synagogue immediately before the Simhath Torah service is described by the delegate Chiang Jung-chi, though it is obviously no longer applicable when he comes to Kaifeng in 1850. "Whenever the day arrives for honoring the Sacred Writings," Chiang writes, "the disciples must all bathe in the place appointed for that purpose, after which they may enter the synagogue. The rabbi then takes his seat on an elevated position, with a large red satin umbrella held over him. The umbrella is still preserved in the synagogue."[28]

The schedule laid out for reading the Torah at worship services remains essentially the same as that followed in Persia, the law being divided by the *kehillah* into fifty-three *parashioth* rather than the fifty-four favored by most Western Jews. The appropriate *haftarah* (portion from the Prophets) is chanted immediately after the reading of the Torah, the roster of passages chosen for this purpose being very much the same as that of Central Asian and Western Jewry.

In some matters, however, the ritual of the Kaifeng Jews is entirely unconventional. Animal sacrifice, officially discontinued by Judaism following the destruction of the Second Temple, is more than a millennium later still practiced in their synagogue. The usage, presumably not part of the ritual brought to the Middle Kingdom by its first Jewish immigrants, is borrowed by their descendants from the Chinese, who engage in it at periodic intervals throughout the year.[29] From the 1489 and 1663a inscriptions, moreover, it becomes evident that offerings of meat and seasonal foods are made by the Jews to the memory of their forebears in the spring, summer, autumn, and winter—also a Chinese practice.[30] Though such offerings are utterly alien to the spirit of Judaism, the references to them in the two inscriptions leave the ordinary Chinese reader with no reason to suspect that this is the case; he is more apt, on the contrary, to conclude that the traditions that determine what is done in the synagogue are very much akin to those governing what goes on in his own temple.

The fact remains that although sacrifices and ancestor adulation are not sanctioned by Jewish law they do become integral parts of the *kehillah*'s way of life within a few generations after its establishment and are systematically practiced in the synagogue. The argument that Judaism is wholly compatible with Confucianism is, for that matter, tactfully but forcefully stated and restated in the various inscriptions, not only because the Jews themselves grow to believe it, but also in order to allay the suspicion that the faith of Israel may be hostile to, or unappreciative of, the virtues inherent in the dominant religious institutions of the country.[31]

But a synagogue is not a Confucian temple, and a Confucian temple cannot be a synagogue. A knowledgable Central Asian or Western Jew, arriving in Kaifeng during the first centuries of Jewish settlement there and observing the *kehillah*'s conduct in the synagogue (and outside it as well), would not have thought it unacceptably different from his own. However, could such a Jew have broken through to the city later on, he would have been utterly dismayed by the Confucian elements that had been permitted to creep into the rite of a house of worship that was supposed to be Jewish. If, on the other hand, he happened to be as compassionate as he was discerning, his sense of chagrin would have been tempered by the realization that the leaders of the synagogue had succeeded in preserving most of the old practices and liturgies—not always in their pristine forms, of course, but not too far removed from them either.

No house of worship, to be sure, can by its mere presence keep a community from falling apart, but for the last half-dozen or so generations in which the synagogue of Kaifeng remained intact it served, at the very least, as a constant reminder to its deteriorating congregation of what once was and could again be. With the synagogue gone, however, the one- or two-hundred adults in Kaifeng who adamantly refused to think of themselves as anything but Jews ceased to have a haven in which they could from time to time come together and take strength from the vestiges of Judaism they saw there. The remarkable thing, really, is that for the better part of a century after the synagogue was finally dismantled there were always a few individuals in the city—and there may still be some today—from whose hearts and minds the yearning for a return to Judaism was never totally eradicated.

15 ❖ THE JEWISH WAY OF LIFE
IN KAIFENG

THE Jewish community of Kaifeng was unquestionably Rabbanite in its outlook and in no way associated with the
schismatic Karaite sect that came into being in eighth-cen-
tury Baghdad when Anan ben David rejected the authority of the
Talmud and instructed his followers to disregard the scriptural
interpretations propounded by the rabbis. Yet in spite of the fact
that it was firmly lodged within the Rabbanite camp, the kehillah
no longer owned as much as a single tractate of either the Babylonian or the Jerusalem Talmud by the time the Jesuits started
visiting Kaifeng, its library of talmudic works (if it had ever acquired one) having apparently disappeared in one or more of the
numerous disasters that befell the city in the course of the centuries.[1] Before the old tomes were lost—assuming, again, that the Jews
actually had any—it is fair to surmise that at least a few members
of the congregation, if only the rabbis and its other leaders,
would have looked into them and gained some appreciation of the
wealth of material that lay within their pages. But with the precious folios gone and all contact with the outside Jewish world
ended, the kehillah's familiarity with their contents—probably
not too extensive to begin with—quickly faded away to the van-
ishing point. The prayer books that survived the various catastrophes, reflecting as they did the theosophical values of the
Talmud and conforming to the prescriptions set forth throughout
its voluminous text, continued, at any rate, to serve as the main-
stays of its synagogal services and private ceremonial observances, even though the participants in these rites may no longer
have had any inkling of the vital role the Talmud played in what
they were doing.

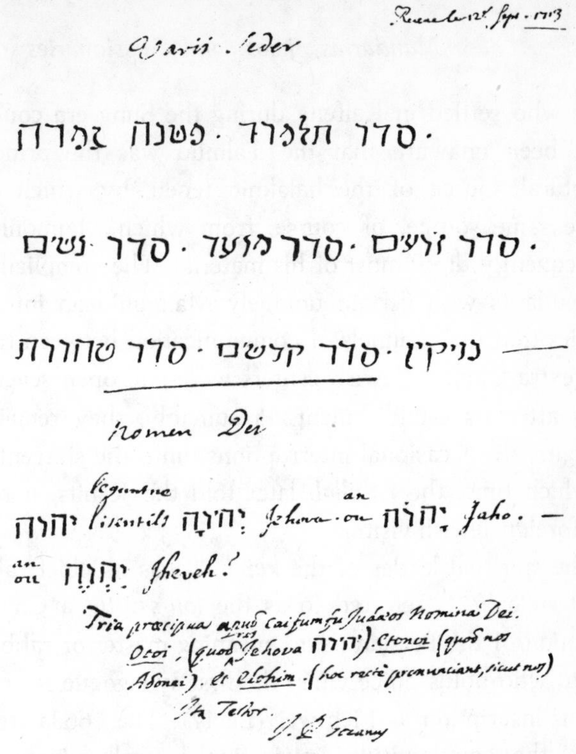

(handwritten, top left) Qavii Seder

סדר זרעים ∙ סדר מועד ∙ סדר נשים

נזיקין ∙ סדר קדשים ∙ סדר טהורות ——

(handwritten)

Nomen Dei

יהוה *leguntur presentils* יְהֹוָה *Jehova — ou* יַהֹוָה *Jaho. —*
ou יְהֹוָֹה *Jheveh !*

Tria praecipua apud Caisum ju Judaeos Nomina Dei.
Ocoi . (quod Jehova יהוה). Cronei (quod non
Adonai). et Elohim . (hoc recte pronunciant, sicut nos)

Ita Tetoir .
J. C. Gozany

38. A list of talmudic works, dated 1713, thought to have been copied by Gozani (who knew no Hebrew), together with the names used by the Kaifeng Jews for God.

In many aspects of its religious life, the usages of the congregation seem also to have fallen within the guidelines postulated by Maimonides in the second half of the twelfth century.[2] There is no proof, to be sure, that Kaifeng Jewry ever had direct access to the works of "the Great Eagle," but it would have had ample time and opportunity to acquire or become acquainted with them well before its reservoir of Jewish learning began to run out. Nor do the Maimonidean leanings of the *kehillah* contradict the historical evidence that has the Jews arriving in Kaifeng no later than 1126, the year in which the Sung fled the city—and nine years before Maimonides was born. In 1163, when the *kehillah* built the first of its synagogues, Maimonides was only twenty-eight years old, so that it is highly unlikely that even his earliest authoritative teachings could by then have reached China, either in written form or by word of mouth. Maimonides's writings codified and interpreted Judaic law and custom. Quite obviously, the

Jews who settled in Kaifeng during the Sung era could scarcely have been unaware that the Talmud was the principal post-scriptural source of the halakhic tenets by which they lived —the same source, of course, from which Maimonides would subsequently draw most of his material. The compliance of their descendants with certain uniquely Maimonidean interpretations implies that the channels of communication between the *kehillah* and extra-Chinese Jewish centers were still open several generations after its establishment. Presumably, they remained open, though with occasional interruptions, until the sixteenth century, at which time, the *kehillah* later told the Jesuits, it received its last foreign Jewish visitor.

The spiritual leader of the *kehillah* was its chief rabbi. In the 1489 stele he is referred to as the *wu-ssu-tu*, a Chinese transliteration of the Persian *ustad*, meaning master or rabbi. The *wu-ssu-tu* who holds office when the first synagogue is built is listed in this inscription as Lieh-wei (Levi?). The 1663a stele, erected when the community's sinicization is well advanced, utilizes the Chinese term *chang-chiao* (leader of the religion)—also employed by the Muslims and the Nestorian Christians—in connection with the chief rabbi who in 1642 supervised the collation of the Torah skins retrieved from the floodwaters which destroyed the synagogue, identifying him as Li Chên (Hebrew name, Jeremiah?). To a substantial degree, the position he occupies is, and will continue to be, hereditary, with a large percent of the incumbents coming from his clan. One exception will be Phineas, probably a member of the Kao, the hard-of-hearing chief rabbi with whom Father Gozani will compare biblical texts in 1704.

Lower ranking rabbis, of whom there are many in the lengthy history of the *kehillah*, are named in the several inscriptions, in the colophons to a number of the surviving synagogal texts, and in the community's Memorial Book. These are frequently men of the Ai and Li clans, the other clans being apparently less prone to educate their sons to the rabbinate.

On a descending scale in the *kehillah*'s synagogal hierarchy, the *man-la* (spiritual leader) comes next. The title, also used by the Muslims for the mullah, is ordinarily bestowed upon individuals who assume an active role in one aspect or another of the *kehillah*'s ritualistic and religio-educational affairs. The *man-la* may be a rabbi. Generally speaking, however, he is a sexton, or *shohet* (ritual slaughterer, responsible for the kosher preparation of meats), *sopher* (scribe), or other synagogal functionary, seemingly a person with a relatively impressive background in Hebraic studies. Domenge, however, extends the honorific even to the ten men who consistently meet at the synagogue to form the *minyan*, or quorum, required for services.[3] Whether the *mohel*, or ritual circumciser, is considered a *man-la* is unresolved, since the office of *mohel* is not mentioned in any of the extant communal writings, in the reports of the visitors to the *kehillah*, or in those conveyed by individual Chinese Jews to Westerners in Shanghai and elsewhere. A conjecture that has been advanced to explain the absence of specific references to the *mohel* is that ritual circumcisions may have been performed by the community's physicians.

Of the various titles conferred by the *kehillah* on its members, the only one which has eluded satisfactory definition is that of *shaliah*, the Hebrew term for envoy. It may represent a communal officer sent, as the occasion demanded, to Jewish centers in and outside of China, or perhaps its emissary in dealings with Chinese officialdom. Or it may apply to the *sheliah ha-zibur*, the member of the congregation who is chosen to conduct the synagogal service.[4]

The theological attitudes and ethical values of the Kaifeng *kehillah* remain essentially Judaic until fairly close to the end, despite the concessions to certain phases of Confucian thought and practice that creep in and mount in importance as the generations go by. Numerous symptoms of a well-developed syncretic relationship with Confucianism are already manifested in 1489, with the text of that year's stele clearly demonstrating the determination of its author to persuade the reader that Confucianism and Judaism have a great deal in common and differ principally in their outward forms. The thought is reiterated in subsequent inscriptions, and the text supplied for the 1512 stele seems even to apologize for the fact that Judaism's sacred books are not written in the same language as Confucianism's. "Although the written characters of the [Hebrew] Scriptures are different from the script of Confucian principles," the non-Jewish composer of the 1512 text declares, "it is found that their ways . . . are similar." The writer of the 1663a inscription is even more anxious to avoid giving offense in the matter of Judaism's alien tongue. "The composition of the Scriptures," he states, "although written in an ancient script and of different pronunciation, is in harmony with the principles of the Six Classics [of Confucianism], and in no case is there anything not in harmony with them." Other favorable allusions are made time and again to the literature and doctrines of Confucianism, and in several instances the moral precepts of Judaism are carefully described as paralleling those enunciated by Confucius and his followers. Held in high esteem by both religions, the various steles proclaim, are such virtues as devotion to sovereign and parent, the reverencing of ancestors, the cultivation of civic responsibility, the pursuit of learning, and the dignity of labor.

Still, while many of the differences between the two faiths are muted, the inscriptions make it very clear that differences do exist. This is most vividly illustrated in connection with the use of images. "As to the modeling of statues and figures," the text of the 1512 stele announces, "and the appointing of forms and colors, they are vain matters and empty practices, made to startle and dazzle the ears and eyes—which is a depraved theory and certainly not worthy of consideration." Here, considering the Chinese predilection for images, the ancient Judaic abhorrence of human and other likenesses as instruments of idolatry is expressed in surprisingly unequivocal and imprudent terms. In 1663a, imagery is again denounced, this time with the statement that Abraham "modeled no images, nor did he allow himself to be deluded by ghosts and spirits." The theme that recurs strikingly throughout the inscriptions is that the basic moral outlooks of Judaism and Confucianism are fully compatible, but the law received by Moses at Sinai is by no means a mirror image of the teachings of Confucius.

By selecting for their points of reference theosophical and ethical matters on which, with the notable exception of graven images, Judaism and Confucianism are not in disagreement, the authors of the Kaifeng lapidary inscriptions are able to convert such towering biblical figures as Abraham, Moses, and Ezra into exponents of a way of life to which no Confucianist could reasonably object. This is prudent and conciliatory, but it would be both unfair and unrealistic to call it mere sycophancy, for over the long time span in which the steles were composed enough Confucianism had become mixed in with the *kehillah*'s Judaism to enable the Jews to feel quite comfortable with certain Confucian doctrines and ritualistic practices. Nevertheless, the *kehillah*'s basic orientation remained unquestionably Jewish during this period. Had the case been otherwise, its members would never have taken it upon themselves to rebuild the synagogue twice, once after the Wan-li conflagration and again after the 1642 flood. Nor did the Confucian ideals expressed in the 1663a inscription mean that the end of Kaifeng Jewry was at hand. The Confucian attitudes revealed from 1489 onward do, however, signal the gradual acculturation of the *kehillah* to the Chinese way of life and are harbingers of the demise that lay in store for it.

In the first quarter of the eighteenth century the Jesuits observed repeatedly that, notwithstanding the inroads being made by Confucianism, the small Jewish enclave in Kaifeng persisted in observing those Judaic teachings it had not yet forgotten. Kaifeng Jewry, it would seem, had already lost an undetermined though substantial number of its people to the religions of its neighbors, but the greatest threats to its survival were its continuing isolation from the rest of the Jewish world and the withering away of its recollection of the tenets and traditions of its ancestors. What frustrated the Jesuits most was that although the Jews were distressingly ignorant of the faith they so obdurately professed, they nonetheless could not be induced to accept the hand that Rome was extending and let themselves be brought into the Christian fold. They maintained friendly relations with the missionaries and listened courteously to what they had to say about religious matters, but the concept of Jesus as the Messiah remained utterly unpalatable to them. Not until the twentieth century would Catholic missionaries be able to announce their first success of any consequence with the Jews, when a letter received in 1943 by Rudolf Loewenthal from Father Antonio Cattaneo, then resident in Kaifeng, brought the tidings, as yet unsubstantiated from other sources, that in 1924 the Shih clan had gone over to Catholicism.[5]

Beginning with Matteo Ricci, nearly all the Jesuits who write about the *kehillah* take note of the grave impairment of its understanding of the Hebrew language and of Jewish law and custom. Their reports support the inference, easily drawn from the erratic orthography and the unconventional scribal styles of the extant synagogal texts, that the congregation's Judaic knowledge is declining rapidly, and add several historical and sociological details not detectable in the Jewish sources. They also present valuable bits of information about the rituals still being practiced by Kaifeng Jewry.

Ricci asserts that in 1605 Ai T'ien complained that a number of aspects of Judaism were much too circumscribing for his taste, that he had been expelled from the synagogue, and that he had narrowly escaped being excommunicated.[6] Four years later, the three young Jews who visit the Peking mission are described by their hosts as chafing under the dietary restrictions imposed upon them by the chief rabbi.[7] Both of these reports seem badly overdone. Ai's devotion to Judaism is attested to by the vertical inscription, which he personally wrote and contributed to the synagogue, identifying himself therein as "a disciple of the religion," and by the fact that his sons were apparently given as good a Jewish education as was then available in Kaifeng. As for the three young men, their discontent with the dietary inconveniences to which they were subjected was not serious enough to persuade them, as their hosts tried to do, that Christianity had more to offer than Judaism.

The Jesuits' descriptions of the Judaism they encountered in Kaifeng must be interpreted with the utmost of care. Because the *kehillah*'s understanding of its faith deteriorated so drastically over the centuries, the common practice of any one generation was not necessarily carried over intact to the next. The Jesuits, scarcely the most impartial or knowledgeable witnesses in matters relating to Judaism, all too often misunderstood or misrepresented what they saw and heard in the course of their contacts with the *kehillah*. Every single authentically Jewish practice noted by the

Jesuits (and by later visitors to Kaifeng), it is true, must have been inherited from previous generations. (How else, after all, could their thoroughly isolated descendants have learned about it?) However, one of the major problems that arises in interpreting the Jesuit reports, even those reports that can be accepted as straight-forward and unbiased, is that when a Jesuit writes that the Jews say they follow a certain practice—for example, refraining from eating pork—it is not always possible to determine precisely what he means. Is this a practice that is still observed by all or nearly all the Jews of Kaifeng? Or is it a rule of Judaism this generation remembers, perhaps with a touch of nostalgia, solely because its antecedents subscribed to it? And does this generation acknowledge the rule merely on a pro forma basis, obeying it only in the synagogue or on special occasions? Or not at all? Whatever the answers may be, the rate at which the individual families making up the *kehillah* abandoned the everyday ritualistic practices of Judaism could not have been uniform, certain of them keeping to the old ways more tenaciously than others.

The Jesuits have little interest in the secular life of the Jews, but are fascinated by their history, their books, and their rituals. The Tetragrammaton, which appears in the synagogal texts, the Jesuits say, is read not phonetically, but as *Etunoi*—a Chinese transliteration, of course, of the universally prescribed reading *Adonai*. The Jews recognize God as eternal and without physical form. He is One, He has been, He is, and He will be. They believe in Heaven and Hell, that the individual will be judged in the hereafter, in the resurrection of the dead, and in the existence of angels. They observe the Sabbath and other festivals, practice circumcision, do not eat pork, and seek and accept no converts (except, presumably, the non-Jewish women who marry into the fold). They give their children traditional Hebrew names, for the most part derived from the Bible, in addition to the conventional names of the country. Some, probably the wealthier ones, indulge in polygamy. A person who contributes books to the synagogue may be excused from attending synagogal services. Although incense is burned in honor of the ancestors, as is the Chinese custom, Chinese-style images are not set up for them in the synagogue. There are special prayers and ceremonies for marriages, circumcisions, interments, and other events that are not part of the ordinary synagogal ritual cycle.

Several details are furnished by the Jesuits with regard to the observances of the holy days. The Jews, Gozani reports, heed the rules surrounding the Sabbath, Passover, "and other Feasts of the ancient Law." They do not, he says, "light fires or dress any victuals on Saturdays, but prepare on Fridays everything necessary for that day." There are occasions during the year, he adds, on which, "all day long they afflict their souls." These would no doubt be Yom Kippur, Tisha b'Av, and perhaps one or two other fast days.[8]

Domenge, who attends services in the synagogue on the Shemini Atzereth day of 1722, speaks of the erection of a *sukkah* in the compound, and in his letter of 1725 conveys the information that the Jews celebrate a holiday in honor of Esther and Mordecai—Purim, of course.

Other information is provided by later visitors, but not always reliably. When the Chinese delegates write about their 1850 visit to Kaifeng, they leave the unjustified impression that the ritual practices they describe are still being adhered to, although the probability is that at this time only the Sabbath (and perhaps Simhath Torah) may still be celebrated, and in a token fashion at best. By 1866, with the synagogue demolished, Martin is able to say of the Jewish holidays merely that recollections of Passover and Shevuoth continue to linger on in the minds of several of the Jews with whom he speaks. A year later, the Jews tell Liebermann that none of their old holy days are still being observed.

The letter which Chao Nien-tsu sends in 1850 to "the chief teacher of the Jewish religion" briefly describes the major festivals of Kaifeng Jewry, obviously as they were celebrated in earlier days. The datings he provides for these holidays are not always correct. Some may be no more than honest errors on his part; others may indicate that the Jews had gotten into the habit of observing certain Chinese holidays having nothing at all to do with Judaism—or that at some point they simply mixed up their calendar. Chao's description of what he calls "the fast of the Judge's day" as a time when "fires are not lit" suggests Yom

Kippur, which falls on the tenth day of the Hebrew month Tishri. Chao has this "fast of the Judge's day" concur with the tenth day of the Chinese sixth moon. But, as Leslie points out, "the time of year is wrong and fits the Fast of the Ninth of Av (9 Av 5610 was the tenth of the sixth Chinese month, July 18, 1850)." Leslie speculates that the Jews may toward the end have amalgamated the two fasts, "celebrating (or at least remembering) them on the ninth of Av."[9] There is no reason why this might not have happened, for well before Chao's time the *kehillah*'s retention of the law and ritual of Judaism was sufficiently diminished to make so egregious an error as the merging of the two totally unrelated fasts possible. Such a merging, if it really took place, would of course be no more than another indication that the end of Judaism's long tenure in Kaifeng was drawing close.

In their conversations with Bishop White, the Jews repeated several details regarding their funerary customs that were already known and added one or two that were new. A deceased Jew, they told him, was shrouded in cloth, placed in a coffin, and buried in a cemetery that, at least until 1642, was located outside the West Gate of the city, "the thought in mind," according to White, "probably being that of the direction of Jerusalem." However, after the loss of the cemetery, either in the flood of 1642 or in a later inundation, and because of "the general disintegration of the Jewish colony," the clans began to inter their dead in separate family plots."[10]

On the whole, more reliable evidence can be derived from the *kehillah*'s extant manuscripts concerning its synagogal and extra-synagogal rituals in the centuries immediately preceding the destruction of its last house of worship than has been extracted from the writings of all the people who visited Kaifeng. In the matter of home observances, for example, the two surviving Haggadahs, one apparently from the seventeenth century and the other copied from it in the next, indicate that the Passover *seder* was celebrated even as the community approached extinction and that the ritual was almost identical with that presently followed throughout the Jewish world.[11] Other surviving manuscripts contain such domestic liturgical texts as the *kiddush* (sanctification) over wine, the benediction and grace recited at

שבל הָעַמִּים שַׁבָּת וּמוֹעֲדֵי
קָדְשְׁךָ בְּשִׂמְחָה וְשָׂשׂוֹן הִנְחַלְתָּנוּ
בָּרוּךְ אַתָּה יי מְקַדֵּשׁ הַשַּׁבָּת
וְיִשְׂרָאֵל וְהַזְּמַנִּים: אמן

וַיְכֻלּוּ הַשָּׁמַיִם וְהָאָרֶץ וְכָל צְבָאָם
וַיְכַל אֱלֹהִים בַּיּוֹם הַשְּׁבִיעִי
מְלַאכְתּוֹ אֲשֶׁר עָשָׂה וַיִּשְׁבֹּת

נעילת ידים : בַּאֲשֶׁר גַּבְהֵילוֹ

כהא ילו יָצָאנוּ מִמִּצְרַיִם הָא לַחְמָא
עַנְיָא דַּאֲכָלוּ אַבְהָתַנָא בְּאַרְעָא
דְמִצְרַיִם כָּל דִּכְפִין יֵיתֵי וְיֵכוּל
וְכָל דְּצָרִיךְ לְפִסְחָא יֵיתֵי וְיִפְסַח
שַׁתָּא הָדָא בְּאַרְעָא הוּא

הִגִּיעָנוּ לִזְמַן הַזֶּה :

בָּרוּךְ אַתָּה יי אֱלֹהֵינוּ מֶלֶךְ
הָעוֹלָם בּוֹרֵא פְּרִי הַגָּפֶן:

בָּרוּךְ אַתָּה יי אֱלֹהֵינוּ מֶלֶךְ הָעוֹלָם
אֲשֶׁר קִדְּשָׁנוּ בְּמִצְוֹתָיו וְצִוָּנוּ עַל

שֶׁבְּכָל הַלֵּילוֹת אָנוּ אוֹכְלִין
חָמֵץ וּמַצָּה וְהַלַּיְלָה הַזֶּה כֻּלּוֹ
מַצָּה : שֶׁבְּכָל
הַלֵּילוֹת אָנוּ אוֹכְלִין שְׁאָר יְרָקוֹת
וְהַלַּיְלָה הַזֶּה מְרוֹרִים :
שֶׁבְּכָל הַלֵּילוֹת אָנוּ אוֹכְלִין
בֵּין יוֹשְׁבִין וּבֵין מְסֻבִּין הַלַּיְלָה

39. Excerpts from the Passover Haggadah of the Jews of Kaifeng. The rubrics are in Judeo-Persian.

meals, and parts of the *hazkarat neshamot* (memorial service for the dead), suggesting that such family rites were still being performed in the seventeenth and early eighteenth centuries, when the manuscripts were copied, and perhaps even later.

The biblical and rabbinic teachings that both the community and the individual must hold themselves responsible for the welfare of the poor and the helpless were deeply imbedded in the *kehillah*'s consciousness and conscience. In the matter of *zedakah* (charity or, better still, good deeds as essential components of ordinary justice), the 1512 inscription carefully and tactfully explains, the ideals of Judaism and Confucianism are happily identical. "Concerning widows and widowers," it declares, "and orphans and childless old men, and the lame and infirm of every sort, there is none that is not succored and relieved by compassion, so that no one becomes shelterless." Moreover, "if anyone through poverty is unable to arrange a marriage, or to carry out a necessary funeral ceremony, there is none but will hasten to bring him help, so that he may have the funds for a wedding, or the needed equipment for a funeral." The author of the 1663a inscription reiterates the community's concern for those of its members who are in distress. "Orphans and childless old men," he writes, "wifeless men and widows, are all helped and relieved."

Leaving aside ritualistic considerations, the everyday life of the Kaifeng Jews was very much the same as that of the people around them, with Jews of a particular economic or cultural level tending to live more or less as non-Jews of corresponding positions in society did. However, most Jews (and, at the outset, probably all of them) had their homes within easy walking distance of the synagogue, not only because Jewish law forbids riding on the Sabbath and other festivals, but also as a matter of personal preference. The Jews continued to cluster themselves about the synagogue until modern times, but as their ties to Judaism waned, some moved to other parts of the city.

That the Jews arrived in Kaifeng bearing tributes of cloth to the emperor does not mean that they were all traders. A number of them probably were, but it is more likely that the group's migration to the Sung capital was instigated by war or oppression rather than by visions of a brighter economic future. The descendants of the original settlers were in any case engaged in an assortment of occupations. Thus, An San, the man who would in the 1420s be elevated to high rank and given the name Chao Ch'eng, started life either as a common soldier or as a physician. His meteoric rise seems to have cleared the way for other Jews to seek governmental office, so that the 1489 stele is already able to list the names of two members of the *kehillah* who hold such posts, as well as to refer to one Jew living in Ning-hsia and another in Ning-po whose families can between them boast of a high civil official and an officer in the imperial army.

The 1489 inscription specifies no other occupations, but it does imply that at least a few Jews were merchants. "Coming down to the accuracy of scales and the dimensions of measures," it declares," they [the Jews] do not, in the slightest degree, dare to cheat other men." The 1512 stele is much more informative about the vocations followed by the *kehillah*. Some Jews, it proudly reports, "bring glory to their parents and acquire renown for themselves; and others, in position of dignity either in or outside [the court], serve their prince and spread benefits among the people. Some are engaged in military operations, both offensive and defensive, and spend themselves in their loyalty and gratitude to the Empire. . . . Moreover, there are farmers who till their fields in the country districts, and draw from the soil the where-withal to pay the public tribute; and artisans who in their trades provide a sufficiency of articles for common use; and traders, who are diligently engaged in commerce in faraway lands, so that their names are famous along the rivers and lakes; and, finally, businessmen who are shopkeepers and make profits in the markets."

The 1663a stele, describing the cessation of everyday activities on Yom Kippur, tells of scholars putting aside their books for the day, farmers leaving their fields, and merchants closing the doors of their shops. It also furnishes the names and ranks of several Jews who were either civil or military officials. The 1663b inscription, by Leslie's count, includes twenty degree holders, fourteen army officers, and four official physicians. For so small a community, he points out (and quite properly), "this is a remarkable achievement."[12]

The successes of individual members of their clan are unabashedly proclaimed in the stele erected by the Chao in 1679. As might be expected, only those Chao who reach relatively high positions are given a place in the inscription, while the Chao whose occupational attainments are of lesser prestige are not so honored.

In Sergeant T'ieh's time, the occupations in which the Jews are engaged are the usual ones. "One of the family of Kao," Sergeant T'ieh tells Consul Layton, "keeps a large spice and perfumery warehouse; and Shih has a large silk shop."[13] T'ieh probably remembers these two men as among the most successful Jews in the city, but the others are no doubt not nearly as well off. They are petty shopkeepers, craftsmen, transportation workers, farmers, scholars, teachers, soldiers. They earn their livelihood, in other words, in the same white-collar and blue-collar occupations as their neighbors. At certain periods in their history, the proportion of Jews who attain fame and fortune exceeds that of the rest of the citizenry of Kaifeng, but in the *kehillah*'s declining years its output of unusually successful individuals becomes far less impressive, and perhaps even proportionally lower than that of the overall community.

While it served as the Sung capital, and for centuries afterwards, Kaifeng was a densely populated city, many times larger than any of the medieval cities of Europe.[14] The Imperial Way, lined on either side by a minicanal and numerous shopping arcades, is said to have cut a swath 300 yards wide from the south entry of the palace to the city wall; but because land was at a premium, most of Kaifeng's streets tended to be narrower than those of other Chinese metropolises. Homes, as a rule, abutted one another. Much of Kaifeng, the Jewish quarter included, was a fire trap. The city, it is true, had organized a fire detection and control system so far ahead of the times that it served as the model that many other great cities, notably Hangchow, would copy, but the threat of fire always posed a serious problem to its inhabitants. Guard stations were set up at intervals of 500 yards, and a hundred soldiers manned each of a series of watch towers replete with hatchets, buckets, ropes, scythes, and other fire-fighting paraphernalia. During daylight hours, at the first sign of a blaze, the watch hoisted flags signifying that help was urgently needed. At night, lanterns were lit. By prearrangement, the number of raised flags or lighted lanterns indicated the location of the fire. In spite of all this, fires still took their toll, keeping the authorities and the citizenry constantly on edge as they wondered when and where the next conflagration would strike. The Jewish quarter was in a particularly vulnerable area of the city. At least one synagogue was burned to the ground, and from time to time many Jewish residences and business establishments must have suffered the same fate. Lives would of course also have been lost.

Under the Sung, Kaifeng was China's foremost cultural and commercial center, and, of course, the seat of government. It boasted a university, the national art academy, a plethora of recreational installations, shops and restaurants of all kinds, the best medical facilities then available, public bath houses and, in short, every amenity that a reasonable man could desire. In fact, for many centuries after it lost its position as China's capital it remained a city with a great deal to offer. But it was not a placid place in which to live and experienced more than its quota of wars, civil unrest, fires, and floods. In all these, the good and the bad, the Jews shared. They were treated, on the whole, no better and no worse than the rest of the population. Still, they seem always to have been concerned about their foreign origins. For this they had some justification, and it explains their anxiety to be regarded by their fellow citizens as members of a community that was deeply and inextricably rooted in the soil of the country.

The inhabitants of the Middle Kingdom—so called because, as everybody knew, it was not only the world's geographic center but its intellectual, economic, and military center as well—were generally agreed that outside the country there lived only uncouth and inferior beings. These they thought of and referred to as barbarians. So xenophobic and self-deluding did the Chinese become in this respect that as late as the nineteenth century, foreign diplomats would not be received by the emperor or his officials unless they came as vassals. In 1824, to give one example, Lord Napier's letter to certain Chinese authorities announcing his appointment as His Majesty's Superintendent of British Trade in China was returned to him unopened, a single line on the envelope brusquely notifying him that it was being "tossed back" because he had failed to identify the message with the character *pin,* or humble petition. John Quincy Adams would later pun that the principal cause of the Opium War was not opium but "a *pin*"—the demeaning document, that is, which placed all other nations in the position of acknowledging that they were inferior to China, an insult that Britain understandably found impossible to swallow. It was this Chinese disdain for foreigners that frightened the Kaifeng Jews and throughout much of their history made them do everything in their power to avoid being suspected of maintaining ties with the despised barbarians.

Actually, the Chinese Jews were visited with relatively few indignities over the centuries simply because they were of alien descent, and adherents of an exotic faith to boot. Certainly, they were treated by the Chinese immeasurably better than their co-religionists in the Christian and Islamic worlds. The handful of restrictive edicts they endured, all of a temporary nature, were not aimed at them specifically, but at all people of recognizably foreign extraction—Muslims mainly. The Jews were, in fact, more often than not thought to be Muslims, and the fourteenth-century bans on ritual slaughter and levirate marriage were in reality directed against the Muslims by Mongol rulers whose sense of propriety was outraged by both practices. These edicts included the Jews, perhaps because the Chinese mistook them for a Muslim sect or perhaps because the Chinese knew that they too were guilty of engaging in the same "distasteful" and "arrogant" acts. After the 1420s, when An San was promoted to high office, the Jews seem to have been left in benign neglect.

When the Manchus conquered China in the middle of the seventeenth century and ordered all Chinese males to wear queues as a symbol of their submission to the new order, the Jews became as bepigtailed as the rest of the population. When, in the nineteenth and twentieth centuries, the anti-Manchu rebels denounced the queue, now grown into a time-honored institution and accepted by millions upon millions of Chinese as such, the Jews reacted like everyone else, some hastening to cut off their pigtails, some not. Similarly, when bound feet came under attack, certain Jewish families stopped binding the feet of their daughters, while others held off doing so for as long as possible. The Jews, in short, were as Chinese in their general outlook as was the indigenous population. They thought very much like the Chinese, dressed like them, spoke the same language, ate the same foods (avoiding only those that were ritually prohibited), attended the same schools, and worked in the same occupations. In their ritual observances and in their yearning to come together again with coreligionists who happened to be non-Chinese, they remained different from their compatriots; but in time, of course, even these two differences disappeared. It is inconceivable, however, that they could at any time in their history have so violated the tenets of their faith as to engage, as many of their neighbors did, in the terrible crime of infanticide.

The language ordinarily spoken by the Kaifeng Jews was of course the local Chinese dialect, which was very much like the dialect heard in Peking. Originally, many of them would have been entirely at home in Hebrew and also capable of translating the Aramaic passages so frequently encountered in the Judaic liturgy; but in later centuries very few members of the *kehillah* were still able to carry on a sustained conversation in Hebrew or read it with much understanding, and the language, as they used it, had long become admixed with inflections and intonations betraying the influence of the Chinese milieu in which they were born and raised. Scholars who have analyzed the Kaifeng pronunciation of various Hebrew words, as preserved in the reports of the Jesuits or inferred from other sources, have been struck by the frequent sinicizations of the Hebrew—sinicizations, incidentally, which often crept into the synagogal texts and resulted in extraordinary spellings. The Hebrew word *hereb* (sword, *h-r-b*) is thus misspelled in the surviving Kaifeng Torah scrolls (in Deut. 32:25) as *halab* or *heleb* (milk, or fat, *h-l-b*, depending on how it is vocalized).[15] This is an understandable carry-over of the Chinese tendency to pronounce the letter *r* (*resh*) as an *l* (*lamed*). Similar errors in both orthography and speech have been noted elsewhere, and in great numbers.[16]

New Persian, for centuries the lingua franca of Central Asia,

וַתֹּאכַל אֶ—ץ וִיבֻלָהּ

אַסְפֶּה עָלֵימוֹ רָעוֹת

מְזֵי רָעָב וּ—לֻ—מֵי

יִשֵּׁן בַּהֵמֹת אֲשַׁלַּח בָּ—

מִחוּץ תְּשַׁכֶּל־חָלָב ➤

בָּחוּר גַּ—בְּתוּלָה

אָמַרְתִּי אַפְאֵיהֶ—

לוּלֵי כַּעַס אוֹיֵב אָגוּר

יֹאמְרוּ יָדֵנוּ רָמָה וְלֹא

כִּי גוֹי אֹבַד עֵצוֹ—

לוּ חָכְמוּ יַשְׂכִּי—וּ

אֵיכָ— יִרְדֹּ—ף

וַעֲלֵיהֶם מוּסְרֵי הָרֵ—

רֶעֵי אֲכֻלָה בְּדַ—

רֶשֶׁף וְקֶטֶב מְרִירִי

עַם חֲמַת זַחֲלֵי עָפָר

וּמֵחֲדָרִים אֵימָה גַּם־

יַק עַד־אִישׁ שֵׂיבָה

אַשְׁבִּיתָה מֵאֱנוֹשׁ זִכְרָם

פֶּן יְנַכְּרוּ עָר—יְמוֹ פֶּן

יְהוָה פָּעַל כָּל־זֹאת

הֵמָּה וְאֵין בָּם תְּבוּנָה

אָרֶץ יָבִינוּ לְאַחֲרִיתָם

אֶ—ד אֶ———ף

40. Excerpt (Deut. 32:22–30) from the Kaifeng Torah scroll at Bridwell Library, Southern Methodist University. In the line indicated by an arrow ("the sword shall deal death without"), the third word is written as *ḥ-l-b* (which can be read as "milk" or "fat") instead of the more usual *ḥ-r-b* ("sword"). At the Kaifeng synagogue in 1722, Jean Domenge, S.J., inspected the Torah scroll known as the "Scroll of Moses" (now missing) and observed that the scribe had written the second word of the same line as *t-'a-k-l* (can be read as *tokhal*, or *te'akhel*, "shall devour") instead of the more usual *t-sh-k-l* (*teshakel*, "shall deal death"). Of the seven extant Kaifeng Torah scrolls, the six that are complete (and therefore contain this portion of the text) spell *t-sh-k-l* correctly but show *ḥ-l-b* in place of *ḥ-r-b*. The present excerpt also contains several other scribal errors.

the Jewish immigrants to Kaifeng undoubtedly knew well, and they probably spoke it in their daily lives. The synagogal texts used by them and their descendants are rich in rubrics and colophonic materials written in Judeo-Persian (Persian in Hebrew script). Longobardi, according to de Gouvea, addressed a group of Kaifeng Jews in "Persian" in the second decade of the seventeenth century, and both Domenge and Gaubil (in the 1720s) could write that the Jews they met in Kaifeng had not yet lost all their knowledge of the language.

Concerning the Jewish training the *kehillah* offered to its young people, all that is known is that it continued to be available, though on the most rudimentary of levels, until at least the early years of the eighteenth century. That not all Jewish parents took advantage of even the limited Hebrew schooling opportunities still open to their children in the second half of the sixteenth century is indicated by the confession made by Ai T'ien in 1605, when he was sixty, of an acquaintance with Hebrew that did not extend beyond a bare ability to recognize the shape of the lettering in Ricci's Hebrew Bible as Hebraic. Gozani, to be sure, was impressed by the fact that many Jewish youngsters were familiar with the language, but since he himself knew no Hebrew at all, his rosy assessment of their facility in the ancient tongue need not be taken seriously. At best, they could falteringly pronounce the words they saw in their Bibles and prayer books, though with little if any understanding of what the words meant. The reactions of Domenge and Gaubil, both of whom had a fair grasp of Hebrew, to the Jews' ignorance of the language are far better measures than Gozani's of the depths into which the *kehillah*'s educational system had sunk. After 1723, when the Jesuits left Kaifeng, the system, bad as it already was, must have gone even further downhill, and at a rapidly accelerating rate, with the rabbi and perhaps a few others still retaining a faint comprehension of the contents of the synagogal books and trying with little success to pass on their own meager knowledge to others. By the first decade of the nineteenth century, the only Chinese Jew who possessed as much as a nodding acquaintance with the language was the rabbi, and when he died in faraway Kansu Province that too came to an end.

If the Jews made their way to Honan as refugees from war-torn lands or from persecution, they probably came in family groups and did not begin to intermarry with their hosts in appreciable numbers for some time. If they arrived essentially as traders—an inference which has been repeatedly drawn (though perhaps unjustifiably) by reason of the cotton they are known to have presented to the emperor—then they presumably brought few or no women with them, and retained their identity only because, although they intermarried almost from the start, they were careful to hand down their Jewish loyalties to the children they fathered. Since the synagogal inscriptions describing the origins of the *kehillah* allude to clans rather than to individuals, the impression emerges that the Jews are more apt to have come to Kaifeng seeking a haven of refuge than as merchant adventurers.

By Ricci's time, intermarriage had been going on for generations. The Jews, he was told by Ai T'ien, himself living proof of the mingling of the races, had "gentile wives and relatives." The *kehillah*'s Memorial Book, Leslie has shown, proves that in the latter part of the sixteenth century and the early part of the seventeenth more than one-fourth of its married women were non-Jewish by birth.[17] By the first quarter of the eighteenth century there was, very likely, more intermarriage than not. How Gozani could have looked into the Oriental Jewish faces about him and say, as he did in 1712, that the Jews "do not marry except among their own men and women," is entirely bewildering—unless, perhaps, he meant that at that particular time they had temporarily given up the practice of espousing non-Jews.[18] And this denial of intermarriage was not a mere slip on his part, for eight years previously he had written, "these families marry one among the other, and never with the *hui-hui*, or Muslims, with whom they have nothing in common, either with regard to books, or religious ceremonies. They even turn up their whiskers in a different manner."[19] Gozani's denial that the Jews married outside their own group was echoed, surprisingly and just as incorrectly, by the Chinese delegates following their return late in 1850 from Kaifeng.[20] Sergeant T'ieh, however, had told Consul Layton a year earlier that six of the Jewish clans in the city customarily intermarried with the Chinese, but that although the

Jews gave their daughters to the Muslims, the Muslims did not give their daughters to the Jews.[21] The evidence of intermarriage, so clearly presented in the Memorial Book, belies, in any case, all claims that there was no intermarriage between Jew and non-Jew in Kaifeng.[22] In such unions, Chinese society being what it was, those Jewish women who married non-Jews were permanently lost to the *kehillah*, while Chinese women who married Jewish men—after conversion, presumably, at least so long as there was still a rabbi functioning in Kaifeng—were absorbed into the *kehillah* and thenceforth counted as Jewish.

To classify the original Jewish settlers as traders presupposes a drastic alteration in the skin color and physiognomies of the very next generation—unless, of course, other Jews arrived soon after they did, and in family groupings. It may have been their imaginations that deceived Ricci, Martin, and others into believing that the individual Kaifeng Jews they met exhibited facial features characteristically Jewish (whatever that may mean), but other observers, at least from the late nineteenth century on, found it impossible to distinguish the Chinese Jews from their compatriots by physical characteristics alone—although some who were blessed with vivid imaginations occasionally insisted that they had done so. The truth, obviously, is that in the end the Chinese Jews became as thoroughly Chinese in their appearance as in their thoughts and emotions. In actuality, of course, they lost their Caucasian features long before they severed their mental and emotional ties to the Judaism of their forefathers.

16 ❖ THE JEWS AND
THEIR NEIGHBORS

A T the time the Jews established their *kehillah* in Kaifeng, the 1489 lapidary inscription plainly states, the number of their clans ran to seventy; but, having provided this figure, it is then able to list the names of only seventeen. For this reason, and because a simple transposition of its two characters turns the Chinese word for seventeen into seventy, it is quite possible that the author of the text really intended to have seventeen inscribed on the stone and that the larger figure was inadvertently substituted.[1] The inscription composed by the Chao in 1679 sets the number of Jewish clans living in the city when its first synagogue was built at seventy-three, containing among them more than 500 families. The demographic statistics supplied in the two stones would thus point to the presence of some 2,500 Jews in Kaifeng in the first centuries of their settlement there. This appears excessive, for it presupposes a migration to Kaifeng of relatively massive and unwieldy proportions. It also suggests, however unintentionally, that the Jewish newcomers to Kaifeng probably made their way there from their original homes entirely by land, and not by a sea and land route, the more complex logistics of which would call for the employment of a small fleet of ocean-going vessels as a preliminary step to the organization of a caravan to take them to Honan from their port of entry.

Just how the two population counts were arrived at is conjectural. The 1489 clan figure, if it was actually meant to be seventy, might well represent a statistic derived from an oral tradition that was generously embellished in the telling and came in time to be given more credence than it deserved. Once cut into stone, the historicity of the overblown figure would have become even more firmly entrenched in the popular mind than before, and accepted without cavil. The three additional clans introduced into the 1679 inscription seem to have gotten there either as the result of a further embellishment, which had the first settlers joined by three other clans, or because of a slipshod transcription of the number engraved on the 1489 stele.

The text of 1663a, composed while the horrors of the 1642 siege and flood were still vivid in the author's memory, speaks of the survival of "hardly more than a couple of hundred families." Under ordinary circumstances this would suggest a thousand or so individuals, but how low the size of an average family had fallen after the substantial human losses sustained by the *kehillah* in the twin catastrophes of 1642 is not revealed by the inscription. Nor does it tell how many Jewish families lived in Kaifeng before the city came under attack by Li Tzu-ch'eng and his rebel forces.

Leslie's studies of the congregation's Memorial Book yield a population breakdown for a typical generation of seventeenth-century Kaifeng Jews of 250 to 300 men, 200 to 250 wives, and perhaps 300 children, making a total of between 750 and 850 individuals.[2] The Ai is the largest clan, with the Li next in size. Smallest are the Chin and the Shih, seemingly because of all seven clans they are the ones who marry least often out of the faith.[3] In 1722, Domenge concludes that the *kehillah* has slightly more than 100 families. A year later, Gaubil puts its strength at 1,000 individuals, about twice the number suggested by Domenge. In 1851, the Chinese delegates can report that 300 Jews (adults, presumably) are present when the agreement is drawn to sell them six of the communal Torah scrolls and several dozen other manuscripts. In 1866, Martin estimates that 300 to 400 Jews (adults?) are left in the city. Twenty-three years later, Mills is told that there are 200 families in the *kehillah*, and after the passage of another seven years Annaud is given two differing estimates of the number of Jewish individuals still living in the old capital—500 (about 100 families) by the Jew Kao, and half as many by unnamed Muslim informants. Other visitors in this period suggest a variety of figures. Around the beginning of the twentieth century, the Jews of Shanghai are told of 140 coreligionists (families?) left in Honan. During World War II, Mikami counts 100 Jews there, while his countryman Sogabe sets the figure at 180. Pokora, after his 1957 visit, writes that 100 Kaifeng families continue to think of themselves as Jewish.

In the Sung era, Kaifeng, with a population that is said to have approached or even exceeded the million mark, was one of the largest metropolises in the world, if not the largest. Its population seems to have remained at more or less that level until 1642, but when Martin came there in 1866, its citizenry had long been reduced to roughly a third of that number. Even if the statistics provided in the 1489 and 1679 steles are accepted as valid, though they probably should not be, the available demographic data would indicate that for every Jew who lived in Kaifeng, there were always from several hundred to well over a thousand non-Jews.

The ratio was no doubt even more disparate in the several other cities of China in which Jews lived, a possible exception being Hangchow, whose *kehillah* may at one time have substantially surpassed Kaifeng's in size. It is not in the least surprising, accordingly, that allusions to Jews occur so infrequently in the Chinese records or that in those occasional instances in which a gazetteer mentions an official who happens to be Jewish he is not identified as such.[4] Understandably, most of the compilers of these records were not quite sure of what a Jew was, and those who were may have thought it prudent to remain silent about the fact that a particular imperial official was tainted with the stigma of barbarian descent. Scholars examining the gazetteers have nevertheless discovered listings for a few individuals who are known to have been Jews from the presence of their names in the steles and in the surviving synagogal books, and have thus been able to sift out occasional nuggets of information, regarding the lives and careers of these men, which would otherwise never have come to light. What is strikingly clear from these sources—both the Jewish and the Chinese (and the Christian visitors' reports as well)—is that once the barriers to civil and military advancement were removed as a byproduct of the emperor's recognition of the services rendered to the Dragon Throne by An San, the Jews took full advantage of the opportunities that had suddenly been thrown open to them and achieved a far greater importance in Chinese society than their small numbers would suggest. But because they were so few and China so immense, the impact of their successes on the overall history of their country was modest.

The first Chinese Jews whose names have survived are Liehwei (Levi?), chief rabbi of Kaifeng in 1163, and An-tu-la (Abdullah?, or Hamdullah?), who in that year was entrusted with the responsibility for building the synagogue. Their names are recorded in the 1489 stele, which also enumerates fourteen men who some two centuries after the construction of the synagogue held the position of *man-la;* identifies several communal leaders and major contributors to the synagogue; tells of two members of the *kehillah* who had attained official posts, the one having first earned the *kung-sheng* degree, the other the *chü-jen;* and also refers to one Jew in Ning-po as well as to another in Ninghsia, each with a relative who had held a government position of some significance.

Many other Jews are given a place of honor in the later inscriptions, with 1663b providing the names of no less than 241 men of varying degrees of prominence. Among these are found listings of the *kehillah*'s religious leaders and of thirty-eight other individuals who had been markedly successful in Chinese life. The roster includes the civil official Chao Kuang-yü and his two distinguished sons Ying-ch'eng and Ying-tou; Majors Chao Ch'êng-chi, Chang Mei, and Chang Shih-jü; Company Commanders Li Yao and Chao Ts'an and nine other army officers; and sixteen scholars and four physicians. The Memorial Book and the colophons to the synagogal manuscripts supply several hundred additional names, though only a few represent individuals of importance. Further information concerning some of the more outstanding personages in the *kehillah* has been made available through the efforts of historians who have screened the likely local and regional gazetteers and other non-Jewish writings for references to names known to them to be those of Jews. Together, the various sources record a mélange of biographical notices and incidents in the community's history that ranges from the trivial to the consequential. Here, for example, as compiled by Leslie, is a list of odds and ends regarding certain Kaifeng Jews (leaving out the most eminent of all, Chao Ying-ch'eng, and his immediate family), which have been extracted from other-than-Jewish documents and in some instances duplicate information also occurring in the Jewish sources:

1. Chao Ch'êng-chi was on duty, with the rank of major (*yü-chi*), in Ku-yüan, Shensi, from 1657 to 1661.
2. Li Yao, Company Commander (*tu-ssu*), died in action, fighting against the rebel Li Tzu-ch'eng, in 1643.
3. Ai Ying-k'uei, *tzu* Wen-so, was special physician to the resident prince of Chou at the beginning of the Ch'ing (1644–), and owned a pharmacy not far from the synagogue.
4. Ai Shih-te was a virtuous youth, honored at the beginning of the Ch'ing (1644–).
5. Ai Hsi's widow, *née* Kao, was honored for her fifty years of chastity in 1734. [She had never remarried.]
6. The mother of Shih Hung-chi, *née* Shen [a convert], was honored for saving her son in the fighting at the end of the Ming (towards 1644), after the death of her husband Shih Tzuhsing. Shih Hung-chi and his son (or nephew) Wen-yao received local scholarships.
7. Chao Shih-fang was the leader of a group of residents concerned in the repair of a Confucian shrine, just next to the [site of the] synagogue, in 1652.[5]

At least three gazetteers praise still another Jewish woman for her exemplary conduct. Her husband, a brother of Chao Ying-ch'eng and Chao Ying-tou, had died around 1650. "Madame (*née*) Kao, wife of Chao Ying-fu," the 1695 Kaifeng chronicle relates, "remained chaste and virtuous after he died for forty-four years. She served her mother-in-law most filially, and looked after her orphan child until he grew up."[6]

Few though they were, by the second half of the seventeenth century the Jews' influence and leadership in commerce, scholarship, and the mandarinate were impressive enough to convince an array of Kaifeng's highest office holders that it would be politic to contribute laudatory tablets to the newly rebuilt synagogue. Yet, perhaps because of their disinclination to publicize the presence of an obscure foreign cult in their community, not one of these same officials apparently saw fit to take note of the energetic *kehillah* and its handsome house of worship in the reports they wrote around the time the new edifice was dedicated.

The swelling resentment of the Chinese toward the merchants and missionaries who had come to the Middle Kingdom from barbarian lands led inevitably to the sweeping imperial edict which in 1724 had expelled nearly every Westerner then in the country and simultaneously encouraged the growth of wide-spread popular movements aimed, among other things, at expunging all alien influences from the Chinese soul and soil. It seems also to have had a deleterious effect on the attitudes of certain of the inhabitants of Kaifeng regarding the tiny community of Jews which had been ensconced in their midst for so many centuries. The Muslims, themselves frequently involved in serious difficulties with the Chinese government, began to display an anti-Jewish bias that was utterly un-Chinese. A few restrictive statutes affecting the Jews had been enacted in the fourteenth century, it is true, but these were neither directed at them alone nor of any lasting consequence. The antagonisms with which the Jews were forced to deal after the expulsion of the Jesuits from Kaifeng were primarily Muslim in origin. The ordinary frictions so often generated between minority ethnic and cultural groups living in close proximity to one another in an environment not of their own making do not totally account for the numerous petty harassments inflicted by the Muslims on the badly outnumbered Jews. The hostile attitude adopted by the Muslims may have stemmed to some degree from a desire to demonstrate that, despite what many Chinese believed, the Jews—frequently called the *lan-mao hui-hui*, or blue-capped Muslims, by their neighbors because of the color of the headgear they habitually wore at prayer—were not in any way affiliated with Islam. The Jews, in short, might be tarred with an alien brush, but they themselves, the Muslims apparently wanted the world to understand, despised everything that was foreign, and their dislike for the Jews should make that clear to all concerned. The Muslims' anti-Jewish stand may have been, in effect, part of a stratagem consciously or unconsciously devised to ward off the danger that their own Islamic faith might come under unwelcome scrutiny and criticism because of its glaringly obvious barbarian derivation.

The Jews, on their side, took whatever feeble precautions they could to let it be known that they were as fiercely loyal to China as was any other segment of the population, their concern for their safety going so far as to induce them to make a small but significant alteration of the text of the 1489 stone still standing on the site of their old synagogue. The story of why this change was made is a pathetic indication of how uneasy the Jews were becoming in the face of the Muslim harassments and the looming threat that they might be denounced as aliens to the various insurgent forces that overran the country in the middle and latter half of the nineteenth century.

The 1489 stele had originally included the names of the seventeen Jewish clans that, as it proudly reported, arrived in Kaifeng during the Sung dynasty, bearing tributes of cotton cloth to the emperor. All seventeen names were still on the stone in the first quarter of the eighteenth century, when the Jesuits obtained transcripts and rubbings of its text, and also as late as 1850, when the Chinese delegates had a copy made for their sponsors in Shanghai.[7] Around 1899, Volonteri, then stationed in Kaifeng with a group of Jesuits from Milan, acquired a new rubbing of the stone and sent it to his colleague, Father Jérôme Tobar, who published its text in Shanghai in 1900.[8] This Volonteri-Tobar version, surprisingly, showed only three clan names—Ai, Li, and Chin. The rest, it was found, had been carefully and neatly honed off the stone, giving rise, of course, to the question: Why, when, and by whom were the other fourteen names removed?

The mystery was resolved in 1906 by Martin who, while in Kaifeng forty years earlier, had personally encountered some indication of the Muslim antipathy to the Jews. Referring to a statement made by a Mr. Wilder concerning the alteration of the stone, Martin observed that "a foreigner came to Kaifeng in 1870 and was well entertained at a good restaurant; but the next day the gentry proceeded to drive the foreigner out." Whoever the visitor was, Wilder had declared, the incident alarmed the Jews and caused them to grind off most of the clan names on the 1489 stele.[9]

As to why the names of the Ai, Li, and Chin were not excised from the old monument, it may be that the three clans decided courageously (or perhaps recklessly) to live with whatever risks the continuing public acknowledgment of their ancestry might bring rather than submit to the indignity of having their origins concealed by so demeaning a subterfuge.

Oliver Bainbridge's account of how he nearly lost his life at the hands of a Muslim mob during his 1906 visit to Kaifeng also tells a great deal about the hatred the Muslims had built up against the Jews. Trying to locate relics from the synagogue, Bainbridge incautiously asked several mullahs if they had any in their mosques. This caused him, he later reported, to be suspected of being "a Jewish rabbi in disguise," a case of mistaken identity that brought together a mob of several thousand excited Muslims who brandished "brick, clubs, or knives" and shouted anti-Jewish imprecations at him. It was, naturally enough, a terrifying experience, and it came to an end only when he convinced the mullahs that he "was not a Jew, but a British traveler." But, he concluded, the Muslim antagonism to the Jews was not shared by the rest of the city's inhabitants. "The Confucians," he wrote, "are more kindly disposed towards the Jews than the Mohammedans, who always pull their gowns to one side if they meet a Jew, which, in China, is a vile insult."[10]

Regardless of the Muslim attitude toward the Jews, the Jews were at no time singled out for maltreatment by the bulk of Kaifeng's residents or subjected to the kind of governmentally inspired persecutions that their brethren in other lands knew only too well. China's treatment of her Jews remained, as always, benign, but the *kehillah* became increasingly fearful—and rightfully so, especially during such uprisings as the Taiping, Boxer, and others that swept the nation—about the prospect of becoming identified in the public mind with the hated barbarian enemies of the country. The cloud under which Kaifeng Jewry labored in the last century or so of its survival as a distinctly recognizable community may, for that matter, have grown even more foreboding because of the decline of its roles in commerce, government, and education. No longer commanding the respect for learning and prosperity, which had been theirs in times gone by, the Jews were now looked upon as ignoramuses and paupers —and, at least by the Muslims, as a powerless group that could be molested with impunity. Legally, there continued to be no distinction between the Jews and their neighbors; politically, culturally, and economically, their position had slipped badly.

In Chinese society, the ambitious young man's goal was to climb the ladder of success by passing the several levels of examinations offered at regular intervals by the government and then enter the civil service as a mandarin. The higher the degree he acquired, the more prestigious and rewarding he could expect his official assignment to be. Since the individual who devoted his efforts to commerce was regarded with disdain by the educated few who ruled the nation and its multifarious subdivisions—and who also wrote its records—it is easy to understand why the fact that a man was prominent in business affairs was not considered worthy of being commemorated in either the Jewish or the Chinese sources. The *kehillah*'s lapidary inscriptions fail completely to pay tribute to any of its members for their attainments in commerce, but quite a few of them were no doubt well-to-do businessmen. The frequent references in the steles to those who contributed heavily to the construction, renovation, and expansion of the synagogal property may be taken, if one reads between the lines, as at least partial enumerations of the wealthier members of the community, though not all these men were necessarily the builders of the fortunes they possessed. From the very beginning of Kaifeng Jewry there must in any case have been individuals who acquired wealth and power by virtue of their entrepreneurial abilities. This would have been especially true in those centuries in which trade between China and her neighbors was still being carried on without the inhibiting restrictions later imposed by the Ming dynasty. The decision of the Ming emperors to discourage travel between their realm and the rest of the world was without doubt more of a blow to the Jews (and to the Muslims) of Kaifeng than to most of their other subjects.

In view of the emphasis that the Chinese placed on scholarship, it is not at all surprising that the mantle of leadership of the country's Jews fell on the shoulders of their scholar-officials and rabbinical notables, with the former, of course, coming to be far better known in Chinese circles than the latter. The most distinguished scholar-official ever to emerge from the ranks of Kai-feng Jewry was Chao Ying-ch'eng (Moses ben Abram), whose career has been reconstructed from details provided in the 1663 and 1679 steles, as well as from biographical notices discovered in various Chinese gazetteers. Born in 1619, he received his *chü-jen* degree in 1645. A year later he became a *chin-shih*, the only Chinese Jew who is definitely known to have earned that coveted academic rank.[11] His *chin-shih* brought him an appointment as department director in the Ministry of Justice. In 1650 he was sent to Fukien Province, there to become the intendant, with the rank of assistant surveillance commissioner, or perhaps surveillance vice-commissioner, for the Chang-nan Circuit, a position carrying with it considerable prestige and commensurate responsibilities. Almost immediately, he was called upon to suppress a rebellion by the "bandits" and "robbers" (as the records describe them) Chang En-hsüan, Su Jung, and Chu I-t'ai. The gazetteers are fulsome in their praise of the energetic and effective manner in which he quelled the revolt and in their recognition of his subsequent efforts to improve the lot of the citizenry who had been affected by the unrest. The Shang-hang District Gazetteer of 1760 reports on Chao's activities in the Chang-nan Circuit:

At the time, the cruel bandit Chang En-hsüan and his band were strongly entrenched in a strategic position; and the robbers Su Jung, Chu I-t'ai and their band from Yung-ting were again burning and killing in K'u-chu and other villages. When Ying-ch'eng first took up his post, it was already right at the end of the year; he considered the extermination of the bandits as his most urgent task. He drew the *Chieh-nan-t'u* [charts of the suffering of the people] in thirty *ts'e* [volumes], and submitted them to the *hsün-fu* [provincial governor] Chang Hsüeh-sheng. Ying-ch'eng personally supervised the village militia, and together with the major Ho Kuo-hsiang launched a direct attack on the bandits' nest. Jung and his companions were all captured; En-hsüan also fled to P'ing-ho and was killed. The hidden ruffians were thus once and for all flushed out. When he had leisure, Ying-ch'eng bought a dwelling place to the west of the district [office?] and made it into a Lecture Hall. He selected the best teacher[s?] and gave him [them?] a public salary to give monthly lessons. After the bandit dis-

41. The Memorial Book of the Kaifeng Jews.

42. Excerpt from the Memorial Book of the Kaifeng synagogue, including the name of the *chin-shih* Chao Ying-ch'eng Moses ben Abram, the most eminent Jew ever born in Kaifeng.

turbances, for the first time the sound of reading was heard among the people, all on an extensive scale.[12]

Chao's civic-mindedness is applauded in other official records. "He . . . promoted schools," reports the 1898 Honan gazetteer, "and cleared up judicial cases";[13] and an 1829 Fukien gazetteer, describing the reactions of the people who benefited from Chao's enlightened policies, makes this observation: "The people were delighted to be free from calamity, and when suddenly they heard the sound of reading, compared it to a lucky star or auspicious cloud, mutually congratulating one another."[14]

In 1653, one of his parents having died, Chao went home to Kaifeng to begin the prescribed three years of mourning. His return enabled him to become active again in Jewish communal affairs. A competent Hebraist, at least by the standards then prevailing in Kaifeng, he took up the task of assisting the rabbi, Li Chên, in the collation of the Torah skins recovered from the flood of 1642. With his brother Ying-tou and their cousin Chao Ch'êng-chi, he searched for and discovered the foundations of the destroyed synagogue. From his income as an official, which must have been substantial, he personally underwrote the entire cost for the building of the three sections of the rear hall of the synagogue. He also wrote his book *Shêng Ching chi pien* (A Record of the Vicissitudes of the Holy Scriptures) which, if it is ever found, should prove to be an invaluable new source of information concerning the *kehillah* and its books. In 1656 he was appointed assistant surveillance commissioner for the Lower Chiang-tang Circuit, in what is now Hupei Province, but died shortly after assuming the post. Age thirty-eight or thirty-nine at the time of his death, he was memorialized in three Chinese gazetteers as a "warm-hearted and calm" personality "who had the air of an ancient and solid minister,"[15] and, as might be expected, left an indelible impression on his own people. His clan, the Chao, erected their stele in 1679 to honor his father Chao Kuang-yü for having given two great sons to the community, Ying-ch'eng and Ying-tou. Nearly two centuries later, Chao Nien-tsu, writing, as he thought, to "the chief teacher of the Jewish religion," took special pride in pointing to Ying-ch'eng and Ying-tou as the two most outstanding men in the history of his clan.[16]

Chao Ying-tou, Ying-ch'eng's younger brother, received his *kung-sheng* degree in 1653 and was later granted an honorary *chin-shih*. His Hebrew name is not known. In the early 1660s he served as district magistrate in Kunming, Yunnan Province, and held the equivalent office in I-liang, also in Yunnan, in the second half of the same decade. While assigned to the latter post, he was instrumental in the rebuilding of a Confucian temple and a Palace of Learning. An undated tablet, entitled "Inscription Recording the Rebuilding of the I-liang Palace of Learning" (and still standing in I-liang shortly before the city was captured by the Mao forces), included Chao among the four individuals credited with the reconstruction of the edifice.[17]

The 1663a inscription reveals that in 1653 Chao Ying-tou, who had returned to Kaifeng that year to take the examination for the *kung-sheng* degree, his brother Ying-ch'eng, and their cousin Major Chao Ch'êng-chi uncovered the foundations of the old synagogue that had been swept away in the flood eleven years earlier and then "set them in order." It also identifies Ying-tou as the author of a ten-chapter book called *Ming-tao-hsu* (A Preface to the Clarification of the Way), apparently a scholarly study of the tenets of Judaism. This may have been the book described by the Jesuits as the work that the *kehillah* presented to the authorities when, as the Jesuits put it, the Jews feared that they might be subjected to "persecution"; but, like his brother's work, it too has disappeared and there is no way of determining whether it actually is the apologia alluded to by the missionaries.[18]

Little else is known of Ying-tou's life. He is called a *chin-shih* "by grace"—an honorary *chin-shih*, that is—in the two inscriptions appearing on the Chao Clan archway, which was erected in the synagogal compound during 1678, and is also referred to in these, the 1679 stele, a 1670 *pien*, and an undated *lien* as district magistrate of I-liang. The 1678 and 1679 texts add that he had been promoted one grade higher, to the *wen-lin-lang* level (an official position of the first degree of the seventh rank). He was probably in Kaifeng for some time in 1670 and again in 1679. His name also appears in the Memorial Book, but only incidentally (since he was presumably still alive when its last obituary notices were inserted), as the husband—perhaps sequentially, perhaps bigamously—of two women of non-Jewish birth who had predeceased him.

As the various synagogal and secular records show, the careers of the Chao brothers Ying-ch'eng and Ying-tou were exceptionally distinguished, but the two were far from being the only Kaifeng Jews to make their mark on Chinese society. The Jewish and Chinese records allude to the ranks and attainments of a fair number of Chinese Jews, but it is doubtful if any of the individuals mentioned in these sources ever did as well for themselves and for their coreligionists (leaving aside An San) as the two Chao, whose clan unquestionably acquired more prominence in Chinese affairs than any of the others. Bishop White, it is true, was able to convince himself that the Li had contributed even more notably than the Chao to the ranks of Chinese military and governmental officialdom, but only because he mistakenly identified Li Kuang-t'ien as a member of the *kehillah*'s Li clan.[19] This Li Kuang-t'ien was commanding general of Kaifeng during the siege of 1642, and also the younger brother of Li Kuang-tso, the eminent scholar who wrote out the characters of the 1663a inscription in vermilion (for the engravers) and composed a *pien* text in 1670. White's identification of the younger Li, the hero of the defense of Kaifeng, as a Jew, taken up enthusiastically by other writers,[20] has, however, been amply disproved by Leslie. White's principal reason for making Li Kuang-t'ien a Jew (and his brother and other individuals named Li as well) is his patronymic. "But," as Leslie has wryly pointed out, while advancing an array of additional and more cogent arguments to counter White's thesis, "there were perhaps more men surnamed Li in China than all the Jews in the world at that time."[21]

Chao Ying-ch'eng's brilliant academic and civil service career, cut short though it was in his prime, came quickly and deservedly to be a source of enduring pride to his coreligionists. If even a single Chinese Jew of an earlier period than his, whether from Kaifeng or elsewhere, had done nearly as well, the *kehillah* would certainly not have permitted his accomplishments to pass unsung in its inscriptional and documentary texts. Nor would it in later years have remained silent about more recent successes of this caliber. As both the written and oral records of the community fail to tell of Jews whose attainments approached or rivaled Chao's, it is his name that overshadows the rest and emerges as the most illustrious in the history of his people.

Yet in spite of the fact that the Kaifeng Jews themselves never claimed to have produced a more important figure in Chinese life than Chao Ying-ch'eng, others have seen fit to do precisely that. Istvan Bakony, as has been noted, chose to make Jews out of the two world-renowned Soong sisters, Mmes. Chiang Kai-shek and Sun Yat-sen. The same distinction was claimed for Hsü Shih-ch'ang, president of China from 1918 to 1922; Liu Shao-chi, president of the People's Republic of China between 1959 and 1968, as well as an earlier figure, Hung Hsiu-ch'üan, instigator and leader of the devastating Taiping Rebellion (1849–64). No convincing evidence was ever offered, however, to support the allegations that these eminences were of Jewish extraction. Their surnames, for that matter, are not among those which have been traced to the Jewish communities of either Kaifeng or any other Chinese city.

The attribution of Jewish ancestry to Hsü Shih-ch'ang is based on nothing more than a statement made early in 1919 to an American reporter by a Mr. Feng, secretary to the Chinese consul in New York, to the effect that the recently inaugurated president of China, though apparently by then a Confucian, was descended from a Jewish family that had once lived in Kaifeng. Feng's statement, when it was publicized, created a mild flurry of excitement in Jewish circles, but it was never substantiated. It is quite possible, actually, that Hsü was born in Honan Province, for it was there that he spent much of his youth and for a time earned his living as tutor to the children of a local district magistrate; and his family, although legally registered as residing in Tientsin, had for several generations provided a succession of minor government officials who served in Honan. Aside from this geographic link, however, there is no apparent reason for attributing Hsü's ancestry to the Jews of Kaifeng.[22]

Much more elaborate and colorful, and even less apt to be true, is the story told in 1961 by the German writer Hans Heinrich

Wetzel who, in a biography of Liu Shao-chi, boldly provides both his subject and Hung Hsiu-ch'üan with Judaic genealogies. As a child in Hunan Province, according to Wetzel, the future president of China was told by his elderly great-uncle Liu Tso-fang, formerly head of the Finance Ministry in Peking, that the Liu clan was of Kaifeng Jewish origin. The Jews who setttled in Kaifeng, Wetzel has Liu Tso-fang explain to the boy, "came to China from Ceylon[!] during the Han era and lived in the country for 2,000 years before becoming as Chinese as the Chinese. Their priests, their *labini* [*rabbanim*], were called 'Aaronites, or Asonites', and belonged to the tribe of Asher. They venerated *Ji-Hi-Wei* [Jehovah]." The elder Liu, Wetzel then adds, also informed the youngster that the Taiping chief, Hung Hsiu-ch'üan, was likewise of Jewish descent. Wetzel embellishes the story by having a treasured relic from the Liu's Kaifeng days—a Hebrew prayer book, no less!—passed on to the boy after the great-uncle's execution.[23]

There must, no doubt, still be numerous untapped sources that are capable of yielding more data regarding the autochthonous Jews of the Middle Kingdom, collectively and individually (and far more reliable data, one may hope, than Feng's and Wetzel's), than those provided in the various synagogal texts and in the Chinese documents so far examined. If and when freer access to the government's archives and scholarly libraries of the People's Republic of China becomes possible, some of this material will almost surely be retrieved, and perhaps also—though this may be expecting too much—copies of one or both of the Judaic theses composed by Chao Ying-ch'eng and his brother Ying-tou. Further study of the currently available synagogal writings, abetted by the continuing interest of Hebraic specialists in comparing them with scriptural and liturgical works originating in old Jewish communities located in countries other than China, should ultimately provide the solutions to several of the many mysteries that now surround the saga of Chinese Jewry. The archives of the Roman Catholic church may also hold a miscellany of hitherto undiscovered or undisclosed documents that could well have been received in Europe, directly or at second hand, from earlier Jesuit visitors to Kaifeng than Gozani, Domenge, and Gaubil—from missionaries, that is, like Figueiredo and Enriquez, whose contacts with the *kehillah* took place in the seventeenth century. Additional Jewish documentation, moreover, the nature of which it is fruitless to attempt to predict, may emerge with the passage of time, either from within China itself or from the literary legacies of non-Chinese communities that had dealings with, or knowledge of, the Jewish communities beyond the Great Wall. That such finds will shed significant new light on the lost Jewish enclaves of Imperial China is highly improbable. However, at the very least, they should serve as further poignant reminders of Israel's longterm presence in that unlikely corner of the globe.

Epilogue ❖ SURVIVAL AND EXTINCTION

W HY, some three-quarters of a millennium after its establishment, did the Jewish community of Kaifeng finally
collapse? More to the point, perhaps, and far more difficult to answer, is the converse of the question: How was it possible for such a tiny cluster of Jews, tucked away in a land so
remote that no one ordinarily thought of it as lying within the
reaches of the Israelite Diaspora, to remain Jewish for as many
centuries as they did?

Although neither problem lends itself to a single simplistic and
all-encompassing solution, there has been no lack of effort to discover one; and the most eminent figure who participated in the
vain search for a specific underlying cause, which would by itself
alone satisfactorily explain the baffling mystery of the lengthy
survival and ultimate disintegration of Kaifeng Jewry, was the
philosopher Immanuel Kant.

In the mid-1790s, pondering the matter from the quiet of his
East Prussian study, Kant found himself in the awkward position
of having to concede that it could not be reconciled with a general-
ized rule of history he was then in the process of formulating.
"Now it is worthy of notice," he reflected, "that . . . the Jews
have continued to maintain themselves as such [as a distinctive
religious body], though scattered throughout the world, whereas
the faith of other religious fellowships has usually been fused with
the faith of the people among whom they have been scattered.
This phenomenon strikes many as so remarkable that they judge
it to be impossible according to the nature of things, but to be an
extraordinary dispensation for a special divine purpose."[1]

As Kant viewed it, however, there was nothing in the least

miraculous about world Jewry's unique success in preserving its integrity over the ages. Judaism, he declared, owed its survival to the fact that it possessed a body of written Scriptures, history having quite clearly demonstrated that "a people which has a written religion never fuses together in one faith with a people . . . possessing no such books, but only rites." This dictum, he insisted, must be regarded as a universally true law of history; and the Jews, moreover, could thank Christianity, and to a lesser extent Islam, for the good fortune they had enjoyed in surviving and keeping their ranks relatively unbroken. "For the Jews," he argued, "could ever and again seek out their old documents among the Christians (who had issued forth from them) whenever, in their wanderings, the skill in reading these books, and so the desire to possess them, was lost, as may often have happened, and when they merely retained the memory of having formerly possessed them."

Still, Kant was compelled to confess, there were two distant and obscure Jewish enclaves whose survival could not be totally accounted for by the thesis he was propounding. The first was the Malabar community of India, but he reasoned that its remarkable record for sustaining its ethnic and cultic solidarity in a setting that was neither Christian nor Islamic stemmed on the whole from its "continuing commercial relation with . . . co-religionists in Arabia" and the numerous opportunities this afforded for replenishing its diminished store of Judaic learning. The second was the Jewish colony of Kaifeng; though here, because he was apparently unaware of the fact that the Kaifeng Jews lived side by side with tens of thousands of adherents of the faith of Jslam, he could find no way of explaining the old *kehillah*'s failure to disappear within the context of the oversimplified religio-historical pattern to which he was committing himself. Kaifeng Jewry, he knew from the Jesuit sources, retained only a feeble grasp of the Hebrew in which its Bible was written and had no means at all of communicating with Jewish, or even Christian or Islamic, centers in other lands. By all rights, if his theory was tenable, Chinese Jewry should therefore have vanished long ago. Yet, it had not disappeared, ancient though it was. It was clear, then, that the experience of the Jews of China presented a jarring exception to his purportedly universal rule. An alternative theory was obviously called for to explain their special situation, one that did not demand as a prerequisite for survival an ongoing capacity for reading the Scriptures of their faith or procuring the assistance of people who could. The alternative he settled on was that although the Chinese Jews had gradually lost most of their knowledge of Judaism, they had managed to last for as many centuries as they did because there was absolutely no "kinship between their faith and the types of belief" prevailing in China.[2] As for the comprehensive body of religious and ethical literature that had been created by the people among whom the Chinese Jews lived, since this, unlike the Old Testament sections of the sacred writings of Christianity and Islam, was entirely unrelated to any of the texts from which Judaism drew its inspiration, it could be of no direct interest to the Jews. It was, in essence, an odd set of speculations that Kant projected, suggesting as it did—unflatteringly to the Jews, and without any evidence whatever to back it up—that the success of Judaism in holding on to its ancient heritage was in great measure contingent upon its physical proximity to the worlds of Christianity and Islam, particularly the former. One of the incidental implications arising from this peculiar twist of Kantian logic would therefore be that if China had been Christian, or even Islamic, its Jews might have remained more actively and more knowledgably Jewish than the Jesuits had reported them to be three-fourths of a century before the eminent German thinker started mulling over their condition.

Kant's arguments notwithstanding, the responsibility for the decline of the Kaifeng Jews' recollection of the tenets and traditions of their religion can no more be ascribed to a lack of "all kinship between their faith" and those of the dominant religious institutions of China than a deterioration of Jewish learning in Christian or Islamic lands can be charged to the glaring incompatibilities existing between many of the essential teachings derived from the Hebrew Scriptures and many of those derived from the New Testament and the Koran. The insensitivity of a minority to the values and ways of its own culture is more apt to arise, on the contrary, as a by-product of temptations which lead some of its members to strive to be thought of as less "different" from their neighbors than the nature of their communal background would suggest. Such temptations chronically beset the Chinese Jews, just as they did Jews living under Christian or Islamic hegemony. The nature of the allurements, however, was not always the same, the stake and the sword having never been employed in China, as they so often were in other regions of the world, to persuade Jews that their physical safety and their spiritual salvation could be simultaneously assured if they would only turn their backs on their own faith and embrace that of the majority. The inducements that in time led many Chinese Jews to become Confucians, Buddhists, or Taoists tended, in short, to be gentler and, in the long run, more effective than those held out by Christianity or Islam—though Chinese Jewry would almost surely not have faded totally away if its numbers had been substantially larger or its isolation less complete. And these—its small size and the fact that it was cut off for too many generations from the outside world—were the principal (though not the only) causes of its eventual dissolution.[3]

The inescapable impression that emerges from even a superficial reading of the Kaifeng synagogal steles is that of a tiny community that is losing its ancestral culture and becoming inextricably absorbed into the culture of the larger community around it. That it managed to stay alive as long as it did is a tribute to the tolerant attitude, or perhaps the courteous indifference, which China generally displayed toward those of her minority citizens who chose to follow their own ancestral creeds and to the burning determination of successive generations of Chinese Jews to keep on being Jewish. It is these two factors, most likely, that made it possible for Kaifeng Jewry to stave off its demise for centuries; and, apparently, for several other Sino-Jewish communities to do the same.

As it struggled to retain its viability, the Kaifeng *kehillah* was faced with assimilatory problems comparable to those encountered by untold numbers of Jewish and other minority communities throughout history. Some of its members were too apathetic about the heritage into which they had been born—often because they knew so little about it—to care very much whether it was passed on to the next generation or not. Others were moved to lose themselves in the majority by a compulsion to cease being regarded as "different." And, no doubt, there were those whose departure from Judaism was motivated by nothing more than conscienceless opportunism. Jewish women who married non-Jews left the fold, of course, though such numerical losses tended on the whole to be offset by the non-Jewish women who became Jewish when they married Jewish men. Only in rare cases, presumably, did an individual undergo conversion to one of the majority faiths because of a conviction, honestly and perhaps maturely arrived at, that its doctrine had more to offer than his own. Such a decision, in all probability, would have aroused strong feelings of suspicion on the part of his former coreligionists that his motives might not be quite as unsullied and above reproach as he pretended.

The odds against the continued survival of the Chinese Jews *qua* Jews were substantially increased by the absence of a national policy, so common in Europe, prohibiting them from participating in the academic life of the country and its civil service or restricting them from employment in any but a few specific fields of endeavor. The attainment of academic degrees—the higher, the better—was the key to securing the greatly coveted appointments to official posts, the degrees being granted through a series of standardized examinations. "By Ming times (1368–1644)," as Sung Nai Rhee reminds his readers in an article devoted to the effects of the Chinese civil service system on the assimilation of Chinese Jewry, "the examinations, based exclusively on the contents of the Confucian *Classics* and their neo-Confucian interpretations, given at three levels (prefectural, provincial, and metropolitan), led to three successive degrees."[4] The higher two, the *chin-shih* and the *chü-jen*, assured the holders of appointment to administrative or judicial posts. What this meant, Rhee explains, was that:

in terms of their special rights and privileges, in addition to appointments to official posts, the degree holders, variously

43. The "Chinese Jew," a portrait by Betty Byrne. Apparently made in the 1920s or 1930s. The subject was a Chinese of Jewish descent who lived in Shanghai.

called "gentry" or "scholar-officials," enjoyed exemption from labor service, freedom from corporal punishments, such as beating with the bamboo, and certain other prerogatives, all of which established them at the very pinnacle of the Chinese sociopolitical structure. In other words, as so graphically described in the famous Ch'ing Dynasty novel *Ju-lin Wai-shih* ("An Unofficial History of the Literati") by Wu Ching-tzu, the civil service system in Confucian China "gave a man a simultaneous access to power, prestige and wealth."

In view of the extraordinary social mobility guaranteed by the civil service system, it was natural that the more ambitious and able Jews of Kaifeng would seek to take advantage of it. The desire to do so would have been especially heightened by the fact that in traditional Chinese society the mercantile occupation, to which most Jews belonged, was the most despised class category. And, indeed, the few available documents from Kaifeng clearly attest to the fact that, beginning in the fourteenth century, a large number of Jews from Kaifeng did join the scholar-official class in increasing numbers as years went by.[5]

But the Jews' success in climbing the academic and civil service ladders, Rhee continues, was not without its penalties, for it was transforming the Jewish intellectuals into Confucian literati:

And being a Confucian literatus signified much more than a mere academic and status achievement, for it affected the person's whole character and his philosophical as well as religious perspective. Once a Jew became a member of the Confucian literati he was expected to (and he invariably did) conduct himself as a Confucian, within the framework of Confucian thought pattern. In other words, a membership in the literati necessarily involved internal as well as external metamorphosis.

The Confucianization of the Jewish intellectuals was, of course, viewed with strong disapproval by the more religiously conscious members of the Jewish community. But as far as the Jewish Confucians were concerned, their acculturation was quite justifiable, for, in their judgment, Confucianism and Judaism were essentially equivalent, as they understood their essence to be wholly embodied in the principles of *wu-lun*, the Five Basic Social Relationships defined by the Confucian *Classics*.[6]

The Jewish scholar-official, like his colleagues, was routinely assigned to a district far from home, a precaution taken to discourage nepotism, favoritism, and other undesirable practices. It follows, then, that a high proportion of the Kaifeng *kehillah*'s brightest and most capable men were compelled to move to other parts of the country where, except in rare instances, they and their children would have absolutely no contact with other Jews and might well end up losing all their ties to Judaism.

Not all of the *kehillah*'s displaced literati—and perhaps, in fact, very few—drifted away irreversibly from their Judaic roots. Chao Ying-ch'eng and his brother Ying-tou, both of whom evidently received relatively good Jewish religious training in their early years, played outstanding roles as adults in the communal and cultural affairs of their people, each involving himself in the rebuilding of what was to be the congregation's last synagogue and also composing a Chinese work devoted to Jewish matters. Their friend Li Chên, presumed by some historians to have earned a *chü-jen* degree and to have been a district magistrate, did not allow his Confucian education, it would appear, to keep him from serving as chief rabbi of Kaifeng.[7]

Nevertheless, the long years of Confucian indoctrination to which many of the city's most brilliant and ambitious Jews were exposed, often to the detriment of their Judaic studies, could not avoid having a shattering impact on the congregation's unity. Ai T'ien, a *chü-jen*, confessed to Ricci that he could barely recognize the characters in a Bible that the priest showed him as Hebrew and was totally incapable of reading them. Yet, in spite of this, he was not altogether unfamiliar with the contents of the Book of Genesis; for had the case been otherwise, he would never have identified the individuals portrayed in the painting in Ricci's church as Old Testament figures. Inadequately tutored though he recognized himself to be in Judaic disciplines, Ai remained loyal to his ancestral faith, notwithstanding the reservations he expressed to Ricci about the dietary and other difficulties that being a Jew imposed on him when he was away from home.

There were, however, some Kaifeng Jews with academic backgrounds similar to Ai's whose Jewishness was nominal at best. The Confucian leanings of these men, as Rhee properly maintains, undoubtedly created considerable dissension within the *kehillah*. Still, their preference for Confucian ways by no means justifies his contention that the numerous non-Jewish sentiments enunciated in the various synagogal steles were put there by the wealthy and powerful literati class in order "to explain and endear Confucianism to those Jews who might have looked unfavorably toward their [the literati's] acculturation."[8] Other scholars, of course, have maintained that one of the primary purposes behind the erection of the steles was to present the *kehillah*'s theological stand in a form that would be pleasing to strangers and thus make Judaism understandable and inoffensive to them.

Although it is highly improbable that the literati went so far as to humiliate their less assimilated kinsmen by setting up the various steles on the synagogal grounds as a means of brainwashing them into believing that Confucianism was "superior" to Judaism, there must nevertheless have been bitter and heart-rending disputes within the congregation regarding the course it was to take vis-à-vis the non-Jewish philosophies and customs that were encroaching on its own, the traditionalists trying desperately to keep all alien influences at bay and the innovators demanding the incorporation of many of them into the Jewish way of life. This was not the first time, of course, that a confrontation of this nature disrupted the solidarity of a Jewish community, and certainly not the last. Similar conflicts had cropped up in ancient Judea during the Greek and Roman occupations of the country, and even earlier, and in any number of the countries in which Israel lived in exile. And it foreshadowed, among others, the struggle between the Orthodox and Reform movements, which divided a people who could ill afford the luxury of fragmentation. The nineteenth- and twentieth-century debates over the direction Judaism was to adopt obviously affected thousands of times as many Jews, but were probably no fiercer than those that scarred the psyche of Kaifeng Jewry. Without question, the insistence of certain Confucian-oriented literati, and other assimilationist-minded Jews as well, that such non-Jewish practices as ancestor adulation be brought into the synagogue was no less repugnant to their traditionally inclined coreligionists than, for example, the insistence by the proponents of Reform that the organ be given a place in communal worship would later be to their Orthodox brethren.[9]

In a sense, the internecine religious clash that arose within Kaifeng Jewry was not unlike the Chinese Rites Controversy, which subsequently shook the foundations of the Catholic church, the primary difference being that the Kaifeng innovators were not interested in taking on Confucian practices for the purpose of converting the Chinese from one faith to another, whereas the Jesuits were. The motives of the Kaifeng dissidents were no doubt mixed. Some, at the one extreme, sincerely believed that Confucian teachings could be harmonized with Jewish doctrine; some, at the other extreme, were time-servers, and intent, whether they openly admitted it or not, on total assimilation. Between the two extremes, as might be expected, there were any number of attitudinal gradations. It would appear, in any case, that the Church's reluctance to present a better face to the Chinese by incorporating certain of their traditional rites into her own may in the end have cost her China. The price paid by the Kaifeng synagogue for its less obdurate stand, taken though it was for quite different reasons, may have been its very existence.

The most clear-cut object lesson derived by historians and sociologists from the ultimate absorption of the Chinese Jews into the ethnic strains and religious cultures of their country has of course been that numerically small peoples transplanted into strange and enormously larger societies that do not grind them down or forcibly segregate them have little or no chance of retaining their own cultures or communal integrity over the long run. Among those who came to this conclusion but believed he knew the solution to the dilemma it posed to the Jews, whether their numbers in any particular country were minuscule or immense, was the intensely concerned scholar-merchant S. M. Perlmann. Having personally met and talked with several Kaifeng Jews in Shanghai, and having immersed himself in the study of the Jewish experience in China, Perlmann argued at considerable length and with great earnestness against the notion that there could be any reasonable hope for the longterm survival of Jewish communities living in societies which treated them well and did not set them apart as pariahs.[10] Deeply dedicated to the cause of Zionism, he saw the record of Chinese Jewry's gradual disappearance into an alien culture as a doleful foretaste of what was bound to happen to the Jews of those enlightened nations that accorded them the rights and privileges of first-class citizens and permitted them to order their lives more or less as they chose. In 1912, taking what was then an understandably optimistic, though tragically unrealistic, view of the prospects for an early world-wide diminution of anti-Semitism and tempering it with an expression of his fear that the dawning of an age of tolerance might catch Judaism offguard, he described the perils he foresaw for his coreligionists in blunt and unequivocal terms. Let the Jews of the world, he pleaded, many of them already living under flags of freedom, and still more living in the hope that the barbaric retstrictions being imposed against them in their respective homelands would soon be removed, take heed of the dire fate of the Israelite settlements of China. The danger that Judaism would shortly disappear, he contended, "is not imminent in those countries where the hostility to the Jews is still strong and effective, because they will fight there and conserve themselves. But we have to look forward, to the time which must come sooner or later, to the time when the Jews will enjoy the same privileges as the dominant people, as the Germans, the Roumanians and the Russians. Then the process of grinding and annihilating the minority will commence all over the world and work rapidly, because there will be heard no more groans of any oppressed to remind the Jews that they were once a strong nation and are about to be destroyed from the face of the earth. Therefore we have to look out for means to prevent the process of absorption, and *the only remedy is . . . a territory for the Jews*."[11] Kindness, Perlmann felt, could become a more effective device for obliterating the Jews than brutality, never dreaming that his brave new world had already spawned a Hitler.

With Jacob leading them, the Bible relates, sixty-six Hebrews crossed into Egypt seeking a haven from the famine that had made life in Canaan intolerable. Once in Egypt, they joined with

Joseph and his sons Manasseh and Ephraim, so that they were now seventy in all. "To sojourn in the land are we come," declared the Patriarch's sons to the Pharaoh; and by this, as the Kaifeng Jews could read each Passover in their Haggadahs, they meant that their little band was not asking permission to dwell permanently in the Pharaoh's domain, but only to be granted a brief respite there.

Seventy Jewish clans—again that mystic number—arrived in Kaifeng, the synagogal stele of 1489 proclaims in a passage reminiscent of the biblical story of the coming of the Hebrews to Egypt, also seeking permission to sojourn there, but with no thought in mind, apparently, though the stele has nothing to say on the matter, that their stay was to be anything but permanent.[12]

On their arrival in Egypt, the Hebrews were greeted by their kinsman Joseph, who had eased the way for them and seen to it that they would be made welcome. If the immigrants who traveled to Kaifeng in the Sung period were greeted by coreligionists already there, the stele does not tell of it. Did the clans simply wander across China without assurance that they would not be turned back? Or did they, like latter-day Joshuas, send emissaries ahead "to view the land" and report back to them before they decided to make Kaifeng their destination? Or had Jewish merchant-adventurers who knew the Sung capital at first hand suggested that it was the most promising Chinese city for them to select as their future home? Here too, the stele is silent.

In Egypt, in time, there arose a new Pharaoh "who knew not Joseph" and enslaved the Hebrews. Three or four hundred years after Jacob led them there, they were still a united people—although, as the Midrash declares, many adopted the slogan, "Let us be Egyptian in all things"—and they had multiplied so greatly that "the land was filled with them."[13] When they went forth from the land of bondage they were, as God had promised Jacob they would be, "a great nation."

In China, no ruler ever singled out the Jews for persecution, and they were never enslaved. The numbers of the Chinese Jews, unlike those of the Hebrews, remained always small; and, again unlike the Hebrews, they never departed from the country to which their forefathers had come. The parallel their stone inscription of 1489 had tacitly drawn, whether by chance or by design, between the two arrivals—theirs at the court of the Sung and that of the Hebrews at the court of the Pharaohs—did not extend beyond either event. In the final analysis, however, the Hebrews who said, "Let us be Egyptian in all things," did not prevail. As for the Jews who said, "Let us be Chinese in all things," they, it would seem, carried the day.

Appendix ❖ INTERVIEWS WITH
SHIH HUNG-MO

I N mid-1974, Rabbi Marvin Tokayer, then rabbi of the Jewish
community of Japan, traveled to Taipei and interviewed
Lt.-Col. Shih Hung-mo(k) (retired), Republic of China Air
Force. Rabbi Tokayer's memoranda of the talks, generously made
available to the author, are summarized below, though several
of the details already incorporated in the text of this book
are omitted.

PERSONAL HISTORY OF LT.-COL. SHIH HUNG-MO

Shih Hung-mo was born on May 20, 1924, in Kunming City,
Yunnan Province, in southwest China. According to official Air
Force records filled out by Shih himself, his father's name was
Shih Shu, but Colonel Shih explains that his father was also
called Shih Tse-i. (The use of more than one name was a common practice in China.) The elder Shih was born on June 4, 1887,
also in Kunming.

At a very early age, Shih Hung-mo was informed that his
family belonged to the so-called Chinese Blue Muhammadan
religious and ethnic group—that is, they were Jews. In his youth
in Kunming, he had personal dealings with only three other male
individuals whom he knew to be Jewish, these being his father,
a much older brother (killed in action in the 1930s while fighting
against the Japanese as a member of the Nationalist Army), and
an uncle. He recalls being told by his father and uncle that there
were one or more other Blue Muhammadan families in Kunming

but does not remember ever meeting them. Although virtually all the Jews who lived in the city, in his time and earlier, were ill-educated and even illiterate, Shih Luan, the elder brother of his paternal great-grandfather, had been able to read enough Hebrew to make out a few simple prayers. Hung-mo's father and uncle claimed that they had seen several Hebrew books in the old gentleman's possession. Hung-mo himself, however, never saw either Shih Luan (he having died long before Hung-mo was born) or the books.

In Shih's childhood, his family did not observe any traditional Jewish practices, except, perhaps, for an occasional cessation of work on the Sabbath; but he was informed that two or three generations back the Sabbath and several other holidays were still being observed, and that Shih Luan had made a particular point of celebrating the Rosh Hashanah festival.

Shih recalls being told by his maternal grandmother that she was in part of Mongol descent. His father had owned the original copy of the genealogical chart of the paternal side of the family, this going back some fifteen or twenty generations to an individual known as Shih Tzu (Ancestor Shih) who came to Kunming from Chekiang Province at the beginning of the Ming dynasty, or not long after 1368. This genealogy was handwritten (an indication of the poverty of the family, the more wealthy families having their genealogies block printed) in Chinese characters.

Because, as Colonel Shih puts it, the Chinese in Kunming thought of the Jews as the most "strange, grotesque, outlandish, and queer believers" in the world, his family taught him at an early age to keep his true identity secret. Even today, he says, his friends are not aware of his ties to Judaism, and he is deathly afraid lest they learn the truth about him. (This seems an odd position for him to take, it must be pointed out, in view of the fact that he submitted two letters and two articles to English-language periodicals proudly and openly declaring his Jewishness.) As a consequence of the fear of Kunming's Jews of being known as Jews, it was inevitable that they eventually disappeared.

Shih's uncle, somewhat better off than his peddler-father, was entrusted with raising the boy from age ten. This man, Shih Cheng-i, his father's elder brother, was a merchant who made frequent trips abroad, especially to India. During 1935 and 1936, when Hung-mo was about eleven, he accompanied Cheng-i on an extensive business trip. Neither would ever see Kunming again.

Uncle and nephew traveled extensively for nearly a decade, their return to China having become impossible or inadvisable during the World War II period. They traveled mainly by caravan, carrying silk, fur, herbs, and other Chinese products to the Middle East. Among the countries they visited were Burma, India, Palestine (Haifa and Jaffa), and Egypt. They spent several months in Palestine. Their itineraries in the Mediterranean area were by sea.

The two Shih passed the war years in India, Burma, and northern Indochina. One of Hung-mo's Air Force files, written in his own hand, indicates that he was in Chungking, working as a civilian with the Chinese military forces from October 1944 to September 1945. Before that time, he very clearly was not in China. The entry in the Air Force file is, however, inconsistent with the information that follows.

Shih graduated from an Indian university on January 1, 1946, with a bachelor's degree in languages (especially English), history, and geography. He also learned Spanish, German, Arabic, and Hebrew, but the latter were self-taught. The name of the university transliterates from the Chinese as Hai-deh-la-ba (Hyderabad?). In view of the information given in the preceding paragraphs, I suspect that the degree was either awarded in absentia or that he went back to India for a brief interval following his stay in Chungking.

After his return to China, Shih worked with his uncle in Shanghai, and later obtained employment with the military in Nanking and Hangchow. He joined the Air Force in 1948 in Hangchow, where he lived for six months prior to his evacuation to Taiwan.

While Shih was in Shanghai, his uncle, mother, and a younger sister died, leaving him with no family but his father. After his arrival in Taiwan he received a copy of the family genealogy from his father, as well as several other items of family interest. (Mail between father, in Red China, and son, in Nationalist China, was relayed by a Christian missionary friend in Hong Kong.) Shih has had no contact with his father since about 1958, and doubts that he is still alive.

In 1946 or 1947, in Shanghai, Shih made the acquaintance of several foreign Jews living in the city, who told him of the fact-finding expedition their community had dispatched to Kaifeng in the 1920s. In 1947 he himself traveled to Kaifeng where, after a few days, he found three native Blue Muhammadans. When he lived in Hangchow, the home of Ancestor Shih, he tried to locate Jews there, but without success. He says, however, that he did find several Jewish tombstones in a cemetery outside the city.

Late in 1948, preparing to leave the mainland with the Nationalist forces, Shih departed from Hangchow with five suitcases of personal belongings and traveled by train to Shanghai, where he was to board a steamer to Taiwan. While his luggage was being loaded aboard the ship, and along with other luggage, three of the suitcases fell into the water, taking his family genealogy chart and other personal memorabilia to the bottom. Because of the near-panic conditions surrounding the evacuation, it was impossible to retrieve the baggage, with the result that all of the evidence regarding his personal background, as well as the notes of his efforts to find other Chinese Jews, were lost once and for all.

On his arrival in Taiwan, Shih was assigned to duty in Kangshan. There he wrote the articles and letters that brought his bizarre story to public attention. Yitzhak Ben-Zvi, later to be president of Israel, was among those who read Shih's accounts. Ben-Zvi, an expert in the history of obscure Jewish diasporic groups, apparently offered to attempt to secure an honorary degree for Shih, but the contact between the two men was somehow broken, and nothing came of the matter.

Shih has resided in Taipei since leaving Kangshan some sixteen or seventeen years ago. He is still single, and lives in a dormitory, having retired from the Air Force about a year ago. He is a quiet man who enjoys reading and solitude. He looks healthy, but claims that he is ill, tires easily, and cannot travel long distances.

He does not plan to leave Taiwan. He has never married, he says, mainly because he was never able to find a Blue Muhammadan girl. Small in stature, he is now about fifty years of age. Having passed virtually all of his personal life in isolation, he does not seem to care whether that isolation is broken or not, and, in fact, to have opted for a continuation of the same quiet life.

INFORMATION OBTAINED FROM SHIH HUNG-MO
CONCERNING THE CHINESE JEWS

The Jews of Kaifeng

In 1947 in Kaifeng Shih visited the site of the old synagogue, hunted in vain for Hebrew writings, and actually met three Jews, two of about forty years of age and one of about sixty, as well as the children of their households. All three men were illiterate and destitute. They observed no Jewish customs and had no family genealogies. He suspected, however, that the sixty-year-old man may have had some Hebrew books in his possession. Two of the men he met belonged to the Li clan, one to the Ai. He was also told of other Jews still living in Kaifeng but did not meet them.

Hangchow

In Hangchow, in 1948, Shih came upon no Jews, but did succeed in finding a cemetery several miles to the west of the city, which he says had belonged to Jews. The tombstones all dated from the Ch'ing dynasty, and particularly from the early mid-Ch'ing to the late Ch'ing periods. In the cemetery he found four or five tombstones that he insists marked the burial places of Jewish individuals, and also rubble from monuments, marking places where other Jews had been interred. Each of the four or five standing monuments contained three lines of engraved characters. The first, in Hebrew, read: "Religion of Israel"; the second was in Arabic, after the custom of the Muslims, and displayed such ordinary Muslim slogans as: "By the name of God. He is the One merciful to the exclusive people. He is merciful to all peoples" (Shih's words); and the remainder was written in Chinese characters, running vertically, and gave the name of the deceased, the year of his death, his surviving relatives, and so forth.

Shih was not able to trace the origins of the old Jewish community of Hangchow, but suggests that it may have come into being when a number of Jews accompanied the Sung Court there from Kaifeng in 1126.

Kunming

Shih has little to add about the Jews of Kunming not already noted above, except that when the Kunming Jews were questioned about their occasional token observances of the Sabbath, they prudently explained that they were following the practice of the Seventh-Day Adventists, apparently because they felt they would be less apt to be despised if they were thought to be Christians rather than Jews.

Colonel Shih has combined the fact that the first member of his family who lived in Kunming arrived there from Chekiang at the beginning of the Ming era with various family legends and certain Kunming historical data to develop two hypotheses regarding the origin of the Jewish community of his native city. Both involve the mass migrations that are known to have taken place from Chekiang to Yunnan by command of the founding emperor of the Ming dynasty.

Shih's first hypothesis: As the Chinese records show, the first Ming emperor ordered three of his generals to lead a multitude of Chinese to Yunnan in order to consolidate his rule over that remote southwestern region. The people selected to make the move came from the eastern provinces of Chekiang and Kiangsu, especially from the great cities of Suchow, Hangchow, and Nanking, which were Ming strongholds. Among these emigres was a large number of Muslims. Colonel Shih theorizes that a contingent of Chinese Jews may well have come with the Muhammadans.

Shih's second hypothesis: This is very similar to the first, differing only with regard to the particular migration, there having been a second population transfer to Yunnan, this one too ordered by the first Ming emperor and this time for the purpose of drawing the fangs of one of his rivals, Chang Shih-chieh, by exiling him and a large body of his supporters to the hinterlands of Yunnan. Since masses of Muslims were likely to have been sent to Yunnan with Chang, Jews may also have been intermingled with them.

Today, there is undoubtedly no vestige of Judaism left in Kunming, but there are perhaps some descendants of the Blue Muhammadans still there. Shih Hung-mo's father, Shih Tse-i, the last man known to have had the Shih family genealogical chart, was in all probability also the last man in the city to think of himself as a Jew.

❖ GLOSSARY OF CHINESE TERMS

Chang	Unit of length, approximately ten feet
Chang-chiao (Chamkiao)	Leader of the Religion, chief rabbi
Cheng-chiao	True Religion
Ch'i-hsing pa-chia	Seven surnames, eight clans (Jews of Kaifeng)
Chiao-ching chiao	Religion that teaches the Scriptures (Judaism)
Chiao-ching Hu-T'ung	Lane of the Religion that teaches the Scriptures
Chin-shih	Academic degree equated with the doctorate
Ch'ing-chen-ssu	Synagogue, mosque
Ch'ing hui-hui	Blue Muslims, that is, Jews
Chü-jen	Academic degree equated with the master's
Etunoi (Etonoi)	Chinese transliteration of Adonai
Fu	Prefecture
Hotaoi	Chinese transliteration of Adonai
Hsi-yü (Si-yü)	Western regions, Persia
Hsien	District
Hsing	Surname
Hui (hui-hui, hui-tzu)	Muslims, including Jews
K'o-t'ou	Kowtow
Kung-sheng	Academic degree equated with the bachelor's degree
Lan-mao hui-hui	Blue-capped Muslims, that is, Jews
Li	Unit of length, varying substantially from place to place and time to time, but invariably a substantial portion of a mile
Li-pai-ssu	Synagogue, mosque
Lien (tui-lien)	Vertical tablet inscriptions

Man-la	Synagogal elder or functionary
Pai-mao hui-hui	White-capped Muslims
Pien (p'ai-pien)	Horizontal tablet inscriptions
San-chih (San-ching, San-tso)	Miscellaneous Writings
Shang-ti	God
Shang-t'ien	God, heaven
Sheng-ching	Holy Scripture
Shih-p'ei	Stele
Ssu	Temple
Ta-ching (Tao-ching)	The Law
T'ang-chia	Sexton, concierge
Tao	The Way
Ti	Lord, ruler
T'iao-chin-chiao	Religion that extracts the sinews (Judaism)
T'iao-chin-chiao Hu-T'ung	Lane of the Sinew-Extracting Religion
T'ien	Heaven
T'ien-chiao	Heavenly religion
T'ien-chu	India, or, a large portion of non-Chinese Asia, including India
T'ien-chu	Lord of Heaven
T'ien-chu-chiao	Indian religion. Also used for Judaism and, with different characters, for Catholicism
Tsu (tzu)	Ancestor
Wan-sui-p'ai	Imperial tablet
Wo-t'o	Chinese transliteration of *Ortaq* (Mongolian), a commercial organization, usually Muslim
Wu-ssu-tu	Chinese transliteration of the Persian *Ustad,* or religious leader
Ye-cho a-cha	Chinese transliteration of Jehovah
Yi-t'zu-lo-yeh	Chinese transliteration of Israel
Yi-t'zu-lo-yeh chiao	Religion of Israel

❖ SELECTED BIBLIOGRAPHY

See Notes for full bibliographical references not provided herein.

Adler, Marcus N. "Chinese Jews: A Lecture delivered by Marcus N. Adler, M.A., at the Jews' College Literary Society, Queen Square House, London, on June 17, 1900." *Jewish Quarterly Review* [London] 13, no. 49 (October 1900) : 18–41. Reprinted in Kublin, *Jews in Old China*, pp. 93–117.

Brotier, Gabriel. "Mémoire sur les Juifs établis en Chine." *Lettres édifiantes et curieuses des missions étrangères*. Vol. 24. Paris, 1781 edition, pp. 56–100.

 A summation of letters pertaining to the Kaifeng Jews received by the Society of Jesus from its missionaries in China.

Brown, David A. "Brown Meets the Chinese Jews." *American Hebrew and Jewish Tribune* (January 27–March 3, 1933), pp. 199, 208, 217, 229, 237, 242, 247, 256, 261, 277, 288. Reprinted in condensed form as "Through the Eyes of an American Jew" in White, vol. 1, pp. 150–64.

Chang Hsiang-wen. "An Early Chinese Source on the Kaifeng Jewish Community." *Folklore Studies* [Peking] 4 (1945): 327–31. Reprinted in Kublin, *Studies*, pp. 214–18.

Chen, Nicholas Mu Yu. "A Comunidade Israelita de Khai Fon: Um Estudo sobre a Assimilação dos Judeus na China." Doctoral dissertation, University of São Paulo, 1976.

 The rise and fall of the Jewish community of Kaifeng, as interpreted by a modern Chinese historian.

Ch'en Yüan. See entry under Ross.

Cordier, Henri. See entry under Yule.

D'Elia, Pasquale M., ed. *Fonti Ricciane*. 3 vols. Rome, 1942–49.

 Matteo Ricci's journals, fully annotated.

Dehergne, Joseph. See entry under Leslie and Dehergne.

Dicker, Herman. *Wanderers and Settlers in the Far East*. New York, 1962.

 A review of the Jewish experience in the Orient in recent times.

Drenger, B. D., ed. *The Haggadah of the Chinese Jews*. New York: The Orphan Hospital Ward of Israel, 1967.

Facsimiles of the Passover Haggadah of the Kaifeng *kehillah*, with comments concerning its text by the editor and by Cecil Roth.

Edrehi, Moses. *An Historical Account of the Ten Tribes Settled beyond the River Sambatyon in the East.* London, 1836.

A rambling, imaginative, and fascinating account of the peregrinations of the Ten Lost Tribes by a picturesque Moroccan Jew who entertained no doubts as to their continued existence as an ethnically identifiable people. The allusions to the Chinese Jews are of mixed value, but still worth reading.

Ezra, Edward I., and Sopher, Arthur. *Chinese Jews.* Shanghai, 1926. Reprinted in Kublin, *Jews in Old China,* pp. 213–95.

Fang Chaoying. "Notes on the Chinese Jews of Kaifeng." *Journal of the American Oriental Society 85,* no. 2 (April–June 1965): 126–29. Reprinted in Kublin, *Studies,* pp. 85–90.

Finn, James. *The Jews in China: Their Synagogue, their Scriptures, their History, &c.* London, 1843. Reprinted in Kublin, *Jews in Old China,* pp. 1–91.

—. *The Orphan Colony of Jews in China.* London, 1872.

Two of the landmark contributions to the literature dealing with the Chinese Jews.

Fryer, John. "The Social and Political Aspect of the Chinese Jews." *New Occident 5,* no. 24 (March 1903): 1–18.

Argues for a Jewish entry into China at the time of the Babylonian Captivity. Worth reading as a representative sample of how early twentieth-century Protestant missionaries viewed the history of the Chinese Jews.

Gallagher, Louis J. *China in the Sixteenth Century: The Journals of Matthew Ricci, 1583–1610.* New York: Random House, 1953.

An English version of Trigault's Latinization of Ricci's journals.

Gaubil, Antoine. *Correspondance de Pékin, 1722–1759.* Renée Simon, ed. Geneva: Librairie Droz, 1970.

A compilation of Gaubil's letters, including numerous references to his 1723 visit to the Kaifeng Jews and his unsuccessful attempts, then and later, to obtain their synagogal books.

Glover, A. Kingsley. *Jewish-Chinese Papers.* Appleton, Wisc., 1884.

A collection of the author's papers on the Jews of China. Interesting, but to be taken cautiously.

Godeby, Allen H. *The Lost Tribes: A Myth.* Durham, N.C.: Duke University Press, 1930. Reprinted in New York by Ktav Publishing House, 1974.

A fascinatingly erudite, though all too often naïve, work which deals at considerable length with the Chinese Jews, inter alia, but is marred by the author's propensity for including whatever data he can find to support his own viewpoints while excluding data that contradict what he believes.

Gozani, Jean-Paul. "Lettre . . . au Père Joseph Suarez." *Lettres édifiantes et curieuses écrites des missions étrangères.* Vol. 18. Paris, 1781 edition, pp. 31–55.

> Gozani's description of his visit to the Kaifeng Jews in 1704, with remarks by the editor.

Hoberman, Barry. "The Early Jews in China: The Origin of the Jewish Community of K'aifeng." Undergraduate honors thesis, Duke University, 1973.

> An analysis of the various routes that may have been taken by early Jewish immigrants to China and the times at which they could have arrived in the country.

Jewish Encyclopedia. 12 vols. New York and London, 1901–5.

> Refer also to entries under Kaifeng, China, Chao, and the like in various standard Jewish encyclopedias. See also *Encyclopaedia of Religion and Ethics* for article under Chinese Jews.

Kramer, Lawrence. "The K'aifeng Jews: A Disappearing Community." *Jewish Social Studies* 18, no. 2 (April 1956) : 125–44. Reprinted in Kublin, *Studies*, pp. 1–22.

> The Kaifeng Jews, from the point of view of a sociologist.

Kranzler, David. *Japanese, Nazis and Jews.* New York: Yeshiva University Press, 1976.

> The Shanghai Jewish community in the World War II years.

Kublin, Hyman, ed. *Jews in Old China: Some Western Views.* New York: Paragon Book Reprint, 1971.

—. *Studies of the Chinese Jews: Selections from Journals East and West.* New York: Paragon Book Reprint, 1971.

> Two convenient collections of important Sino-Judaic studies, most of which are difficult to obtain, supplemented by the editor's highly informative comments. Each anthology is indispensable to the serious student of Chinese Jewish history.

Laufer, Berthold. "A Chinese-Hebrew Manuscript: A New Source for the History of the Chinese Jews." *American Journal of Semitic Languages and Literature* 46, no. 3 (April 1930) : 189–97. Reprinted in Kublin, *Studies,* pp. 159–69.

> A preliminary analysis of the Kaifeng *kehillah*'s Memorial Book.

Leslie, Donald Daniel. "The Chinese-Hebrew Memorial Book of the Jewish Community of K'aifeng." *Abr-Nahrain* 4 (1963–64) : 19–49; 5 (1964–65) : 1–28; 6 (1965–66) : 1–52.

> A seminal investigation, yielding extensive data regarding the Kaifeng *kehillah* as a whole and many of its members as well.

The Memorial Book covers the period from the beginning of the fifteenth century to 1670, or somewhat later.

——. "The Judaeo-Persian Colophons to the Pentateuch of the K'aifeng Jews." *Abr-Nahrain* 8 (1968–69) : 1–35.

The contents of the colophons to the synagogal texts are examined for the information they provide regarding the *kehillah*.

——. "The K'aifeng Jew Chao Ying-ch'eng and his Family." *T'oung Pao* 53, nos. 1–3 (1967) : 147–79. Reprinted in Kublin, *Studies*, pp. 101–37.

Reconstructions of the careers and genealogies of individuals belonging to the Chao clan.

——. "The Kaifeng Jewish Community: A Summary." *Jewish Journal of Sociology* 9, no. 2 (December 1969) : 175–85. Reprinted in Kublin, *Studies*, pp. 187–97.

——. *The Survival of the Chinese Jews.* Leiden: E. J. Brill, 1972.

The most comprehensive scholarly study of Chinese Judaism ever attempted, this work includes hundreds of bibliographical references. The prime text for the serious student of Sino-Judaica.

Leslie, Donald Daniel, and Dehergne, Joseph. *Juifs de Chine*, forthcoming.

A selection of important letters by early Jesuit visitors to the Jewish community of Kaifeng, several not hitherto published. Some of the material has been printed under the title "Les Juifs de Chine au XVIIIᵉ Siècle," in *Rencontre: Chrétiens et Juifs* (Paris) 10, no. 47 (1976) : 238–44; 10, no. 48 (Supplement) (1976) : 310–12; 11, no. 49 (1977: 45–50.

Lockman, John. *Travels of the Jesuits.* London, 1762.

Selections in English from the *Lettres édifiantes*, augmented by Lockman's comments on the quest of the Jesuits for information regarding the practices of the Kaifeng Jews in matters related to the Terms and Rites affairs.

Loewenthal, Rudolf. "The Early Jews in China: A Supplementary Bibliography." *Folklore Studies* [Peking] 5 (1946) : 353–98.

——. "An Imaginary Illustration of the Kaifeng Jewish Synagogue." *Oriens Extremus* 19, nos. 1–2 (December 1972) : 95–99.

——. "Jews and China in Eighteenth-Century Literature." *Historia Judaica* 12 (1950) : 67–76.

——. "The Jews in China: An Annotated Bibliography." *Chinese Social and Political Science Review* 24 (1940) : 113–234.

——. "The Nomenclature of Jews in China." *Monumenta Serica* 12 (1947) : 91–126. Reprinted in Kublin, *Studies*, pp. 53–84.

Loewenthal's bibliographies, supplemented by the bibliographical listings in Leslie's *Survival*, are the most reliable and detailed guides to the literature dealing with the Chinese Jews yet published.

Manasseh ben Israel. See entry under Wolf.

Margoliouth, David S. "An early Judaeo-Persian Document from Khotan in the Stein Collection, with Other Early Persian Documents." *Journal of the Royal Asiatic Society of Great Britain and Ireland* 55 (1903) : 735–60. Reprinted in Kublin, *Studies*, pp. 23–51.

> The announcement of the discovery and significance of the eighth-century Judeo-Persian document discovered by Sir Marc Aurel Stein at Tun-huang.

Martin, W. A. P. "Account of a Visit to the Jews in Honan." *The Chinese: Their Education, Philosophy, and Letters*. New York, 1881.

> The story of Martin's visit to the Kaifeng Jews in 1866. Originally published in December 1866 in the *Journal of the North China Branch of the Royal Asiatic Society*, the article was frequently reprinted in several other works by Martin and others.

Metziat Aseret ha-Shebatim [Discovery of the Ten Tribes]. Warsaw, 1900. Reprinted as *Sefer ha-Brit ha-Hadash* [Book of the New Covenant]. Petrikov, White Russia, 1911.

> A collection, in Hebrew, of three articles contributing to Sino-Judaic lore—by Adolph Stempel, Uzziel Haga, and Aaron Halevi Fink. The first two are fantasies; the third may be true. Interesting examples of the kind of reportage about Chinese Jews with which Hebrew readers were repeatedly regaled in the nineteenth century and in the early part of the twentieth.

Moule, Arthur C. *Christians in China before the Year 1550*. New York, 1930.

> Some material about the Chinese Jews, but more important for the background it provides regarding Chinese relationships with Christian residents and travelers before Ricci's arrival in China.

Murr, C. von. *Versuch einer Geschichte der Juden in Sina*. Halle, 1806.

> In its time, the most informative and dependable review of the subject. Superseded by later works, but still valuable.

Neubauer, Adolph. "Jews in China." *Jewish Quarterly Review* 8, no. 29 (October 1895) : 123–39. Reprinted in Kublin, *Studies*, pp. 139–57.

> Reprints much of Martin's report and analyzes the Kaifeng synagogal liturgy, which is described as "near the Yemen rite."

Pelliot, Paul. "Le Juif Ngai [Ai], Informateur du P. Matthieu Ricci." *T'oung Pao*, 2d ser., 20 (1921) : 32–39. Reprinted in Kublin, *Studies*, pp. 91–100.

A brilliant investigation of the available data regarding Ai T'ien's visit to Ricci in 1605.

Pfister, Louis. *Notices biographiques et bibliographiques sur les Jésuites de l'ancienne Mission de Chine, 1552–1773.* 2 vols. Shanghai, 1932–34.

For biographical data regarding many of the Jesuits who had contact with, or wrote about, the Chinese Jews.

Perlmann, S. M. *The History of the Jews in China.* London, 1912. Reprinted in Kublin, *Jews in Old China,* pp. 119–211.

Full of unwarranted assumptions regarding the time of arrival of the first Jews in China and other historical matters concerning them and their descendants, but important because of the author's account of his personal meetings with Jews from Kaifeng in the opening years of the twentieth century.

Pollak, Michael. *The Discovery of a Missing Chinese Torah Scroll.* Dallas: Bridwell Library, Southern Methodist University, 1973.

—. *The Torah Scrolls of the Chinese Jews: The History, Significance and Present Whereabouts of the Sifrei Torah of the Defunct Jewish Community of Kaifeng.* Dallas: Bridwell Library, Southern Methodist University, 1975.

Popper, William. *The Censorship of Hebrew Books.* 2d ed. New York: Ktav Publishing House, 1969.

Recommended as background reading for understanding the Christian attitudes toward Hebrew literature in the period during which the Jesuits made their visits to the Kaifeng Jews.

Rabinowitz, L. *Jewish Merchant Adventurers: A Study of the Radanites.* London: Edward Goldston, 1948.

Interesting and informative, but with a tendency to be speculative.

Rhee, Song Nai. "Jewish Assimilation: The Case of the Chinese Jews." *Comparative Studies in Society and History* 15 (1973): 115–26.

Presents the argument that the principal cause for the deterioration of Judaism in Kaifeng was China's Confucian-oriented educational system and the rewards it offered to those who were interested in climbing the ladder of officialdom.

Ricci, Matteo. See entries under D'Elia, Gallagher, and Tacchi-Venturi.

Ross, Allan Edward, ed. and tr. "An Annotated Translation and Critical Analysis of *K'ai-feng J'tz'u-lo-yeb Chiao* (by Ch'en Yüan): A Study of the K'aifeng Israelites." Master's thesis, University of Southern California, June 1970.

A well-annotated translation of Ch'en's seminal study of Kaifeng Jewry.

Rowbotham, Arnold H. *Missionary and Mandarin.* Berkeley and Los Angeles: University of California Press, 1942.

Discusses the Chinese Rites Controversy and the Terms Question as they affected the Catholic church.

Sassoon, David S. D. "Inscriptions in the Synagogue in Kai-fung-foo." *Jewish Quarterly Review*, n.s., 11 (1920–21) : 126–44.

Semmedo, Alvarez. *Imperio de la China*. Madrid, 1642.

—. *The History of that Great and Renowned Monarchy of China*. London, 1655.

The 1655 edition is a translation of the 1642 Latin version.

Smith, George, ed. *The Jews at K'ae-fung-foo: Being a Narrative of a Mission of Inquiry to the Jewish Synagogue at K'ae-fung-foo on behalf of the London Society for Promoting Christianity among the Jews*. Shanghai, 1851.

Contains the journals of the two Chinese delegates who went to Kaifeng in 1850 and an introduction by Smith, plus the announcement of the delegates' success in purchasing six Torah scrolls and numerous smaller documents in the course of their 1851 visit to the Kaifeng Jews.

Sokobin, Samuel. "The Simson-Hirsch Letter to the Chinese Jews, 1795." *Publications of the American Jewish Historical Society* 49, no. 1 (September 1959) : 39–52. Reprinted in Kublin, *Studies*, pp. 171–86.

Discusses the first interest manifested by American Jews in the Jews of China.

Sopher, Arthur. See entry under Ezra and Sopher.

Tacchi-Venturi, Pietro, ed. *Opere storiche del P. Matteo Ricci, S. J.* 2 vols. Macerata, Italy, 1911–13.

A carefully annotated reprint of Ricci's journals and letters. Contains numerous references to the Chinese Jews.

Tobar, Jérôme. *Inscriptions juives de K'ai-fong-fou*. Shanghai, 1900. Reprinted in Shanghai in 1912.

An outstanding work. Includes the Chinese texts (with French translations) of the 1489, 1512, and 1663 Kaifeng synagogal lapidary inscriptions; the texts and translations of numerous horizontal and vertical synagogal tablet inscriptions; and various other materials pertinent to the history of Chinese Jewry.

White, William Charles. *Chinese Jews*. 3 vols. Toronto: University of Toronto Press, 1942. Reprinted (3 vols in 1), Cecil Roth, ed., New York, Paragon Book Reprint, 1966.

An essential contribution to the story of the Kaifeng Jews. The author was bishop of Honan for about a quarter of a century before his retirement in 1933. His reminiscences of personal talks with the Kaifeng Jews are highly informative. The numerous extracts he provides from other pertinent works offer the reader a handy single source for investigating the subject, but must be approached with caution, as these are often reprinted in abridged form without adequate warning. White's errors, for the most part in his misidentification of individual Chinese as Jews, are corrected in Leslie's studies.

Wolf, Lucien, ed. *Menasseh ben Israel's Mission to Oliver Cromwell*. London, 1901.

A reprint of the 1651 English edition of Manasseh's *Hope of Israel* and the 1656 edition of his *Vindiciae Judaeorum*. Thoroughly annotated, superb introduction.

Wylie, Alexander. *Chinese Researches*. Shanghai, 1897.

Important because of Wylie's insistence that the term *Hsien-chiao* encountered in numerous Chinese annals refers to Jews when, in fact, it refers to Parsis. It was this error that led writers like Perlmann and others to claim that there were Jewish houses of worship in China long before there could have been any.

Yule, Henry. *Cathay and the Way Thither*. 2 vols. London, 1866. Revised by Henri Cordier and reissued in London, 1913–16.

Medieval travelers to the Orient, with allusions to their contacts with, and references to, Jewish settlements in China.

❖ NOTES

Works for which full bibliographical references are provided in these Notes are not included in the Selected Bibliography. Where the original item has been reprinted in a more readily accessible source, the pagination indicated here is generally that of the reprint.

Prologue *Encounter in Peking*

1. Leslie, "Memorial Book," pt. 3, pp. 21–22.
2. For references to Ricci's accounts of his dealings with Ai and his subsequent contacts with the Chinese Jews, see below, pt. 1, chap. 1, nn. 1, 2, 8. The time of Ai's visit to Ricci has been calculated by Pelliot as falling between June 25 and June 31 [*sic*], 1605 (Pelliot, in Kublin, *Studies*, pp. 96–97). Ch'en Tseng-hui provides circumstantial evidence suggesting that Ai also visited Peking in 1604, though apparently not its Catholic mission. (Leslie, "Memorial Book," pt. 3, p. 22; cited by Leslie from Ch'en's "On the Chinese Jew Ai in Matteo Ricci's *Opere Storiche*," *Hsieh-ta Hsüeh-pao* 1 [1949], pp. 171–80, and especially pp. 178–79.)
3. Nigel Cameron, *Barbarians and Mandarins* (New York and Tokyo: Walker-Weatherill, 1970), p. 187.
4. The brothers alluded to by Ai may be Rabbis Judah and Mordechai. There is also reason to believe that Ai's father (Abariah?) was a rabbi and that Ai had a son, Uzziel, who became one too. Ai's Hebrew name may have been Shaphat. (Leslie, "Memorial Book," pt. 1, facing p. 4; pt. 3, pp. 24–25.)

1 *The European Reaction*

1. Tacchi-Venturi, vol. 2, pp. 289–93. An English translation of Ricci's letter appears in Loewenthal, "Early Jews," pp. 396–98, and is reprinted in Kublin, *Studies*, pp. 212–13.

2. Tacchi-Venturi, vol. 2, p. 344.

3. Ibid., p. 493. The portion of Longobardi's letter that refers to the Chinese Jews is reprinted in both the original Italian and in an English translation in Loewenthal, "Early Jews," pp. 390–91.

4. Aleni's experiences in Kaifeng are reported very briefly by Semmedo, although some doubt exists as to whether Aleni did actually go to Kaifeng in 1613. An alternate date would be 1621, or even slightly later. See Semmedo, *History*, pp. 152–54. (Reprinted in Loewenthal, "Early Jews," pp. 392–93.)

5. Finn, *Orphan Colony*, pp. 3–4. See also his *Jews in China* (in Kublin, *Jews in Old China*, pp. 12–13; 13, n. 1; 31; 80; 80, nn. 1, 2).

6. Unpublished translation by Leslie and Dehergne, from a manuscript held in Rome of de Geuvea's *Asia Extrema*, composed in 1644. See also Leslie, *Survival*, p. 177.

7. Gozani, *Lettres édifiantes*, (1781 ed.) vol. 18, pp. 39–40.

8. Various editions of Ricci's journals have been reprinted on numerous occasions and in several languages, e.g., Trigault, Tacchi-Venturi, D'Elia, and Gallagher. Several pertinent extracts from the Tacchi-Venturi (Italian) edition have been made available by Loewenthal in his "Early Jews," pp. 393–98. (Reprinted in Kublin, *Studies*, pp. 209–13.) Those parts of Ricci's journals that deal with the Chinese Jews were apparently written some time after the events which they portray, and differ in several minor details from the letters, which he wrote while the memory of these occurrences was still quite fresh. The letters are considered more reliable than the journals, and are followed in the present work wherever discrepancies arise.

9. Emmanuel Diaz, *Relatione delle cose più notabili scritte ne gli anni 1619, 1620 et 1621 della Cina* (Rome, 1624). Loewenthal, "Early Jews," p. 389, has an English translation of the pertinent passages from Diaz.

10. Cited by Leslie (*Survival*, pp. 176–77), possibly from a letter said to have been written by Semmedo and published in 1627.

11. There is some question as to whether the book was originally published in Portuguese in 1642, or in Spanish (in the same year), no copy of a Portuguese edition having apparently survived. The Spanish version appeared in Madrid under the title *Imperio de la China*. See Loewenthal, "Early Jews," pp. 380–81, for a listing of early editions of the work.

12. Leslie, *Survival*, pp. 166–67. See also Rabinowitz, pp. 185–86. However, in a review of Rabinowitz's *Jewish Merchant Adventurers* in *Historia Judaica* 11, no. 2 (October 1949): 163–65), Lowenthal points out that Paul Pelliot in an article in *T'oung Pao* 21 (1922): p. 399ff., questions whether such a person as Suleiman ever existed.

13. Rabinowitz, pp. 8–11. See also Elkan Nathan Adler, *Jewish Travel-*

lers (London, 1930), pp. 2–3. Claude Cahen, however, casts some doubts on the interpretations given to ibn Khurdadhbih's account in his "Y a-t-il eu des Rahdanites?" *Revue des Études Juives* 3, fasc. 3–4 (July–December 1964) : 499–505.

14. Leslie, *Survival*, pp. 7, 168.

15. Ibid., pp. 7–8, 166–67.

16. Gabriel Ferrand, *Voyage du Marchand Arabe Sulaymân en Inde et en Chine, Rédigé en 851, Suivi de Remarques par Abu Zayd Hasan (vers 916)* (Paris, 1922), pp. 85–92.

17. Leslie, *Survival*, pp. 8, 168–69.

18. Ibid., pp. 15, 169.

19. Elkan Nathan Adler, "A Jewish Merchant in China at the Beginning of the Tenth Century," *Abhandlungen zur Erinnerung an Hirsch Perez Chajes* (Vienna, 1933), pp. 1–5. Reprinted in Jacob R. Marcus, *The Jews in the Medieval World* (Philadelphia: The Jewish Publication Society of America, 1938), pp. 355–59.

20. Elkan Nathan Adler, *Jewish Travellers* (London, 1930), pp. 6–7.

21. Benjamin of Tudela, *The Itinerary of Benjamin of Tudela,* Marcus Nathan Adler, ed. (London, 1907), pp. 66; 67, n. 1 (pp. 60; 60, n., in Hebrew text). Benjamin's report of the existence of Jewish settlements within relatively easy reach of China was, of course, not the only one of its kind to be published in Europe before Ricci's discovery that a Jewish colony had survived in China, but Benjamin was one of the very few Westerners who had personally visited any of the Jewish settlements from which travelers might well have proceeded to the Middle Kingdom. In 1524, the Jewish geographer Abraham Farissol, working from non-Jewish sources, listed various Jewish communities in Asia from which travel to China would have been quite feasible (although he did not make the point), including one called the "Kingdom of Belor." See Farissol's *Iggeret Orhot Olam* (Ferrara, 1524), chap. 28; or his *Itinera Mundi,* a Hebrew and Latin text of the *Iggeret,* Thomas Hyde, trans. and ed. (Oxford, 1591), p. 177. See also Paul Pelliot, *Notes on Marco Polo* (Paris, 1959), pp. 91–92, for a discursus on the identity of Belor.

22. Marco Polo, *The Travels,* Ronald Latham, trans. and ed. (Hammondsworth, Middlesex: Penguin Books, 1958), pp. 118–19.

23. Leslie, *Survival*, pp. 15, 171.

24. Yule, vol. 1, p. 225.

25. Ibid., vol. 2, p. 341.

26. See Loewenthal, "Early Jews," pp. 391–92; see also Loewenthal, "Jews in China," p. 143.

27. Yule, vol. 2, pp. 533–34.

28. Richarde Eden. ed., *The History of Travayle in the West and East Indies, and other countreys lying eyther way* (London: Richard

Jugge, 1577), leaf 343a. Another European who was in China at about the same time that Perera was incarcerated there was the Jewish physician, botanist, and author Christoval Acosta. Born in North Africa to parents who had been exiled from Spain, Acosta traveled extensively throughout Africa and Asia, spending a good deal of time in China. He met and talked with leading physicians everywhere his wanderings took him, but there is no way of knowing whether he ever became aware of a Jewish presence in China. On his return, he established himself in Burgos, presumably after accepting baptism. See *Jewish Encyclopedia* 1:166.

In his *The Jews in New Spain* (Coral Gables, Fla.: University of Miami Press, 1970), Seymour Liebman alludes several times to Mexican Jewish merchants trading in China. "One of the persons included in the 1601 auto-da-fé [in Mexico City] . . . ," he thus states, "was Manuel Rodríguez, nicknamed *El Chiquito,* the Little One; he had come to New Spain from China" (p. 197). At the beginning of the seventeenth century the Mexican Marrano Fernández Tristan, Liebman also relates, gave his coreligionist and countryman Luis Díaz merchandise "worth more than 7,000 pesos on credit"; and this Luis Díaz, according to Liebman, "traded in China" (p. 205). Mexican Inquisition records from the 1640s indicate that the Marrano Gaspar Méndez testified that many Mexican crypto-Jews were then engaged in trade with China (pp. 225–26). Interestingly, a Marrano named Váez and known as *El Cachopo* (the Religious Observer) had testified before the Mexican Inquisition in the 1620s of having been told by the Marrano Ana Gómez that a Jew recently arrived in Mexico from China had reported that "in China there are many [Caucasian] Jews who met together secretly for religious purposes" (p. 231). "The Jewish traveler," Liebman explains, "must have alluded to groups of Iberian crypto-Jews in the Philippines and on the coast of China where agents of the Inquisition were functioning, since both colonies were then under Spanish dominion." He also cites Robert Ricard's statement in "Pour une étude de judaisme portugais au Mexique pendant la période coloniale," *Revue d'Histoire Moderne* 14 (August 1939): 524 to the effect that "one passage of a proceso specified that Sebastion Rodríguez [a Jew] carried on trade between New Spain and China," and that "one [Jewish] merchant left [Mexico] for Macao," which, of course, lay only a few dozen miles from Canton (p. 151). It should be pointed out, however, that in connection with the Mexican Marrano Antonio Díaz de Cáceres another writer in the field of Mexican Jewish history, Martin A. Cohen, reports that in 1589 this man "decided to take a business trip to the Philippine archipelago, indiscriminately called China by many contemporary Spaniards." See Martin A. Cohen, *The Martyr*

(Philadelphia: The Jewish Publication Society of America, 1973), p. 186. Not all of the Mexican Marranos who are said to have visited China may therefore actually have done so.

29. A similar, if less sweeping, phrase is used in a letter written to Bouvet on December 13, 1707, by Leibniz: "Il y a des Juifs habitués dans la Chine depuis fort longtemps." Cited by Lowenthal, "Early Jews," p. 374.

30. Attacks on the trustworthiness of the Hebrew Scriptures started with the early Church Fathers; e.g., Justin Martyr (second century). Jerome (circa 337–420), more competent in Hebrew than most patristic writers, rejected the charge, already common in his time, that the Jews had deliberately corrupted their biblical texts. Jerome, as he explained in his *Epistolae* (36.1), secured a Torah scroll from a synagogue in Rome because he considered the Hebrew text the only reliable one then available. (*Jewish Encyclopedia* 4:86, 7:117.) But in at least one instance, Jerome preferred to question the authenticity of the Hebrew text because it did not agree with a point he was trying to make. A fairly typical Christian charge was that made in the tenth century by the chronicler Agapius. To him, however, the culprits who altered the Torah were the high priests Caiaphas and Annas rather than the rabbis of the Talmud. Agapius had certain of the Emperor Constantine's Jewish subjects confess to Constantine that the two priests had changed much of the chronology of the Hebrew Scriptures in order to make it appear that Jesus could not be the Messiah. He then alluded to several specific examples of the falsifications allegedly made by the two priests. See B. Graffin, "Kitab al-Unvan ('Histoire universelle'), écrite par Agapius (Mahboub) de Menbidj," *Patrologia Orientalis* 5, fasc. 4, pt. 1 (Paris, 1947), pp. 645–57.

31. For a list of biblical texts claimed by Islamic writers to have been altered by the rabbis, see M. Steinschneider, *Jewish Literature from the Eighth to the Eighteenth Century* (London, 1857), pp. 129; 318–19, n. (Reprinted in New York by Hermon Press, 1970.) One of the Islamic polemicists who attacked the Jews for "corrupting" Holy Writ had himself been born a Jew. He was Sa'id ben Hassan of Alexandria, who lived in the latter part of the thirteenth and the early part of the fourteenth centuries. As he saw the matter, agreeing in this respect with many other Islamic scholars, the Jews had systematically expunged Muhammad's name every time it occurred in their Scriptures, and occasionally Ishmael's, replacing these with other names. He himself, however, was not above inserting words into the biblical text when it suited his purpose. (*Jewish Encyclopedia* 10:637.) On the Christian side, the realization that inquiring too deeply into the authenticity of the Hebrew Bible might boomerang

and lead Christians to question the authority of the Church became a matter of deep concern to a number of clerics. In the mid-fifteenth century, in fact, the Franciscan monk Alfonso de Espina preached in Spain against those Christian heretics "who tried to point out the existence of forgeries in the New Testament because it contained quotations from the Prophets which did not appear in the same form in the Hebrew Bible." Yitzhak Baer, *A History of the Jews in Christian Spain*, 2 vols. (Philadelphia: The Jewish Publication Society of America, 1961), vol. 2, p. 286.

32. Popper, pp. 23–24.

33. Reuchlin, Hutten, and Erasmus, it has been claimed, were moved to support the Jews for intellectual rather than humane reasons. Poliakov thus asserts that "the Dominican inquisitors and their allies, though consigning the Hebrew books to the flames, showed greater Christian charity" toward the Jews than the humanists who, "though they had become champions of the Jewish books, attacked the Jew Pfefferkorn and all his coreligionists, baptized or not." Léon Poliakov, *The History of Anti-Semitism* (New York: Schocken Books, 1974), vol. 1, p. 215.

34. Selma Stern, *Yossel of Rosheim* (Philadelphia: The Jewish Publication Society of America, 1963), p. xvi.

35. Popper, p. 55.

36. David Kaufmann, "Lazarus de Viterbo's Epistle to Cardinal Sirleto Concerning the Integrity of the Text of the Hebrew Bible," *Jewish Quarterly Review* 7 (1895): 278–96.

37. Semmedo, *History*, p, 153.

38. Loewenthal, "Early Jews," p. 374. However, in the very same month that Leibniz was urging Verjus to do his utmost to get the Kaifeng texts examined, doubt was being expressed as to whether the Chinese Jews still retained any scriptural book at all. "I do not know," wrote François Froger in January 1700, "if these Jews are indigenous to China, and since they are so few in number it would seem improbable that they could have succeeded in preserving their books." The statement, which refers to Chinese Jewry as a whole, was made by Froger upon learning that a few Chinese Jews had recently been found in Tsi-ning-chou, Shantung Province. François Froger, *Relation du premier voyage des François à la Chine, fait en 1698, 1699, et 1700 sur le vaisseau "L'Amphrite"* (Leipzig, 1926), p. 140.

39. François Bernier, *Voyage de Cachemore* (The Hague, 1672), p. 140.

40. Loewenthal, "Early Jews," p. 374.

41. The *Lettres* were reprinted many times and in several languages. In the 1781 edition (Paris), ordinarily cited in the present work, le Gobien's preface appears in vol. 18.

42. *Lettres édifiantes* (1781 ed.), vol. 18, pp. 31–55.

43. Wolf, p. 30.
44. See Rowbotham, pp. 175; 322–23, nn.
45. Longobardi, first Ricci's assistant and later his successor, was perhaps the most notable exception among the Jesuits in this respect, holding that the Chinese would have to enter the Roman Catholic church without the sweeping concessions Ricci was willing to grant them—or stay out. Longobardi expounded his views in a treatise that was eventually published by the Dominican polemicist Domingo Navarreté as part of an attack on the Jesuit Order. Another Jesuit opponent of the policy advocated by Ricci, the French priest Jean-François Foucquet, was driven out of the Order several decades after Ricci's death for insisting that Confucianism was idolatrous. Ibid., pp. 122–23, 132.
46. Joseph R. Rosenbloom, "The Rites Controversy," *America* 110, no. 16 (April 18, 1964): 544–45. Protestant missionaries, arriving in China in the first half of the nineteenth century, wrestled with their own equivalents of the Terms and Rites questions but were not nearly as disastrously divided over them as the Catholics.

2 *Ricci's Jews and Cromwell's Puritans*

1. Richarde Eden, ed., *The History of Travayle in the West and East Indies, and other countreys lying eyther way* (London: Richard Jugge, 1577), leaf 2b.
2. Expelled from England in 1290, Jews occasionally managed to find a precarious home there in the centuries before it again became legal for them to live in the country. Rodrigo Lopez, for example, was physician to Queen Elizabeth; Jacob of Oxford opened England's first coffee shop in 1650 or thereabouts; and the famous Gracia Mendes of the House of Nasi and her entourage stopped over in London around 1536 on their way to Antwerp. She, as well as the few Jews who lived in London, then and in the next century or so, were, however, ostensibly Catholic.
3. Wolf, p. xxii.
4. Franz Landsberger, *Rembrandt, the Jews and the Bible,* 2d ed. (Philadelphia: The Jewish Publication Society of America, 1961), pp. 96–102.
5. Wall's translation of the Latin edition (1651) is reprinted in its entirety in Wolf, pp. 1–56.
6. Ibid., pp. 11–17. The version of Montezinos's story, which is presented in the present work, differs slightly from that given by Wolf, having been derived from the Wall translation, the Latin account, and the Spanish—not all of which are precisely the same. The Span-

ish version, incidentally, was rendered into English in 1853 by Elias Hayyim Lindo, and was published for the first time in Elisabeth Levi de Montezinos's "The Narrative of Aharon Levi, alias Antonio de Montezinos." *The American Sephardi* 7–8 (Autumn 1975): 62–83. Miss Montezinos is a collateral descendant of Antonio de Montezinos.

7. Miss Montezinos has discovered records in the Archivo Historico Nacional, Madrid, showing that one Antonio de Montezinos was actually imprisoned in Cartagena from September 3, 1639, until shortly after February 19, 1641. See p. 75 of her article on Montezinos (ibid.) for her comments, and pp. 82–83 for a facsimile of the archival text. The Inquisition prison in which Montezinos was incarcerated still stands.

8. The case for Amerindian Israelitism was originally presented in Diego de Landa's *Relácion de las cosas de Yucatan,* written in 1566 but not published until the eighteenth century. The author was a Spanish monk who arrived in the New World with a band of Conquistadores and later became bishop of Yucatan. The earliest printed claim for an Israelite origin for the Indians appeared in Joannes Fredericus Lumnius's *De Extremo Dei Judicio et Indorum Vocatione,* the first edition of which was published at Antwerp in 1567. The thesis that the Indians were of Jewish descent was widely accepted. The Quaker leader and founder of Pennsylvania, William Penn, believed that the Indians with whom he dealt were members of the Lost Tribes of Israel. Later, the Indians were viewed as descendants of the ancient Israelites by various commentators on the Book of Mormon. A bemusing syllogism to counter the claim that the Indians were Israelites was constructed by Hamon L'Estrange in his *Americans No Jewes,* published in London in 1652. As is well known, L'Estrange observed, Jews are not permitted to marry harlots; all Indian women are harlots; hence the Indians cannot be Jews. Cited by Henry Steele Commager, *The Empire of Reason* (Garden City, N.Y.: Anchor Press–Doubleday, 1977), p. 77.

9. For Manasseh's discussion of the Trigault and Semmedo reports, see Wolf, pp. 29–31. Manasseh agrees with Semmedo that the Chinese Jews are really Jews, because, as he gathers from Semmedo, "those *Chineses* observe many *Jewish* Rites, which you may see in a manuscript, which the noble *Joaochimus Wicofortius* hath."

10. Ibid., p. 29. A Lost Tribe passage across the "Strait of Anian" had been suggested in 1607 by Gregorio Garcia in his *Origen de las Indios de el Nuevo mundo e Indias Occidentales,* published in Valencia.

11. Quivira is the never-never land of gold that inspired Coronado's wild-goose chase to Kansas in the 1540s.

12. Wolf., p. 31.

13. Ibid., pp. 54–55.

14. Ibid., p. 31. Modern biblical scholarship attributes Isa. 49:12 to Deutero-Isaiah, whose prophetic career is ascribed to circa 525–500 B.C.E.

15. Cf. the report entitled "La présence Juive en Chine," which was delivered by Dr. P. Azoulay on September 4, 1957, before the XXIV⁰ Congrès International d'Orientalisme, in Munich; or the statement made by Dr. Josef Zeitlin in the *Miami Herald*, August 1, 1975.

16. Leslie, *Survival*, p. 9. See also Rabinowitz, pp. 65; 65, n. 6; and 70–71, for additional comments concerning the translation of Sinim.

17. *The Interpreter's Bible* (New York: Abingdon Press, 1956), vol. 5, p. 575. There was a sizable settlement of Jews in the vicinity of Aswan in Isaiah's lifetime, and it had been there since the early part of the sixth century B.C.E., when the Babylonians had either hired or impressed thousands of Jews to guard the Egyptian border—the region, specifically, in which the Sevaniyyim lived—against incursions by the Ethiopians. The Aswan garrison, later reinforced by the arrival of contingents of Jewish farmers and artisans, survived as an important Jewish center until about 410 B.C.E. This arcane bit of history would not have been known to Manasseh, for it was not chanced upon until the latter part of the nineteenth century. It was the Jews of the Aswan region, it would appear, of whom Isaiah was thinking as potential returnees to Zion. To this day, incidentally, many of the black Falashan Jews of Ethiopia trace their descent in part from the Judean troops once stationed in Aswan.

18. See Perlmann (in Kublin, *Jews in Old China*, p. 145) and pt. 2, chap. 13, below, for the Hieronomach Alexei W(V)inogradoff's suggestion that Hebrews might have traveled to China even before the birth of Moses.

19. Wolf, p. 46. The Jewish impatience for the arrival of the Messiah had only recently (in 1648) enabled Sabbatai Zevi to declare himself the Messiah and to attract an enormous following of Jews desperately seeking relief from the persecutions to which they were then being subjected. Huge numbers of Jews—and Christians—were convinced that 1666 was to be the messianic year. To the Christians, of course, the Messiah was a divine figure; to the Jews, he was a human being whose basic accomplishment would be to free them and lead them back to their own land.

20. In his *Hope of Israel*, Manasseh had initially singled out Portugal—not England—as the biblical "end of the earth." (See Wolf, p. 48.) It occurred to him after publication of the work, however, that transferring the distinction to Britain would enable him to introduce a powerful and novel weapon into his campaign for persuading the

English to let the Jews come back to the British Isles. Exactly when this particular flight of fancy was broached to the English is not clear. It may have been communicated to them through the non-Jewish intermediaries with whom Manasseh dealt; or perhaps through Manasseh's son Samuel and his nephew David Dormido, both of whom he sent to London for the purpose of negotiating with Cromwell. The contention that England was one of the two biblical ends of the earth appeared in print for the first time in Manasseh's *Vindiciae Judaeorum,* published in London on April 10, 1656, about six months following his own arrival in the city. (The pertinent passage from the *Vindiciae* is reprinted in Wolf, pp. 143–44, which also reprints the entire pamphlet on pp. 105–47.) For a provocative discussion of how the *Hope of Israel* came to be written and an analysis of the subsequent shift in Manasseh's approach to the meaning of the biblical "end of the earth," see Ismar Schorsch's "From Messianism to Realpolitik: Menasseh ben Israel and the Readmission of the Jews to England," *Proceedings of the American Academy for Jewish Research* 45 (1978) : 187–208.

21. Marcus Arkin argues that "Cromwell and his advisers were attracted more by the potential economic value of the Jews than by any religious or humanitarian feelings flowing from the Puritan outlook on life," and agrees with Werner Sombart's seemingly extreme statement that Cromwell "was actuated solely by considerations of an economic nature" in inviting the Jews back to England. Marcus Arkin, *Aspects of Jewish Economic History* (Philadelphia: The Jewish Publication Society of America, 1975), pp. 105–6. Arkin's contention notwithstanding, the messianic argument presented by Manasseh was an important factor in the negotiations surrounding the matter of readmitting the Jews to England, and certainly brought Cromwell support he may not have had if Manasseh had failed to bring it up.

22. Léon Poliakov, *The History of Anti-Semitism* (New York: Schocken Books, 1974), vol. 1, p. 205, n. 2.

3 *Testaments in Stone*

1. Gallagher, p. 107.
2. Tacchi-Venturi, vol. 2, pp. 292–93. An English translation is given by Loewenthal, in "Early Jews," p. 397.
3. It has been suggested that each of the 1489 and 1512 texts was originally inscribed on a stone of its own and that both texts were later recopied from other sources onto a single stone, the original two stones having been lost or damaged in the flood that swept away

the synagogue in 1642. (Leslie, *Survival,* pp. 30, 131–32.) Lowenthal, "Early Jews," p. 371, cites an article by Liu Lung-kuang in a Japanese journal (*The Kabun Osaka Mainichi,* February 15, 1941), which is itself largely derived from *A Guide to Kaifeng,* written about 1921 by a Japanese. The author of the *Guide* is reported by Liu to have stated that a synagogal stele set up during the Yüan era (1280–1368) was sold several decades before the publication of his *Guide* to a Shanghai curio dealer. However, no trace of this stele—if it ever existed—has yet been found.

4. White, vol. 2, pp. 3, 7.

5. Ibid., p. 96.

6. The text actually reads "seventy" rather than "seventeen," but the former is surely incorrect. Three of the surnames given—Li, Chang, and Chin—are each borne by two clans. The matter is discussed below, pt. 2, chap. 14.

7. "Amongst the names given to Kaifeng throughout the centuries were Ta-liang, Pien-chou, Liang-chou, Nan-ching, Pien-liang, Pien. Hsiang-fu was the name of the central district (*hsien*) in Kaifeng prefecture." (Leslie, *Survival,* p. 22, n.) When *fu* is added to a city's name, as in Kaifeng-fu, it indicates that the city is a prefectural capital. (Actually, Kaifeng itself formed a prefecture, and was the capital of Honan Province.) Kaifeng, by the rules of the Wade-Giles transliteration system, should be spelled K'aifeng, the apostrophe indicating that the K is to pronounced as in *key*. The K, when not followed by an apostrophe, is usually given the sound of the letter g. However, it has become an acceptable practice to spell Kaifeng without the apostrophe, the tacit understanding being that the first letter is pronounced here as in English.

8. The complete texts of both the 1489 and 1512 inscriptions are available in Chinese and English in White, vol. 2, pp. 7–54; in Chinese and French in Tobar, pp. 36–64; and in Chinese and Portuguese in Chen.

9. Kaifeng was captured in 1126–27 by Jurchen invaders. A Sung prince who escaped was able to establish a "temporary" capital at Hangchow, from which he and his successors ("the Southern Sung") ruled a shrunken empire which no longer included Honan Province. Chin Chung's use of a Southern Sung dating corresponding to the Christian year 1163—when Kaifeng was no longer ruled over by the Sung—was not uncommon. Some scholars, incidentally, have understood Chin's account to mean that the Jews came to Kaifeng in 1163 and built their synagogue there in the same year; but why then should the Jews be reported as bringing a tribute "to the Sung" in a capital city from which the Sung had been gone some three dozen years? It has been plausibly speculated that a portion of

Kaifeng's Jewish community fled to Hangchow with the defeated Sung, but no concrete evidence is available to support the conjecture. (Dr. Kublin has, however, pointed out, in a conversation with the author, that there are grounds for believing that for some decades following the 1126 expulsion of the Sung from Kaifeng, Honan remained a "no-man's land," alternately held and lost by the Sung.)

10. "The street running north and south on the western side of the synagogue enclosure is still [in 1940 or thereabouts] known by the name of Earth Street," according to White, vol. 2, p. 24, n. 18, "and probably derived from a time when an earth-market was located there. Earth for the filling in of low courtyards is always in demand in Kaifeng, because the district is subject to heavy sand storms, and after each storm the sand and refuse that is swept up is thrown out on the streets. This means that the streets in time become higher than the courtyards and floors of the houses, necessitating the filling in of soil whenever a house should require to be rebuilt."

11. Around 1940, White reported that the old synagogal site was at the time about 250 by 350 feet. Ibid., p. 24, n. 18.

12. An San's career is discussed below, pt. 2, chap. 14.

13. The fact that the scholars who prepared the text of the stele were non-Jews is not overly surprising. The *kehillah*'s employment of non-Jews to prepare the 1512 inscription, as well as later ones, was explained in this fashion by Charles D. Tenney: "It is the custom in China, when a tablet is to be set up to honor any temple or public building, to invite some scholar of local reputation to compose or write it. He is then posted upon such facts as it is desired shall be contained in the inscription, and he draws it up in such a way that it may have the necessary literary flavor." Tenney's statement is taken from an article in the *Scribe*, April 30, 1920, pp. 4, 8–9, this article having apparently been copied from *Millard's Review of the Far East* [Shanghai] 12, no. 1 March 6, 1920: 6, 8, 10–12. See also, Loewenthal, "Early Jews," p. 383.

14. In the 1489 stele, the synagogue is referred to as the *Ch'ing Chen Ssu* (Temple of Purity and Truth), but in the 1512 inscription it becomes the *Tsun Ch'ung Tao Ch'ing Ssu* (Temple for the Veneration of the Law). The historian Ch'en Yüan points out that the former term was identical with that used by the Muslims to denote a mosque. Around 1506, strong antagonisms to Muslims and other people of foreign descent or ties began to develop at the imperial court. It may well be that in using the latter term for the synagogue the composer of the 1512 text was trying to help protect the Jews by dissociating them from the far better known Muslims. See Ross, pp. 16–18.

15. Ch'en Yüan argues that the Han dynasty referred to is the Han that

ruled between 946 and 950 C.E., during the Five Dynasty period. His point is not accepted by other scholars, one reason being that the Abu Zaid account of a massacre at Khanfu in 877/78 includes Jews among the victims. Ibid., pp. 36–37; p. 36, n. 15.

16. The author of the inscription does not seem to understand that Abraham was first called Abram, as he has Abraham receiving the Scriptures and Abram handing them down. The sentence immediately following the reference to Ezra pays tribute to the Scribe's restoration of the ancient Hebrew texts to Israel.

17. These six allusions to Jews are summarized by Leslie, *Survival,* pp. 11–15.

18. The reason for this prohibition against the ritual slaughter of meat is cited ibid., p. 14, from the *Yüan Shih* of the same date, though Jews are not specifically mentioned: "The *Hui-hui* [Muslims], who pass by and are offered food, will not eat a sheep that they themselves have not killed. The people are upset by this. The emperor said: 'They are our slaves. How dare they not eat and drink what our court eats and drinks?' He forbade it." Marco Polo, Leslie points out (p. 15), "also notes that Muslims were forbidden to practice the ritual slaughter involving slitting the animal's throat."

19. Ibid., pp. 15, 20.

20. Ibid., p. 16.

21. Cited by Pfister, vol. 1, pp. 158–59.

22. The Chinese texts and the English translations of 1663a and 1663b are given in White, vol. 2, pp. 57–95. Tobar, pp. 65–87, gives the Chinese texts and the French translations. The Chinese text of 1663a and a Portuguese translation are available in Chen, pp. 64–72, 76–77 and in unnumbered pages following p. 77. The text of 1663b does not include the date of its composition, but was no doubt completed close to the same time as that of 1663a.

23. The "tens of items of miscellaneous Scriptures" could have been pieced together from the "twenty-six items of Scriptures" reported in 1663b only if the "tens of items" were made up by binding together salvagable leaves from the twenty-six books into smaller volumes. Thus, enough usable leaves may have been obtained from, say, a Book of Genesis to make up two or three separate booklets, each comprising one section, or *parashah*, of Genesis. Presumably, some of the recovered texts were also prayer books and Passover Haggadahs, and they must have included the Memorial Book as well. In all probability, either the figures given in the steles are not precise or numerous other books, perhaps kept in private dwellings, also survived.

24. The author's earlier statement that "when, in 1653, a new synagogal center was dedicated on the site of the old one, a total of thirteen

Torahs was installed in the sanctuary" is in error and requires correction. Apparently, the new synagogue was dedicated in 1663, or shortly before that year. The twelve Torahs that were rewritten after the flood of 1642 were probably completed between 1653 and 1663. See Pollak, *Torah Scrolls*, p. 26.

25. White, vol. 2, p. 4. The Chinese text of the 1679 stele and an English translation are provided in White, vol. 2, pp. 96–107.

26. The 1489/1512 and 1679 steles were seen in 1957 on the premises of the former Canadian Anglican mission by Prof. René Goldman. See pt. 1, chap. 12, n. 22, below. Mr. and Mrs. Guy Weill, visiting Kaifeng with a group of American historians and archeologists on July 16, 1978, were unable to inspect either the steles or the synagogal site. There was nothing to be gained by going to the site, their Chinese guide informed them, for worker's apartment buildings had been raised over it. As for the steles, the guide declared, they were undergoing repair and were not available for examination. (Letters from Mr. Weill to the author, November 9 and December 21, 1978.)

4 *Guidelines for Rome*

1. In the end, the weight of Jewish opinion turned unfavorable to Henry. For a description of Croke's negotiations with the Jewish scholars, see Cecil Roth's *Jews in the Renaissance* (Philadelphia: The Jewish Publication Society of America, 1959), pp. 158–61.

2. There was a similar disagreement in connection with the Malabar Rites, this being the collective term that was applied to the concessions which the Jesuit missionaries offered to both potential and actual converts in the subcontinent of India. The Malabar Rites dispute, however, generated considerably less friction within the Church than the Chinese Rites Controversy.

3. Some Jesuits even suggested that the Mount Ararat on which the Ark landed was located in "Tartary," and that Noah, separating himself from his family, wandered off soon after the flood in an easterly direction and founded the first Chinese dynasty. This Jesuit theory was endorsed in the opening years of the nineteenth century by John Barrow, secretary to Lord Macartney, the English ambassador who came to Peking in 1793. Barrow's stand on the matter is discussed in his *Travels in China* (London, 1804). See also Rowbotham, pp. 121–24, for a Jesuit claim that the descendents of Noah's eldest son, Japheth, brought the "Ancient (pre-Torah) Law" to northeast Asia.

4. Rowbotham, pp. 122–23.

5. Ibid., p. 296.

6. Ibid., pp. 145–46.

7. Ibid., p. 147.

8. Robert Browning, *The Ring and the Book*, vol. 10, lines 1589–1604.

9. Rowbotham, p. 147.

10. Joseph R. Rosenbloom, "The Rites Controversy," *America* 110, no. 16 (April 18, 1964) : 544–45.

11. The translation of Gozani's Portuguese text for the most part followed here is derived from *Juifs de Chine*, by Donald Daniel Leslie and Joseph Dehergne, forthcoming. Gozani's 1704 report to Suarez first appeared in print, in a French translation, in vol. 7 of the 1707 edition of the *Lettres édifiantes*, pp. 1–28. White has a condensed English version, vol. 1, pp. 39–46, extracted from Lockman's 1743 translation, vol. 2, pp. 11–22.

12. Gozani may have exaggerated this prohibition against allowing other congregants than the rabbi to have access to the Ark—a "prohibition," apparently, reminiscent of the Temple practice in which the high priest alone entered the Holy of Holies on the Day of Atonement. Liebermann reported being told by the Jews of Kaifeng in 1867 that *kohanim* (members of the priestly clan) officiated in the Bethel on the Sabbath, festivals, and the New Moon. See *Annual Report of the Anglo-Jewish Association, 1878–79*, p. 93.

13. In the Jesuit Archives at Chantilly there is a bilingual listing of the biblical and apocryphal books that may have been known to (though, almost surely, not all of them were owned by) the Kaifeng Jews in 1704–5. Ecclesiasticus is included in this list, but no conclusion can be drawn of course as to whether the synagogue actually had a copy of it when the list was made up. The Hebrew titles are in the handwriting of Rabbi Phineas. The Western equivalents are in a handwriting that may be Gozani's. (Leslie, *Survival*, pp. 150, 153.) Ecclesiasticus is one of the several books that are listed in this document only by their Western titles.

14. Ibid., p. 49.

15. That the tribes whom Gozani refers to as "others" would have had to come from the Northern Kingdom of Israel, and not from the Southern Kingdom of Judea, does not seem to have crossed his mind.

16. Published in Prague. Pp. 168–69 of this edition contain references to the Chinese Jews.

17. Brotier's report was written in French in the 1750s and was printed in a Latin translation in vol. 3, pp. 567–80, of the 1771 edition (Paris) of *G. Cornelli Taciti Opera*, a work that Brotier edited. The French text, "Mémoire sur les Juifs établis en Chine," appeared in 1774, in vol. 31, pp. 296–372, of the *Lettres édifiantes*, and was re-

printed a number of times in French and in other languages. A condensed English version is provided in White, vol. 1, pp. 49–68.

5 *An Illusion Shattered*

1. See Lockman, vol. 2, pp. 14, n.; 18, n.; 34, n.

2. Domenge's original drawing of the reading of the Torah in the Kaifeng synagogue is reproduced herein (see Illus. 37, p. 291), together with the revision made by Brucker. Brucker's revisions of Domenge's two synagogal plans are herein reproduced (see Illus. 32, p. 282, and Illus. 33, p. 283). A black-and-white reproduction of a hand-colored etching of the interior of the Kaifeng synagogue, as imagined by an anonymous Italian artist of the first half of the nineteenth century, appears on p. 279. A model of the exterior of the synagogal building, based on Domenge's sketches but still essentially imaginative, is displayed in Beth Hatefusoth (Museum of the Jewish Diaspora), Tel Aviv. It is reproduced herein (see Illus. 10, p. 87).

   That Domenge should have shown the Jews worshipping shoeless—like Muslims—is not surprising. "In all Muslim countries," the famous Italian rabbi Obadiah Bertinoro had written from Alexandria to his father in 1488, "no man enters a synagogue with his shoes on, but barefooted." Cited by Jacob R. Marcus, *The Jew in the Medieval World* (Philadelphia: The Jewish Publication Society of America, 1938), p. 397. The Kaifeng Jews, almost certainly the descendants of immigrants from Muslim-dominated lands, could be expected to have carried on this custom of their ancestors.

3. The longer passages quoted in this chapter from Domenge are taken from Leslie and Dehergne's forthcoming *Juifs en Chine*. See Brotier, *Lettres édifiantes*, 1781 ed., vol. 24, pp. 56–100, for a recapitulation of the experiences of both Domenge and (almost a year later) Gaubil with the Kaifeng Jews; and White, vol. 1, pp. 49–68, for a condensed version of the Brotier article.

4. Translated from pp. 99–100 of vol. 24 of the 1781 edition of the *Lettres édifiantes*.

5. Renée Simon, who edited Gaubil's correspondence, has the manuscript addressed to Father Jean-Baptiste du Halde (pp. 51–59, in Gaubil's *Correspondance*), but Leslie (*Survival*, p. 181) states that a manuscript in the *Fonds Brotier*, vol. 149, pp. 29–36, held at the Archives de la Compagnie de Jésus, Province de Paris, Chantilly, shows that it was written to Souciet.

6. Phrase quoted in Gaubil, p. 563.

7. Dehergne (and Leslie), *Rencontre* 6, no. 48, supplement (1976), p. 311. (To appear, also, in their forthcoming *Juifs de Chine*.)

Rabbi Phineas, who had compared his Bible with Gozani's in 1704, could obviously read Hebrew, even if imperfectly. Hebrew texts written in his hand still exist, and may be seen in the collection of Kaifeng synagogal manuscripts held at the Hebrew Union College, Cincinnati.

8. Gaubil, p. 63.
9. Ibid., pp. 423–24.
10. Ibid., p. 63.
11. Ibid. p. 68.
12. Gaubil tells the story of his attempts to induce the princes to requisition the Kaifeng materials in his letter of November 8, 1749, to the French academician Dortous de Mairan. Ibid., pp. 598–601.
13. Cited in Loewenthal, *Jews in China*, pp. 142–43.

6 *Interlude of Silence*

1. Gaubil, p. 75.
2. Pfister, vol. 1, p. 160.
3. See, for example, the totally fallacious 1804 report of John Barrow to the effect that there was at that time a considerable number of Jews in Hangchow, "where they carry on the principal trade, and have acquired the reputation of fabricating the best stuffs of this material [silk?] that are made in China." Many of these Hangchow Jews, he goes on, "forsake the religion of their forefathers, and arrive at high employment in the State. Few among them, I understand, except the Rabbis, have any knowledge of the Hebrew language, and they have so intermixed with the Chinese that the priests of the present day are said to find some difficulties in keeping up their congregations." Cited in the *Hebrew* (July 15, 1864), p. 4, from Barrow's *Travels in China* (London, 1804). Another report, this one from the 1840s and perhaps more accurate than Barrow's, has it that "according to the accounts of the French attaché at China, two Jews of that Empire requested the English and French ambassadors to afford them assistance in the visiting of their respective countries, for the purpose of enquiring into the political and religious condition of their European brethren." In *Jewish Chronicle* [London], March 6, 1846, p. 96.
4. Most of Europe's early information about China came, of course, from the missionaries, whose writings, as one sinologist has put it, "seem to have had a greater immediate effect on Europe than on China. It was through them that Europe first became really acquainted with the Middle Kingdom." Kenneth Scott La Tourette, *A History of Christian Missions in China* (London, 1929), p. 196.

5. See Loewenthal, "Jews and China in Eighteenth-Century Literature," for a discussion of the allusions in eighteenth-century European literature to the Chinese Jews. Of these allusions, only d'Argens's and Voltaire's specifically deal with the Kaifeng *kehillah.*

6. *Jewish Encyclopedia* 12:266, citing from Voltaire's *Mélanges,* vol. 3, p. 344.

7. Cited (in the original Latin) by Cecil Roth on p. viii of his Preface to the second edition of White's *Chinese Jews.*

8. See vol. 1, pp. 59–60, of Daniel Fenning's *A New System of Geography,* 2 vols. (London, 1764–65).

9. *Ha-Me'asef* (April 1790), p. 134.

10. Ibid. (May–June 1790), p. 262. Weinstein points out that the Jews of Cochin have occasionally been misrepresented as residents of Cochin China (Vietnam) or even of China. Myron M. Weinstein, "A Putative Ceylon Rite," *Studies in Jewish Bibliography, History and Literature in Honor of J. Edward Kiev* (New York: Ktav Publishing House, 1971), p. 504, n. 7. See also S. Koder, "A Hebrew Letter of 1768 [actually, 1767]," *Journal of the Rama Varma Archaeological Society* [*Cochin*], 15 (April 1949), pp. 3–6. The original Hebrew text of the letter was printed by Wessely in *Ha-Me'asef* (May–June 1767), p. 3. The same page contains the letter written by Ezekiel Rahabi of Cochin to Tobias Boaz of The Hague.

11. Edrehi, p. 181. For details regarding van Dort, see pp. 38–40 and n. 88 in Myron M. Weinstein's "A Hebrew Qur'an Manuscript," *Studies in Bibliography and Booklore* 10, nos. 1–2 (Winter 1971–72) : 19–52.

12. Claudius Buchanan, *Christian Researches in Asia* (New York, 1812), p. 120.

13. Ibid., p. 123. According to Godeby, an Afghanistani legend describes the Chinese Jews as descendants of the Lost Tribe of Manasseh. Godeby, pp. 17, 372.

14. Claudius Buchanan, *Christian Researches in Asia* (New York, 1812), p. 122.

15. Walter J. Fischel, ed., *Unknown Jews in Unknown Lands: The Travels of David d'Beth Hillel (1824–1832)* (New York: Ktav Publishing House, 1973), pp. 115–16.

16. The covering letter is reprinted in Loewenthal, "Jews in China," pp. 206–7. Leslie (*Survival,* p. 189, n. 2) suggests that it may have been written by George Mendes da Costa. Copies of the covering letter and the letter intended for the *kehillah* are preserved in the British Museum (Add. ms. 29868).

17. Edrehi, pp. 191–92. Edrehi's exotic background seems to have intrigued Henry Wadsworth Longfellow, who came to know Edrehi's

son Isaac when the latter was in Boston somewhat before 1858. "The Jew described by Longfellow in the *Prelude* to *Tales of a Wayside Inn*," writes Sol Liptzin, "was probably a synthetic poetic figure based not only on the poet's recollection of the living younger Edrehi but also on the portrait of the older Edrehi, which looked out from the frontispiece of the strange volume published in Boston [the second edition of the elder Edrehi's book]." Sol Liptzin, *The Jew in American Literature* (New York: Bloch Publishing, 1966), pp. 42–44. Longfellow describes "Edrehi" as "A Spanish Jew from Alicant,/ With aspect grand and grave. . . ."

18. The letter written to the Chinese Jews in 1760 is printed, in English, by Edrehi, pp. 183–91. The statement regarding his search for the reply allegedly preserved in India House occurs on p. 191.

19. Marcus N. Adler (in Kublin, *Jews in Old China*, p. 107).

20. Benjamin Kennicott, *Dissertatio Generalis in Vetus Testamentum Hebraicum*, vol. 2 (Oxford, 1776–80), p. 65. See also his *The Ten Annual Accounts of the Collation of the Hebrew MSS of the Old Testament* (Oxford, 1770), pp. 129–30, 162–63.

21. Finn (in Kublin, *Jews in Old China*, p. 19).

22. For a discussion of the effect of Grosier's book on the New York Jewish community, see Sokobin (in Kublin, *Studies*, pp. 171–86); Hyman B. Grinstein, *The Rise of the Jewish Community of New York, 1654–1860* (Philadelphia: The Jewish Publication Society of America, 1945), pp. 418–19; *American Hebrew*, May 21, 1897, p. 89; and Benjamin II, *Three Years in America*, 2 vols. (Philadelphia: The Jewish Publication Society of America, 1956), pp. 62–64. Benjamin gives both the Hebrew text of the letter and an English translation.

23. Finn (in Kublin, *Jews in Old China*, p. 19).

24. Smith, p. 25.

7 Enter James Finn

1. Gaubil, pp. 140–42.

2. The entire work is reprinted in Kublin, *Jews in Old China*, pp. 1–92.

3. Ibid., pp. xii–xiii.

4. Published in London, 1872.

5. Cited by Finn (in Kublin, *Jews in Old China*, pp. 13; 13, n. 1; 80; 80, n. 2).

6. Ibid., p. 31.

7. Ibid., pp. 12; 80; 80, n. 1.

8. Ibid., pp. 16–17.

9. Ibid., p. 83.

10. Ibid., p. 4.

11. Godeby, p. 371. Bokhara and China are also interconnected in a tradition held by the Jews of the Transcaucasian city of Derbent, who told the traveler Joseph Levi Tchorni that many of their people had in centuries gone by migrated to Bokhara and China. See A. Neubauer, "Where are the Ten Tribes?" *Jewish Quarterly Review*, o.s. (July 1889) : 422, citing Tchorni's *Sefer ha-Masaot* (St. Petersburg, 1884), p. 585.

12. The text appears in an English translation in Finn's *Orphan Colony*, pp. 15–20, and in the Hebrew original, pp. 121–24.

13. Layton's letter of January 15, 1849, is cited, ibid., pp. 21–27.

14. Several writers have asserted that there were two branches of the Chao clans, both sharing the same surname. White, vol. 3, p. 3, thus has the Kaifeng Jews of the first quarter of the twentieth century speak of "seven surnames and eight families." Leslie, however, rejects this, stressing instead that there were two clans surnamed Li. *Survival*, p. 110.

15. Finn, *Orphan Colony*, p. 25. Uzziel Haga, in *Metziat Aseret ha-Shebatim*, p. 36, quotes a Lemberg newspaper dated 1817 as containing a report from an English traveler to the effect that a Chinese Muslim had told him that the Kaifeng Jews observed the eighth day as their Sabbath. Haga (whose account, it should be pointed out, is not trustworthy and seems, moreover, to have been pirated from an equally questionable German source—and who may himself, for that matter, be the creature of someone's imagination) suggests that "the Mohammedan made this statement because in his faith our sixth day is his Sabbath—that is to say, his equivalent of the seventh day. Hence he would call our Sabbath the eighth day." The English traveler would appear to be the missionary Robert Morrison, whose personal journal contains an entry dated October 10, 1816, describing a meeting with a Muslim who told him the same story that was cited by Haga from an 1817 issue of the Lemberg newspaper. The pertinent passage from Morrison's journal is quoted in Leslie's *Survival*, p. 53. In both accounts—Morrison's, and also Haga's paraphrase of the Lemberg item—no mention is made of the sixth day as a day of rest. Layton may of course have misunderstood T'ieh on this.

16. For Mrs. Layton's letter and Finn's account of its peregrinations, see Finn's *Orphan Colony*, pp. 35–38.

17. Smith, p. 24.

18. Leslie, *Survival*, p. 190; Finn, *Orphan Colony*, p. 15.

19. Finn, *Orphan Colony*, pp. 44–45.

20. Ibid., p. 14.

21. Chao Nien-tsu's letter is printed in an English translation, ibid., pp. 39–44.

8 *The Chinese Delegates*

1. George J. Miller, "David A. Borrenstein: A Printer and Publisher at Princeton, N.J., 1824–28," *The Papers of the Bibliographical Society of America* 30 (1936): 1–56. Borrenstein, a convert from Judaism to Christianity, was taught the printing trade in London by the London Society. For Miller's account of Frey's activities, see pp. 1–6.

   Some further notion of the intensity of the conversionary efforts of this period vis-à-vis the Jews in the English-speaking countries may be gleaned from the fact (according to a contemporary Jewish estimate) that in New York City alone there were twenty organizations whose goal it was to Christianize the Jews of America. The total number of Jews in New York City in 1825—men, women and children—was approximately 500, and in all the United States there were then no more than a few thousand. See Hyman A. Grinstein, *The Rise of the Jewish Community of New York, 1654–1860* (Philadelphia: The Jewish Publication Society of America, 1945), pp. 382–88.

2. Barbara W. Tuchman, *Bible and Sword* (New York: New York University Press, 1956), p. 187.

3. Thomas D. Halstead, *Our Missions: being a History of the Principal Missionary Transactions of the London Society for Promoting Christianity amongst the Jews from its Foundation in 1809 to the Present Year* (London, 1866), p. 36.

4. The London Society's missionaries were by no means unique in their willingness to go to extremes to make converts, whether out of Jews or anyone else. It is doubtful, however, whether any representatives of the London Society went quite as far as the eccentric Prussian Protestant missionary Karl (Charles) Gutzlaff, who in 1832–33 twice accepted employment as an interpreter for a British shipping firm engaged in the smuggling of opium into China. Gutzlaff, having participated personally in the smuggling, justified his conduct on the grounds that the income derived from it would be used to save souls that would otherwise be lost forever. See Maurice Collis, *Foreign Mud: the Opium Imbroglio at Canton in the 1830's and the Anglo-Chinese War* (New York: W. W. Norton & Company, 1968), pp. 69–74. Another famous missionary who acted as a paid interpreter for opium smugglers was the Englishman Robert Morrison. Nigel Cameron, *Barbarians and Mandarins* (New York and Tokyo: Walker-Weatherill, 1970), p. 316.

5. *Jewish Encyclopedia*, 4:252.

6. Sassoon, pp. 142–44.

7. Smith, p. 24.

8. In 1853, the Jews, together with their townsmen, would weather still another of the many disasters of which Kaifeng seems to have had more than its fair share. This time the catastrophe was of a military nature, the Taiping rebels having besieged the city. The Taipings did not capture it, but only because of a sudden downpour that flooded their encampment, killed several thousand of them, and destroyed much of their equipment. The personal and material damages suffered by the besieged, naturally enough, had lasting effects.

9. Cf., the 1856 statement by Townsend Harris, first American consul and minister to Japan: "I may remark that, while the Chinese Buddhists have retained the *sound* of these pious ejaculations, they have entirely lost the meaning of the words, and this remark will apply to all the books they have in the Pali character. They have preserved the sound by writing it in Chinese, but the sense is lost. The same has taken place with the Mahometans at Ningpo with the Koran, and with the Jews in Kaifeng and the Pentateuch." Townsend Harris, *The Complete Journals of Townsend Harris*, 2d ed., rev. (Rutland, Vt., and Tokyo: Charles E. Tuttle, 1959), p. 44. It may be that Harris, talking with missionaries, was told by them that the delegates had informed them that the Kaifeng Jews, or some of them, could still make out a few words in Hebrew but had no notion of what these words meant.

10. Smith, pp. 26, 47–48.

11. The details of Chao's discussion with the delegates are furnished by Ch'iu, in Smith, pp. 28–30 and 47–48.

12. Ibid., p. 28.

13. Ibid., pp. 47–48.

14. Ibid., p. 53.

15. One particularly imaginative article appeared in the *Asmonean* (New York), May 9, 1851. Taken "from a letter in the *South China Advocate,* dated Shanghai, China, Jan. 14, 1851 [seven days after the delegates' return to the city from their initial visit to Kaifeng], and addressed to the Rev. Wm. M. Wightman, D. D., by the Rev. D. Jenkins of the American China Mission," it alleges that "there is another synagogue in Hangchow, in the Province of Chekiang, about eight days' journey from Shanghai and back." How had Jenkins learned this? "My Mandarin teacher tells me he has seen the inscription there—but has never been in it." Cf., a similar claim by Barrow, chap. 6, n. 3, above.

16. The original article was published in *Household Words*, August 2, 1851, pp. 452–56. It was reprinted in *International Magazine* 4, p. 264 and *passim*, and in *Entertaining Miscellanies*, vol. 6 (New York, 1853). It also appeared in the *Weekly Gleaner*, an English-language San Francisco Jewish newspaper, in two installments (April

10 and April 17, 1857). The same periodical featured reproductions of Hebrew texts taken from the books the delegates acquired during their first visit to Kaifeng in its issues of June 19 and June 26, 1857. The *Gleaner*, incidentally, was edited by Rabbi Julius Eckman, who had hoped to go personally to China and become the Kaifeng *kehillah's* teacher.

17. See below, pt. 1, chap. 9, for a discussion of the letter to the chief rabbi of Alsace and the Londoner's report.

18. See pt. 1, chap. 9, below, for the story of Liebermann's visit to Kaifeng and the possibility that it may have been pirated from the story told by another purported visitor to the *kehillah*, Aaron Halevi Fink, who also claimed that he had been told by the Jews that they had reason to believe that the men who acquired the manuscripts were Jewish.

19. White, vol. 1, p. 133; vol. 3, pp. 156–57.

20. For the story of the Kaifeng Torah scrolls, see Pollak, *Discovery*, and Pollak, *Torah Scrolls*. Currently (1979), each of the following institutions has a Kaifeng Torah: American Bible Society, New York (incomplete); Jewish Theological Seminary, New York; Österreichisiche Nationalbibliothek, Vienna; Bridwell Library, Southern Methodist University, Dallas; British Museum, London; Cambridge University Library, Cambridge; and Bodleian Library, Oxford. Of these, the last four were obtained from the Kaifeng Jews by the delegates, and the first three by subsequent purchase (see pt. 1, chap. 9, below). The rest are unaccounted for. Hebrew Union College, Cincinnati, has thirty-four section books of the Law, twenty-nine liturgical manuscripts (two of which are Haggadahs for Passover), and the *kehillah's* Memorial Book. One section book is owned by the Royal Ontario Museum, Toronto, and another by the John Rylands Library, Manchester. (The Cincinnati holdings apparently include a few booklets obtained in the years following the 1851 trip of the delegates to Kaifeng. The Toronto and Manchester exemplars seem also to have been acquired after 1851.)

9 *The Orphan Colony*

1. The details presented here of Martin's journey to Kaifeng are taken from his "Account of a Visit to the Jews in Honan," as reprinted in his book *The Chinese* (New York, 1881), pp. 287–98. Originally prepared for the North China Branch of the Royal Asiatic Society, Martin's paper was read at a special meeting of the society held in Shanghai on March 29, 1866, and was then published in the society's

Journal and republished on several occasions. A condensation is provided in White, vol. 1, pp. 184–87.

2. In 1842, the official schedule for the express transportation of mail from Peking to Kaifeng by couriers mounted on horse was eight days. Lord Macartney, the British diplomat who came to China in the last decade of the eighteenth century, described the country's courier system as efficient and swift. Michael Loewe, *Imperial China* (New York: Frederick A. Praeger, 1966), pp. 216, 237. Because horses were expensive, they were usually used only by government functionaries, the military, and people of wealth. Martin might have made better time if he had traveled on horseback. Nevertheless, his complaints about the difficulties of travel in China indicate why relatively few Caucasians at this time cared to make the journey to Kaifeng, even when the countryside was relatively peaceful.

3. *Jewish Times*, March 26, 1869, p. 5.

4. The letter was written by Martin to the Rev. Mr. Kaufmann, a chaplain to Protestant sailors passing through Shanghai. Dated February 11, 1867, in Peking, it was printed in the English-language missionary journal *Jewish Intelligence* and then cited in the *Jewish Chronicle* [London], September 20, 1867, p. 7, and again (this time in a French translation) in *Archives Israélites* 28 (1867): 932–34. As late as 1890, having long given up all hope of making Christians out of the Kaifeng Jews, Martin again suggested to the Jews of America that they look into the matter of reconstituting the ancient *kehillah* of Kaifeng—pointing out, however, that it was by then probably too late to expect much success. See Martin's letter to the editor in *Jewish Messenger*, October 30, 1890. (Martin's name is erroneously printed as W. H., rather than W. A. P. Martin.)

5. Finn, *Orphan Colony*, p. 96, contains one version of this story, taken from the *Jewish Record*, November 14, 1862, Finn's attention having presumably been directed to this source by a rewriting of the tale that appeared in the *Jewish Chronicle*, February 28, 1868, where it was credited (if that is the appropriate verb) to the issue of the *Jewish Record* noted by Finn. The story was also picked up by the *Archives Israélites* 25 (1864): 664, from *Le Courrier de Saigon* (April 10, 1864), a periodical identified by the *Archives Israélites* as "the official journal of the French inhabitants of Cochin China." The Saigon version included the claim that the British sea captain (who, even in its version, remained anonymous) was Jewish. As late as 1911, the captain was still being described as a Jew (in *Sefer ha-Brit ha-Hadash*, printed in Petrikov, White Russia).

6. The book appeared originally as *Cinq Années en Orient (1846–51)*. Revised and enlarged, it was republished in German under the title

Acht Jahre in Asien und Afrika (Hanover, 1858). Subsequent editions were based on the Hanover version. The Hebrew edition, *Sefer Ma'asei Yisrael* (Lyck, 1859), was further expanded by its editor, David Gordon, to include a digest of an article that had appeared in a Hebrew periodical in North Germany and which gave the gist of the Jesuit dealings with the Chinese Jews. Benjamin's odd tale regarding the Chinese Jews is told on pp. 70–73 of the Lyck edition. See also the version appearing in the *Jewish Progress,* April 27, 1888.

7. J. C., "The Jews in China," *Jewish Messenger,* May 13, 1859, p. 139.

8. Leslie, *Survival,* p. 67.

9. The story of Adler's efforts on behalf of the *kehillah* has been extracted here in the main from the details provided by Marcus Nathan Adler's lecture "Chinese Jews" (in Kublin, *Jews in Old China,* pp. 93–117); Finn, *Orphan Colony,* pp. 94–95, 112; Leo Shpall, "Americans and the Lost Chinese Jews," *Jewish Center Review,* February 1954: 12–13; and various articles in the *Occident* cited below.

10. Some Jewish leaders, however, were as woefully ignorant of the number of Jews who lived in China as of the conditions in which these lost brethren found themselves. In the mid-1920s, the rabbi of Harbin, Moshe Kishilev, having received a letter from the celebrated Hofetz Hayyim (Rabbi Israel Meir Cohen of Vilna) inquiring about the Jews of Honan, showed it to M. Birman. He then observed to Birman that 130 years previously (actually in 1845, five years before the delegates' first trip to Kaifeng) Rabbi Israel Lipshutz of Danzig had stated in his *Tiferet Yisrael* (a commentary on the Mishnah) that there were many millions of Jews in China. Reported by Birman in *Der Amerikaner,* December 11, 1953, p. 20. The fable of the million Chinese Jews found by the British sea captain may, moreover, have reached Europe even earlier than the time indicated in n. 5 above, and this too could have left certain Jewish supporters of the movement to save the Chinese Jews with the notion that the people they hoped to help were very numerous indeed.

11. *Occident,* April 10, 1852, pp. 37–39. Actually, Carpenter's exhortations did little other than induce a few of the ministers of his denomination to pass around the collection plate at their services, but the amount collected on behalf of his project to make Seventh-Day Baptists out of the Chinese Jews never amounted to more than a pittance.

12. "Hebrew Prayers Used by the Jews of China," ibid., March 1853, pp. 586–97, especially p. 588. The article was taken from *Jewish Intelligence* 19 (January 1853) and, as its title indicates, is devoted to the texts recently acquired by the delegates. A similar analysis also

appeared in the *Jewish Chronicle,* January 28 and February 11, 1853.

13. *Occident,* March 1853, p. 587.

14. Leeser's summation of the letter and his comments appear ibid., November 1853, pp. 409–13.

15. But Rabbi Adler, alas, later complained that only £20 were remitted to him. *Jewish Chronicle,* February 7, 1868.

16. Finn, *Orphan Colony,* p. 94. See also Eckman's article in *Hebrew Observer* May 7, 1869. For biographical details regarding Eckman, see Robert E. Levinson, "Julius Eckman and the *Weekly Gleaner:* The Jewish Press in the Pioneer American West," *A Bicentennial Festschrift for Jacob Rader Marcus* (Waltham, Mass.: American Jewish Historical Society, 1976), pp. 323–40. In a letter to the author, dated November 22, 1977, Dr. Levinson states that "the folklore surrounding Eckman's desire to get to China "is really fascinating. Some authors have actually supposed he got there, and have taken that point of view. I have no proof of it myself." According to Sharfman, Eckman was dissuaded from proceeding to China by Rabbi James K. Gutheim of New Orleans (concerning whose efforts on behalf of the Chinese Jews, see below, this chapter). In the mid-1850s, says Sharfman, the two most immediate external philanthropic concerns of American Jewry were the alleviation of the plight of the 20,000 Jews in Palestine left destitute by the effects of the Crimean War and the rescue of the Chinese Jews. I. Harold Sharfman, *"Nothing Left to Commemorate": The Story of the Pioneer Jews of Jackson, Amador County, California* (Glendale, Calif.: Arthur H. Clark, 1969), pp. 19–21. Sharfman also observes that the Rev. Samuel S. Schuck of the Seventh-Day Baptist Mission at Shanghai (one of the missionaries, incidentally, who would not or could not help Samuel Hyman Cohen get a passport that would permit him to travel to Kaifeng) returned to the United States with the intention of raising funds for converting the Kaifeng Jews. "When he lectured at Sacramento in 1854, on the subject of the Chinese Jews," Sharfman states (p. 20), "he noted that none had yet been converted."

17. Stories of Chinese Jews living in California have cropped up from time to time. Here is Benjamin II's version of two reports of this nature which he ran into during his travels in America, 1859–62: "During my stay in Sacramento, a friend told me that he met a Chinese Jew in the mountains. It was clear from the conversations of this Chinese that he was well acquainted with Jewish customs, and this, as well as the fact that he was circumcised, was proof enough that he was a Jew. It could also be seen in his features. He said that he was born in Manila, in the piratical islands . . . where —a fact unknown to me until then—a large number of Israelites

were living. Another Chinese who called himself a Jew was said to be in Sacramento. He would refuse to light a fire on the Sabbath and explained that, although he was a working man, he did not want to do anything that his religion forbade him." I. J. Benjamin, *Three Years in America,* 2 vols. (Philadelphia: The Jewish Publication Society of America, 1965), vol. 2, p. 10. The second of the two Chinese Jews whom Benjamin places in or near Sacramento is apparently the man described by the *Chronicle* as the individual "who did not work on the Sabbath day."

An item akin to the two presented by Benjamin in his *Three Years in America,* and at least as dubious, was later sent to the *American Israelite,* which printed it in its issue of February 13, 1880, p. 2. The writer, Isidor N. Choynski, using the pseudonym Maftir, claimed that during a conversation he had once had with a Chinese, whom he identified as "Ahling Moh," in his bookstore at 34 Geary Street, San Francisco, the Oriental, noticing a Hebrew book lying on a table, immediately asked Choynski if he was a "Hebrew." When Choynski answered in the affirmative, the man told him that he himself came from a Jewish group living in Ning-po that observed, as Choynski reported his customer's statement, "many of the rites . . . practiced among the Western Jews." His people had a "Tolah," the man declared, "and manuscripts of the Bible stamped on rice paper."

But it was left to an organization calling itself the Native Sons of British Columbia to tell of Chinese Jews—Jews, moreover, from Kaifeng—who came much earlier than the nineteenth century to America. Certain writers had claimed that the Chinese, not Columbus, were the discoverers of the New World. In the 1920s, the Native Sons, having noted that the Indians of British Columbia employed a number of words and customs, which appeared to be of ancient Hebrew origin, concluded that these Indians had picked up their Hebraic words and customs from Kaifeng Jewish merchant adventurers who were part of one or more of the pre- and post-Columbian Chinese expeditions to America. Cited, though skeptically, in *American Hebrew,* March 12, 1926, pp. 537, 556.

18. *Occident,* August 1866, pp. 229–34. Benjamin II, however, states in his *Three Years in America* (see n. 17, above), vol. 1, p. 318, that Touro left the society $6,000, and that when he, Benjamin, arrived in New Orleans in 1860 its endowment had grown to $10,000.

19. The understandable reluctance of many Jews in America to take on the financial burden of rehabilitating the Kaifeng *kehillah* while people closer to home were in dire need of assistance was voiced on numerous occasions. The highly respected rabbi, Sabbato Morais, for example, urged more than two decades after the end of the

Civil War that it was more important for American Jewry to apply all of its available funds to the needs of Jews fleeing to the United States from persecution in their native lands than to the rescue of the Chinese Jews. *American Hebrew,* November 2, 1888, p. 204.

20. Max J. Kohler, "The Board of Delegates of American Israelites, 1859–1878," *Publications of the American Jewish Historical Society,* 29 (1925) : 75–135, especially p. 88. See also *Jewish Chronicle,* February 7, 1868. The British Jews had collected £400 for Halévy's projected trip to China, the sum to be forwarded to the Alliance Israélite Universelle as soon as Halévy, then on a mission to the Falashan Jews of Abyssinia, declared himself ready to depart for the Orient.

21. Benjamin's account of his dealings with the Jews of New Orleans appears in his *Three Years in America* (see n. 17, above), vol. 1, pp. 318–33.

22. *Cornerstone* 12, (May 19, 1860).

23. On the whole, the European authorities indicated that it would indeed be better if the New Orleans Jews found another means of memorializing Touro than erecting a bust in his honor.

24. The Torah scroll kept by Martin is now at the Jewish Theological Seminary, New York. Williams's is at the American Bible Society, also in New York. Von Scherzer's is at the Österreichische Nationalbibliothek, Vienna. Had the young men from Kaifeng offered any of their communal scrolls to Caucasian Jews living in China they would no doubt have found a ready market for them. Replying in 1866 to a letter from M. Simon, a French official then in China on a scientific mission for his government who claimed to have met Chinese Jews in both Peking and Ning-po (seemingly Jews of Kaifeng origin), the Alliance Israélite had suggested that he ask them a series of questions about their history, ritual, and the like, and that he also try to acquire facsimiles of specified passages in their synagogal manuscripts. The tone of the Alliance's response indicates that it was also interested in buying whatever texts the Jews might be willing to relinquish. Whether Simon was ever able to ask his Chinese Jewish contacts (if he had really made any) the questions posed by the Alliance is not known. Simon also claimed that there were other Jews in China, particularly in the northern provinces, and more than one might suspect. The Jews had in the past been hunted down, he said, as putative members of such insurrectionary societies as the White Lotus League, and they now found it prudent to let people think they were Muslims. Simon claimed too that a Chinese Jewish employee of his had reported the presence in Tientsin of 250–300 Jews, where they had "a small oratory and a rabbi." He himself had met the rabbi, Simon added, and was told by him that two or three

Jewish families lived in Hangchow. The original text of Simon's fanciful letter, written in Kiangsi Province on September 4, 1863, was printed in *Archives Israélites* 24 (1865) : 970–71. It had been previously printed in the *Jewish Chronicle,* December 4, 1863, which would also publish the Alliance's response on May 4, 1866. In his letter, Simon had stated that he intended to leave in a month or so for Kaifeng and there visit the Jews. At any rate, an entry in *Archives Israélites* 28 (1867) : 933, suggests that its editors had given up all hope of hearing again from their elusive correspondent. The Alliance had earlier anticipated that it would be able to communicate with the *kehillah* through a non-Jewish traveler, Count Stanislas d'Escayrac de Lauture, who was planning to visit China and whose itinerary included Kaifeng; but nothing came of this. Ibid., 22 (1861) : 454–56.

25. Cited in James Arthur Miller's *Apostle of China* (New York and Milwaukee: Morehouse Publishing Company, 1937), p. 71. That the three young visitors from Kaifeng should—in 1867—think that Christianity and Judasim were the same is understandable, considering the time and circumstances. However, the next generation of Kaifeng Jews would know better.

26. Ibid., p. 72.

27. Ibid., pp. 72–73. Reprinted in White, vol. 1, pp. 188–89.

28. *The Eighth Annual Report of the Anglo-Jewish Association in Connection with the Alliance Israélite Universelle, 1878–79,* Appendix E, pp. 90–96. See also Löwy's statement that he condensed ten letters from Liebermann rather than one in *Jewish Chronicle,* June 22, 1900, p. 21.

29. *Report of the Anglo-Jewish Association,* p. 90, cited in n. 28, above.

30. *Jewish Chronicle,* February 7, 14, and 21, 1868.

31. "These papers [Fink's letter]," the editors wrote, "are of a highly personal character and repay perusal. Fortunately, circumstances permit of an editorial guarantee of their authenticity. The statements of the writer are not fanciful inventions, but plain, unvarnished matters of fact." Ibid. (February 28, 1868), p. 4.

32. In the author's *Torah Scrolls of the Chinese Jews,* pp. 119–21, Fink's claim to have visited the Kaifeng Jews in 1864 is prematurely characterized as fraudulent, the fact that Fink's account had perhaps been published before Liebermann's not having been realized when the book was written. To the best of the author's knowledge, the authenticity of Liebermann's account has never been questioned in print until the present. One point in Liebermann's favor, incidentally, is that Martin, who met the Kaifeng Jews in February 1866, failed to record any statement on their part of being visited by an Occidental coreligionist only a year and a half earlier. This is perhaps a

mark against Fink, but neither Martin's silence nor, presumably, his hosts' necessarily means that Fink was not in Kaifeng in 1864.

33. Fink also notes the presence of a pool of water on the old synagogal site, a fact later confirmed by other writers. In the middle of this pool, he says, "stands a large stone rising about five feet above the level of the water, which seems to be exceedingly ancient. On it are engraved on both sides, from the top to the bottom, Chinese characters; but I could not prevail upon anyone to go into the water to read the inscription for me." *Jewish Chronicle,* February 14, 1868, p. 2. Fink, incidentally, claims a knowledge of Chinese—but was apparently not sufficiently interested in the inscriptions to get his feet wet or, if the pool was deep, to find a boat and row out to the monument. Martin, who saw the 1489/1512 stele in 1866, addressed a crowd of Jews and others standing nearby, one hand resting on the monument. Could the pool have dried out, at least temporarily, since Fink was there (if he was)?

34. The same colophon appears in one of the booklets obtained by the delegates and now at the Hebrew Union College. See also Leslie's "Judaeo-Persian," p. 16, and his *Survival,* p. 94, for further discussions of this colophon.

35. The allegation that the Kaifeng Jews displayed one of their Torah scrolls in a marketplace appears in other nineteenth-century reports, though not always in the same form, and even in a recent novel, Stephen Becker's *Dog Tags* (New York: Random House, 1973), pp. 41–42. Here a Chinese medical student at an American university tells a Jewish classmate in the early post-World War II years that an English traveler in Victorian times came to Kaifeng where, in the marketplace, "he saw a vendor . . . holding up a scroll, and he went to look at the scroll and it was in Hebrew. The Englishman went crazy with excitement, and in time he got the whole story. Hundreds of years before, a bunch of Jews had fled from someplace and crossed all of Asia and settled in Kaifeng. After a while they were assimilated and forgot who they were, but there were always those weird scrolls and books that nobody could read anymore. So every market day one of them went out and stood there, holding up the scroll, hoping that some traveler could enlighten him. Funny thing was, they still kept the Sabbath. It was on a Wednesday or some such day because the western calendar had changed and the Chinese never cared too much about the day of the week anyway, but they kept it."

36. Fink does not speak of any specific number of Jews in Peking, but says that the Kaifeng Jews actually gave him a letter to them. He says nothing, however, about delivering this letter to the Peking

addressees, but closes his own communication to the *Jewish Chronicle* (which printed that portion of it on February 21, 1868) with an impassioned description of his unhappy financial situation and a declaration of his intention to travel to various coastal cities in China and ask the Occidental Jews living in these cities to supply him with funds for returning to Kaifeng. Nothing more is subsequently heard of this, or of him.

10 *Too Little, and Much too Late*

1. However, Fink, although he claimed to have encountered great peril during his stay in Kaifeng, expressed the desire to return there and work with the Jews. Kaifeng, incidentally, was the last of all the provincial capitals of China to admit Protestant missionaries on a permanent basis.

2. Fink, who placed his visit to Kaifeng in 1864, said that he alternated between posing as a Chinese and appearing openly as an Occidental. Like Schereschewsky and Liebermann, he too reported having had to face considerable hostility in Kaifeng, but unlike Liebermann he said nothing about carrying a weapon. Fink also claimed to have been driven out of the city.

3. The letter was printed in *Jewish Chronicle* [London], July 27, 1888, p. 6. There is reason to suspect that the author was the missionary A. Kingsley Glover, who wrote extensively, and often without much accuracy, about the Chinese Jews.

4. Other odd reports about the Kaifeng Jews trickled in to the West somewhat before and somewhat after the *Jewish Chronicle's* publication of the letter from the traveler who was turned back at the city's gates. An unnamed Jewish visitor to China, though apparently not to Kaifeng, is cited in the July 30, 1868, issue of the *Jewish Chronicle* as saying that the Jews of Kaifeng "reside in a separate quarter of the town, and are placed under the jurisdiction of a special Chief of Police, who acts at the same time as a magistrate. . . . The houses in the Jewish quarter are built according to the Chinese system of architecture, and even the wooden ornaments on the roofs, which are considered to be a protection against evil spirits, are not wanting." The Jews, this report goes on, are active in commerce, industry and agriculture. As craftsmen, they engage in silk weaving, sword cutlery, wood carving, and jewelry work. E. T. Williams, writing from China, is quoted in the *Jewish Chronicle*, August 23, 1889, as claiming that there are several thousand Jews in Kaifeng, most of whom are "lapsing into heathenism." According to Williams, who does not seem to have gone to Kaifeng himself, the Jews were on the whole "in comfortable circumstances."

5. Dennis J. Mills, "An Eventful Itineration," *China's Millions* (London, 1891), p. 47. The murder may have been related to the blood feud that is said to have broken out between the Chang and the other clans, the Chang having been accused of selling the old synagogal ark to a mosque.

6. Leslie, *Survival*, p. 65.

7. Pollak, *Torah Scrolls*, pp. 69–71.

8. Marcus N. Adler (in Kublin, *Jews of Old China*, pp. 114–15).

9. Ibid., pp. 115–16.

10. For additional details regarding Jonas Lehmann, see Pollak, *Torah Scrolls*, pp. 127–28.

11. *Allgemeine Zeitung des Judenthums* [Berlin], no. 78, 1914, pp. 28–29; no. 79 (1915), pp. 472–74.

12. Marcus N. Adler (in Kublin, *Jews of Old China*, p. 115). Large portions of Adler's lecture, as well as the comments of several of his auditors, are reported in *Jewish Chronicle*, June 22, 1900, pp. 21–22.

13. *Chicago Inter-Ocean*, December 31, 1899.

14. *American Hebrew*, January 12, 1900.

15. *Der Israelit* [Mainz], April 21, 1890, pp. 553–55. The father had been editor of *Der Israelit*. The post was subsequently taken over by Jonas's younger brother Oskar.

16. Cf., the statement made in 1910 to the Chinese scholar Chang Hsiang-wen by a Jew named Chao: "The district magistrate wanted to take away from us a site of the synagogue and intended to move our stele. We protested violently, and the project was abandoned." Chang Hsiang-wen (in Kublin, *Studies*, pp. 214–18).

17. Leslie, *Survival*, pp. 65–66, 197.

18. Godeby, p. 418.

19. Oliver Bainbridge, "The Chinese Jews," *National Geographic Magazine* 18, no. 10 (October 1907): 621–32. The article was also printed in *Israel's Messenger*, October 19, 1906, pp. 8–10; in *A Short Account of the Calcutta Jews, etc.*, pt. 5 (Calcutta, 1917); and in French in *A travers le Monde* 14 (1908), p. 20.

20. An undated clipping from an unidentified newspaper pasted into the Hebrew Union College's copy of Bishop Smith's *Narrative* provides the information concerning the presence (apparently for the purpose of sale) of both the case and the petition in Jacob's store. Several of the Kaifeng synagogal artifacts owned by the Royal Ontario Museum, including the Torah case, as of 1979 are on indefinite loan to Toronto's Holy Blossom Synagogue.

21. An English translation of the letter is provided by Marcus N. Adler (in Kublin, *Jews in Old China*, pp. 116–17).

22. David A. Brown, who visited the Kaifeng Jews in 1932, provided a

summary of the society's history in articles published in the United States in the following year. (See Selected Bibliography, under Brown.) His articles are condensed in White, vol. 1, pp. 150–64. See also, Frederick W. Eddy, "First Mission to Colony of Chinese Orthodox Jews," *New York Times,* May 3, 1903, sec. 3, p. 8.

23. Walter Fuchs, "The Chinese Jews of K'ai-Fêng Fu," *T'ien Hsia Monthly* 5 (August 1937): 35–40. Fuchs's article is condensed in White, vol. 1, pp. 165–68.

24. "From Shanghai," an unidentified Kaifeng (non-Jewish) convert to Christianity, a painter, later wrote William Geil, "Mr. Powell wrote that the Jews there wished to get some of the Kaifeng Jewish boys, so I took two down [actually, one adult, Li, and his young son] to be educated. When they wrote again, I tried to get more, but they will not be helped; they care only for money." William Edgar Geil, *Eighteen Capitals of China* (Philadelphia, 1911), pp. 362–63. Unlike the painter, however, the elder Li apparently encountered no real difficulty in persuading six friends to accompany him to Shanghai.

25. Fuchs (in White, vol. 1, p. 168). See also n. 23, above. The figure of £5,000 is also given in two letters to the *American Hebrew* appealing for funds, the first (August 22, 1902, pp. 377–78) by L. Moore, president of the Society, and the second (February 13, 1903, p. 430) by N. E. B. Ezra.

26. *Israel's Messenger,* October 19, 1906.

27. "Letter to the Editor," *Emanu-El,* March 14, 1913, p. 2. Signed by N. E. B. Ezra.

28. *Jewish Chronicle,* October 12, 1962, p. 20.

29. In the same year, 1902, Edward Isaac Ezra's study, "Chinese Jews," was published in the *East of Asia Magazine* 1 (1902): 278–96. The article was later revised and expanded by Arthur Sopher, the new version being published in 1926 at Shanghai. The Ezra-Sopher text was reprinted in 1971 in Kublin's *Jews in Old China,* pp. 213–95.

30. Perlmann's major work on the Chinese Jews, which includes the details of his personal contacts with the visitors to Shanghai, is a booklet called *The History of the Jews in China* (London, 1912). It has been reprinted in Kublin's *Jews in Old China,* pp. 119–211.

31. Perlmann (in Kublin's *Jews in Old China,* p. 143).

32. Eddy, *New York Times* article cited in n. 22, above.

11 *Beyond the Point of No Return*

1. White, vol. 1, Preface.

2. Ibid., pp. 20–21; vol. 3, pp. 4–5. The same Chao Yün-chung wrote a letter sometime before 1914 to Bruno Schindler, a German

Jewish sinologist, asking for help in reconstituting the *kehillah*. Had the *kehillah* actually been revived and the synagogue rebuilt, the Canadians would have been obligated under the terms of the agreement they had made with the Kaifeng Jews to return the steles. See Bruno Schindler, "Berichte über die Juden in China," *Die Erde* (February 1914) : 63.

Chao's reason (as reported by White) for letting the Canadians have the steles was that he would rather see them in Christian hands than in the possession of the Muslims or any other group. White tried hard to convert Chao, but met with no success. Although he realized that Judaism was coming to an end in Kaifeng, Chao's attachment to the tradition of his ancestors apparently remained steadfast, and this despite the fact that he knew very little about it. "Chao Yün-chung came to see me this afternoon," White wrote in 1918 to a Shanghai Jewish newspaper editor, "and although I am glad to be able to tell you he does not worship idols, yet I am sorry to say it looks as if all human trace of the Chinese Jews will soon be completely lost. . . . He says they have only the ancestral tablets as a record, which they do not worship as the Chinese do but use only as a memorial to their parents, and as this generation is the first generation following the final destruction of the synagogue [*sic*], the next generation will find them lost as a race." White's letter, dated October 23, 1918, was printed in *Israel's Messenger*, March 14, 1919, p. 31.

3. See White's letter, ibid., and J. Preuss, *The Chinese Jews of Kaifeng-fu* (Tel Aviv: Museum Haaretz, 1966), p. 25.

4. *Chinese Recorder* [Shanghai], November 1919, pp. 780–82. Cited in White, vol. 1, pp. 194–95. Additional details regarding the meetings are given in an article captioned "Chinese Jews found by Christian Missionaries," *Scribe*, February 20, 1920, pp. 5, 7, which states that of the 200 Jewish families remaining in Kaifeng only about forty were represented. To call them together, White inserted advertisements in the local newspapers, the *Scribe* reports, "inviting bona fide Jews to enroll at the Anglican church and to receive tickets entitling them to the lantern lectures, free meals and the general meetings. Special men were sent to known Jews inviting them personally and getting them to give the names and addresses of other Jews known to them. Many were too suspicious to have anything to do with the movement, especially those who had so drifted away from their clan connection that they had forgotten, or practically so, their relationship with the Jews."

5. White, vol. 3, p. 154. White is referring to individual contacts continued until the late 1930s or the early 1940s.

6. Tenney was American chargé d'affaires at Peking. His report con-

cerning the Kaifeng Jews appears in the *Scribe,* April 30, 1920, pp. 4, 8–9, which apparently copied it from *Millard's Review of the Far East* [Shanghai] 12, no. 1 (March 6, 1920) : 6, 8, 10–12. See also, Loewenthal, "Early Jews," p. 383.

7. Ibid., p. 209.

8. *Wisconsin Jewish Chronicle,* September 1924, cites Berthel's article in the *North China Herald,* but does not give the date on which it appeared in the *Herald.*

9. Sopher (in Kublin, *Jews in Old China,* p. 276).

10. A. Horne, "Kaifengfu," *Israel's Messenger,* July 4, 1924, p. 18.

11. Leslie, *Survival,* p. 71.

12. George E. Sokolsky, "The Jews in China," *The Menorah Journal* 15, no. 5 (November 1928) : 453–54.

13. The story of Levy's experiences in Kaifeng and the information imparted to the society on his return to Shanghai are dealt with in Sopher's *Chinese Jews* (reprinted in Kublin, *Early Jews,* the Levy story appearing on pp. 285–91). Sopher's booklet was published in 1926. Sokolsky's article, which says nothing about Levy's return to Shanghai but leaves him somewhere in the interior of China, was printed in 1928. Apparently, Sokolsky was not aware of the fact that Levy had managed to get safely to Kaifeng, although the information provided by Sokolsky was published three or four years after Levy's reappearance in Shanghai.

14. Noach Mishkowsky, *Ethiopia: Jews in Africa and Asia* (New York: Borochoff Yugend Bibliotek, 1936), p. 134.

15. Ibid., p. 132. Mishkowsky identifies the town, in a Yiddish transliteration as "Yah-uh-min."

16. Meat is salted as part of the process whereby it is made kosher. No other allusion to the salting of meat than this one seems to appear in the literature dealing with the Chinese Jews.

17. Ibid., pp. 132–34. Mishkowsky's story of meeting two Jews in Manchuria is, of course, strange, and should perhaps not be taken seriously. But there were unquestionably Jews here and there throughout the wide expanse of China. In fact, a letter was written in 1923 by a member of the Ai clan, who happened to be stranded in Szechuan Province, to the Jews of Shanghai, asking them to provide him with the means to visit them and then find him employment. Rabbi W. Hirsch, to whom the letter was turned over, attempted without success to get in touch with the man. W. Hirsch, "Los Judios de Kaifangfu," *La Luz* [Buenos Aires], February 19, 1965, pp. 4–6.

18. Leslie, *Survival,* p. 117, n. 2.

19. The articles written by Brown that describe his trip to Kaifeng are listed in the Selected Bibliography. White, vol. 1, pp. 150–64, presents a truncated version of Brown's articles under the title, "Through

the Eyes of an American Jew." The bulk of the story of Brown's visit to the *kehillah,* as presented herein, is contained in the White version.

20. Who could this Jewish visitor have been? The timing suggests David Levy, A. Horne, Arthur Sopher, or Harry A. Franck (one of whom may have been mistaken for a Jew and who seems to have been a guest in this particular Chao home). See n. 7, above. If however, the younger Chao's estimate of the elapsed time since the last visit by a Jew was exaggerated by some three years, the visitor may have been a Mr. Solotsky, a Russian-American Jew who was sent to China, presumably by an American relief organization, to help his coreligionists there (though probably the Western rather than the Chinese Jews). It is not certain, however, that Solotsky went personally to Kaifeng or, if he did, that he was able to contact the city's Jews. He succeeded, in any case, in obtaining this information about them from White's mission: "The number of Jews in Kaifeng is about 80, including women and children. In addition, there are about 40 Jews scattered in certain districts of the province of Honan. Most of them are very poor, not much better off than beggars. But two or three families are comparatively wealthy, and one man, named Shih, is very rich. Mr. Shih owns two large houses, some shops and some land. He has adopted Christianity and is a silversmith by profession. Many of the Jews are street peddlers, and three or four of them are merchants. Very few are farmers or scholars. Most of the young ones are serving as apprentices in one trade or another. They look very much like the bona fide Chinese; indeed it is practically impossible to distinguish the Chinese Jews from the Mongolian Chinese. . . . They have no synagogues. In their homes, the usual Chinese household gods are kept and worshipped in genuine Chinese fashion. . . . Very few of the Jews can read Chinese, and none can read the Hebrew Scriptures." William Klemm, "A Faltering Remnant of Israel," *B'nai B'rith Magazine* 42, no. 3 (December 1927) : 58–59.

12 *Outright Lies, Tall Tales, and a Few Truths*

1. A report from Bombay, published in *Jewish Chronicle* [London], June 8, 1906, p. 17, thus tells of two Chinese boys, neither from Kaifeng, who went through the ceremony of conversion to Judaism, though one of them, whose name was Feba, always insisted that he had been born a Jew. Feba's parents were killed by the Taiping rebels in 1862, when he was eight years old. Shortly afterward, he and a homeless friend of about the same age were picked up by Solomon

Reuben, a member of a British volunteer corps. The two were sent by some Shanghai Jews to Bombay, where they underwent the, rite of circumcision, Feba taking the new name of Salem Shaloam David. The other boy died two years later. Feba became in time an active member of the Bombay *kehillah,* and also of the Shanghai Society for Rescuing the Chinese Jews. In the 1906 *Jewish Chronicle* article, bylined as "from a Bombay correspondent," Feba is specifically identified as of Jewish birth. "He comes from a family of Chinese Jews," the *Jewish Chronicle's* informant writes, "and is the eldest of three children. His original name was Feba. Owing to his Jewish birth, he had to suffer great social ostracism in the interior of China. Thus, he was prevented by his Chinese playmates from entering the heathen places of worship." One wonders, however, whether Feba's recollections of his childhood were not custom tailored to suit the fancies of his Bombay benefactors.

2. The details of Stempel's story, as given here, are extracted from *Jewish Chronicle,* December 20 and 27, 1867, and the Hebrew version appearing in *Metziat Aseret ha-Shebatim* (Warsaw, 1900), pp. 3–9. In the Hebrew text, Stempel's name is listed as Abraham. The Hebrew texts are reprints of articles on China that appeared in the journal *Ha-Maggid.* The Stempel story was initially published in French, in *Archives Israélites* 28, no. 21 (November 1, 1867): 992–95; 28, no. 23 (December 1, 1867): 1087–89; 28, no. 24 (December 15, 1867): 1131–36; and 29, no. 1 (January 1, 1868): 24–28. A portion of the French text was translated into English and published in *Jewish Chronicle.* The Hebrew version appeared originally in *Ha-Maggid* during 1868. A German version, containing the same sections of the Stempel letters as the *Ha-Maggid* text, was published in *Der Israelit,* 1867 and 1868.

3. There are numerous variants of the Sambatyon legend. The one presented here (and recounted by Stempel) is the best known.

4. Stempel was not the first to place the Sambatyon in China. A traveler's account written in 1847 by a Jew who, preparing to start on a journey from Tiberias, went to have his passport approved by the governor of Aden, was told by the governor "that in China . . . there is a Jewish kingdom, and the Sambatyon is found there." Cited by A. Neubauer, "Where are the Ten Tribes?" *Jewish Quarterly Review,* o.s. (July 1889): 418–19.

5. The rabbi and Stempel also discuss the place of the Talmud in Jewish life. This aspect of their conversation appears only in the *Archives Israélites* presentation 29, no. 1 (January 1, 1868): 24–28.

6. See p. 189, above.

7. The story of the florist is told by the Zionist writer Leon Ilutovich

who, surprisingly, believed that the man was actually Jewish and planned to observe the Yom Kippur holiday. Ilutovich tells the tale in at least two of his articles: "Oriental Fragments," *The Zionist Observer*, December 1949, pp. 24–26; and "The Chinese Jews of Kaifeng," *The American Zionist*, May 1972, pp. 29–30. A variant of the synagogue story is given by Dun J. Li, who presents it for what it is—a tongue-in-cheek anecdote, and nothing more. "A story was told during World War II," Li writes, "that an American soldier of Jewish faith went to visit a Chinese synagogue, only to be reminded of his 'mistake' at the entrance. 'Sir, this is a Jewish synagogue, not a Christian church,' said the Chinese usher, bowing and smiling. As far as he was concerned, the fact that the American soldier was a white man automatically ruled him out as a Jew." *The Ageless Chinese*, 2d ed. (New York: Charles Scribner's Sons, 1971), pp. 371–72. One wonders, however, how the American Jewish businessman Shmuel ben-Ari was persuaded to swallow whole the story he heard in 1937, while he was in China, of 400 Chinese Jews who, he was told, were employed at the time in mines in Honan Province—and were particularly scrupulous in their observance of the Sabbath. Ben-Ari's story appears in *Jewish Chronicle*, September 3, 1937, p. 44.

8. Shizuo Sogabe, "The Kaifeng Jews," *The Gaiko Jibo* [*Revue Diplomatique*] [Tokyo] 97, no. 4 (February 15, 1941): 65–67; and Teichō Mikami, "Report on the Actual Conditions of the Kaifeng Jewish Community," *Shina Bukyō Shigaku* [Tokyo] 5, no. 1 (June 25, 1941): 76–77. For a brief summary of the contents of the two articles, see Loewenthal, "Nomenclature" (in Kublin, *Studies*, pp. 67–68), and also Loewenthal, "Imaginary Illustration," pp. 98; 98, n. 4. Oddly enough, another discussion of the Chinese Jews appeared in a Japanese periodical on the same day as Sogabe's. The author was Liu Lung-kuang, his essay was called "The Myth of the Jews in Kaifeng," and it was printed in *The Kabun Osaka Mainichi*, pp. 23–24. (See pt. 1, chap. 3, n. 3, above.)

Another reason for the Japanese interest in the Kaifeng Jews, as suggested to the author by Marvin Tokayer and David Kranzler, stems from a plan promulgated by certain Japanese military officers and approved by the Japanese cabinet in December 1938 for settling nearly 1 million harassed European Jews in Manchuria, then under Japanese domination. These officers, badly misled by Nazi propaganda and such works as *The Protocols of Zion*, had convinced themselves that the Jews exercised an overpowering influence on the government of the United States and the governments of various European nations. It was therefore in Japan's interests, these officers contended, to win the friendship of the Jews, who might then be expected to bend every effort to persuade the West to withdraw its objections to Japan's expansionist program in Asia. An influx of Jews into Manchuria, moreover, would strengthen that satellite militarily and economically and enable it to serve as an effective buffer against the Soviet Union. In the pre-World War II years, accordingly, the Japanese interest in the Jews—not excluding those Jews who lived in Kaifeng—went far beyond what one might ordinarily expect. Once the war was on and the Manchurian venture was no longer feasible, Japan still chose to keep on reasonably good terms with the Jews. She thus sheltered some 30,000 of them in Shanghai, nearly all of whom were refugees from lands held by her anti-Semitic partner Germany. Japan's aims here were twofold: (1) to influence American policy by currying favor with the supposedly all-powerful American Jews and perhaps avoid war with the United States; and, even more improbably, (2) in the years after Pearl Harbor, to arrange peace feelers through the good offices of world Jewry and to induce world Jewry to intercede in her behalf should the fortunes of war go against her. This highly unrealistic estimate of the role of the Jewish people in international affairs may well have induced Japanese Intelligence to have its agents look into the history and status of Kaifeng Jewry. See Marvin Tokayer and Mary Sagmaster Swartz, *The Fugu Plan: The Untold Story of the Japanese and the Jews During World War II* (New York and London: Paddington Press, 1979). See also Kranzler, pp. 169–266, or his adaptation of these pages published under the title, "Japanese Policy Toward the Jews, 1938–1941," in *Japan Interpreter* 11, no. 4 (Spring 1977): 493–527.

9. Loewenthal, in his "Imaginary Illustration" article, p. 98, suggests that the Jews could have misrepresented their religious affiliations to Mikami because "they may have been motivated by fears of political persecution if the Japanese suspected them of links with the West."

10. For the Japanese attitudes and conduct toward the Caucasian Jews who spent the war years in occupied China, see the entries in the Selected Bibliography under both Kranzler and Dicker.

11. Salvotti earned his spurs as a "scholar" in anti-Semitic and Fascist circles with such virulent publications as "Das faschistische Italien und die Juden," *Wille und Macht*, January 15, 1937, pp. 25–28; *Documentario ebraico* (Lucca, 1939); and "I Giudei in Cina," *La Difesa della Razza*, April 5, 1940 and May 5, 1940. For an article by a Nazi on the Chinese Jews, which surprisingly, considering the source and the nature of the publication in which it was printed, does not heap imprecations on them or on Jewry at large, see Matthias Werner's "Judische Gemeinden in Inner-China," *Der Weltkampf: Monatsschrift für Weltpolitik, völkische kultur und*

die Judenfrage in aller Welt 16 (1939) : 325–26. The writer's summing up of the story of the Chinese Jews is, however, far from accurate. According to Loewenthal ("Early Jews," p. 385), Werner's article also appeared in *Passe* 6, no. 5. (1939) : 190–91.

12. *Juden in Ostasien*, pp. 13–20.

13. Swift's booklet, *The Mystery of Iniquity*, is one of a series of rabidly anti-Semitic works issued in Marietta, Ga., by an organization calling itself The Thunderbolt. Bakony's reasons for casting the Chinese Jews as villians intent on suborning not only "the Chinese Gentiles" but also the rest of the world are presented in a pamphlet entitled *Chinese Communism and Chinese Jews*, which was published in Metairie, La., either in 1977 or 1978, by Udecan Editions. One can only speculate to what heights Bakony's imagination might have soared if he had been aware (as he apparently was not) that T. V. Soong, the Chinese finance minister who provided Brown with an airplane when the latter expressed a desire to visit the Jews of Kaifeng, was a brother of Mmes. Sun Yat-sen and Chiang Kai-shek.

14. As far as is known, however, no Western Jew after Brown visited them until the end of World War II. The extent to which they were affected by the famine that killed off an estimated 15 percent of Honan's population in the early part of 1943 has not been determined.

15. Harrison Forman, *Changing China* (New York, 1948), p. 147. Forman died in February 1978. In a letter to the author (August 8, 1978), Mrs. Forman notes that "many" of the photographs her late husband took of the Kaifeng Jews in 1938 have as yet not been published. "The black and white negatives on the Kaifeng Jews," she writes, "are in the files and are awaiting cataloguing. At this time we would have no way of locating them."

16. Yitzhak Ben-Zvi, "The Stone Tablets of the Old Synagogue in Kai-Feng-Fu," *Sefunot* 5 (1961) : 5–66. See p. 35, n. 13.

17. The contents of Cattaneo's letter and the matter of the Jewish enrollee at the seminary are discussed by Loewenthal in his "Nomenclature." (See Kublin, *Studies*, p. 66.)

18. Ben-Zvi, p. 35, n. 13. See n. 16, above.

19. Leslie, *Survival*, p. 74.

20. Ibid., pp. 74, 107.

21. Ibid., p. 74.

22. Stated in a letter to the author, dated August 25, 1978, and responding to a query suggested by Anson Laytner, who learned of Prof. Goldman's visit to Kaifeng during a conversation with Goldman some years ago and subsequently went to China as an exchange student from Canada (1973–74). Unlike Goldman and his companions, however, Laytner was unable to obtain permission from the

authorities to visit Kaifeng. The two Jewish steles that Goldman reports seeing in the no-longer functioning Canadian Anglican church were of course the 1489/1512 and the 1679 stones. See chap. 3, n. 26, above. In a later letter (December 15, 1978), Prof. Goldman states that he was accompanied to the Li household by Pokora, six East German students, and, of course, the members of the Communist Party cadre mentioned in his earlier letter. Laytner, it should be added, is not as inclined as Goldman to dismantle the cadres' estimate of the presence of 700 Jews in Kaifeng as a gross exaggeration.

23. Lev Rubashov, "The Jews of China," *Jewish Frontier* 35, no. 7 (July–August 1968) : 24–27.

24. Leslie, *Survival*, p. 74.

25. Walter Spiegel, "Gibt es noch chinesische Juden?" *Die Welt*, no. 8 (January 10, 1976). Still, while Spiegel's luncheon companions were unaware of the fact that their country had long sheltered compatriots who were Jews, other Chinese did know about them. Bernard Goldstein, formerly director of the Jewish Family Service of Dallas, has thus informed the author that during a visit to Peking in April 1978 he and Mrs. Goldstein were introduced to the internationally known sociologist Prof. Fei Hsiao-tung, who informed them and several other American tourists that one of his students was then writing a doctoral dissertation on the subject of the Chinese Jews and, moreover, that a number of artifacts of Jewish origin have in recent years been unearthed in archaeological excavations in Kaifeng, presumably at the site of the synagogue. One of these artifacts, as the Goldsteins recall being told, displays a Star of David. However, at the time the *kehillah* was cut off from communication with the West the symbol had no special Jewish connotation and was used by Jews and non-Jews alike. Prof. Leonard J. Duhl, University of California (Berkeley), who was also present at the Fei talk, notes (in a letter to the author dated August 9, 1978) that a tape recording, which he made of a personal interview with Prof. Fei, contains a statement by Fei to the effect that portions of a Torah scroll were recovered in the course of the excavations.

26. Bernard S. Raskas, "The First Rabbi in Red China," *Hadassah Magazine* (June–July 1977) : 13, 36–38.

27. The story was told by Robert M. Lury to Marvin Tokayer while the latter was rabbi of the Jewish community of Japan and later communicated to the author by Rabbi Tokayer. Also worth mentioning is the tale related to Rabbi Tokayer and repeated by him to the author—this one originating with two Catholic nuns whom the rabbi met in Okinawa. Before their expulsion from Mainland

China by the Maoist regime, the nuns declared they had met a number of Chinese who, they were given to understand, lived on an island and there raised sheep from whose wool prayer shawls were made for use in Kaifeng.

An earlier story about a Chinese sailor, which has a direct though unconfirmed tie to Chinese Judaism, appeared in the *Hebrew* July 28, 1911, having been reprinted or extracted from a recent issue of the *Boston Advocate*. This man, Li Han-ti, was a member of the crew of the *Seneca*, a British vessel that put in at a Boston harbor in the summer of 1911, following a voyage from the Orient. Li identified himself as a Jew from Kaifeng and, according to the report, "seemed to be well informed because he refused to celebrate a Chinese religious festival, claiming that as a Jew he had no business to pray to the Dragon." Nothing more is revealed about Li, the *Advocate* having learned secondhand the little it did concerning the man.

28. From a letter to Rabbi Tokayer written by Rabbi Rabinowitz August 5, 1974, and subsequently made available to the author by Rabbi Tokayer.

29. *Peony*, Pearl Buck's romantic, if historically muddled, novel (New York: John Day, 1948) dealing with Kaifeng Jewry in the decades immediately preceding the destruction of its last synagogue, ends with this exaggerated view of the lingering impact of Judaism on modern-day China, as articulated by an elderly Chinese woman who had once been in love with a member of the Chao clan: " 'Nothing is lost,' " she repeated. " 'He lives again and again, among our people,' " she mused. " 'Where there is a bolder brow, a brighter eye, there is one like him; where a voice sings most clearly, there is one; where a line is drawn most cleverly to make a picture clear, a carving strong, there is one; where a statesman stands most honorable, a judge most just, there is one; where a scholar is most learned, there is one; where a woman is both beautiful and wise, there is one. Their blood is lively in whatever frame it flows, and when the frame is gone, its very dust enriches the still kindly soil. Their spirit is born anew in every generation. They are no more and yet they live forever.' "

13 *The Beginnings of Judaism in China*

1. Cited by Perlmann (in Kublin, *Jews in Old China,* pp. 124, 139) from Vinogradoff's *Istoria Biblii na Wostoke* (St. Petersburg, 1895).
2. White, vol. 1, p. 10.
3. For example, Godeby, p. 369.

4. See William F. Leggett, *The Story of Silk* (New York: Lifetime Editions, 1949), p. 145, for a typical legend of this kind, this one dealing with Solomon, a magic carpet, and a silkworm in his gardens, which he commanded to bore a tiny hole through a costly diamond sent to him by the Queen of Sheba. Several other legends suggesting the presence of silk in Israel in biblical times are provided in Louis Ginzberg's *The Legends of the Jews,* 7 vols. (Philadelphia: The Jewish Publication Society of America, 1909–38). For alleged references to silk in the Bible itself, see Amos 13:12, Ezek. 16:10, Ezek. 16:13, and associated commentaries.

5. Cited from Pliny's *Natural History* by L. Boulnois, *The Silk Road* (London, 1966), pp. 45–46. Silk is thought to have reached the Middle East by the first century B.C.E., but not directly, according to Ying-shi Yü, *Trade and Expansion in Han China* (Berkeley and Los Angeles: University of California Press, 1967), p. 158. The trade, such as it was, Yü indicates, was effected through intermediaries, and even as late as Pliny's day there was no direct commercial traffic between Rome and China. In Pliny's century, Yü states, "no single Chinese merchant . . . is known to have ever set foot on Roman soil." The first Romans who are reported to have appeared in a Chinese capital were merchants who arrived in 166 C.E. at the Han court and tried to pass themselves off—as merchants were apt to do even as late as the sixteenth century—as diplomatic envoys from Europe. Ibid., p. 161.

6. See pt. 1, chap. 2, above.

7. See Perlmann (in Kublin, *Jews in Old China,* pp. 149–52) for the case favoring a pre-talmudic arrival of Jews in China on the grounds, inter alia, that they brought levirate marriage there without the modifications subsequently made in it by the talmudic tractate Yebamot. For a concise summation of levirate marriage as it affected the Chinese Jews themselves and their neighbors, see Leslie, *Survival,* pp. 12–14, n. 2.

8. See pt. 1, chap. 3, above.

9. See, for example, Wylie, pp. 1–23.

10. White, vol. 1, pp. 134–35, 142–43, reproduces four such figurines. Preuss, following White, takes the figurines as possible likenesses of Jewish merchants traveling in China. J. Preuss, *The Chinese Jews of Kaifeng-Fu* (Tel Aviv: Museum Haaretz, 1961), pp. 4–5.

11. Perlmann (in Kublin, *Jews in Old China,* pp. 130–31). The Sung period to which Perlmann refers is not to be confused with a much later period beginning in 960 of the same name.

12. Brotier, *Lettres édifiantes* (1781 ed.), vol. 24, pp. 96–97, notes that the Kaifeng Jews informed the Jesuits that the Jews entered China

during the reign of Ming Ti. "Such a dating," he then says, "could not better agree with the destruction of Jerusalem which took place in the year 70." The settlement of Jews in Kaifeng is, of course, far less ancient.

13. See Margoliouth (in Kublin, *Studies*, pp. 23–51). Rabbi Marvin Tokayer, in a personal communication to the author, pointed out K. Z(S)aleman's article in *Zapiski Vo* 16 (1904) : 46–57, which while questioning the precision of a 718 dating for the Dandan-Uilig document agrees that it must have been written no later than the end of the eighth century.

14. Cited by Jeannette Mirsky in "Discovering Ancient Treasures in 'Caves of 1,000 Buddhas,'" *Smithsonian* 8, no. 2 (May 1977) : 94–103.

15. Leslie, *Survival*, pp. 5, 165; White, vol. 1, pp. 139–40. The find is discussed in detail in Ph. Berger and M. Schwab, "Le Plus Ancien Manuscrit Hébreu," *Journal Asiatique* (July–August 1913) : 139–75. Dr. Eric F. L. Ray, Rabbi Tokayer informed the author, has concluded that this manuscript was written in the sixth, rather than the eighth or ninth centuries. Among the items discovered by Stein in Tun-huang was a copy of the *Diamond Sutra* (a selection from the Buddhist Scriptures). Dated 868, it is the world's oldest surviving printed book, preceding Gutenberg's first typographic efforts (using movable type, of course, rather than the block type employed by the Chinese printers of the *Diamond Sutra*) by nearly six centuries. Remarkably well preserved, the book is now in the British Museum.

16. Cited by Leslie, *Survival*, p. 6.

17. Ibid., p. 11.

18. Ibid., p. 19. Similar statements concerning these Bokharan and Samarkandian traditions are also repeated by Joseph Wolff, Marcus N. Adler, Moses Edrehi, and Allen H. Godeby.

19. The reference to "various places" occurs in the "skilled archer" document of May–June 1354. Cited by Leslie, *Survival*, p. 13.

20. List derived from Leslie, ibid., pp. 15–16.

21. Leslie, "Judaeo-Persian," p. 8; *Survival*, pp. 21–22.

22. An excellent summation of the theories dealing with the origins of the Kaifeng Jews was prepared by Hobermann. See Selected Bibliography. Laufer, unlike most Jewish historians, believes that the Jews came to China by sea. "Two facts are conspicuous in the history of the Chinese Jews," he writes. "They hailed from Persia and India, and reached China by way of the sea." Laufer (in Kublin, *Studies*, p. 163). In a review of White's *Chinese Jews*, L. Carrington Goodrich suggested that Indian Jews may have sailed to China from

Quilon or other Indian coastal cities in which Jews lived. See Kublin, *Studies*, pp. 201–3.

23. *Jerusalem Post*, March 31, 1952.
24. *National Jewish Monthly* (January 1953).
25. *India & Israel* 17 (June 1953). In a letter to the author, Rabbi Tokayer, who met Shih when the latter was in his early fifties, remarks that Shih was unquestionably a very handsome man. See Appendix for a synopsis of Tokayer's interviews with Shih.
26. *Orient* 5 (November 1954).
27. The Shih of Kaifeng considered their name to mean "stone."
28. The several other languages that Shih claims to know are listed in his other published pieces. In none of these printed accounts, however, does he say that he has a knowledge of Hebrew. This he claims in conversations and correspondence with Tokayer. In his military service record, a copy of which Tokayer has kindly sent to the author, Shih states that he knows Hebrew.
29. 1056 B.C.—a slip on Shih's part? Or a typographical error?
30. Here, strangely, Shih omits the Kaifeng clan that bore the same surname as his own.
31. The information regarding the loss of the tablet and the broken engagement is contained in a letter to the author from Rabbi Tokayer, December 2, 1975.
32. Leslie notes Fang Hao's success in finding references in three Yunnan gazetteers to Chao Ying-tou's service in 1663–68 in Kunming as magistrate. Chao Ying-tou was the younger brother of Chao Ying-ch'eng, the most important Jew to emerge from the Kaifeng *kehillah*. Both men are mentioned in the 1663a inscription. Ying-tou's name also appears in the 1679 stele. For additional information regarding Ying-tou, see chap. 16, below.
33. Letter to the author from Shih, August 20, 1975. The discrimination to which Shih refers is presumably that inflicted on the Kaifeng Jews by the Muslims among whom they lived, not the authorities.
34. Ibid.
35. In a letter to the author from Donald D. Leslie, October 16, 1975.
36. Prof. Zeev W. Falk of the Hebrew University, Jerusalem, who has met and talked with Shih, was deeply moved by the latter's patent "craving to belong to the Jewish people," but has his doubts as to whether Shih is actually of Jewish descent. "I would rather assume," Falk states in a letter to the author, March 7, 1978, "that his family has sympathized with Jews and Judaism and has made the claim [of being Jewish] to justify its solidarity" with the House of Israel. Like Rabbi Tokayer, Falk feels drawn to Shih the man, but would require additional evidential data as a precondition for accepting him as a Jew by ethnic descent.

14 *The Synagogue on the Earth-Market Character Street*

1. For the precise location of the synagogue and the names of the streets in its vicinity, see Leslie, "Chao" (in Kublin, *Studies,* pp. 114–15).

2. See Ross, pp. 60–61, and, on the same pages, Ross's n. 4 for the citation from Dr. Eber and for further details regarding An San. The reason for An's meteoric rise in rank, ingeniously glossed over by the writer of the 1489 inscription in order to camouflage An's plebeian origins and his betrayal of a superior, was clarified in a study published in 1965 by Chaoying Fang, whose article on the subject is reprinted in Kublin, *Studies,* pp. 85–90.

3. Chang Hsiang-wen (in Kublin, *Studies,* p. 217).

4. Ross, p. 64.

5. The numerals that have been inserted in Domenge's sketches of the synagogue are in parentheses. In the last of a six-volume Italian anthology of selections from the *Lettres édifiantes,* which was published in Milan beginning in 1825 under the title *Scelti de lettere edificanti,* there is a drawing (facing p. 107 in the Italian text) unabashedly captioned "Sinagoga degli Ebrei cinesi" ("Synagogue of the Chinese Jews"). It is an amusingly naive fake, prepared by an anonymous artist who knew little or nothing about Chinese architecture and dress, and was equally ignorant of Jewish customs, Oriental or Occidental. The synagogal interior and its furnishings, as he depicts them, are entirely European. Several male figures are attired in what appears to be nineteenth-century Catholic clerical garb, Italian style. Several other men are wearing conical peasant hats. The women seated in the "sinagoga" are clad in styles appropriate to the Middle East, and have their heads covered by scarves. For a more detailed description of this bogus representation of the Kaifeng synagogue, see Loewenthal's "Imaginary Illustration." (See also pt. 1, chap. 5, n. 2, above, regarding the synagogal model in the Beth Hatefusoth, Tel Aviv.)

6. White, vol. 1, p. 3.

7. The bowls were probably used as receptacles for flowers. They were at least eight such bowls in the compound, but Domenge shows only two. Ibid., p. 4.

8. There was a curbing around the well. Nearby was a building, not included in Domenge's sketch, which was used for ablutions, apparently as a *mikveh,* or ritual bathhouse. Ibid.

9. After the destruction of the synagogue, the balustrades were acquired by a local Confucian temple. Ibid., p. 3.

10. The description provided here of the synagogue and the compound is derived in the main from Gozani's 1704 letter, Domenge's sketches,

Brotier's condensation of the reports of Domenge and Gaubil, the journals of the Chinese delegates, and the data provided by Tobar and by White.

11. The term *dragon's pavilion* was widely used in China. It refers to the area in which the imperial tablet (*wan-sui-p'ai*) was located. Tablets of this kind were usually ornamented with elaborate dragon carvings, thus accounting for the name.

12. White, vol. 2, pp. 24–25, n. 23.

13. Each of the thirteen Torah scrolls stood on its own table, according to the Jesuit visitors. "Each *Ta Ching* [Torah scroll]," says Brotier (*Lettres édifiantes*, 1781 ed., vol. 24, p. 66), "is rolled around a rod, and forms a kind of tent covered by a curtain of silk." MacLaurin equates these curtains with veils, which makes it possible for him to advance this interesting, though not necessarily justifiable, speculation: "In these Holy of Holies they had an ark kept in complete darkness and containing thirteen veiled scrolls—does this preserve a memory of the thirteen veils in Solomon's Temple?" See E. C. B. MacLaurin, "The Beginnings of the Israelite Diaspora," *Australian Journal of Biblical Archaeology* 1, no. 4 (1971) : 82–95. The fact that the *kehillah* had thirteen scrolls in its synagogal Ark may of course have some relationship with these Solomonic veils, but its decision to keep that number in the Ark is more apt to have been arrived at in this manner: the one Torah scroll pieced together from skins salvaged from the 1642 floodwaters was consecrated, as is definitely known, to the memory of Moses; and each of the other twelve (as noted by Brotier, *Lettres édifiantes*, 1781 ed., vol. 24, p. 66) represented one of the tribes of Israel. The "tribal" scrolls, incidentally, were numbered, each copy bearing a Hebrew figure, from *aleph* to *yod-beth* (one to twelve), on the reverse side of its last skin.

14. These terms were identified by Christian scholars as angels, and were so noted on p. 27 of the *Narrative* assembled by Bishop Smith from the journals of the delegates he had sent to Kaifeng. However, the distinguished Jewish bibliographer Joseph Zedner preferred to read *shemesh* as "sun," its intrinsic Hebrew meaning. As to *kamon*, Zedner wondered whether the word could not have been miscopied by the delegates or if it might not have represented a Hebraicization of the Arabic *qamar*, or moon. But why *sun* and *moon* were painted atop each tablet, Zedner could not say. (Nor, for that matter, could Smith explain why the Chinese Jews should choose to inscribe the names of two very obscure angels—assuming, of course, that they had even heard of them—on the two plaques.) See Joseph Zedner, "Neueste Mittheilungen über eine Judengemeinde in China," *Monatsschrift für Geschichte und Wissenschaft des Judenthums* (Leipzig,

1853) : 56–61, particularly p. 59. One possible explanation in support of Zedner's speculation, farfetched though his guess appears to be, is that the Jews thought of the *Shema* as a declaration not only of their belief in monotheism, but also as a statement of their faith that God's omnipotence extends to all that exists in the world—to all, in brief, that lies below the sun and the moon.

15. The horizontal and vertical tablets are discussed later in this chapter.

16. See Leslie, *Survival*, pp. 81–82, for his reference to Gozani's description of the incense bowls.

17. It is possible, however, that the Jews had access to Chinese versions of selected portions of the Scriptures that may have been prepared by the Jesuits. From the mid-nineteenth century onward, the Jews were of course repeatedly offered Chinese Bibles—not excluding the New Testament—by Protestant missionaries.

18. The Chinese texts of the horizontal and vertical tablets, together with their French translations, appear in Tobar, pp. 8–30. The Chinese texts and their English translations are available in White, vol. 2, pp. 110–54. See also Leslie, *Survival*, pp. 136–38.

19. The fifty-three "Heavenly Writings" are the *parashioth*, into which the Chinese Jews, like the Persian Jews, divided the Pentateuch. Western Jews divide it into fifty-four sections. The younger Ai is including the five final letter forms of the Hebrew alphabet in his count of twenty-seven characters. His allusion to the display of Hebrew characters on the doors (doorposts?) of Jewish homes seems to indicate that the Jews of Kaifeng placed *mezuzoth* on the doorposts of their dwellings.

20. White, vol. 1, p. 16. A synagogal chime, obtained by White in Kaifeng, is preserved at the Royal Ontario Museum, Toronto.

21. 1489 and 1663a lapidary inscriptions.

22. 1663a stele.

23. Ibid.

24. Cf., pt. 1, chap. 11, n. 15, for the Widow Shih's recollection, in 1932, of being told by her father-in-law that men and women wore long white gowns while at prayer.

25. Brotier, *Lettres édifiantes*, 1781 ed., vol. 24, p. 67.

26. Ibid., Cf., Chao Nien-tsu's 1850 letter to "the Chief Teacher of the Jewish Religion," which states that "in the synagogue are worn a blue cap and shoes with soft soles." Finn, *Orphan Colony*, p. 42. The Muslims wore white caps in their mosques. This difference in the color of the headgear used at prayer served the people of Kaifeng as a means of distinguishing the Jews from the Muslims, the former often being called the *Lan-mao hui-hui* (blue-capped Muslims), and the latter the *Pai-mao hui-hui* (white-capped Muslims).

27. Swaying, stepping forward and backward, and bowing are, of

course, still commonly done in the synagogue. Kneeling, except on the High Holy Days, was banned from most synagogues some centuries after the destruction of the Second Temple. For a description and explanation of these and other symbolic synagogal gestures, see pp. 356–60 of Abraham Milgrim's *Jewish Worship* (Philadelphia: The Jewish Publication Society of America, 1971).

28. Smith, p. 51. There had not been a rabbi in Kaifeng, when the delegates came there, for nearly fifty years. The ritual bathing and the seating of the rabbi in a place of honor are of course customs that were no longer carried on in 1850, notwithstanding the delegate Chiang's use of the present tense to describe them.

29. "They told me," Gozani wrote to Suarez in 1704, "that in the spring and autumn they rendered to their ancestors the same honors that are customarily offered in China, doing this in the chamber near the sanctuary; though, in truth, they do not offer up any swine's flesh, but of other meat; and that in their ordinary ceremonies they merely present porcelain vessels full of meats and confitures, together with perfumes." Gozani, *Lettres édifiantes*, 1781 ed., vol. 18, pp. 42–43. The 1663a inscription is more specific about the animal offerings. The *kehillah*, it says, uses "oxen and sheep and seasonal foods" in its ceremonials. A number of Diaspora Jews, it should be added, have at various times also engaged in animal sacrifices.

30. Leslie (*Survival*, p. 87) suggests that these sacrifices were offered at Passover, Shevuoth, Sukkoth, and Hanukkah. In a review of Leslie's *Survival*, Ware disagrees with Leslie's choice of holidays. The holidays on which the Kaifeng Jews offered sacrifices, Ware argues, are the "Ching Ming and the Feast of Hungry Ghosts in the Chinese ritual calendar." James H. Ware, Jr., *Journal of Church and State* 19, no. 2 (Spring 1977) : 334.

31. See chap 15, below, for a more extensive discussion of the *kehillah's* adaptation to the ways of Confucianism.

15 *The Jewish Way of Life in Kaifeng*

1. A list of the titles of several talmudic tractates, dated September 12, 1713, and followed by Gozani's autograph, is reproduced by Leslie; but because the titles are in a handwriting other than Gozani's, Leslie suggests that the list may have been sent to the Jesuits from Europe so that he could present it to the Jews and find out if they recognized the titles. Gaubil, however, was told by the Jews that they still owned some fragments of the mishnaic portions of the Talmud. Leslie, *Survival*, pp. 153–54, pl. 20.

2. The Kaifeng synagogue's division of the Pentateuch into fifty-three *parashioth*, Persian style, Leslie points out, was also advocated by Maimonides. The Kaifeng prayer books and the Passover Haggadah closely resemble those of the Jews of Yemen, who were themselves strongly and directly influenced by Maimonides. Ibid., pp. 20, 24, 156–57. See also Stephen F. K. Moch's study of a Kaifeng section book in "The Ben Aser and Ben Naftali Traditions as Seen in the Hebrew Union College MS. 958 and Other Biblical Manuscripts" (thesis submitted at Hebrew Union College-Jewish Institute of Religion, 1978), especially chap. 3.

3. Leslie, *Survival*, p. 95.

4. On the basis of evidence derived from the Memorial Book, Leslie concludes that the *shelihim* were all "of one direct descent," and, presumably, "hereditary leaders all born in Kaifeng." Ibid., pp. 116–17. The *shelihim* whose names occur in the Memorial Book are the brothers Rabbi Shadar and Rabbi Jeremiah (Li Chên?); their father, Rabbi Jacob; their grandfather, Rabbi Abishai; and his father, Rabbi Eldad. Leslie, "Memorial Book," pt. 3, p. 49.

5. Loewenthal, "Nomenclature" (in Kublin, *Studies*, p. 67). In 1932, it will be recalled, Brown met several of the Shih, none of them Catholic.

6. See Laufer's statements (in Kublin, *Studies*, pp. 168–69) regarding Ricci's assertion that Ai had been expelled from the synagogue. Laufer suggests that Ricci may have misunderstood Ai.

7. Gallagher, pp. 190–91.

8. Gozani, *Lettres édifiantes*, 1781 ed., vol. 18, p. 45.

9. Leslie, *Survival*, p. 89.

10. White, vol. 1, p. 16. Burial and mourning customs were apparently strictly observed by the ancestors of the Jews with whom White talked. "If anyone is in mourning," the 1512 stele thus declares, "meat and wine are forbidden to him, and at funerals he does not make ostentatious display, but follows the ritual regulations, for he does not believe at all in superstitious practices." Early in the twentieth century, Perlmann was told by several Kaifeng Jews of the funerary customs still followed by their people. "They bury their deceased in coffins," he wrote, "but of a different shape than those of the Chinese, and do not attire the dead in secular clothes, as the Chinese do, but in linen." See Perlmann (in Kublin, *Jews in Old China*, p. 143). In 1932 Brown was informed that "on the anniversary of the death of an ancestor, they burned incense and made special offerings before a tablet in the house. When a death occurred, the body was clothed in a simple cloth, placed in a coffin, and buried in the earth." (White, vol. 1, p. 162.) The statement in 1663a, "in

matters concerning capping [bar mitzvah], marriage, deaths, and funerals, the Chinese rites are followed," need not be taken too literally.

11. The two Haggadahs, now held by the Hebrew Union College, Cincinnati, were substantially reproduced in 1967 under the title *The Haggadah of the Chinese Jews*. In his introduction to the text, Cecil Roth points out that the Kaifeng text is "basically . . . the same as that generally familiar today. Nevertheless, there are a number of striking differences in unessential points—some of them known in other Oriental rites, some of them quite unfamiliar." The order of the service, he notes, is somewhat different. A number of hymns, most of them dating back to the Middle Ages, are absent; the ancient *Dayyenu* is inexplicably not included; and the service is shorter than that of many other communities. The Kaifeng Haggadahs do, however, contain two relatively unfamiliar hymns. One, beginning with the words *bahar banu* ("He chose us"), is introduced into the *kiddush*. (It appears also in such Haggadahs as those used in Yemen, Aleppo, and others, in fragments discovered in the Cairo genizah, and in the liturgy compiled by Saadiah Gaon in tenth-century Baghdad). The other, beginning with the words *ata ga'alta* ("Thou hast redeemed"), occurs in the same Haggadahs and in several others.

12. Leslie, *Survival*, p. 101.

13. Finn, *Orphan Colony*, p. 23.

14. For an excellent portrayal of life in a large thirteenth-century Chinese city—Hangchow, in this case—see Jacques Gernet, *Daily Life in China on the Eve of the Mongol Invasion, 1250–1276* (New York: Macmillan, 1962).

15. The number of errors committed by the Kaifeng scribes as they prepared the twelve Torah scrolls that were to replace those lost in the 1642 flood was awesome. Two centuries after the Kaifeng copying project was completed, S. M. Schiller-Szinessy, examining the Kaifeng scroll given by the London Society to Cambridge University, was moved to rare heights of indignation by the hundreds of errors he encountered in it. *"Lu lo ra'iti lo he'emanti!"* he exclaimed in Hebrew—"If I hadn't seen it with my own eyes, I'd never have believed it!" Pollak, *Torah Scrolls*, p. 46.

16. Leslie has compiled a list of Hebrew-Chinese transliterations to illustrate the impact of Chinese pronunciation on certain well-known Hebrew terms. Thus: *Thaulaha, Taula,* or *Thaulatse,* for Torah; *Moltohi,* for Mordechai; *Tucunda,* for Judah; and so forth. *Survival,* pp. 120–24.

17. Leslie, "Memorial Book," pt. 2, p. 7.

18. Cited by Leslie, *Survival,* p. 105.
19. Gozani, *Letttres édifiantes,* 1781 ed., vol. 18, p. 41.
20. Smith, p. 29.
21. Finn, *Orphan Colony,* p. 23.
22. The term *intermarriage,* as used in Jewish law, refers to marriages between individuals of differing faiths, so that if a woman was converted to Judaism before she married a Jew, this would not constitute intermarriage from the religio-legal point of view. The term, as it is being used here, is meant, of course, to be interpreted as involving marriage between a person who was born Jewish and another who was not.

16 *The Jews and Their Neighbors*

1. Leslie, "Memorial Book," pt. 2, p. 2.
2. Ibid., pt. 3, pp. 39–43.
3. Ibid., pt. 1, pp. 30–31.
4. The *Ju-meng-lu* [A record as in a dream], a book attributed (although perhaps incorrectly) to Li Kuang-t'ien, describes Kaifeng as it was in the years immediately before the 1642 siege and flood. It mentions the synagogue in passing. The work is not a gazetteer, however; nor does it specifically identify any individual in Kaifeng as a Jew. It does, nevertheless, list a general pharmacy belonging to Ai Wen-so, who appears in the Jewish records as Ai Ying-k'uei, and also a small pharmacy located on the south side of the Earth Street purveying optical medications and belonging to the Ai. The notes made by Li Kuang-t'ien, who supervised the defense of Kaifeng in 1642 and has been mistakenly identified by White (vol. 3, pp. 128–32, 149) as a Jew, seem to have been used for the compilation, later on, of the *Shou Pien Jih-chih* [A diary of the defense of Kaifeng], but this work contains few references of value to the city's Jewish community. It does mention, however, a Muslim (or possibly a Muslim-Jewish) company, and also troops led by Li Yao, a Jewish company commander. Leslie, *Survival,* p. 204. See also Loewenthal, "Early Jews," p. 388.
5. Leslie, *Survival,* pp. 43, 201–08.
6. Cited by Leslie, "Chao" (in Kublin, *Studies,* p. 131). The Hsiang-fu gazetteers of 1739 and 1898 also applaud the Widow Chao's devotion to the memory of her deceased husband and the responsible manner in which she raised her child and looked after her mother-in-law.
7. For the present locations of the various rubbings and transcripts, see Leslie, *Survival,* pp. 130–35.

8. Tobar, pp. 36–54. The present 1489/1512 and 1679 steles are probably still in Kaifeng, where the Canadian Anglicans left them on their departure from the city after it was taken by the Maoist forces, and where they were seen by Goldman in 1957. See pt. 1, chap. 3, n. 26, and chap. 12, n. 22, above.

9. Cited by Ross, p. 8, n. 2. The stranger may have been Schereschewsky, who was in Kaifeng in 1867, but only if Martin and Wilder were in error in ascribing their Occidental visitor's brief stay in the city to the year 1870. Like Martin, Ch'en Yüan was convinced that the Jews themselves had removed the names. "It was some time between the Muslim Rebellion during the T'ung Chih reign (1862) and the Boxer Rebellion during the Kuang Hsu reign (1900)," Ch'en wrote, "that the descendants of the Israelites obliterated the names in order to avoid some kind of calamity." (Ross, p. 8.) Godeby agrees, stating that the names were erased "because of Mohammedan persecutions and Boxer outrages." (Godeby, p. 418.)

10. Oliver Bainbridge, "The Chinese Jews," *Israel's Messenger*, October 19, 1906, pp. 8–10. Also published in *National Geographic Magazine* 18, no. 10 (October 1907) : 621–32, and elsewhere.

11. Leslie, in a letter to the author (and in *Survival*, p. 40), holds that the only earned *chin-shih* in the history of Kaifeng Jewry was Chao Ying-ch'eng's. White, Kramer, and Rhee, however, assert that the Kaifeng Jews produced several *chin-shih* degree holders, but they are undoubtedly erroneously including individuals who were not Jewish. White, vol. 3, pp. 110–43; Kramer (in Kublin, *Studies*, p. 13); Rhee, p. 120.

12. Cited by Leslie, "Chao" (in Kublin, *Studies*, pp. 121–22). The same 1760 gazetteer also includes two short essays by Chao Ying-ch'eng himself, the one telling of his suppression of the rebels, the other of the lecture hall which he established. Ibid., p. 127.

13. Ibid., p. 120.

14. Ibid., p. 122, n. 3.

15. Ibid., p. 124. The citation is from gazetteers of 1775, 1852, and 1882.

16. Finn, *Orphan Colony*, p. 41.

17. Leslie, "Chao" (in Kublin, *Studies*, p. 130).

18. Brotier, *Lettres édifiantes* 1781 ed., vol. 24, p. 100.

19. White, vol. 3, opening four unnumbered pages, and pp. 103–4, 128–32, 149–53, 158–60, 201–8, 221–24.

20. The editor of *The Haggadah of the Chinese Jews*, for example, reproduces the full-page drawing from White, which is captioned "The Chinese Jew, Li Kuang-t'ien, Hero of the Defense of Pien [Kaifeng]."

21. Leslie, "Memorial Book," pt. 2, pp. 11–12.

22. "China's President of Jewish Birth," *Jewish Tribune*, February 28, 1919, p. 1. The story is taken from "a recent issue" of the *Jewish Daily News*, whose reporter, G. Zilikowitz, had picked up the rumor about Hsü's Jewish ancestry from Feng. For further details concerning Hsü's life and career, see pp. 136–40, vol. 2, *Biographical Dictionary of Republican China*, Howard L. Boorman, ed., 4 vols. (New York and London: Columbia University Press, 1967–71). The *Dictionary* does not connect Hsü with Judaism.

23. Hans Heinrich Wetzel, *Le Moine Rouge* (Paris: Éditions Denoel, 1961), pp. 45–53, 61. Priests *(kohanim)* would, of course, be of the tribe of Levi, not Asher, while rabbis might be of any tribe. Seven years after Wetzel's book was published, and two months before Liu was purged by Mao and stripped of the last of his very extensive powers, an American rabbi, taking the German's highly romanticized biography of Liu much too seriously, permitted himself to indulge in a bit of unwarranted fantasy. "Could it be," he asked, in a brief article dealing with Wetzel's book, "that anti-Semitism has reared its ugly head in the struggle for power between Mao Tse-tung and President Liu Shao-chi?" Having asked this question, he closed his article with the suggestive words, "The possibility that anti-Semitism is a factor in the Chinese struggle for power today is of course rather remote. But, then, only the Lord truly knows. . . ." Arthur A. Chiel, "The Red Friar," *Jewish Digest* (August 1968): 7–8. Chiel had several months earlier already pointed out Wetzel's identification of Liu as a descendant of Jews living in Kaifeng, this in a letter to the editor of *The Reconstructionist*, February 9, 1968, pp. 26–27.

Epilogue *Survival and Extinction*

1. This, as well as the citations from Kant which follow, is taken from his *Religion Within the Limits of Reason Alone*, 2d ed. (La Salle, Ill.: The Open Court Publishing, 1960), p. 127.

2. Kaifeng Jewry, even as Kant was writing about it, was of course much closer to its end as a structured religious community than he realized, there having been no news from the *kehillah* since 1723. Had he been aware of the impending dissolution of the *kehillah* and of the fact that it was even less capable of understanding its Scriptures than when the Jesuits were still in Kaifeng, he would have been spared the problem of searching for an alternate theory that would explain why the city's Jewish community persisted in surviving even though it could not comprehend its Scriptures.

3. These factors tended, of course, to weaken the Jewish educational system of Kaifeng, and with dire consequences. Chen (pp. 37–41) lists three other major causes for the withering away of Judaism in Kaifeng: (1) the gradual shift of the center of gravity of China's economy from the north to the south; (2) the damage done to Kaifeng by the recurring floodings of the Yellow River; and (3) the invasions to which Honan was repeatedly subjected. These, understandably, stimulated migrations—presumably by Jews as well as by non-Jews—from Honan to more secure and economically attractive parts of the country. Still another contributing factor to the demise of Kaifeng Jewry, the adverse effect of China's academic system on the stability of the *kehillah,* as outlined by Sung Nai Rhee, is discussed below, in the text of this Epilogue.

4. Rhee, p. 119.

5. Ibid., pp. 119–20.

6. Ibid., p. 121.

7. Thus, White (vol. 3, p. 126) specifically states that Li "received appointment as a district magistrate." However, Leslie, in a letter to the author, questions the validity of identifying Li as an official.

8. Rhee, p. 122.

9. Instrumental music was banned from use in synagogal worship services in commemoration of the destruction of the Temple and also because the tuning and playing of musical instruments are considered work of the kind that may not be done on the Sabbath and certain other holidays. In the struggle between the Orthodox and Reform factions, the latter insisted on bringing the organ into the synagogal service, an innovation that the former found repugnant. Some Jewish authorities have claimed that a primitive form of the organ was used in the Second Temple, and that Christianity was originally reluctant to permit its use in church services because it was looked upon as "a Jewish instrument." In time, of course, the organ became the central musical instrument of the Church, a fact which now made Orthodox Jewry reject it as "a Christian instrument." The Reform faction's yearning for the inclusion of the organ in synagogal services, the Orthodox Jews charged, was no more than an expression of an unspoken desire to ape Christian ways, a step to the final goal of total assimilation. The organ thus became a cause célèbre in the long war between Orthodoxy and Reform, and remains so to this day. The analogy between this struggle and the one that must have gone on in Kaifeng over the introduction of Confucianist ways into Jewish practices is striking. See *Jewish Encyclopedia* 9: 134, 432–33, for a summary of the dispute over the organ.

10. Perlmann (in Kublin, *Jews in Old China,* pp. 200–11).

11. Ibid., pp. 209–10. The italics are Perlmann's.

12. The parallels outlined here between the arrival of the Hebrews in Egypt and the arrival of the Jews in Kaifeng are pointed out by B. D. Drenger in the Editor's Notes in the 1967 reprint of the Kaifeng Haggadahs.

13. The citation from the Midrash is taken from the gloss to Exod. 1:8 in J. H. Hertz's *The Pentateuch and Haftorahs*, vol. 1 (s.l, n.d.).

❖ INDEX

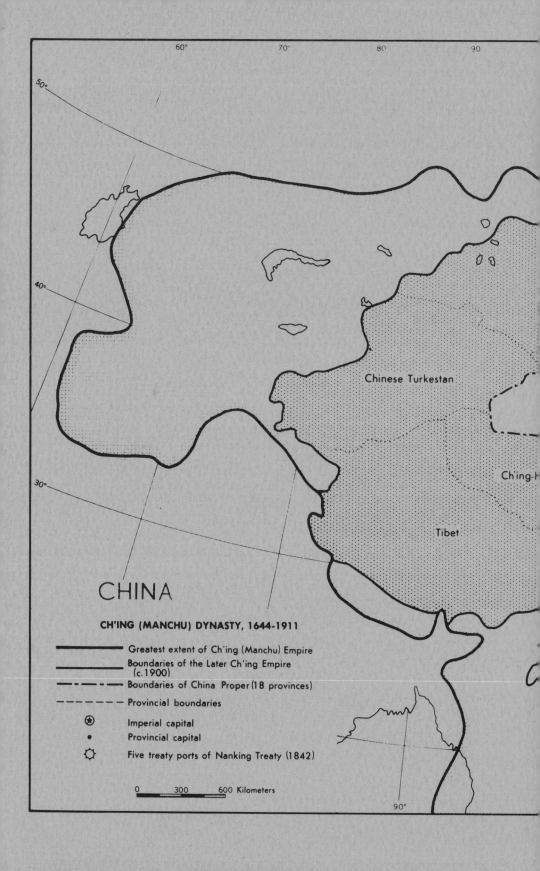

CHINA

CH'ING (MANCHU) DYNASTY, 1644-1911

Chinese Turkestan

Ch'ing-H

Tibet

Greatest extent of Ch'ing (Manchu) Empire

Boundaries of the Later Ch'ing Empire
(c.1900)

Boundaries of China Proper (18 provinces)

Provincial boundaries

Imperial capital

Provincial capital

Five treaty ports of Nanking Treaty (1842)

0   300   600 Kilometers